D1459703

.

Major Bible Themes

**52 VITAL
DOCTRINES OF THE SCRIPTURE
SIMPLIFIED AND EXPLAINED**

Lewis Sperry Chafer

REVISED BY
John F. Walvoord

Academie
Books from Zondervan Publishing House
1415 Lake Drive, S.E., Grand Rapids, Michigan 49506

Major Bible Themes

First edition copyright © 1926, 1953 by
Dallas Theological Seminary.
Revised edition copyright © 1974 by
Dallas Theological Seminary.
Published by Zondervan Publishing House,
Grand Rapids, Michigan.

ACADEMIE BOOKS is an imprint of Zondervan
Publishing House, 1415 Lake Drive, S.E.,
Grand Rapids, Michigan 49506

Library of Congress Catalog Card Number 73-17641

ISBN 0-310-22390-3

Printed in the United States of America

88 89 90 91 92 / DC / 28 27 26 25 24

Contents

Foreword to the Revised Edition

For more than half a century *Major Bible Themes* has blessed thousands of readers throughout the world. In fulfilling the purpose of its author, Lewis Sperry Chafer, the book has stated in simple and concise terms the major themes of biblical revelation. As such, it has opened the comprehensive truths of the Word of God to countless students of Scripture.

A quarter of a century after producing *Major Bible Themes,* Lewis Sperry Chafer wrote his monumental eight volume *Systematic Theology.* This presented in an extensive treatise biblical doctrine in comprehensive and systematic form. It seems entirely fitting that these fruits of the lifelong study of Scripture by Lewis Sperry Chafer should be to some extent incorporated in his *Major Bible Themes.*

In its revised form, large use has been made of the later writings of Lewis Sperry Chafer. Some chapters have been combined, and a number of new chapters have been added. In this new edition, *Major Bible Themes* presents in simplified form the mature conclusions of a lifetime of study by Lewis Sperry Chafer.

While some chapters in the revision are quite similar to the

7

original publication, about seventy-five percent of the work is new. Many additional scripture passages have been added, and subjects omitted in the original work are now included.

The purpose of the revised edition is to present in comprehensive and simplified form the major themes of the Bible. The work is designed for self-study, with appropriate questions at the end of each chapter. The new edition provides fifty-two chapters, one chapter for each week of the year. As such it is a suitable text for private study, for home Bible classes, and church study groups. It is designed as well as an introductory study in biblical truth for Bible institutes and colleges. The revised edition is published in the hope that it will increase and extend the usefulness of this volume for a new generation of Bible students.

JOHN F. WALVOORD

Introduction to the First Edition

This book is in no sense intended to be a treatise on systematic theology. In its preparation, a limited number of the most vital and practical doctrinal themes have been chosen, and an attempt has been made to adapt these brief discussions to the needs of the untrained Christian.

To each chapter a list of questions has been added which, it is hoped, may make the studies more useful both to individuals and to groups. The student who would be versed on these subjects should look up every passage cited and continue the study of each theme until all the questions can be answered from memory.

Bible doctrines are the bones of revelation, and the attentive Bible student must be impressed with the New Testament emphasis on "sound doctrine" (Matt. 7:28; John 7:16-17; Acts 2:42; Rom. 6:17; Eph. 4:14; 1 Tim. 1:3; 4:6, 16; 6:1; 2 Tim. 3:10, 16; 4:2-3; 2 John 9-10). Not knowing the doctrines of the Bible, the child of God will be, even when sincere, "tossed to and fro, and carried about with every wind of doctrine, by the sleight of men, and cunning craftiness, whereby they lie in wait to deceive"; the many well-meaning believers who are drawn into modern cults and heresies being sufficient proof. On the other hand, the divine purpose is that the servant of Christ shall be fully equipped to "preach the word; be instant in season, out of season; reprove, rebuke, exhort with all longsuffering and doctrine."

These chapters are published with the prayer that they may honor Him whose glory and grace are supreme, and that some among the children of God may be helped more accurately "to speak the things which become sound doctrine."

LEWIS SPERRY CHAFER

1

The Bible: The Word of God

Even a casual reader of the Bible soon discovers he is reading a most unusual book. Although covering thousands of years of human history and written by more than forty human authors, the Bible is not simply a collection of writings but one book with amazing continuity. It is called "The Bible" from the Greek word *biblos* meaning "a book." Its unusual character is due to the fact that it is indeed the Word of God even though written by human authors.

Two lines of evidence are usually offered supporting the conclusion that the Bible is the Word of God: (1) the internal evidence, the facts found in the Bible itself and the Bible's own claim concerning its divine origin; (2) the external evidence, the nature of the facts given in the Scripture which support its supernatural character.

A. Internal Evidence

In hundreds of passages, the Bible declares or assumes itself to be the Word of God (Deut. 6:6-9, 17-18; Josh. 1:8; 8:32-35; 2

11

Sam. 22:31; Pss. 1:2; 12:6; 19:7-11; 93:5; 119:9, 11, 18, 89-93, 97-100, 104-5, 130; Prov. 30:5-6; Isa. 55:10-11; Jer. 15:16; 23:29; Dan. 10:21; Matt. 5:17-19; 22:29; Mark 13:31; Luke 16:17; John 2:22; 5:24; 10:35; Acts 17:11; Rom. 10:17; 1 Cor. 2:13; Col. 3:16; 1 Thess. 2:13; 2 Tim. 2:15; 3:15-17; 1 Pet. 1:23-25; 2 Pet. 3:15-16; Rev. 1:2; 22:18). The Scriptures in so many ways declare that the Bible is the Word of God, that its claims are clear to anyone. The constant assumption of the writers of the Old Testament, the writers of the New Testament, and Christ Himself is that the Bible is the inspired Word of God. For instance, Psalm 19:7-11 declares that the Bible is indeed the Word of the Lord and names six perfections with six corresponding transformations of human character which the Word accomplishes. Jesus Christ declared that the law had to be fulfilled (Matt. 5:17-18). Hebrews 1:1-2 not only affirms that God spoke in the Old Testament to the prophets in the Word of God but to His Son in the New Testament. The Bible can be rejected only by rejecting its constant claims to being God's Word.

B. External Evidence

The Bible not only claims to be the Word of God but supports these claims by abundant evidence which has often convinced even the most skeptical of readers.

1. *The continuity of the Bible.* One of the most amazing facts about the Scripture is that though it was written by more than forty authors living over a period of about 1,600 years, the Bible is nevertheless one book, not simply a collection of sixty-six books. Its authors came from all walks of life, kings, peasants, philosophers, fishermen, physicians, statesmen, scholars, poets, and farmers. They lived in different cultures, in different experiences and often were quite different in character. The Bible has a continuity which can be observed from Genesis to Revelation.

The continuity of the Bible can be seen in its historical sequence which begins with creation of the present world to the creation of the new heavens and the new earth. The Old Testament unfolds doctrinal themes such as the nature of God Himself, the doctrine of sin, the doctrine of salvation, and the programs of God for the world as a whole, for Israel, and for the church. Doctrine is progressively presented from its first or elementary introduction to its more complex development. Type is followed by antitype, prophecy by fulfillment. One of the continued themes of the Bible is the anticipation, presentation, realization, and exaltation of the most perfect person on earth or in heaven, the Lord Jesus Christ. To account for such an amazing book with its continuity of development on natural means would demand a greater miracle than inspiration itself. Accordingly, believers in Scripture, while recognizing human authorship of the various books, account for its continuity by the guidance and inspiration of the Holy Spirit.

2. *The extent of biblical revelation.* In its unfolding of truth, the Bible is inexhaustible. Like a telescope it sweeps the universe from the heights of heaven to the depths of hell and traces the works of God from the beginning to their end. Like a microscope the minutest details of the plan and purpose of God and the perfection of His creation are revealed. Like a stereoscope, it places all beings and objects, whether in earth or in heaven, in right relation the one to the other. Although many books of the Bible were written in the early days of human knowledge when its authors were not aware of modern discoveries, nevertheless what they wrote is never contradicted by later discovery, and ancient writings of Scripture are amazingly adapted to modern situations. In extent of its revelation, biblical truth goes far beyond human discovery, reaching as it does from eternity past to eternity future and revealing facts which only God could know. No other book in all the world even attempts to present comprehensive truth as the Bible does.

3. *The influence and publication of the Bible.* No other book has ever been published in as many languages and for as many different peoples and cultures as the Bible itself. Its pages were among the first to be printed as printing presses were invented. Millions of copies of Scripture have been published in all the principal languages of the world, and every written language has at least some portion of the Bible in print. Although skeptics, like the French infidel, Voltaire, have often predicted that the Bible would be obsolete within a generation, and even twentieth-century authors have predicted that the Bible would soon be a forgotten book, it continues to be published in increasing numbers in more languages than ever before. Other religions have surpassed Christianity in number of followers, but they have not been able to offer any written revelation comparable to Scripture. In our modern day, the influence of the Bible continues to be transforming. To the unsaved it is the "sword of the Spirit" (Eph 6:17), and to the saved it is a cleansing, sanctifying, and effective power (John 17:17; 2 Cor. 3:17, 18; Eph.

5:25-26). The Bible continues to be the only divine basis for law and morality.

4. *Subject matter of the Bible.* The supernatural character of the Bible is seen in the fact that it deals as freely with the unknown and otherwise unknowable as it does with that which is known. It describes eternity past including creation before man was even in existence. The nature and works of God are revealed. In biblical prophecy the whole program for the world, for Israel, and for the church is unfolded, culminating in that which is eternal. On every subject presented, its statement is final, accurate, and timeless. Its comprehensive nature has made its readers wise in truth that is related both to time and to eternity.

5. *The Bible as literature.* Considered as literature, the Bible is also supreme. It contains not only graphic history but detailed prophecy, beautiful poetry and drama, stories of love and war, the speculations of philosophy as over against the finality of biblical truth. The variety of its authorship is matched by the variety of its subject matter. No other book as literature has so entranced readers of all ages and of all degrees of intelligent scholarship.

6. *The unprejudiced authority of the Bible.* The human authorship of the Bible has not resulted in prejudice in favor of man. The Bible unhesitatingly records the sin and weakness of the best of men, and graphically warns those who rely on their own virtues of their ultimate doom. Although recorded by human pens, it is a message from God to man rather than a message from man to man. While sometimes speaking of earthly things and human experience, it also describes with clarity and authority things of both heaven and earth, things seen and unseen, revealing facts about God, about angels, about men, about time and eternity, about life and death, of sin and salvation, of heaven and hell. Such a book could not be written by man if he chose to write it, and even if he could, man would not choose to write it, apart from divine direction. Accordingly, the Bible, though written by men, is a message from God with the certainty, assurance, and peace that only God can give.

7. *The supreme character of the Bible.* Above all else, the Bible is a supernatural book revealing the person and glory of God as manifested in His Son. Such a person as Jesus Christ could never have been the invention of a mortal man, for His perfections could never have been comprehended by the wisest and holiest of this earth. The supreme character of the Bible is

supported by its revelation of the supreme character of history in the person of Jesus Christ.

Because of the combination of human and supernatural qualities which enter into the Bible, a similarity may be observed between the Bible as the written Word and the Lord Jesus Christ as the living Word. They are both supernatural in origin, presenting an inscrutable and perfect blending of that which is divine and that which is human. They both exercise a transforming power over those who believe, and are alike allowed of God to be set at nought and rejected by those who do not believe. The untainted, undiminished divine perfections are embodied in each. The revelations which they disclose are at once as simple as the mental capacity of a child, and as complex as the infinite treasures of divine wisdom and knowledge, and as enduring as the God whom they reveal.

Questions

1. What is the meaning of the word "Bible"?
2. What are the two general lines of evidence that the Bible is the Word of God?
3. Name five passages in the Old Testament and five passages in the New Testament in which the Bible declares or assumes itself to be the Word of God.
4. Name six perfections with six corresponding transformations of human character which the Word accomplishes, according to Psalm 19:7-11.
5. Why is the continuity of the Bible an evidence of its inspiration?
6. What are some of the evidences of continuity in the Bible?
7. How does the Bible differ from other books in the extent of its revelation of truth?
8. How does the extensive publication of the Bible relate to its transforming power?
9. Relate the supernatural character of the Bible to its subject matter.
10. Evaluate the Bible as literature.
11. How can the human authorship be related to the unprejudiced authority of the Bible?
12. Relate the Bible as a supernatural book to Jesus Christ as a supernatural person.

2

The Bible: Inspired of God

The Bible is the only book ever written that was inspired of God in the sense that God personally guided the writers. The inspiration of the Bible is defined as teaching that God so directed the human authors that, without destroying their own individuality, literary style, or personal interest, His complete and connected thought toward man was recorded. In forming Scriptures, it is true that God employed human writers; but these men, although they may not have understood all that they were writing, nevertheless under the guiding hand of God produced the sixty-six books that form the Bible in which there is amazing unity and constant evidence of the work of the Holy Spirit in directing what was written.

Accordingly, although written by human pen, the Bible is God's message to man rather than a message of man to his fellow man. Regardless of whether Scripture records words which God actually dictated, the copying of ancient records, the results of research of the human author, or the thoughts, aspirations, and fears of the writer, in every particular God guided the men so that what they wrote was precisely what God intended for them to write with the result that the Bible is indeed the

Word of God. Although passages of the Bible may differ greatly in their character, every word of Scripture is equally inspired of God.

The doctrine of inspiration, because it is supernatural, presents some problems to human understanding. How can a human author, recording his own thoughts and knowledge, be guided to write exactly what God directs him to write? Because of questions like this, various opinions have been advanced as to the extent of the divine control over the human authors. These have been called "theories of inspiration," and all interpreters of the Bible follow one or more of these theories. The view of inspiration that is accepted is the foundation upon which all Bible interpretation is built, and accordingly, careful attention must be given to the true view of inspiraton.

A. Theories of Inspiration

1. *Verbal, plenary inspiration.* In the history of the church the orthodox view of inspiration has been described as verbal and plenary. By verbal inspiration it is meant that the Spirit of God guided in the choice of the words used in the original writings. Scripture, however, indicates human authorship. Various books of the Bible reflect the writers' personal characteristics in style and vocabulary, and their personalities are often expressed in their thoughts, opinions, prayers, or fears. However, although the human elements are evident in the Bible, inspiration contends that God directed so that all the words that were used were equally inspired of God. This is brought out by the use of the word "plenary" which means "full inspiration," as opposed to views that claim only partial inspiration for the Bible.

Additional descriptive words are often added to make it clear what the orthodox doctrine is. Scripture is declared to be infallible in the sense of being unfailingly accurate. Scripture is also declared to be inerrant, meaning that the Bible does not contain any error as a statement of fact. Although the Bible may record on occasion the statements of men which are untrue or even the false teaching of Satan as in Genesis 3:4, in all these cases, while the statement attributed to Satan or men is faithfully recorded, it is clear that God does not affirm the truth of these statements. In stating that the Bible is verbally and fully inspired, and infallible and inerrant in its statement of truth, it is held that God's supernatural and perfect guidance is given to every word of Scripture so that the Bible can be trusted as an accurate statement of divine truth.

The claim of inspiration, of course, applies to the original writings only and not to copies, translations, or quotations. As there is no original manuscript in existence, scholars have gone to great lengths to determine the accuracy of the text of the Bible that we now have. For the purpose of learning truth, it may be assumed that our present copies of the Bible are accurate reproductions of the original writings. Although many minor variations in text exist, these very rarely affect any teaching of the Bible, and as further manuscripts are discovered, they tend to confirm this conclusion.

For all practical purposes, the Old Testament, written in Hebrew, and the New Testament, written in Greek, may be accepted as the very Word of God and a true statement of what God intended to communicate to man.

2. *Mechanical or dictation theory.* In contrast to the true doctrine of inspiration, which allows for human authorship and personality writing under the direction of God, some have held that God actually dictated the Scripture and that the writers of the Bible were only stenographers. If God had dictated the Bible, however, the style of writing and the vocabulary of the Bible would be the same throughout. In many cases the authors of Scripture expressed their own fears and feelings, or their prayers for God's deliverance, and in other ways injected their personalities into the divine record. Paul's heart-felt prayer for Israel in Romans 9:1-3, for instance, would lose its meaning if it were dictated by God.

Accordingly, while inspiration extends to every word of Scripture, it does not rule out human personality, literary style, or personal interest. The Bible affirms human authorship just as much as it does the divine authorship of the Bible. God accomplished the accuracy He desired by directing the human authors, but without the mechanical process of dictation. Some portions of the Bible were dictated by God and these are recorded as such, but most of the Bible was written by the human authors without evidence of direct dictation.

3. *The concept theory.* Some have attempted to weaken the complete inspiration of the Bible and allow for human authorship by saying that God inspired the concept but not the precise words. This view, however, has grave problems, as the human authors may have only partially understood what God was re-

vealing to them, and in restating it in their own words could inject considerable error.

The Bible expressly contradicts the idea that only concepts were given to the human authors. Again and again, emphasis is given to the words of Scripture as being inspired. The importance of words is frequently mentioned (Exod. 20:1; John 6:63; 17:8; 1 Cor. 2:13). In quotations from the Old Testament, it is frequently assumed that the very words are inspired of God as in John 10:34-35; Galatians 3:16; and the frequent mention of the Bible as the Word of God as in Ephesians 6:17; James 1:21-23; and 1 Peter 2:2. A solemn curse is pronounced upon anyone who takes away from the Word of God (Rev. 22:18-19). The concept theory, accordingly, falls far short of what the Scriptures claim as the true doctrine of inspiration.

4. *Partial inspiration.* Various theories affirming that only parts of the Bible are inspired are also advanced. For instance, some have claimed that the revelatory portions of the Bible dealing with divine truth are accurate, but that we cannot accept historical, geographical, or scientific statements in Scripture. Coupled wth partial inspiration is the idea that some portions of Scripture are more inspired than others, so that truth and error become a matter of degree. This is sometimes applied to what is known as "mystical inspiration," or the idea that God, in varying degrees, assisted the authors in what they were writing but fell short of giving them the capacity to write Scripture without error. All forms of partial inspiration leave the reader the final judge, and accordingly, the authority of Scripture becomes the authority of the person reading the Scripture, with no two readers agreeing exactly as to what is truth and what is not.

5. *Neoorthodox view of inspiration.* In the twentieth century a new view of divine revelation has been advanced, beginning with Karl Barth, which is called neoorthodox. While not necessarily denying that supernatural elements exist in the writing of Scripture, this view acknowledges that there are errors in the Bible and thus the Bible cannot be taken as literally true. Neoorthodoxy holds that God speaks through the Scriptures and uses them as a means by which to communicate truth to us. Accordingly, the Bible becomes a channel of divine revelation much as a beautiful flower or a lovely sunset communicates the concept that God is the Creator. The Bible under this theory becomes true only as it is comprehended and truth is realized by the individual reader. The history of this view demonstrates

that no two of its advocates exactly agree as to what the Bible actually teaches, and, like the view of partial inspiration, leaves the individual as the final authority concerning what is true and what is false.

6. *Naturalistic inspiration.* This is the most extreme view of unbelief and holds that the Bible is just like any other book. Although God may have given to the authors unusual ability to express concepts, it is after all a human production without supernatural divine guidance. The Bible under this concept becomes merely another book on religion, expressing ancient views of spiritual experience of men in the past. This view destroys any distinctive claim for the divine authority of the Bible and leaves without explanation the amazing factual accuracy of the Bible.

Ultimately, the reader of Scripture must make a choice. Either the Bible is what it claims to be — the inspired Word of God — and a book to be trusted as if God had written it Himself without human authors, or it must be regarded as a book which does not substantiate its claims and is not indeed the Word of God. While many proofs can be amassed in support of the inspiration of the Bible, the best evidence is found in the fact that the Book supports its claims. Its power has been manifested in the transformed lives of millions of those who have put their trust in the words and promises of Scripture.

B. The Testimony of Christ

The fact that the Bible is inspired of the Holy Spirit is supported by many internal evidences that it is indeed the Word of God and is confirmed by the power of the Word of God to influence and transform men. Of all the evidences, however, one of the most important is the testimony of Jesus Christ Himself to the fact that the Bible is inspired of God. Whenever Christ quoted Scripture — as He did frequently — He quoted it as having authority and in full recognition that it had come by the inspiration of the Holy Spirit. According to Matthew 5:18, Christ affirmed that not one jot or one tittle of the law would remain unfulfilled. By this He was saying that not one jot (the smallest letter of the Hebrew alphabet) or one tittle (the smallest part of a letter which would change the meaning) would be left unfulfilled. If accuracy and inspiration extended to the very letter, Christ was obviously affirming the inspiration of the entire Old Testament.

In John 10:35 Christ affirmed "the scripture cannot be broken." Again and again the New Testament affirms accurate fulfillment of the Old Testament, as in Matthew 1:22-23 (cf. Matt. 4:14; 8:17; 12:17; 15:7-8; 21:4-5, 42; 22:29; 26:31, 56; 27:9-10, 35). These references from the gospel of Matthew are typical of what extends throughout the entire New Testament. Even when affirming a dispensational change or a modificaton of a rule of life, the authority and inspiration of the original statement in Scripture are not questioned (Matt. 19:7-12).

Quotations from the Old Testament extend to every important section and frequently are from books that are most disputed by liberal critics, such as Deuteronomy, Jonah, and Daniel (Deut. 6:16 — cf. Matt. 12:40; Dan. 9:27; 12:11 — cf. Matt. 24:15). It is logically impossible to question the inspiration of the Old Testament without questioning the character and veracity of Jesus Christ. It is for this reason that denial of the inspired Word of God leads to the denial of the incarnate Word of God.

Jesus Christ not only affirmed the inspiration and infallible accuracy of the Old Testament, but He predicted the writing of the New Testament. According to John 16:12-13, the disciples were to receive truth from the Holy Spirit after Christ had ascended to heaven. Christ stated that the disciples would be witnesses to the truth (Matt. 28:19; Luke 10:22-23; John 15:27; Acts 1:8). Jesus gave to the disciples authority in their speaking of the truth (Luke 10:16; John 13:19; John 17:14, 18; Heb. 2:3-4).

As the New Testament was written, the writers were conscious that they were guided by the Spirit of God and freely claimed that the New Testament was inspired equally with the Old. Just as David wrote by the Spirit (Matt. 22:43) and as the psalmist was inspired (Heb. 3:7-11; cf. Ps. 95:7-11), so the New Testament likewise claims inspiration. In 1 Timothy 5:18, both Deuteronomy 25:4 and Luke 10:7 are quoted as equally inspired Scripture. In 2 Peter 3:15-16, the epistles of Paul are classified as Scripture which should be received as the Word of God like all other Scripture. The New Testament obviously claims to have the same inspiration as the Old Testament.

C. Important Passages on Inspiration

One of the central passages on the inspiration of the Bible is found in 2 Timothy 3:16 where it is affirmed, "All scripture is given by inspiration of God, and is profitable for doctrine, for reproof, for correction, for instruction in righteousness." By "scripture" the apostle is referring to "the holy scriptures" mentioned in 2 Timothy 3:15 and including both the Old and New Testaments. The expression "by inspiration of God" is one word in the New Testament Greek, *theopneustos*, meaning "God-breathed." By this it is meant Scripture proceeds from God and by this fact takes on the same perfections that characterize God Himself. It would be impossible for God to be the author of error. The inspiration extends not so much to the authors but to the Word of God itself. While the authors were fallible and subject to error, God breathed through them His infallible Word, and by divine power and guidance so directed the human authors that what they wrote was indeed the infallible Word of God. Because it is the Word of God, it is profitable for doctrine or teaching, and for reproof, correction, and instruction in righteousness.

One of the important questions that is frequently raised is, How could God inspire Scripture while on the one hand allowing for human authorship and individuality and on the other hand producing the inspired Word of God without error? The question of how God performed a supernatural act is always inscrutable, but some light is cast on this question in 2 Peter 1:21 where, in connection with discussion of prophecy in the Scripture, it is stated, "For the prophecy came not in old time by the will of man: but holy men of God spake as they were moved by the Holy Ghost." Whether they were oral prophets or writing prophets, the explanation is that they were "moved by the Holy Ghost." The word translated "moved" is the word for carrying a burden. In this statement, accordingly, the human authors are carried along to the destination intended by God much as a boat will carry its passengers to its ultimate destination. Although passengers on a boat have some human freedom and can move freely within the boat, they nevertheless surely and inevitably are carried to the destination of the boat itself.

While this explanation is not complete, as the work of inspiration is beyond human comprehension or explanation, it makes clear that the human authors were not left to their own devices and were not simply exercising ordinary power. God was working through them, breathing out His word with them as the channels. Some Scripture, to be sure, was dictated expressly by God, as for instance the giving of the law in Exodus 20:1-17. Again and again the Old Testament declares that "God said" (Gen. 1:3). Another frequent expression is that "the word of the LORD came" to one of the prophets (cf. Jer. 1:2; Hos. 1:1; Jonah 1:1; Mic. 1:1; Zeph. 1:1; Hag. 1:1; Zech. 1:1). In other instances God spoke through visions or dreams (Dan. 2:1) or appeared in a vision (Dan. 7:1). While the form and circumstances of divine revelation varied, in it all God speaks authoritatively, accurately, and inerrantly. Accordingly, the Word of God partakes of the same qualty of absolute truth as is in the person and character of God Himself.

D. Qualifying Considerations

In stating that the entire Bible is true and inspired of God, allowance must be made for the fact that sometimes the Bible records a lie as a lie, as in the case of the lie of Satan in Genesis 3:4. The Bible can also record the experiences and reasonings of men as illustrated in the Book of Job and Ecclesiastes. Here what the Scripture actually quotes them as thinking or saying must be tested by the clear affirmations of truth elsewhere in the Bible. Accordingly, some of the statements of Job's friends are wrong, and some of the philosophizing of Ecclesiastes does not go beyond human wisdom. Whenever the Bible states a fact as a fact, however, it must be true whether this is in a revelation of God's own being, His moral standards, or His prophetic program, or whether it involves history, geography, or facts that are related to science. It is an amazing testimony to the accuracy of the Word of God that though the authors could not anticipate modern scientific discoveries and did not use technical language, they nevertheless do not contradict anything that man discovers to be certainly true.

There are problems in the Bible which may raise questions. Sometimes because of lack of information, the Bible seems to contradict itself, as for instance in the account of the healing of the blind men at Jericho, where varying accounts indicate two or one blind man (Matt. 20:30; Mark 10:46; Luke 18:35) and where the incident is set as going into (Luke 18:35) or going out of Jericho (Mark 10:46; Luke 19:1). Problems of this kind, however, yield to patient study, and the difficulty could be solved if all the facts were known. For example, there were two cities of Jericho — one ancient, the other more modern. Christ could be going out of one Jericho while entering the other.

Many supposed errors in the Bible have been cleared up by archaeological discoveries.

Actually no one knows enough to contradict the statements of Scripture, whether they refer to the creation of the world or the creation of man or whether they extend to some detail in narrative. Properly understood, the Bible stands as the monument of God's own veracity and truth and can be trusted in the same way as if God Himself were speaking directly to the individual reading Scripture. Although every attempt has been made to undermine and destroy the Bible, to those seeking truth about God it continues to be the only authoritative and inerrant source of divine revelation.

Questions

1. Define what is meant by the inspiration of the Bible.
2. To what extent is the Bible inspired?
3. What is meant by verbal, plenary inspiration?
4. To what extent is the Bible infallible and inerrant, and what do these terms mean?
5. How can you explain that the Bible records untrue statements of men?
6. To what extent does inspiration extend to copies and translations of the Bible?
7. Define the mechanical or dictation theory of inspiration and indicate why it is inadequate.
8. What are the problems of the concept theory of inspiration?
9. What are the problems of theory of partial inspiration or degrees of inspiration?
10. How does the neoorthodox view of inspiration differ from the orthodox view?
11. Why must the naturalistic view of the Bible be rejected?
12. What did Christ teach concerning the inspiration of the Bible?
13. How do quotations of the Old Testament uphold the inspiration of the Old Testament?
14. What indications are given in the New Testament that it is also inspired of God?
15. Discuss the contribution of 2 Timothy 3:16.
16. What does 2 Peter 1:21 contribute as to the method of inspiration?
17. Indicate the extent to which the Bible affirms its own inspiration.
18. How does inspiration relate to the truth of human experiences and reasonings as illustrated in the Book of Job and Ecclesiastes?
19. What should be our response to seeming contradictions in the Bible?
20. Taking the subject of inspiration as a whole, why is it so important?

3

The Bible:
Its Subject and Purpose

A. *Jesus Christ as the Subject*

The Lord Jesus Christ is the supreme subject of the Bible. In reading Scripture, however, the perfections of Christ in His Person and work are presented in many ways.

1. *Jesus Christ as the Creator.* The early chapters of Genesis record the creation of the world as accomplished by God, using the word *elohim* which includes God the Father, God the Son, and God the Holy Spirit. It is not until one reaches the New Testament that it is revealed clearly that all things were made by Christ (John 1:3). According to Colossians 1:16-17, "By him were all things created, that are in heaven, and that are in earth, visible and invisible, whether they be thrones, or dominions, or principalities, or powers: all things were created by him, and for him: and he is before all things and by him all things consist." This does not mean that God the Father and God the Holy Spirit had no part in creation, but it does give to, Christ the place of being the main actor in the creation of the universe. Accordingly, the perfections of the universe reflect His handiwork.

2. *Jesus Christ as the supreme ruler of the world.* Because He is the Creator, Jesus Christ also has the place of being the supreme ruler of the universe. While Scripture attributes supreme sovereignty to God the Father, it is clear that it is His purpose that Christ should rule the world (Ps. 2:8-9). It is the purpose of God that every tongue shall confess that Christ is Lord and every knee will bow (Isa. 45:23; Rom. 14:11; Phil. 2:9-11). The history of man, although it records his rebellion against God (Ps. 2:1-2), reveals that Christ is awaiting the day when His full sovereignty is expressed over the entire world (Ps. 110:1). The day will come when Christ will be Lord of all, sin will be judged, and the sovereignty of Christ revealed (Rev. 19:15-16).

In fulfilling His purpose, God has permitted earthly rulers to occupy their thrones. Great nations have risen and fallen such as Egypt, Assyria, Babylon, Medo-Persia, Greece, and Rome, but the final kingdom will be the kingdom from heaven over which Christ will rule (Dan. 7:13-14).

Not only is Christ the King over the nations, but He will reign on the throne of David as the Son of David and especially will be the King of Israel (Luke 1:31-33). This will become evident when He returns in His second coming to establish His millennial kingdom and will reign over the entire world including the kingdom of Israel.

His sovereignty is also expressed in His relationship to the church of which He is the head (Eph. 1:22-23). As the supreme sovereign over the world, over Israel, and over the church (Eph. 1:20-21), Christ is the supreme judge of all men (John 5:27; cf. Isa. 9:6-7; Ps. 72:1-2, 8, 11).

3. *Jesus Christ as the Incarnate Word.* In the New Testament especially, Jesus Christ is revealed as the Incarnate Word, the physical embodiment of what God is, and a revelation of the nature and being of God. In Christ are revealed all the attributes that belong to God, especially His wisdom, power, holiness, and love. Jesus Christ is the Word (John 1:1), the expression of what God is. Through Jesus Christ, men can come to know God in a more accurate and detailed way than in any other means of divine revelation. According to Hebrews 1:3, Christ "being the brightness of his glory, and the express image of his person, and upholding all things by the word of his power, when he had by himself purged our sins, sat down on the right hand of the Majesty on high." It is a central purpose of God that He reveal Himself to His creatures through Jesus Christ.

4. *Jesus Christ as Savior.* In the drama of history, beginning with man's creation and fall and ending in the new heaven and the new earth, the work of Jesus Christ as the Savior is a prominent theme of Scripture. Christ is the promised seed who would conquer Satan (Gen. 3:15). In the Old Testament, Christ is pictured as the servant of Jehovah who would bear the sins of the whole world (Isa. 53:4-6; cf. John 1:29). As a sacrifice for sin, He was to die on the cross and suffer the judgment of the sin of the whole world (1 Cor. 15:3-4; 2 Cor. 5:19-21; 1 Pet. 1:18-19; 1 John 2:2; Rev. 1:5). As Savior He is not only the sacrifice for sin but also our High Priest (Heb. 7:25-27).

One of the central purposes of God, as revealed in Scripture, is to provide salvation through Jesus Christ for a lost race. Accordingly, from Genesis to Revelation, Jesus Christ is presented supremely as the only Savior (Acts 4:12).

B. The History of Man in the Bible

While the Bible is preeminently designed to glorify God, it records the history of man in keeping with that purpose. The creation narrative in the early chapters of Genesis culminates in the creation of Adam and Eve. Scripture as a whole unfolds God's plan and purpose for the human race.

As later chapters will disclose, God's sovereign purposes for the nations of the world are majestically unfolded in the history of the race. The immediate descendents of Adam and Eve are blotted out in the flood in the time of Noah. Genesis 10 records the descendants of Noah as they formed the three major divisions of the human race. Then, as the descendants of Noah also failed and were judged at the Tower of Babel, God selected Abraham to fulfill His purpose of revealing Himself through the people of Israel. Beginning in Genesis 12, a dominant theme of the Bible is the emergence and history of the nation of Irsael. Most of the Old Testament is occupied with this fairly small nation in relation to the mass of Gentiles about it. In the purposes of God, this culminates in the New Testament in the coming of Jesus Christ who supremely fulfilled the promise given originally to Abraham that through his seed all nations of the world would be blessed.

In the New Testament, another major division of humanity emerges, that is, the church as the body of Christ, comprising both Jew and Gentile who believe in Jesus Christ as their Savior.

Thus the New Testament is occupied especially in the Acts and epistles with God's dealings with the church. The Book of Revelation is the grand climax to it all. The succession of great empires — beginning with Egypt and Assyria and continuing with Babylon, Medo-Persia, Greece, and Rome — is climaxed by the kingdom which comes from heaven at the second coming of Christ. Jew and Gentile alike are found in the millennial kingdom, with Israel finding its fulfillment in possessing the land under its Messiah King and the nations of the world enjoying also the blessings of the millennial kingdom.

While the subject of Scripture centers in Jesus Christ and relates the history of the world to God's purpose to glorify Himself, the major movements of God can, accordingly, be seen in the demonstration of His sovereignty in relation to the nations, His faithfulness in relation to Israel, and His grace in relation to the church. The consummation of it all is found in the new heavens, the new earth, and the new Jerusalem as history recedes and eternity begins.

C. The Purpose of the Bible

According to the written Word of God, one supreme purpose is revealed in all that God has done or will do, from the beginning of creation to the farthest reaches of eternity. This supreme purpose is the manifestation of the glory of God. For this one purpose angels were created, the material universe was designed to reflect that glory, and man was created in the image and likeness of God. In the inscrutable wisdom of God, even sin was permitted and redemption was provided with a view toward the realization of this supreme purpose.

For God to manifest His glory is in keeping with His infinite perfections. When man attempts to glorify himself, it is always questionable because man is so imperfect. For God to manifest His glory is to express and reveal truth which has infinite blessing for the creature. Because God is infinite in His being and absolute in His perfection, He is worthy of infinite glory, and it would be an injustice of infinite proportions should His creation withhold from Him the full expression of that honor and glory which are rightfully His. In manifesting His glory, God is not self-seeking, but rather is expressing His glory for the benefit of His creation. The revelation of God to His creatures has provided them with a worthy object for love and devotion, has given them ground for faith and peace of mind, and has given man assurance of salvation in time and eternity. The more man comprehends the glory of God, the greater is the blessing that accrues to man.

Since the Bible is God's message to man, its supreme purpose is His supreme purpose — which is, that He may be glorified. The Bible records:

1. That "all things . . . that are in heaven, and that are in earth, visible and invisible, whether they be thrones, or dominions, or principalities, or powers: all things were created by him, and for him" (for his glory, Col. 1:16). *Angels and men, the material universe and every creature, are all created for His glory.* "The heavens declare the glory of God" (Ps. 19:1).

2. *The nation Israel is for the glory of God* (Isa. 43:7, 21, 25; 60:1, 3, 21; 62:3; Jer. 13:11).

3. *Salvation is unto the glory of God* (Rom. 9:23), even as it will be a manifestation of the grace of God (Eph. 2:7), and is now a manifestation of the wisdom of God (Eph. 3:10).

4. *All service should be unto the glory of God* (Matt. 5:16; John 15:8; 1 Cor. 10:31; 1 Pet. 2:12; 4:11, 14). The Bible itself is God's instrument by which He prepares the man of God unto every good work (2 Tim. 3:16-17).

5. *The Christian's new passion is that God may be glorified* (Rom. 5:2).

6. *Even the believer's death is said to be to this one end* (John 21:19; Phil. 1:20).

7. *The saved one is appointed to share in the glory of Christ* (John 17:22; Col. 3:4).

Taken as a whole, the Bible differs in its subject and purpose from any other book in the world. It stands supreme as reflecting the place of man and his opportunity of salvation, the supreme character and work of Jesus Christ as the only Savior, and gives in detail the infinite glories that belong to God Himself. It is the one book that reveals the Creator to the creature and discloses the plan by which man in all his imperfections can be reconciled and in eternal fellowship with the eternal God.

Questions

1. What evidence is found that Christ participated in creation?
2. In what sense is Christ the supreme ruler of the world and how is it expressed?
3. Explain how Christ is the supreme revelation of God.
4. Trace the line of Scripture dealing with Christ as Savior, including the mention of some New Testament passages.
5. What does the Bible record concerning the history of man in Genesis 1-11?
6. For what purpose did God select Abraham?
7. How does the history of Israel culminate in Christ?
8. What new purpose is revealed in the New Testament?
9. What great nations characterize history?
10. Distinguish the purposes of God as they relate to the nations, Israel, and the church.
11. In what respects does the Bible reveal the glory of God as its supreme purpose?

4

The Bible:
As a Divine Revelation

A. *Forms of Divine Revelation*

The Bible is intended to be a revelation of the being, works, and program of God. That an infinite God would seek to reveal Himself to His creatures is reasonable and is essential to God's fulfilling His purpose in creation. It is only natural that rational beings should attempt to learn something about the Creator who made them. If man is the highest order of creature, who has the capacity to recognize and have fellowship with the Creator, it is reasonable to expect that the Creator will communicate with His creature revealing His purpose and will. Three major ways have been used by God to reveal Himself.

1. *Revelation of God in creation.* The eternal power and character of God are revealed by the things which are created (Rom. 1:20). The natural world being a work of God discloses that God is a God of infinite power and wisdom and has designed the physical world for intelligent purposes. The revelation of God through nature, however, has its limitations, as there is no clear disclosure of the love of God or the holiness of God. While the revelation of God in nature is sufficient so that God

31

can judge the heathen world for not worshiping Him as their Creator, it does not reveal a way of salvation by which sinners can be reconciled to a holy God.

2. *Revelation in Christ.* A supreme revelation of God was provided in the person and work of Christ, who was born in God's appointed time (Gal. 4:4). The Son of God came into the world to reveal God to men in terms which they could understand. By His becoming man in the act of incarnation, facts about God which otherwise would have been difficult for man to understand are translated into the limited range of human comprehension. Accordingly, in Christ not only is the power and wisdom of God revealed, but also the love of God, the goodness of God, His holiness, and His grace. Christ stated, "He that hath seen me hath seen the Father" (John 14:9). Therefore, one who knows Jesus Christ also knows God the Father.

3. *Revelation in the written Word.* The written Word of God is able, however, to reveal God in even more explicit terms than can be observed in the person and work of Christ. As previously brought out, it is the Bible that introduces Jesus Christ to us both as the object of prophecy and as the fulfillment of prophecy. Yet the Bible goes far beyond giving details about Christ, discloses God's program for Israel, for the nations, and for the church, and deals with many related subjects as the history of mankind and of the universe unfolds. The Bible not only presents God as its supreme subject, but also unfolds His purposes. The written revelation is all-inclusive. It restates all the facts concerning God which are revealed through nature and gives the only record concerning God's manifestation in Christ. It also enlarges the divine revelation into great detail regarding God the Father, the Son, the Spirit, angels, demons, man, sin, salvation, grace, and glory. The Bible, accordingly, may be regarded as completing the intended divine revelation of God partially revealed in nature, more fully revealed in Christ, and completely revealed in the written Word.

B. Special Revelation

Throughout the history of man, God has given special revelation. Many instances are recorded in the Word of God of His speaking directly to man as He did in the Garden of Eden or to the prophets of the Old Testament or the apostles in the New Testament. Some of this special revelation was recorded in the Bible and forms the only authoritative and inspired record that we have of such special revelation.

Upon completion of the sixty-six books in the Bible, special revelation in the ordinary sense seems to have ceased. No one has ever been able successfully to add one verse to the written Scriptures as a normative statement of truth. Apocryphal additions are clearly inferior and without the inspiration which has attended all writing of Scripture itself.

In place of special revelation, however, a work of the Spirit has especially characterized the present age. As the Spirit of God illuminates or casts light upon the Scriptures, this is a legitimate form of present tense revelation from God in which the teachings of the Bible are made clear and applied to individual life and circumstances. Coupled with the work of illumination is the work of the Spirit in guidance as general scriptural truths are applied to the particular needs of an individual. While both guidance and illumination are genuine works of God, they do not guarantee that an individual will perfectly understand the Bible or in all cases will understand accurately God's guidance. Thus, while illumination and guidance are a work of the Spirit, they do not possess the infallibility of Scripture as they are being received by fallible human beings.

Apart from this work of the Spirit of God, however, in revealing what Scripture means, there is no real understanding of the truth as stated in 1 Corinthians 2:10. The truth of the Word of God needs to be revealed to us by the Spirit of God, and we need to be taught by the Spirit (1 Cor. 2:13). According to 1 Corinthians 2:14, "The natural man receiveth not the things of the Spirit of God: for they are foolishness unto him: neither can he know them, because they are spiritually discerned." Accordingly, the Bible is a closed book, as far as its real meaning is concerned, to one who is not a Christian and not taught by the Spirit. It also requires on the part of the individual student of Scripture a close fellowship with God in which the Spirit of God is able to reveal His truth.

C. Interpretation

In receiving revelation which comes through the Holy Spirit as He teaches the Word of God to a believer in Christ, the problems of interpretation of the Bible are evident. Certain basic rules are necessary if one is to understand the science of interpretation, called "hermeneutics." While there is reliance upon the Holy Spirit for instruction in the Word of God, certain principles may be enumerated.

1. *The purpose of the Bible as a whole.* In interpreting the Bible, every text must be taken in the light of the total content of Scripture, as the Bible does not contradict itself.

2. *The particular message of each book of the Bible.* The interpretation of Scripture must always take into consideration the purpose of the book of which it is a part. A study of Ecclesiastes is, accordingly, quite different than a study of the book of Revelation or the Psalms, and interpretation must be in keeping with the purpose of the book.

3. *To whom addressed.* While all Scripture is given by equal inspiration of God, not all Scripture is equally applicable. Much false doctrine has come through applying Scripture wrongly. Thus the question must be raised concerning who is in view in a particular passage. Here primary and secondary application must be distinguished. Primary application might extend only to the individual or group to whom the Scripture is addressed, as for instance the epistle to the Galatians or a psalm written by David. There is almost always a secondary application, as the particular truths set forth in the scriptural text are found to have a general application beyond the one to whom it is actually addressed. So, while the Old Testament law was addressed to Israel, Christians in this dispensation can study it with profit as a revelation of God's holiness with due allowance for the particulars which may be changed in their application to us.

4. *The context.* One of the important considerations in the exposition of any text is to consider the immediate context. Often this gives the clue to what was intended in the particular statement. Scripture which precedes and follows any given verse helps the reader understand the verse itself.

5. *Similar teachings elsewhere in the Word of God.* Because the Bible cannot contradict itself, when a theological statement is made in one verse it should be harmonized with any other similar theological statement elsewhere. This is the particular task of systematic theology, which attempts to take all the divine revelation and restate it in doctrinal form which is not contradictory of any portion of Scripture. Often books will complement each other. For instance, the Book of Revelation often depends for its interpretation on the Book of Daniel or other Old Testament prophecies. If the Holy Spirit is the author of the entire

Word of God, what is said in one place should help us understand what is said in another place in Scripture.

6. *Accurate exegesis of the words of a particular text.* The Bible was originally written in Hebrew and Greek, and often there is difficulty in precise translations. Thus a knowledge of the original language is helpful in determining exactly what the text says. Students of Scripture who do not have these technical tools can often be helped by commentaries and expositions by writers who are able to give added light upon a particular text. While for most purposes a good translation is sufficient, a careful student will sometimes consult authorities who are able to shed light on a specific text.

In addition to determining the actual meaning of the words, proper interpretation assumes that each word has its normal literal meaning unless there are good reasons for regarding it as a figure of speech. For instance, the land promised Israel should not be considered a reference to heaven, but rather as a literal reference to the Holy Land. Likewise, promises given to Israel should not be spiritualized to apply to Gentile believers in Christ. The rule of interpretation is that words should be given their normal meaning unless the context clearly indicates that a figure of speech is intended.

7. *Guard against prejudice.* While it is proper for any interpreter of Scripture to approach a passage with theological convictions arising from a study of the entire Bible, care should be taken not to twist a text into what it does not say in order to harmonize it with preconceived ideas. Each text should be allowed to speak for itself even if it leaves temporarily some unresolved problems of harmonization with other Scripture.

In interpreting the Bible it is important to regard Scripture as a comprehensive revelation intended to be understood by all who are taught by the Spirit. The Bible was intended to communicate truth, and when properly interpreted it yields a system of doctrine which is harmonious and not contradictory.

Questions

1. Why is it reasonable to assume that God would desire to reveal Himself to man?
2. What is the extent and the limitation of revelation in nature?
3. To what extent is Christ a revelation of God?
4. Why was the written Word necessary to reveal God completely?
5. What are some of the major subjects of divine revelation which could not be learned in nature?
6. What is meant by special revelation?
7. What work of the Spirit has replaced special revelation today, and why is this necessary?
8. Why must the purpose of the Bible as a whole, as well as the particular message of each book of the Bible, be taken into consideration?
9. What are the dangers of misapplying Scripture, and why must primary and secondary application be distinguished?
10. What is contributed by the context of any passage?
11. Why must interpretation of one text be in harmony with other biblical passages?
12. To what extent is accurate exegesis required?
13. To what extent should the normal meaning of words determine the meaning of a passage?
14. What are the dangers of prejudice in interpreting Scripture?

5

God the Trinity

A. Belief in the Existence of God

The belief that a divine being exists greater than man has been common to all cultures and civilizations. This has been due in part to the fact that man reasons there must be an explanation for our world and for human experience, and that a being greater than man would serve to explain this. Man seems intuitively, by his very religious nature, to reach out to some sort of higher being. This also can be explained in part by the work of the Holy Spirit in the world which extends to every creature, a work which is designated in theology as common grace, in contrast to the special work of the Spirit relating to man's salvation. The modern phenomenon of many who claim to be atheists arises from the perversion of man's mind and the denial that any rational explanation of the universe is possible. Accordingly, the Bible declares an atheist to be a fool (Ps. 14:1).

Ordinarily men do not ask for proofs of their own existence nor the existence of material things which they recognize by their senses. Although God is unseen as to His person, His existence is so evident that men generally require no proofs for the fact of God. Doubt of God's existence is evidently due to man's own perversity and blindness and to satanic influence. The evidence for the existence of God in creation is so clear that rejection of it is the ground of condemnation of the heathen world which has not heard the Gospel. According to Romans 1:19-20, their condemnation is, "Because that which may be known of God is manifest in them; for God hath shewed it unto them. For the invisible things of him from the creation of the world are clearly seen, being understood by the things that are made, even his eternal power and Godhead; so that they are without excuse."

The revelation of God through prophets before Scripture was written, and the revelation coming from Scripture, have to some degree penetrated the total consciousness of man today. Although the world in general is ignorant of scriptural revelation, some concepts of God have pervaded the thinking of the entire world so that belief in some sort of a higher being is generally true even among men untouched directly by Scripture.

Although ancient Greek philosophers were unfamiliar with biblical revelation, some attempts were made to explain our universe on the basis of a higher being. Various systems of thought have evolved: (1) polytheism, the belief in many gods; (2) hylozoism, that identifies the life principle found in all creation as being God Himself; (3) materialism, which argues that matter is self-functioning according to natural law and no god is necessary to its functioning, a theory supporting modern evolutionism; and (4) pantheism which holds that God is impersonal and identical with nature itself, that God is immanent but not transcendent. Many variations of these concepts of God exist.

In arguing for the existence of God from the facts of creation apart from the revelation of Scripture, four general classes or lines of reason may be observed: (1) The ontological argument holds that God must exist because man universally believes that He exists. This is sometimes called an *a priori* argument. (2) The cosmological argument holds that every effect must have its sufficient cause and, therefore, the universe, which is an effect, must have a Creator as its cause. Involved in this argument is the complexity of an ordered universe which could not have come into existence by accident. (3) The teleological argument points out that every design must have its designer, and as the whole creation is intricately designed and interrelated, creation must have a great designer. The fact that all things work together indicate that this designer must be one of infinite power and wisdom. (4) The anthropological argument argues from the nature and existence of man as being unexplained apart from creation by God who has a nature similar to but greater than man's. Involved in this is the fact that man has intellect (capacity to think), sensibility (capacity to feel), and will (capacity to make moral choices). Such extraordinary ability points to One who has similar but greater abilities who has created man.

Although these arguments for the existence of God have considerable validity and man may be justly condemned by God for rejecting them (Rom. 1:18-20), they have not been sufficient to bring man into proper relationship to God or to produce a real faith in God unassisted by scriptural revelation. It is in the Bible that the complete revelation of God is given, confirming all the facts found in nature but adding to natural revelation many truths which natural revelation could not have disclosed.

B. The Unity of the Divine Trinity

In general, the Old Testament emphasizes the unity of God (Exod. 20:3; Deut. 6:4; Isa. 44:6), a fact which is also taught in the New Testament (John 10:30; 14:9; 17:11, 22, 23; Col. 1:15). Both the Old Testament and to a greater extent the New Testament, however, also indicate that God exists as a Trinity — God the Father, God the Son, God the Holy Spirit. Many believe that the doctrine of the Trinity is implicit in the use of the word *elohim*, as a name for God which is in a plural form and seems to refer to the triune God.

Early in Genesis there are references to the Spirit of God, and the plural personal pronouns are used for God as in Genesis 1:26; 3:22; 11:7. Frequently in the Old Testament there are distinctions within the nature of God in terms of the Father, the Son and the Holy Spirit. Isaiah 7:14 speaks of the Son as the Immanuel, "God with us," who was to be distinct from the Father and the Spirit. This Son is called in Isaiah 9:6 "the mighty God, the everlasting Father, the Prince of Peace."

In Psalm 2:7 God the Father, referred to as "I," indicates that it is His purpose to have His Son as the supreme sovereign over the earth. Just as the Father and the Son are distinguished, so God is also distinguished from the Holy Spirit as in Psalm 104:30 where the Lord God sends His Spirit. To these evidences may be added all the references to the Angel of Jehovah, which indicate the appearances of the Son of God in the Old Testament as one sent by the Father, and references to the Spirit of the Lord as the Holy Spirit distinct from the Father and the Son.

To these Old Testament evidences the New Testament gives additional revelation. Here in the Person of Jesus Christ is God incarnate, conceived by the Holy Spirit and yet Son of God the Father. At the baptism of Jesus, the distinctions in the Trinity are evident with God the Father speaking from heaven, the Holy Spirit descending like a dove and lighting upon Him, and Jesus Himself being baptized (Matt. 3:16-17). These distinctions in the Trinity are also observed in such passages as John 14:16, where the Father and the Comforter are distinguished from Christ Himself and in Matthew 28:19 where the disciples are instructed to baptize believers "in the name of the Father, and of the Son, and of the Holy Ghost."

The many indications in both the Old and New Testaments that God exists or subsists as a triune being have made the doctrine of the Trinity a central fact of all orthodox creeds from the early church until modern times. Any departure from this is considered a departure from scriptural truth. Although the word "trinity" does not occur in the Bible, the facts of scriptural revelation permit no other explanation.

While the doctrine of the Trinity is a central fact of Christian faith, it is also beyond human comprehension and has no parallel in human experience. It is best defined as holding that, while God is one, He exists as three persons. These persons are equal, have the same attributes, and are equally worthy of adoration, worship, and faith. Yet the doctrine of the unity of the Godhead makes clear that they are not three separate gods, like three separate human beings such as Peter, James, and John. Accordingly, the true Christian faith is not tritheism, a belief in three Gods. On the other hand, the Trinity must not be explained as three modes of existence, that is, one God manifesting Himself in three ways. The Trinity is essential to the being of God and is more than a form of divine revelation.

The persons of the Trinity, while having equal attributes, differ in certain properties. Hence, the First Person of the Trinity is called the Father. The Second Person is called the Son and is sent forth by the Father. The Third Person is the Holy Spirit who is sent forth by the Father and the Son. This is called in theology the doctrine of procession, and the order is never reversed, that is, the Son never sends the Father and the Spirit never sends the Son. In the nature of the uniqueness of the Godhead, there is no illustration or parallel in human experience. Thus this doctrine should be accepted by faith on the basis of scriptural revelation even if it is beyond human comprehension and definition.

C. The Names of God

In the Old Testament, three principal names are ascribed to God. The first name, "Jehovah" or "Yahweh" is the name of God applied only to the true God. The name first appears in connection with the Creation in Genesis 2:4, and the meaning of the name is defined in Exodus 3:13-14 as the "I am that I am," that is, the self-existent, eternal God.

The most common name for God in the Old Testament is *elohim,* a word which is used both for the true God and for gods of the heathen world. This name is introduced in Genesis 1:1. The meaning of this name has been debated, but seems to include the idea of being the "strong one" and being one to be feared or reverenced. Because it is in a plural form, it seems to include all the Trinity, although it can also be used of individual Persons of the Trinity.

The third name for God in the Old Testament is *adonai,* which commonly means "master" or "lord" and is used not only of God as our Master but also of men who are masters over their servants. It is frequently joined to *elohim,* as in Genesis 15:2, and when so used emphasizes the fact that God is our Master or Lord. Many combinations of these names of God are found in the Old Testament. The most frequent is Jehovah Elohim or Adonai Elohim.

To these combinations of the three primary names of God are many other compounds found in the Old Testament such as Jehovah-jireh, meaning "the LORD will provide" (Gen. 22:13-14); Jehovah-rapha, "the LORD who healeth" (Exod. 15:26); Jehovah-nissi, "the LORD my banner" (Exod. 17:8-15); Jehovah-shalom, "the LORD our peace" (Judg. 6:24); Jehovah-tsidkenu, "the LORD our righteousness" (Jer. 23:6); Jehovah-shammah "the LORD is present" (Ezek. 48:35).

In the New Testament additional titles of God are found, the First Person being distinguished as "the Father," the Second Person distinguished as "the Son," and the Third Person distinguished as "the Holy Spirit." These titles, of course, are also

found in the Old Testament but are more common in the New
Testament. Discussion of these terms will follow in chapters
dealing with the three persons of the Trinity.

D. *The Attributes of God*

In the essential being of God, there are certain inherent attributes or essential qualities of God. These attributes are eternally
held by the Triune God and are equal for each person of the
Godhead. Included in the attributes is the fact that God is a
Spirit (John 4:24), God is life (John 5:26), God is self-existent
(Exod. 3:14), God is infinite (Ps. 145:3), God is immutable or
changeless (Ps. 102:27; Mal. 3:6; James 1:17), God is truth
(Deut. 32:4; John 17:3), God is love (1 John 4:8), God is eternal (Ps. 90:2), God is holy (1 Pet. 1:16; 1 John 1:5), God is
omnipresent (Ps. 139:8); Jer. 23:23-24), God is omniscient (Ps.
147:4-5), and God is omnipotent (Matt. 19:26.

Variations of these attributes can be seen in the fact that
God is good, God is merciful, and God is sovereign. All perfections are ascribed to God to infinity, and His works as well as
His being are perfect. The great detail and design of the universe are evidence of His sovereignty, power, and wisdom; His
plan of salvation, as revealed in the Scriptures, is evidence of
His love, righteousness, and grace. No aspect of creation is too
large for Him to be in complete control, and no detail, even to
the falling of a sparrow, is too small to be included in His
sovereign plan.

E. *The Sovereignty of God*

The attributes of God make clear that God is supreme over all.
He yields to no other power, authority or glory, and is not subject to any absolute greater than Himself. He represents perfection to an infinite degree in every aspect of His being. He
can never be surprised, defeated, or uncertain. However, without sacrificing His authority or jeopardizing the final realization
of His perfect will, it has pleased God to give to men a measure
of freedom of choice, and for the exercise of this choice God
holds man responsible.

Because man in his depraved state is blind and insensitive to
the work of God, it is clear from Scripture that men do not turn

to God apart from the moving of His Spirit in their hearts (John 6:44; 16:7-11). On the human side, however, man is held responsible for unbelief and is commanded to believe on the Lord Jesus Christ in order to be saved (Acts 16:31). It is also true that in the affairs of men, especially of Christians, God works to accomplish His will (Phil. 2:13). Yet He does not force men to yield themselves to God but rather beseeches them to do so (Rom. 12:1-2).

The fact that God has given to men certain freedom does not introduce an element of uncertainty into the universe, as God anticipates in advance and knows to infinity all that man will do in response to the divine and human influences which come into his life. His sovereignty therefore infinitely extends to every act even if it be to the temporary permission of evil that ultimately God might be glorified.

F. The Decree of God

The sovereign purpose of God is defined theologically as the decree of God, referring to the comprehensive plan that includes all events of every classification which will occur. The decree of God includes those events which God does Himself and also includes all that God accomplishes through natural law, over which He is completely sovereign. More difficult to comprehend is the fact that His sovereign decree also extends to all the acts of men, which are included in His eternal plan.

While incomprehensible to us, it is evident that the all-wise God, having complete knowledge of what man would do in his freedom, in electing to give man freedom of choice does not introduce any element of uncertainty. The divine plan, accordingly, included permitting man to sin as Adam and Eve did with all the resultant acts of sin. It included the divine remedy of Christ dying on the cross and all the work of the Holy Spirit in bringing men to repentance and faith.

Although the working of God in human hearts is inscrutable, the Bible is plain that on the one hand what man does has been included in God's eternal decree and on the other hand man operates with freedom of choice and is held responsible for his choices. The decree of God is not fatalism — a blind, mechanical control of all events — but is an intelligent, loving, and wise plan in which man, responsible for his choices, is held accountable for what he does and rewarded for his good works.

The decree of God may be divided into subdivisions such as His decree to create, His decree to preserve the world, His decree of providence, or His wise guidance of the universe. His decree includes the promises or covenants of God, the dispensations or outworkings of God's purpose, and supremely His grace manifested toward man. Before such a God, man can only bow in submission, love and adoration.

Questions

1. How can we account for the common belief in the existence of God?
2. Why is atheism unreasonable?
3. How clear is the revelation of God in nature?
4. Define four systems of thought which attempt to explain the universe on the basis of a higher being.
5. What is the ontological argument for the existence of God?
6. What is the cosmological argument for the existence of God?
7. What is the teleological argument for the existence of God?
8. What is the anthropological argument for the existence of God?
9. To what extent does the Old and New Testament emphasize the unity of God?
10. To what extent does the Old Testament teach the doctrine of the Trinity?
11. To what extent does the New Testament teach the doctrine of the Trinity?
12. Distinguish the doctrine of the Trinity from tritheism.
13. Why is the Trinity not to be explained as three modes of existence of God?
14. Explain how the Trinity is distinguished by certain properties.
15. State and define the three most important names for God in the Old Testament.
16. What are some of the compound names for God in the Old Testament?
17. What are the distinguishing titles of the three persons of the Trinity in the New Testament?
18. Name some of the important attributes of God as revealed in Scripture.
19. What is meant by the sovereignty of God?
20. What is meant by the decree of God?
21. How can the decree of God be subdivided?
22. How can the decree of God be distinguished from fatalism?
23. Why does the biblical revelation of God demand our submission, love and adoration in relation to Him?

6

God the Father

A. *The Father as the First Person*

In the revelation of the three persons who constitute the Holy Trinity — the Father, the Son, and the Holy Spirit — the First Person is designated as the Father. As such, the Father is not the entire Trinity just as the Son is not the Trinity nor the Spirit the Trinity. The Trinity includes all three persons. Although the doctrine of the Father, the Son, and the Holy Spirit is presented in the Old Testament and these terms are given to the persons of the Trinity, the New Testament defines and reveals the full doctrine. The Father is presented as electing, loving, and bestowing. The Son is presented as suffering, redeeming, and upholding the universe. The Holy Spirit is presented as regenerating, indwelling, baptizing, energizing, and sanctifying. New Testament revelation centers in revealing Jesus Christ, but in presenting the Christ as the Son of God, the truth of God the Father is likewise revealed. Because of the irreversible order of the Father sending and commissioning the Son, and the Son sending and commissioning the Holy Spirit, the Father is properly designated in theology as the First Person without lessening in any way the ineffable deity of either the Second Person or the Third Person.

In the revelation concerning the fatherhood of God, four distinct aspects may be observed: (1) God as the Father of all creation; (2) God the Father by intimate relationship; (3) God as the Father of our Lord Jesus Christ; and (4) God as the Father of all who believe in Jesus Christ as Savior and Lord.

B. Fatherhood Over Creation

Although all three persons participated in the creation and upholding of the physical universe and creatures who exist in it, the First Person, or God the Father, in a special way is the Father of all creation. According to Ephesians 3:14-15, Paul writes, "For this cause I bow my knees unto the Father of our Lord Jesus Christ, of whom the whole family in heaven and earth is named." Here the whole family of moral creatures including angels and men is declared to constitute a family of which God is the Father. In a similar way in Hebrews 12:9, the First Person is referred to as "the Father of spirits," which would seem again to include all moral beings such as angels and men.

According to James 1:17, the First Person is "the Father of lights" a peculiar expression which seems to indicate that He is the originator of all spiritual light. In Job 38:7 angels are described as sons of God (Job 1:6; 2:1). Adam is referred to as of God by creation in Luke 3:38, by implication, a son of God. Malachi 2:10 asks the question, "Have we not all one father? hath not one God created us?" Paul in addressing the Athenians on Mars Hill included in his argument, "Forasmuch then as we are the offspring of God" (Acts 17:29). In 1 Corinthians 8:6, the declaration is made, "But to us there is but one God, the Father, of whom are all things."

On the basis of these texts, there is sufficient ground to conclude that the First Person of the Trinity as the Creator is the Father of all creation and that all creatures, having physical life, owe their origin to Him. In this sense only, it is proper to refer to the universal fatherhood of God. All creatures in this sense participate in the universal brotherhood of creation. This does not justify, however, the misuse of this doctrine by liberal theologians to teach universal salvation or that every man has God as his Father in the spiritual sense.

C. Fatherhood by Intimate Relationship

The concept and relationship of father and son are used in the Old Testament in several instances to relate God to Israel. According to Exodus 4:22, Moses instructed Pharoah, "Thus saith the LORD, Israel is my son, even my firstborn." This was more than merely being their Creator and was less than saying that they were regenerated, for not all Israel had spiritual life. It does affirm a special relationship of divine care and solicitude for Israel similar to that of a father to a son.

In predicting God's special favor on the house of David, God revealed to David that His relationship to Solomon would be like a father to a son. He said to David, "I will be his father, and he shall be my son" (2 Sam. 7:14). In general God declares that His care as a Father will be over all who trust in Him as their God. According to Psalm 103:13, the statement is made "Like as a father pitieth his children, so the LORD pitieth them that fear Him."

D. The Father of Our Lord Jesus Christ

The most important and extensive revelation in regard to the fatherhood of God involves the relationship of the First Person to the Second Person. The First Person is described as "the God and Father of our Lord Jesus Christ" (Eph. 1:3). The most comprehensive theological revelation of the New Testament is that God the Father, the First Person, is the Father of the Lord Jesus Christ, the Second Person. The fact that Jesus Christ is referred to frequently in the New Testament as the Son of God and that the attributes and works of God are constantly assigned to Him constitutes at once the proof of the deity of Jesus Christ and the doctrine of the Trinity as a whole, with Christ as the Second Person in relationship to the First Person as a son is related to a father.

Theologians ever since the first century have wrestled with a precise definition of how God is the Father of the Second Person. Obviously the terms "father" and "son" are used of God to describe the intimate relationship of the First and Second Persons without necessarily fulfilling all the aspects that would be true in a human relationship of father and son. This is especially evident in the fact that both the Father and the Son are eternal. The early error of Arius in the fourth century, that the Son was the first of all created beings, was denounced by the early church as heresy in view of the fact that the Second Person is just as eternal as the First Person.

Some theologians, while affirming the preexistence of the Second Person, have attempted to begin the role of the Second Person as a *Son* at some point in time either at the Creation, at the Incarnation, or at some subsequent point of special recognition of the Second Person such as His baptism, His death, His resurrection, or His ascension. All these alternate views, however, are faulty, as Scripture seems clearly to indicate that the Second Person has been a Son in relation to the First Person from all eternity past. As such He is the "only begotten Son" (John 3:16) whom God "gave" as a Son to the world when the Son became incarnate. Scripture seems to indicate that He was given as a Son — not given in order to become a Son. Isaiah 9:6 states, "For unto us a child is born, unto us a son is given." This is especially brought out in Colossians 1:15 where Christ is declared to be "the image of the invisible God, the firstborn of every creature." If Christ was the firstborn of every creature, that is, a Son before any other creature was created, then it is clear that He was a Son from all eternity past.

The relationship of Father and Son, therefore, relates to the deity and unity of the Holy Trinity from all eternity, in contrast to the Incarnation, in which the Father was related to the humanity of Christ which began in time. Within orthodoxy, accordingly, the words of the Nicene Creed (A.D. 325) — in answer to the Arian heresy of the fourth century — states, "the only-begotten Son of God, begotten of the Father before all worlds; God of God, Light of Light, very God of very God; begotten, not made, being of one substance with the Father." In like manner, the Athanasian Creed states, "The Son is of the Father alone; not made nor created, but begotten . . . generated from eternity from the substance of the Father."

In using the terms "Father" and "Son" to describe the First and Second Persons, the terms are elevated to their highest level, indicating oneness of life, oneness of character and attributes, and yet a relationship in which the Father can give and send the Son even though this involves ultimately the obedience of the Son in dying on the cross. The obedience of Christ is based upon His sonship not on any inequality with God the Father in the unity of the Trinity.

While the relationship between the First and the Second Persons of the Trinity is actually that of a father to a son and a son to a father (2 Cor. 1:3; Gal. 4:4; Heb. 1:2), the fact of this relationship is an illustration of vital truth which accommodates itself to the mode of thought of a finite mind. The truth that the Father is the Father of our Lord Jesus Christ, though mentioned infrequently in the Old Testament (Ps. 2:7; Isa. 7:14; 9:6-7), is one of the most general teachings of the New Testament.

1. *The Son of God is said to have been begotten of the Father* (Ps. 2:7; John 1:14, 18; 3:16, 18; 1 John 4:9).

2. *The Father acknowledged the Lord Jesus Christ to be His Son* (Matt. 3:17; 17:5; Luke 9:35).

3. *The Father is acknowledged by the Son* (Matt. 11:27; 26:63-64; Luke 22:29; John 8:16-29, 33-44; 17:1).

4. *The fact that God the Father is the Father of the Lord Jesus Christ is acknowledged by men* (Matt. 16:16; Mark 15:39; John 1:34, 49; Acts 3:13).

5. *The Son acknowledges the Father by being subject to Him* (John 8:29, 49).

6. *Even the demons recognize this relationship between the Father and the Son* (Matt. 8:29).

E. The Father of All Who Believe in Christ

In contrast to the concept of God the Father as the Creator which extends to all creatures is the truth that God is the Father in a special sense of those who believe in Christ and have received eternal life. The fact that God is the Father of all creation does not assure the salvation of all men or give them eternal life. Scripture is clear that there is salvation only for those who have received Christ by faith as their Savior. The claim that God the Father is the Father of all mankind and that there is therefore a universal brotherhood among men does not mean that all are saved and will go to heaven. Scripture teaches instead that only those who believe in Christ unto salvation are the sons of God in a spiritual sense. This is not on the ground of their natural birth into the human race, nor on the ground that God is their Creator, but rather is based upon their second, or spiritual, birth into the family of God (John 1:12; Gal. 3:26; Eph. 2:19; 3:15; 5:1).

By the regenerating work of the Spirit the believer is made a legitimate child of God. God being actually his Father, he is impelled by the Spirit to say, "Abba, Father." Being born of

God, he is a partaker of the divine nature, and on the ground of that birth, he is heir of God and a joint-heir with Christ (John 1:12-13; 3:3-6; Rom. 8:16-17; Ttus 3:4-7; 1 Pet. 1:4). The impartation of the divine nature is an operation so effective that the nature thus imparted is never removed for any cause whatsoever.

When the teachings of Scripture relative to the present power and authority of Satan are considered, added proof is given that all men are not children of God by their natural birth. In this connection the most direct and faithful sayings of Christ are in evidence. Speaking of those who disbelieved He said, "Ye are of your father the devil" (John 8:44). Likewise, when describing the unregenerate, He said, "The tares are the children of the wicked one" (Matt. 13:38). The Apostle Paul wrote of the unsaved as "the children of disobedience" and "the children of wrath" (Eph. 2:2, 3).

Emphasis should be placed on the fact that it is not in the power of anyone to make himself a child of God. God alone can undertake such a transformation, and He undertakes it only on the one condition which He Himself has imposed, that Christ shall be believed upon and received as Savior (John 1:12).

The fatherhood of God is an important doctrine of the New Testament (John 20:17; 1 Cor. 15:24; Eph. 1:3; 2:18; 4:6; Col. 1:12-13; 1 Pet. 1:3; 1 John 1:3; 2:1, 22; 3:1). The assurance of the love and care of our Heavenly Father is a great comfort to Christians and an encouragement to faith and prayer.

Questions

1. How are the works of the Father, the Son, and the Holy Spirit contrasted in the New Testament?
2. What are the four distinct aspects of the fatherhood of God?
3. Summarize the evidence that God is the Father of all creation.
4. What is meant by the fatherhood of God by intimate relationship?
5. Discuss the question of the eternity of the relationship of father and son between God the Father and Jesus Christ.
6. What are some of the evidences supporting the concept of God the Father in relation to Jesus Christ the Son?
7. What is meant by God being the Father of all who believe in Christ?
8. How does a man become a son of God?
9. What are some of the results of becoming a son of God?
10. What is the error involved in stating that all men are the children of God?
11. How does the fatherhood of God provide comfort to a believer in Christ?

7

God the Son:
His Deity and Eternity

The Scriptures present the Lord Jesus Christ as being at the same time perfectly human and perfectly divine. Because of this, He was both like and unlike other men. According to John 1:14; 1 Timothy 3:16; and Hebrews 2:14-17, Jesus was revealed to be a man among men who was born, who lived, who suffered, and who died. Scripture is equally clear He was unlike man in that He was eternally preexistent, He was entirely sinless in His human life, His death was a sacrifice for the sins of the whole world, and He manifested His divine power in His glorious resurrection and ascension.

On the human side, He had a beginning and was conceived by the Holy Spirit and was born of the Virgin Mary. On the divine side, He had no beginning because He was from all eternity. In Isaiah 9:6 the prediction was given, "For unto us a child is born, unto us a son is given." The distinction is obvious between a child who was *born* and the Son who was *given*. In like manner, it is stated in Galatians 4:4, "But when the fulness of the time was come, God sent forth his Son, made of a woman, made under the law." Accordingly, the eternal Son became in His incarnation "made of a woman."

Although stating that Christ was preexistent merely claims that He existed before He was born, for all practical purposes it is also affirming that He existed from all eternity past. The idea that He was preexistent only in the sense of being the first of all created beings (the so-called Arian heresy from the fourth century) is not a modern teaching. Thus proofs of His preexistence and proofs for His eternity may be grouped together. It is also evident that if Christ is God He is eternal, and if He is eternal He is God, and proofs for the deity of Christ and His eternity support each other.

The eternity and deity of Jesus is established by two lines of revelation: (1) direct statements, and (2) implications from Scripture.

A. Direct Statements of the Eternity and Deity of the Son of God

The eternity and deity of Jesus Christ are asserted in an extensive body of Scripture which affirms His infinite person and His eternal existence coequal with the other persons of the Godhead. This fact is not affected by His incarnation.

Scripture states in John 1:1-2, "In the beginning was the Word, and the Word was with God, and the Word was God. The same was in the beginning with God." According to Micah 5:2, "But thou, Bethlehem Ephratah, though thou be little among the thousands of Judah, yet out of thee shall he come forth unto me that is to be ruler in Israel; whose goings forth have been from of old, from everlasting." Isaiah 7:14 affirms His virgin birth and gives Him the name Immanuel, which means "God with us." According to Isaiah 9:6-7, although Jesus was a child born, He was also given as a Son and is specifically called "the mighty God." When Christ stated in John 8:58, "Verily, verily, I say unto you, Before Abraham was, I am," the Jews understood this to be a claim for deity and eternity (cf. Exod. 3:14; Isa. 43:13). In John 17:5, Christ in His prayer stated, "And now, O Father, glorify thou me with thine own self with the glory which I had with thee before the world was" (cf. John 13:3). Philippians 2:6-7 states that Christ was "in the form of God" before His incarnation. A more explicit statement is made in Colossians 1:15-19 where Jesus Christ is declared to be before all creation, the Creator Himself, and the express image of the invisible God. In 1 Timothy 3:16, Jesus Christ is declared to be "God . . .

manifest in the flesh." In Hebrews 1:2-3 the fact that the Son is the Creator and the express image of God is again stated, and His eternity is affirmed in 13:8 (cf. Eph. 1:4; Rev. 1:11). Scripture states so often that Christ is eternal and that He is God. Contemporary scholarship which accepts the Bible as authoritative overwhelmingly — a few cults excepting — affirms the eternity and deity of Christ.

B. Implications That the Son of God is Eternal

The Word of God constantly and consistently implies the preexistence and eternity of the Lord Jesus Christ. Among the obvious proofs of this fact several may be noted:

1. *The works of creation are ascribed to Christ* (John 1:3; Col. 1:16; Heb. 1:10). He therefore antedates all creation.

2. *The Angel of Jehovah whose appearance is often recorded in the Old Testament is none other than the Lord Jesus Christ.* Though He appears at times as an angel or even as a man, He bears the unmistakable marks of deity. He appeared to Hagar (Gen. 16:7), to Abraham (Gen. 18:1; 22:11-12; note John 8:58), to Jacob (Gen. 48:15-16; note also Gen. 31:11-13; 32:24-32), to Moses (Exod. 3:2, 14), to Joshua (Josh. 5:13-14), and to Manoah (Judg. 13:19-22). He it is who fights for, and defends, His own (2 Kings 19:35; 1 Chron. 21:15-16; Ps. 34:7; Zech. 14:1-4).

3. *The titles of the Lord Jesus Christ indicate His eternal being.* He is precisely what His names imply. He is "The Son of God," "The Only Begotten Son," "The First and the Last," "The Alpha and Omega," "The Lord," "Lord of All," "Lord of Glory," "The Christ," "Wonderful," "Counsellor," "The Mighty God," "The Father of Eternity," "God," "God With Us," "Our Great God," and "God Blessed Forever."

These titles relate Him to the Old Testament revelation of Jehovah-God (cp. Matt. 1:23 with Isa. 7:14; Matt. 4:7 with Deut. 6:16; Mark 5:19 with Ps. 66:16; and Matt. 22:42-45 with Ps. 110:1).

The New Testament names of the Son of God are associated with titles of the Father and the Spirit as being equal with them (Matt. 28:19; John 14:1; 17:3; Acts 2:38; 1 Cor. 1:3; 2 Cor. 13:14; Eph. 6:23; Rev. 20:6; 22:3), and He is explicitly called God (John 1:1; Rom. 9:5; Titus 2:13; Heb. 1:8).

4. *The preexistence and eternity of the Son of God are im-*

plied in the fact that He has the attributes of God — life (John 1:4), self-existence (John 5:26), immutability (Heb. 13:8), truth (John 14:6), love (1 John 3:16), holiness (Heb. 7:26), eternity (Col. 1:17; Heb. 1:11), omnipresence (Matt. 28:20), omniscience (1 Cor. 4:5; Col. 2:3), and omnipotence (Matt. 28:18; Rev. 1:8).

5. *In like manner the preexistence and eternity of Christ are implied in the fact that He is worshiped as God* (John 20:28; Acts 7:59-60; Heb. 1:6). It follows that since the Lord Jesus Christ is God, He is from everlasting to everlasting.

The theme of the deity and eternity of the Son of God should be closely connected with the humanity of Christ through the Incarnation, which is the subject of the next chapter.

Questions

1. Contrast the evidence for the human and the divine natures of Christ.
2. What are some of the evidences for the eternity of the Son of God?
3. How does the eternity of God prove His deity?
4. What additional implications are there from His works that the Son of God is eternal?
5. How do the works of the Son of God prove His deity?
6. How is the eternity of Christ supported by His titles?
7. How is the eternity of Christ supported by His other attributes?
8. How do the attributes of Christ prove His deity?
9. How important to our Christian faith is the doctrine of the deity and eternity of Jesus Christ?

8

God the Son: His Incarnation

When considering the Incarnation, two important truths should be realized: (1) Christ became at the same time and in the absolute sense very God and very man, and (2) in becoming flesh He, though laying aside His glory, in no sense laid aside His deity. In His incarnation He retained every essential attribute of deity. His full deity and complete humanity are essential to His work on the cross. If He were not man, He could not die; if He were not God, His death would not have had infinite value.

John states (John 1:1) that Christ who was one with God and was God from all eternity, became flesh and tabernacled among us (1:14). Paul likewise states that Christ, who was in the form of God, took upon Himself the likeness of men (Phil. 2:6-7); "God was manifest in the flesh" (1 Tim. 3:16); and He who was the full revelation of God's glory was the exact image of His person (Heb. 1:3). Luke, in greater detail, presents the historical fact of His incarnation, as to both His conception and His birth (Luke 1:26-38; 2:5-7).

The Bible presents many contrasts, but none more striking than that Christ in His person should be at the same time very

56

God and very man. Illustrations of these contrasts from Scripture are many: He was weary (John 4:6), yet He called the weary to Himself for rest (Matt. 11:28). He was hungry (Matt. 4:2), yet He was "the bread of life" (John 6:35). He was thirsty (John 19:28), yet He was the water of life (John 7:37). He was in agony (Luke 22:44), yet He healed all manner of disease and soothed every pain. He "grew, and waxed strong in spirit" (Luke 2:40), yet He was from all eternity (John 8:58). He was tempted (Matt. 4:1), yet He, as God, could not be made to sin. He became self-limited in knowledge (Luke 2:52), yet He was the wisdom of God. He said (with reference to His humiliation, being made for a little time lower than the angels — Heb. 2:6-7): "My Father is greater than I" (John 14:28), yet also "he that hath seen me hath seen the Father" (John 14:9) and "I and my Father are one" (John 10:30). He prayed (Luke 6:12), yet He answered prayer (Acts 10:31). He wept at the tomb (John 11:35), yet He called the dead to arise (John 11:43). He asked, "Whom do men say that I the son of man am?" (Matt. 16:13), yet He "needed not that any should testify of man: for he knew what was in man" (John 2:25). He said, "My God, my God, why hast thou forsaken me?" (Mark 15:34), yet it was the very God to whom He cried who was at that moment "in Christ, reconciling the world unto himself" (2 Cor. 5:19). He died, yet He is eternal life. He was God's ideal man, and man's ideal God.

From this it may be seen that the Lord Jesus Christ sometimes functioned within the sphere of that which was perfectly human and sometimes within the sphere of that which was perfectly divine. His divine being was never limited in any degree by the fact of His humanity, nor did He minister to His human need from His divine resources. He could turn stones into bread to feed His human hunger, but this He never did.

A. The Fact of Christ's Humanity

1. *The humanity of Christ was purposed from before the foundation of the world* (Eph. 1:4-7; 3:11; Rev. 13:8). The significance of Christ being called a lamb is to call attention to His sacrifice and shedding of blood which required a physical body.

2. *Every type and prophecy of the Old Testament concerning Christ was an anticipation of the incarnate Son of God.*

3. *The fact of the humanity of Christ is seen in His annuncia-tion and birth* (Luke 1:31-35).

4. *His life here on earth revealed His humanity*: (1) by His human names: "The Son of man," "The man Christ Jesus," "The Son of David," and the like; (2) by His human parentage: He is mentioned as "the fruit of the loins," "her firstborn," "of this man's seed," "seed of David," "seed of Abraham," "made of a woman," "sprang from Judah"; (3) by the fact that He pos-sessed a human body, soul, and spirit (Matt. 26:38; John 13:21; 1 John 4:2, 9); and (4) by His self-imposed human limitations.

5. *The humanity of Christ is seen in His death and resurrec-tion.* It was a human body that suffered death on the cross, and it was the same body which came forth from the tomb in resurrection glory.

6. *The fact of the humanity of Christ is seen in that He ascended to heaven and is now, in His human glorified body, ministering for His own.*

7. *When He comes again it will be the "same Jesus" coming as He went, in the same body (though glorified) in which He became incarnate.*

B. Reasons for the Incarnation

1. *He came to reveal God to men* (Matt. 11:27; John 1:18; 14:9; Rom. 5:8; 1 John 3:16). By the incarnation the incom-prehensible God is translated into terms of human understanding.

2. *He came to reveal man.* He is God's ideal man and as such is an example to believers (1 Pet. 2:21); but He is never an example to the unsaved, since God is not now seeking to reform the unsaved, but rather to save them.

3. *He came to provide a sacrifice for sin.* For this reason He is seen thanking God for His human body and this in relation to true sacrifice for sin (Heb. 10:1-10).

4. *He came in the flesh that He might destroy the works of the Devil* (John 12:31; 16:11; Col. 2:13-15; Heb. 2:14; 1 John 3:8).

5. *He came into the world that He might be a merciful and faithful high priest in things pertaining to God* (Heb. 2:16-17; 8:1; 9:11-12, 24).

6. *He came in the flesh that He might fulfill the Davidic covenant* (2 Sam. 7:16; Luke 1:31-33; Acts 2:30, 31, 36; Rom. 15:8). In His glorified human body He will appear and reign

as "KING OF KINGS, AND LORD OF LORDS," and will sit on the throne of His father David (Luke 1:32; Rev. 19:16).

7. *As incarnate, He becomes Head over all things to the church, which is the new creation, the new humanity* (Eph. 1:22).

In the incarnation the Son of God took upon Himself not only a human body, but also a human soul and spirit. Thus becoming both the material and immaterial sides of human existence, He became entire man, and so closely and permanently related to the human family that He is rightly called "the last Adam" (1 Cor. 15:45) and "the body of his glory" (Phil. 3:21 ASV) is now an abiding fact.

He who is the eternal Son, Jehovah-God, was also the Son of Mary, the boy of Nazareth, the teacher and healer of Judea, the guest of Bethany, the Lamb of Calvary. He will yet be the King of Glory, as He is now the Savior of men, the High Priest, the coming Bridegroom and Lord.

Questions

1. What two important truths must be realized in understanding the incarnation of the Son of God?
2. Why is it important to uphold both the full deity and the full humanity of Christ?
3. What evidence is there that Christ had a full humanity?
4. What evidence is there that Christ had normal human experiences?
5. How is the fact of His deity also asserted even while Christ was on earth?
6. How is the incarnation related to God's revelation to man?
7. How is the incarnation related to Christ's sacrifice for sin?
8. What is the relationship between destroying the works of the devil and the incarnation?
9. How is the incarnation related to Christ's office as High Priest?
10. What is the relationship of the Davidic covenant to the incarnation?
11. How is the position of Christ as Head over the church related to the incarnation?

9

God the Son:
His Substitutionary Death

In Scripture the death of Christ is revealed to be a sacrifice for
the sins of the whole world. Accordingly, John the Baptist introduced Jesus with the words, "Behold the Lamb of God, which
taketh away the sin of the world" (John 1:29). Jesus in His
death was actually the substitute dying in the place of all men.
Although "substitute" is not specifically a biblical word, the
idea that Christ is the sinner's substitute is constantly affirmed
in Scripture. By His substitutionary death the unmeasured,
righteous judgments of God against a sinner were borne by
Christ. The result of this substitution is itself as simple and
definite as the transaction. The Savior has already borne the
divine judgments against the sinner to the full satisfaction of
God. In receiving the salvation which God offers, men are asked
to believe this good news, recognizing that Christ died for their
sins and thereby claiming Jesus Christ as their personal Savior.

The word "substitution" only partially expresses all that is
accomplished by the death of Christ. Actually no all-inclusive
term is used in the Bible. The word "atonement" is frequently
used in theology as an all-inclusive term, but there is no word
corresponding to it in either the Old or New Testament. In the

Old Testament the concept of atoning for sin referred to the temporary covering of sin by the sacrificial offerings. This provided a basis for temporary forgiveness "of sins that are past, through the forbearance of God" (Rom. 3:25). In forgiving sins in the Old Testament period, God was acting in perfect righteousness, since He anticipated the coming of His own Son as a sacrificial Lamb who would in no way pass over or cover sin temporarily but would take it away forever (John 1:29).

A. What the Son's Death Accomplishes

In attempting to consider the full value of the death of Christ, a number of important facts are revealed in Scripture.

1. *The death of Christ assures us of the love of God toward the sinner* (John 3:16; Rom. 5:8; 1 John 3:16; 4:9). The fact that God loves us should influence believers in Christ to live on a high moral standard impossible for an unbeliever (2 Cor. 5:15; 1 Pet. 2:11-25).

2. *The death of Christ is said to be a redemption or ransom paid to the holy demands of God for the sinner and to free the sinner from just condemnation.* It is significant that the discriminating word "for," meaning "instead of" or "on behalf of," is used in every passage in the New Testament where mention of Christ's death as a ransom appears (Matt. 20:28; Mark 10:45; 1 Tim. 2:6). The death of Christ was a necessary penalty which He bore for the sinner (Rom. 4:25; 2 Cor. 5:21; Gal. 1:4; Heb. 9:28).

In paying the price of our ransom, Christ redeemed us. In the New Testament, three important Greek words are used to express this idea: (1) *agorazo,* meaning "to buy in the market" (*agora* means "market"). Man in his sin is considered under the sentence of death (John 3:18-19; Rom. 6:23), a slave "sold under sin" (Rom. 7:14), but in the act of redemption purchased by Christ through the shedding of His blood (1 Cor. 6:20; 7:23; 2 Pet. 2:1; Rev. 5:9; 14:3-4); (2) *exagorazo,* meaning "to buy out of the market" which adds the thought not only of purchase but removal from sale (Gal. 3:13; 4:5; Eph. 5:16; Col. 4:5), indicating that redemption is once for all; (3) *lutroo,* "to let loose" or "set free" (Luke 24:21; Titus 2:14; 1 Pet. 1:18). The same idea is found in the noun form *lutrosis* (Luke 2:38; Heb. 9:12), another similar expression *epoiesen lutrosin* (Luke 1:68), and another form used frequently, *apolutrosis,* indicating freeing a slave (Luke 21:28; Rom. 3:24; 8:23; 1 Cor. 1:30; Eph. 1:7, 14; 4:30; Col. 1:14; Heb. 9:15; 11:35). The concept of redemption accordingly includes the purchase, removal from sale, and the complete freedom of the ransomed individual through the death of Christ and the application of redemption by the Holy Spirit.

The death of Christ was an offering for sin, not like the animal offerings of the Old Testament, which could cover sin only in the sense of delaying the time of righteous judgment. In His sacrifice Christ bore our sins forever (Isa. 53:7-12; John 1:29; 1 Cor. 5:7; Eph. 5:2; Heb. 9:22, 26; 10:14).

3. *The death of Christ is represented on His part as an act of obedience to the law which sinners have broken, which act constitutes a propitiation or satisfaction of all of God's righteous demands upon the sinner.* The Greek word *hilasterion* is used for the "mercy seat" (Heb. 9:5), which was the lid of the ark in the Holy of Holies and which covered the law in the ark. On the Day of Atonement (Lev. 16:14) the mercy seat was sprinkled with blood from the altar and this changed the judgment seat into a mercy seat (Heb. 9:11-15). In like manner, the throne of God becomes a throne of grace (Heb. 4:14-16) through the propitiation of Christ's death. A similar Greek word *hilasmos* refers to the act of propitiation (1 John 2:2; 4:10); the meaning is that Christ in dying on the cross completely satisfied all of God's just demands for judgment on human sin. In Romans 3:25-26 God is accordingly declared righteous in His forgiving sins before the cross on the basis that Christ would eventually die and satisfy completely the law of righteousness. In all of this God is not pictured as a God delighting in vengeance upon the sinner, but rather a God who because of His love delights in mercy to the sinner. In redemption and propitiation, therefore, the believer in Christ is assured that the price has been paid in full, that he has been set free as a sinner, and that all of God's righteous demands for judgment upon him because of his sin have been satisfied.

4. *The death of Christ not only redeemed and propitiated a holy God, but provided the basis by which the world was reconciled unto God.* The Greek word *katallasso*, meaning "to reconcile," has the thought of bringing God and man together by thoroughly changing man. It appears in various forms frequently in the New Testament (Rom. 5:10-11; 11:15; 1 Cor. 7:11; 2 Cor. 5:18-20; Eph. 2:16; Col. 1:20-21). The rendering in Romans 5:11, where it is translated "atonement" in the King James Version, should be translated "reconcilation." The con-

cept in reconciliation is not that God changes, but that His relationship to man changes because of the redeeming work of Christ. Man himself is forgiven, justified, and raised spiritually to the level where he is reconciled to God. The thought is not that God is reconciled to the sinner, that is, adjusted to a sinful estate, but rather that the sinner is adjusted to God's holy character. Reconciliation provisionally is for the entire world, just as God redeemed the whole world and is the propitiation for the sins of the whole world (2 Cor. 5:19; 2 Pet. 2:1; I John 2:1-2). So complete and far-reaching is this marvelous provision of God in redemption, propitiation, and reconciliation that the Scriptures state that God is not now imputing sin unto the world (2 Cor. 5:18-19; Eph. 2:16; Col. 2:20).

5. *The death of Christ removed all moral hindrances in the mind of God to saving of sinners in that sin has been redeemed by the death of Christ, God has been propitiated, and man has been reconciled to God.* There is no further hindrance to God freely accepting and justifying anyone who believes in Jesus Christ as his Savior (Rom. 3:26). Since in the death of Christ God's infinite love and power are released from restraint by the accomplishment of every judgment which His righteousness could demand against a sinner, God is more advantaged by the death of Christ than all the world combined.

6. *Christ, in His death, became the Substitute bearing the penalty belonging to the sinner* (Lev. 16:21; Isa. 53:6; Matt. 20:28; Luke 22:37; John 10:11; Rom. 5:6-8; 1 Pet. 3:18). This fact is the ground of assurance for all who would come unto God for salvation. It presents something for every individual to *believe* concerning his own relation to God on the question of his own sin. A general belief that Christ died for the whole world is not sufficient; a personal conviction that one's own sin has been perfectly borne by Christ the Substitute is required — a belief which results in a sense of relief, joy, and appreciation (Rom. 15:13; Heb. 9:14; 10:2). Salvation is a mighty work of God which is wrought instantly for the one who *believes* on Christ.

B. Fallacies Concerning the Son's Death

The death of Christ is often misinterpreted. Every Christian will do well to understand thoroughly the fallacy of those misstatements which are so general today.

1. *It is claimed that the doctrine of substitution is immoral on the ground that God could not in righteousness lay the sins of the guilty on an innocent victim.* This statement might be considered if it could be proved that Christ was an *unwilling* victim; but Scripture presents Him as being in fullest sympathy with His Father's will and actuated by the same infinite love (John 13:1; Heb. 10:7). Likewise, in the inscrutable mystery of the Godhead, it was God Himself who was in Christ reconciling the world unto Himself (2 Cor. 5:19). Far from the death of Christ being an immoral imposition, it was God Himself, the righteous Judge in infinite love and sacrifice, bearing the full penalty that His own holiness required of the sinner.

2. *It is claimed that Christ died as a martyr and that the value of His death is seen in the example He presented of courage and loyalty to His convictions even unto death.* The sufficient answer to this error is that, since He was God's provided Lamb, no man took His life from Him (John 10:18; Acts 2:23).

3. *It is claimed that Christ died to create a moral effect.* Since the cross displays the divine estimate of sin, men who consider the cross will be constrained to turn from lives of sin. This theory, which has no foundation in Scripture, assumes that God is now seeking the *reformation* of men; while, in reality, the cross is the ground of *regeneration*.

Questions

1. What is meant by the assertion that Christ is the sinner's substitute?
2. What is the Old Testament doctrine of atonement?
3. How is the death of Christ related to the love of God?
4. What are the three basic concepts included in the doctrine of redemption?
5. Define the doctrine of propitiation and explain what is accomplished by it.
6. Define the doctrine of reconciliation and explain what is accomplished by it.
7. If the entire world is reconciled to God, why are some lost?
8. How does redemption, propitiation, and reconciliation free God to save the sinner?
9. Why does the New Testament emphasize that salvation is by faith alone?
10. Name some of the wrong interpretations of the death of Christ and explain why they are wrong.

10

God the Son: His Resurrection

A. Resurrection in the Old Testament

The doctrine of resurrection of all men as well as the resurrection of Christ is taught in the Old Testament. The doctrine appears as early as the time of Job, probably a contemporary of Abraham, and is expressed in his statement of faith in Job 19:25-27, "For I know that my redeemer liveth, and that he shall stand at the latter day upon the earth: and though after my skin worms destroy this body, yet in my flesh shall I see God: whom I shall see for myself, and mine eyes shall behold, and not another; though my reins be consumed within me." Here Job affirms not only his own personal resurrection, but the truth that his Redeemer already lives and should later stand upon the earth. That all men will ultimately be raised is taught in John 5:28-29 and Revelation 20:4-6, 12-13.

Specific prophecies in the Old Testament anticipate the resurrection of the human body (Job 14:13-15; Ps. 16:9-10; 17:15; 49:15; Isa. 26:19; Dan. 12:2; Hos. 13:14; Heb. 11:17-19). The resurrection of Christ is specifically taught in Psalm 16:9-10, where the psalmist David declared, "Therefore my heart is glad, and my glory rejoiceth: my flesh also shall rest in hope. For thou will not leave my soul in hell; neither wilt thou suffer thine Holy One to see corruption." Here David affirms not only that he hopes personally of resurrection but that Jesus Christ, described as the "Holy One," should not see corruption, that is, stay in the grave long enough for His body to decay. This passage is quoted by Peter in Acts 2:24-31 and by Paul in Acts 13:34-37 as indicating the resurrection of Christ.

The resurrection of Christ is also indicated in Psalm 22:22, where following His death Christ declares He will declare His name unto His "brethren." In Psalm 118:22-24, the elevation of Christ to become the headstone of the corner is defined in Acts 4:10-11 as signifying the resurrection of Christ. The resurrection of Christ seems also to be anticipated in the typology of the Old Testament in the priesthood of Melchizedek (Gen. 14:18; Heb. 7:15-17, 23-25). In a similar way the typology of the two birds (Lev. 14:4-7) where the living bird is released, the feast of firstfruits (Lev. 23:10-11) indicating Christ is the firstfruits of the harvest of resurrection, and Aaron's rod that budded (Num. 17:8) speak of resurrection. The doctrine of the resurrection of all men, as well as the resurrection of Christ, is thus well established in the Old Testament.

B. Christ's Predictions of His Own Resurrection

Frequently in the gospels, Christ predicts both His own death and His resurrection (Matt. 16:21; 17:23; 20:17-19; 26:12, 28-29, 31-32; Mark 9:30-32; 14:28; Luke 9:22; 18:31-34; John 2:19-22; 10:17-18). The predictions are so frequent, so explicit, and given in so many different contexts that there can be no question that Christ predicted His own death and resurrection, and the fulfillment of these predictions verifies the accuracy of the prophecy.

C. Proofs of the Resurrection of Christ

The New Testament presents overwhelming proof of the resurrection of Christ. At least seventeen appearances of Christ occurred after His resurrection. These are as follows: (1) appearance to Mary Magdalene (John 20:11-17; cf. Mark 16:9-11); (2)

appearance to the women (Matt. 28:9-10); (3) appearance to Peter (Luke 24:34; 1 Cor. 15:5); (4) appearance of Christ to the disciples on the road to Emmaus (Mark 16:12-13; Luke 24:13-35); (5) appearance of Christ to the ten disciples, referred to collectively as "the eleven" as Thomas was absent (Mark 16:14; Luke 24:36-43; John 20:19-24; (6) appearance to the eleven disciples a week after His resurrection (John 20:26-29); (7) appearance to seven disciples by the Sea of Galilee (John 21:1-23); (8) appearance to five hundred (1 Cor. 15:6); (9) appearance to James the Lord's brother (1 Cor. 15:7); (10) appearance to eleven disciples on the mountain in Galilee (Matt. 28:16-20; 1 Cor. 15:7); (11) appearance to His disciples on the occasion of His ascension from the Mount of Olives (Luke 24:44-53; Acts 1:3-9); (12) appearance of the resurrected Christ to Stephen prior to Stephen's martyrdom (Acts 7:55-56); (13) appearance to Paul on the road to Damascus (Acts 9:3-6; cf. Acts 22:6-11; 26:13-18; 1 Cor. 15:8); (14) appearance to Paul in Arabia (Acts 20:24; 26:17; Gal. 1:12, 17); (15) appearance of Christ to Paul in the temple (Acts 22:17-21; cf. 9:26-30; Gal. 1:18); (16) appearance of Christ to Paul in prison in Caesarea (Acts 23:11); (17) appearance of Christ to the Apostle John (Rev. 1:12-20). The number of these appearances, the great variety of the circumstances, and the confirming evidences that surround these appearances all constitute the strongest kind of historical evidence that Christ actually arose from the dead.

In addition to the proofs provided in His appearances, much supporting evidence can be cited. The tomb was empty after His resurrection (Matt. 28:6; Mark 16:6; Luke 24:3, 6, 12; John 20:2, 5-8). It is evident that the witnesses to the resurrection of Christ were not gullible, easily deceived people. In fact, they were slow to comprehend the evidence (John 20:9, 11-15, 25). Once convinced of the reality of His resurrection, they were willing to die for their faith in Christ. It is also evident that there was a great change in the disciples after the resurrection. Their sorrow was replaced with joy and faith.

Further, the Book of Acts testifies to the divine power of the Holy Spirit in the disciples after the resurrection of Christ, the power of the Gospel which they proclaimed, and the supporting evidence of miracles. The day of Pentecost is another important proof, as it would have been impossible to have convinced three thousand people of the resurrection of Christ who had had opportunity to examine the evidence if it were merely a fiction.

The custom of the early church to observe the first day of the week, the time to celebrate the Lord's Supper and bring their offering, is another historic evidence (Acts 20:7; 1 Cor. 16:2). The very fact that the early church came into existence in spite of persecution and death of the apostles is left without adequate explanation if Christ did not rise from the dead. It was a literal and bodily resurrection which rendered the body of Christ suitable for its heavenly function.

D. Reasons for the Resurrection of Christ

At least seven important reasons may be cited for the resurrection of Christ:

1. *Christ arose because of who He is* (Acts 2:24).
2. *Christ arose to fulfill the Davidic covenant* (2 Sam. 7:12-16; Ps. 89:20-37; Isa. 9:6-7; Luke 1:31-33; Acts 2:25-31).
3. *Christ arose to be the giver of resurrection life* (John 10:10-11; 11:25-26; Eph. 2:6; Col. 3:1-4; 1 John 5:11-12).
4. *Christ arose that He might become the source of resurrection power* (Matt. 28:18; Eph. 1:19-21; Phil. 4:13).
5. *Christ arose to be head over the church* (Eph. 1:20-23).
6. *Christ arose because our justification had been accomplished* (Rom. 4:25).
7. *Christ arose to be the firstfruits of resurrection* (1 Cor. 15:20-23).

E. The Significance of the Resurrection of Christ

The resurrection of Christ because of its historical character constitutes the most important proof for the deity of Jesus Christ. Because it was a great victory over sin and death, it also is the present standard of divine power as stated in Ephesians 1:19-21. Because the resurrection is such an outstanding doctrine, the first day of the week in this dispensation has been set apart for commemoration of the resurrection of Jesus Christ, and, accordingly, supercedes the law of the Sabbath which had set aside the seventh day for Israel. The resurrection is, therefore, the cornerstone of our Christian faith, and as Paul expressed it in 1 Corinthians 15:17, "If Christ be not raised, your faith is vain; ye are yet in your sins." Because Christ is raised, our Christian faith is sure, the ultimate victory of Christ is certain, and our Christian faith is completely justified.

Questions

1. Does the Bible teach that all men who die will be resurrected?
2. Summarize the Old Testament teaching on the resurrection of the human body.
3. To what extent does the Old Testament anticipate the resurrection of Jesus Christ?
4. To what extent did Christ predict His own resurrection?
5. How many appearances of Christ occurred between His resurrection and ascension?
6. What appearances of Christ occurred after His ascension?
7. Why are the many appearances of Christ and the circumstances surrounding them a strong confirmation of the fact of His resurrection?
8. What support do the empty tomb, the character of the witnesses of His resurrection, and the extent of their convictions contribute to the doctrine of His resurrection?
9. What changes took place in the disciples after the resurrection of Christ, and how were they used as witnesses of the resurrection?
10. What evidence may be found in the day of Pentecost for the resurrection of Christ?
11. How do the custom of the early church to observe the first day of the week and the continued existence of the early church in spite of persecution support the doctrine of resurrection?
12. Name at least seven reasons why Christ rose from the dead.
13. Why is the resurrection of Christ important to Christian faith?
14. How is the resurrection of Christ related to the present standard of divine power?

11

God the Son: His Ascension and Priestly Ministry

A. The Fact of the Ascension of Christ

Since the resurrection of Christ is the first in a series of exaltations of Christ, the ascension of Christ to heaven may be considered the second important step. This is recorded in Mark 16:19; Luke 24:50-51; and Acts 1:9-11.

The question has been raised whether Christ ascended to heaven prior to His formal ascension. The word of Christ to Mary Magdalene in John 20:17 is often cited, in which Christ said, "I ascend unto my Father, and your Father; and to my God, and your God." The typology of the Old Testament where the priest, after sacrifice, brought blood into the holy place is also cited (Heb. 9:12, 23-24). Although expositors have differed in their opinions, most evangelicals interpret the present tense of John 20:17, "I ascend," as a vivid future. The expressions in Hebrews that Christ entered heaven with His blood are better translated "by His blood" or "through His blood." The physical application of blood occurred only on the cross. The benefits of the finished work continue to be applied to believers today (1 John 1:7).

A further question has been raised whether the ascension in Acts 1 was a literal act. The passage fully supports the fact that Christ literally went to heaven, just as literally as He came to earth when He was conceived and born. Acts 1 uses four Greek words to describe the ascension: "He was taken up" (v. 9); "a cloud received him out of their sight" (v. 9); "he went up" (v. 10); and "is taken up from you into heaven" (v. 11), better translated "received up" (cf. 9). These four statements are significant because in verse 11 it is predicted that His second coming will be in like manner; that is, His ascension and His second coming will be gradual, visible, bodily, and with clouds (Acts 1:9-11). This refers to His coming to set up His kingdom rather than to the rapture of the church.

B. Evidence for the Arrival of Christ in Heaven

Although the evidence for His ascension from earth to heaven is complete, the fact that Christ is repeatedly said to have arrived in heaven confirms the fact of His ascension. Many passages testify that Christ is seen in heaven after His ascension (Acts 2:33-36; 3:21; 7:55-56; 9:3-6; 22:6-8; 26:13-15; Rom. 8:34; Eph. 1:20-22; 4:8-10; Phil. 2:6-11; 3:20; 1 Thess. 1:10; 4:16; 1 Tim. 3:16; Heb. 1:3, 13; 2:7; 4:14; 6:20; 7:26; 8:1; 9:24; 10:12-13; 12:2; 1 John 2:1; Rev. 1:7, 13-18; 5:5-12; 6:9-17; 7:9-17; 14:1-5; 19:11-16).

C. The Meaning of the Ascension

The ascension marked the end of His earthly ministry. As Christ had come, born in Bethlehem, so now He had returned to the Father. It also marked the return to His manifested glory which was hidden in earthly life even after His resurrection. His entrance into heaven was a great triumph, signifying the completion of His work on earth, and an entering into His new sphere of work at the right hand of the Father.

The position of Christ in heaven is one of universal lordship while awaiting His ultimate triumph and His second coming, and Christ is frequently pictured at the right hand of the Father (Ps. 110:1; Matt. 22:44; Mark 12:36; 16:19; Luke 20:42-43; 22:69; Rom. 8:34; Eph. 1:20; Col. 3:1; Heb. 1:3-13; 8:1; 10:12;

12:2; 1 Pet. 3:22). The throne which Christ occupies in heaven is the Father's throne, not to be confused with the Davidic throne which is earthly. Earth yet awaits the time when it will be made His footstool and His throne will be set up on earth (Matt. 25:31). His present position is, of course, one of honor and authority, and in keeping with His position as Head of the church.

D. The Present Work of Christ in Heaven

In His position at the right hand of the Father, Christ fulfills the seven figures relating Him to the church: (1) Christ as the last Adam and head of the new creation; (2) Christ as the Head of the body of Christ; (3) Christ as the Great Shepherd of His sheep; (4) Christ as the True Vine in relation to the branches; (5) Christ as the Chief Cornerstone in relation to the church as stones of the building; (6) Christ as our High Priest in relationship to the church as a royal priesthood; (7) Christ as the Bridegroom in relation to the church as the bride. All of these figures are full of meaning in describing His present work. His chief ministry, however, is as our High Priest representing the church before the throne of God.

Four important truths are revealed in His work as High Priest.

1. *As High Priest over the true tabernacle on high, the Lord Jesus Christ has entered into heaven itself there to minister as Priest in behalf of those who are His own in the world* (Heb. 8:1-2). The fact that He, when ascending, was received by His Father in heaven is evidence that His earthly ministry was accepted. That He sat down indicated that His work for the world was completed.

That He sat down on His Father's throne and not on His own throne reveals the truth, constantly and so consistently taught in the Scriptures, that He did not set up a kingdom on the earth at His first advent into the world, but that He is now "expecting" until the time when that kingdom shall come in the earth and the divine will shall be done on earth as it is done in heaven. "The kingdoms of this world' are yet to become "the kingdoms of our Lord, and of his Christ; and he shall reign for ever and ever" (Rev. 11:15); the kingly Son will yet ask of His Father and He will give Him the heathen for His inheritance and the uttermost parts of the earth for His possession (Ps. 2:8).

However, Scripture clearly indicates that He is not now establishing that kingdom rule in the earth (Matt. 25:31-46), but that He is rather calling out from both Jews and Gentiles a heavenly people who are related to Him as His body and bride. After the present purpose is accomplished He will return and "build again the tabernacle of David, which is fallen down" (Acts 15:16; cf. vv. 13-18). Though He is a King-Priest according to the Melchisedec type (Heb. 5:10; 7:1), He is now serving as Priest and not as King. He who is coming again and will then be King of Kings, is now ascended to be "head over all things to the church, which is his body" (Eph. 1:22-23).

2. *As our High Priest Christ is the bestower of spiritual gifts.* According to the New Testament, a gift is a divine enablement wrought in and through the believer by the Spirit who indwells him. It is the Spirit working to accomplish certain divine purposes and using the one whom He indwells to that end. It is in no sense a human undertaking aided by the Spirit.

Though certain general gifts are mentioned in the Scriptures (Rom. 12:3-8; 1 Cor. 12:4-11), the possible variety is innumerable, since no two lives are lived under exactly the same conditions. However, to each believer some gift is given; but the blessing and power of the gift will be experienced only when the life is wholly yielded to God (cf. Rom. 12:1-2, 6-8). There will be little need of exhortation for God-honoring service to the one who is filled with the Spirit; for the Spirit will be working in that one both to will and to do of His good pleasure (Phil. 2:13).

In like manner, certain men who are called his "gifts unto men" are provided and locally placed in their service by the ascended Christ (Eph. 4:7-11). The Lord did not leave this work to the uncertain and insufficient judgment of men (1 Cor. 12:11, 18).

3. *The ascended Christ as Priest ever lives to make intercession for His own.* This ministry began before He left the earth (John 17:1-26), is for the saved rather than for the unsaved (John 17:9), and will be continued in heaven as long as His own are in the world. His work of intercession has to do with the weakness, the helplessness, and the immaturity of the saints who are on the earth — things concerning which they are in no way guilty. He who knows the limitations of His own, and the power and strategy of the foe with whom they have to contend, is to them as the Shepherd and Bishop of their souls. His care of Peter is an illustration of this truth (Luke 22:31-32).

The priestly intercession of Christ is not only effectual, but unending. The priests of old failed because of death; but Christ, because He ever lives, has an unchanging priesthood. "Wherefore he is able also to save them to the uttermost [without end] that come unto God by him, seeing he ever liveth to make intercession for them" (Heb. 7:25). David recognized the same divine shepherding care and its guarantee of eternal safety (Ps. 23:1).

4. *Christ now appears for His own in the presence of God.* The child of God is often guilty of actual sin which would separate him from God were it not for his Advocate and what He wrought in His death. The effect of the Christian's sin upon himself is that he loses his fellowship with God, his joy, his peace, and his power. On the other hand, these experiences are restored in infinite grace on the sole ground that he *confess* his sin (1 John 1:9); but it is more important to consider the Christian's sin in relation to the holy character of God.

Through the present priestly advocacy of Christ in heaven there is absolute safety and security for the Father's child even while he is sinning. An advocate is one who espouses and pleads the cause of another in the open courts. As Advocate, Christ is now appearing in heaven for His own (Heb. 9:24) when they sin (1 John 2:1). His pleading is said to be with the Father, and Satan is there also, ceasing not to accuse the brethren night and day before God (Rev. 12:10). To the Christian, the sin may seem insignificant; but a holy God can never treat it lightly. It may be a secret sin on earth; but it is open scandal in heaven. In marvelous grace and without solicitation from men, the Advocate pleads the cause of the guilty child of God. What the Advocate does in thus securing the safety of the believer is so in accordance with infinite *justice* that He is mentioned in this connection as "Jesus Christ the righteous." He pleads His own efficacious blood, and the Father is free to preserve His child against every accusation from Satan or men and from the very judgments which sin would otherwise impose, since Christ through His death became the propitiation for our sins (1 John 2:2).

The truth concerning the priestly ministry of Christ in heaven does not make it easy for the Chirstian to sin. On the contrary, these very things are written that *we be not sinning* (1 John 2:1); for no one can sin carelessly who considers the necessary pleading which his sin imposes upon the Advocate. The priestly ministries of Christ as Intercessor and as Advocate are unto the eternal security of those who are saved (Rom. 8:34).

E. The Present Work of Christ on Earth

Christ is also at work in His church on earth while He is bodily at the right hand of God in heaven. In numerous passages Christ is said to indwell His church and to be with His church (Matt. 28:18-20; John 14:18, 20; Col. 1:27). He also abides in His church in the sense that He is the giver of eternal life to His church (John 1:4; 10:10; 11:25; 14:6; Col. 3:4; 1 John 5:12). In addition to Christ's own ministry to the church, He has sent His Holy Spirit to accomplish a present work in the believer, and the Father, likewise, indwells all believers in this age (John 14:23).

It may be concluded that the present work of Christ is the key to understanding God's present undertaking, that of calling out a people to form the body of Christ, and the empowering and sanctifying of this people to be a witness to Christ to the ends of the earth. His present work is preliminary to that which will follow in the events related to His second coming.

Questions

1. How does the ascension of Christ relate to His exaltation?
2. Discuss the question of whether Christ ascended on the day of His resurrection.
3. What evidence may be offered to prove that the ascension in Acts 1 was a literal ascension?
4. To what extent does Scripture testify to the arrival of Christ in heaven after His ascension?
5. How does the ascension of Christ relate to His earthly ministry?
6. In what sense was the ascension of Christ a triumph?
7. Distinguish the throne of Christ in heaven from the Davidic throne.
8. Name the seven figures relating Christ to His church.
9. What is the significance of Christ now being seated on the Father's throne?
10. How is Christ as our High Priest related to the bestowal of spiritual gifts from men?
11. Contrast the priestly intercession of Christ with the priests of the Old Testament.
12. Describe the work of Christ as our Advocate in heaven.
13. To what extent is Christ also working on earth during the present age?

12

God the Son:
His Coming for His Saints

A. Unfulfilled Prophecy

The doctrine chosen for this chapter is one of the most important themes of unfulfilled prophecy. The student should be reminded that prophecy is God's prewritten history and is therefore as credible as other parts of Scripture. Almost one-fourth of the Bible was in the form of prediction when it was written. Much has been fulfilled, and in every case its fulfillment has been the most literal realization of all that was prophesied. As announced many centuries before the birth of Christ, He, when He came, was of the tribe of Judah, a son of Abraham, a son of David, born of a virgin in Bethlehem. In like manner, the explicit details of His death foretold in Psalm 22, a thousand years before, were precisely fulfilled.

The Word of God also presents much prophecy which at the present time is unfulfilled, and it is reasonable as well as honoring to God to believe that it will be fulfilled in the same faithfulness which has characterized all His works to the present hour.

The fact that Christ is to return to this earth as He went —

"this same Jesus," in His resurrection body, and on the clouds of heaven (Acts 1:11) — is so clearly and extensively taught in the prophetic Scripture that this truth has been included in all the great creeds of Christendom. However, the doctrine of the return of Christ demands most careful and discriminating consideration.

In considering prophecy as it relates to the future coming of Jesus Christ, many Bible students distinguish Christ coming *for* His church, referring to the rapture (the catching up of the saints to heaven), from His coming *with* His saints to set up His kingdom (His formal second coming to the earth) to reign for a thousand years. Between these two events many important events are predicted such as the emergence of a world church, the formation of a world government with a world dictator, and a gigantic world war which will be underway at the time Christ comes to set up His kingdom. Christ coming for His church is the first event in this series, if the prophecies are interpreted literally.

Although the end-time events, which occur after the rapture of the church, are given in many prophecies in both the Old and New Testaments, the truth that Christ would come for His church first was not revealed in the Old Testament and is distinctly a New Testament revelation.

B. Prophecies of the Rapture

The first revelation that Christ would come for His saints before end-time events were fulfilled was given to the disciples in the Upper Room the night before Christ's crucifixion. According to John 14:2-3, Christ announced to His disciples, "In my Father's house are many mansions: if it were not so, I would have told you. I go to prepare a place for you. And if I go and prepare a place for you, I will come again, and receive you unto myself; that where I am, there ye may be also."

The disciples were totally unprepared for this prophecy. They had been instructed in Matthew 24:26-31 concerning the glorious return of Christ to set up His kingdom. Up to this time they had had no intimation that Christ would come first to take them from earth to heaven and by this means remove them from the earth during the time of trouble which characterizes the end of the age. In John 14 it is clear that the Father's house refers to heaven, that Christ was leaving them to prepare a place for His disciples there. He promises that having prepared a place He would come again to receive them. The implication is that His purpose is to take them from earth to the Father's house in heaven. This preliminary announcement is given further detail by the Apostle Paul.

In writing to the Thessalonians concerning their questions of the relationship of the resurrection of the saints and Christ's coming for saints living on earth, Paul gives the details of this important event (1 Thess. 4:13-18). He declares in verses 16-17, "For the Lord himself shall descend from heaven with a shout, with a voice of the archangel, and with the trump of God: and the dead in Christ shall rise first: Then we which are alive and remain shall be caught up together with them in the clouds, to meet the Lord in the air: and so shall we ever be with the Lord."

The order of events for Christ coming for His saints begins with the Lord leaving His throne in heaven and descending to the air above the earth. He will give a shout — literally, "a shout of command." This will be accompanied by the triumphant voice of the archangel Michael and the sounding of the trump of God. In obedience to the command of Christ (John 5:28-29), Christians who have died will be raised from the dead. The souls of the dead have accompanied Christ from heaven as indicated in 1 Thessalonians 4:14 — "them also which sleep in Jesus will God bring with Him" — and will enter their resurrected bodies. A moment after the dead in Christ are raised, living Christians "shall be caught up together with them in the clouds, to meet the Lord in the air." In this manner the entire church will be removed from the scene of earth and will fulfill the promise of John 14 of being with Christ in the Father's house in heaven.

Further details are given in 1 Corinthians 15:51-58. Here the truth of Christ's coming for His church is declared to be "a mystery," that is, a truth not revealed in the Old Testament but revealed in the New Testament (cf. Rom. 16:25-26; Col. 1:26). In contrast to the truth of Christ coming to the earth to set up His kingdom, which is revealed in the Old Testament, the rapture is revealed only in the New Testament. Paul, in 1 Corinthians 15, indicates that the event will take place in a moment of time, "in the twinkling of an eye," that the resurrection bodies of the dead which will be raised will be incorruptible, that is, will not grow old and will be immortal, not subject to death (1 Cor. 15:53).

It is clear from Scripture that our new bodies will also be sinless (Eph. 5:27; cf. Phil. 3:20-21). The bodies of those in the graves as well as those living on earth are not suited for heaven. That is why Paul declares "we shall all be changed" (1 Cor. 15:51).

In contrast with the resurrection and rapture of the church, the resurrection of saints who died before Pentecost, or who die after the rapture, is apparently delayed until the time of Christ's coming to set up His kingdom (Dan. 12:1-2; Rev. 20:4). The wicked dead, however, are not raised until after the thousand year reign of Christ (Rev. 20:5-6, 12-13).

C. Contrasts Between Christ Coming for His Saints and His Coming With His Saints

The view that the rapture occurs before end-time events is called the pretribulational view, in contrast with the posttribulational view which makes Christ's coming for His saints and with His saints one event. The question of which of these two views is right depends on how literally prophecy is interpreted.

A number of differences can be seen between the two events:

1. *Christ coming for His saints to take them to the Father's house in heaven is obviously a movement from earth to heaven,* while His coming with His saints is a *movement from heaven to the earth* when Christ returns to the Mount of Olives and sets up His kingdom.

2. *At the rapture, living saints are translated,* while no saints are translated in connection with the second coming of Christ to the earth.

3. *At the rapture, the saints go to heaven,* while at the second coming saints remain in the earth without translation.

4. *At the rapture, the world is unchanged and unjudged and continues in sin,* while at the second coming the world is judged and righteousness is established in the earth.

5. *The rapture of the church is a deliverance from the day of wrath which follows,* while the second coming is a deliverance of those who have believed in Christ during the time of trouble and have survived.

6. *The rapture is always described as an event which is imminent, that is, could occur at any moment,* while the second

coming of Christ to the earth is preceded by many preceding signs and events.

7. *The rapture of the saints is a truth revealed only in the New Testament* while Christ's second coming to the earth with events preceding and following is a prominent doctrine of both testaments.

8. *The rapture relates only to those who are saved,* while the second coming of Christ to the earth deals with both saved and unsaved.

9. *At the rapture Satan is not bound but is very active in the period which follows,* while at the second coming Satan is bound and rendered inactive.

10. *As presented in the New Testament, no unfulfilled prophecy is given as standing between the church and the time of its rapture, which it is presented as an imminent event,* while many signs must be fulfilled before Christ's second coming to set up His kingdom.

11. *Concerning the resurrection of saints in relation to Christ coming to set up His kingdom in both the Old and New Testaments, no mention is ever made of the translation of living saints at the same time.* In fact, such a doctrine would be impossible as the living saints need to retain their natural bodies in order to function in the millennial kingdom.

12. *In the sequence of events describing the second coming of Christ to the earth, there is no adequate place for an event like the rapture.* According to Matthew 25:31-46, believers and unbelievers are still intermingled at the time of this judgment, which comes after Christ's coming to the earth, and it is obvious that no rapture or separation of the saved from the unsaved has taken place in the descent of Christ from heaven to the earth.

13. *A study of the doctrine of Christ's coming to set up His kingdom with the events which precede and follow make clear that these events do not relate to the church but rather to Israel and Gentile believers and unbelievers.* This will be explained in the next chapter.

The truth of the imminent coming of Christ for His church is a very practical truth. The Thessalonian Christians were instructed in 1 Thessalonians 1:10 "to wait for his Son from heaven, whom he raised from the dead, even Jesus, which delivered us from the wrath to come." Their hope was not survival through the tribulation, but deliverance from the wrath of God which would be poured out upon the earth (cp. 1 Thess. 5:9 and Rev. 6:17). As presented in the New Testament, the rapture is a comforting hope (John 14:1-3; 1 Thess. 4:18), a purifying hope (1 John 3:1-3), and a blessed or happy expectation (Titus 2:13). While the world will not see Christ until His second coming to set up His kingdom, Christians will see Christ in His glory at the time of the rapture and to them it will be "the glorious appearing of the great God and our Saviour Jesus Christ" (Titus 2:13). For a detailed study of the doctrine of the rapture see *The Rapture Question* by Walvoord (Grand Rapids: Zondervan, 1957).

Questions

1. What proportion of the Bible was prophecy when it was written?
2. What is the significance of the fact that many prophecies have already been literally fulfilled?
3. What is the distinction between Christ coming for His saints and Christ coming with His saints?
4. What important events will occur between these two events?
5. When did Christ first announce the rapture of the church, and what did He reveal about it?
6. Why did the disciples have difficulty understanding the first mention of the rapture?
7. Describe the order of events for Christ coming for His saints as given in 1 Thessalonians 4:13-18.
8. Why does Christ bring the souls of Christians who have died with Him from heaven at the time of the rapture?
9. Why is the truth of Christ coming for His church declared to be a mystery in 1 Corinthians 15:51-52?
10. What additional facts concerning the rapture are brought out in 1 Corinthians 15:51-58?
11. What kind of bodies will those translated or raised from the dead receive?
12. If Old Testament saints will not be raised at the rapture, when will they be raised?
13. When will the wicked dead be raised?
14. In view of the teaching of Scripture on the subject of rapture and resurrection, why must the view that all people are raised at the same time be rejected?
15. Name some of the important contrasts between the rapture of the church and the second coming of Christ to the earth to set up His kingdom.
16. In the light of these contrasts, what arguments can be advanced in favor of the pretribulational rapture as opposed to the post-tribulation rapture?
17. What practical application of the truth of the rapture is made to our lives in Scripture?

13

God the Son:
His Coming With His Saints

Since the theme of this chapter is so commonly confused with Christ's coming for His saints, it is important that the two events be studied together in order that the contrast which appears at almost every point may be seen.

A. Important Events Preceding the Second Coming of Christ

As will be discussed later in connection with prophecies of the end-time, the period between the rapture of the church and Christ's second coming to set up His kingdom is divided into three well-defined periods.

1. *A period of preparation will follow the rapture in which ten nations will be formed into a confederacy in a revival of the ancient Roman Empire.* Out of this will emerge a dictator who will control first three then all ten of the nations.

2. *A period of peace will be brought about by the dictator in the Mediterranean area, beginning with a covenant with Israel planned for seven years* (Dan. 9:27).

3. *A time of persecution for Israel and for all believers in Christ will be brought about when the dictator breaks his covenant after the first three and one half years.* At the same time he becomes a world dictator, abolishes all religions of the world in favor of the worship of Himself, and seizes control of all business operations in the world so that no one can buy or sell without his permission. This period of three and one half years is called the great tribulation (Dan. 12:1; Matt. 24:21; Rev. 7:14). In this period God will pour out great judgments (described in Rev. 6:1 — 18:24). The great tribulation will climax in a great world war (Rev. 16:14-16). At the height of this war, Christ will come back to deliver the saints who have not yet been martyred, to bring judgment on the earth, and to bring in His righteous kingdom. From the many passages that describe this period, it is evident that these great and stirring events must precede the second coming of Christ, and it would be impossible to regard the second coming to the earth as imminent inasmuch as these events have not yet taken place.

B. Vital Facts Relating to the Second Coming

1. *The Bible teaches that the Lord Jesus Christ will return to the earth* (Zech. 14:4), *personally* (Matt. 25:31; Rev. 19:11-16), *and on the clouds of heaven* (Matt. 24:30; Acts 1:11; Rev. 1:7). According to all biblical passages, it will be a glorious event which the entire world will see (Rev. 1:7).

2. *According to the revelation given by Christ Himself recorded in Matthew 24:26-29, His glorious appearing will be like lightning shining from the East to the West.* In the days preceding, described as "the tribulation of those days," there will be disturbances in the heaven, the sun darkened, the moon not giving her light, and the stars falling from heaven, and the heavens themselves shaken. More details are given in Revelation 6:12-17; 16:1-21. Christ's return will be seen by everyone on earth (Matt. 24:30; Rev. 1:7) "and then shall all the tribes of the earth mourn" (Matt. 24:30), because the great majority of them are unbelievers who are awaiting judgment.

3. *In His second coming to the earth, Christ is accompanied by saints and angels in a dramatic procession.* This is described in detail in Revelation 19:11-16. Here John writes, "And I saw heaven opened, and behold a white horse; and he that sat upon

him was called Faithful and True, and in righteousness he doth
judge and make war. His eyes were as a flame of fire, and on
his head were many crowns; and he had a name written, that
no man knew, but he himself. And he was clothed with a vesture
dipped in blood: and his name is called The Word of God.
And the armies which were in heaven followed him upon white
horses, clothed in fine linen, white and clean. And out of his
mouth goeth a sharp sword, that with it he should smite the
nations: and he shall rule them with a rod of iron: and he
treadeth the winepress of the fierceness and wrath of Almighty
God. And he hath on his vesture and on his thigh a name written, KING OF KINGS, AND LORD OF LORDS."
The fact that this is a procession in which Christ is accompanied by all the saints and holy angels indicates that it is
gradual and may take many hours. During this period the earth
will rotate, permitting the entire world to see the event. The
second coming itself will terminate on the Mount of Olives, the
same place from which Christ ascended into heaven (Zech.
14:1-4; Acts 1:9-12). At the moment His feet touch the Mount
of Olives, it will cleave in two and form a great valley extending
from Jersualem east to the Jordan valley.

4. *At His coming, Christ will first judge the armies of the
world deployed in battle* (Rev. 19:15-21). As He sets up His
kingdom, He will regather Israel and judge them (Ezek. 20:34-
38) relative to their worthiness to enter the millennial kingdom.
In a similar way He will gather the Gentiles or "the nations"
and judge them (Matt. 25:31-46). He will then bring in His
kingdom of righteousness and peace on the earth, with Satan
bound and all open rebellion judged. Further details will be
given in later chapters.

C. The Second Coming Contrasted With the Rapture

As seen in the preceding chapter, many contrasts exist between
the coming of Christ for His saints and His coming with His
saints.

The two events — Christ's coming *for* His saints and His coming *with* His saints — may be distinguished thus (for brevity, the
first event will be indicated by *a*, and the second event by *b*):

(a) "Our gathering together unto him"; (b) "The coming of
our Lord Jesus Christ" (2 Thess. 2:1).

(a) He comes as the "Morning Star" (Rev. 2:28; 22:16; 2 Pet. 1:19); (b) as the "Sun of Righteousness" (Mal. 4:2).

(a) The "Day of Christ" (1 Cor. 1:8; 2 Cor. 1:14; Phil. 1:6, 10; 2:16); (b) the "Day of the Lord" (2 Pet. 3:10).

(a) A signless event; (b) its approach to be observed (1 Thess. 5:4; Heb. 10:25).

(a) A timeless event – at any moment; (b) fulfillment of prophecy to precede it (2 Thess. 2:2, 3; note, "day of Christ" should be "day of the Lord" in verse 2).

(a) No reference to evil; (b) evil ended, Satan judged, the Man of Sin destroyed (2 Thess. 2:8; Rev. 19:20; 20:1-4).

(a) Israel unchanged; (b) all her covenants fulfilled (Jer. 23:5-8; 30:3-11; 31:27-37).

(a) The church removed from the earth; (b) returning with Christ (1 Thess. 4:17; Jude 14-15; Rev. 19:14).

(a) The nations unchanged; (b) judged (Matt. 25:31-46).

(a) Creation unchanged; (b) delivered from the bondage of corruption (Isa. 35; 65:17-25).

(a) A "mystery" not before revealed; (b) seen throughout the Old and New Testaments (Dan. 7:13-14; Matt. 24:27-30; 1 Cor. 15:51-52).

(a) Hope centered in Christ – "the Lord is at hand" (Phil. 4:5); (b) the kingdom is to come (Matt. 6:10).

(a) Christ appears as Bridegroom, Lord, and Head of the church (Eph. 5:25-27; Titus 2:13); (b) He appears as King, Messiah, and Immanuel to Israel (Isa. 7:14; 9:6-7; 11:1-2).

(a) His coming unseen by the world; (b) coming in power and great glory (Matt. 24:27, 30; Rev. 1:7).

(a) Christians judged as to rewards; (b) the nations judged as to the kingdom (2 Cor. 5:10-11; Matt. 25:31-46).

Important Scripture: (a) John 14:1-3; 1 Corinthians 15:51-52; 1 Thessalonians 4:13-18; Philippians 3:20-21; 2 Corinthians 5:10; (b) Deuteronomy 30:1-10; Psalm 72. Note all the prophets; Matthew 25:1-46; Acts 1:11; 15:13-18; 2 Thessalonions 2:1-12; 2 Peter 2:1 – 3:18; Revelation 19:11 – 20:6.

Questions

1. Describe the period of preparation which will follow the rapture of the church.
2. What is the extent of the period of peace which will follow the period of preparation, and how will it be brought about?
3. What are the major characteristics of the time of persecution for Israel which will follow the time of peace?
4. What is the precise meaning of the time of the great tribulation, and what will bring this period to a close?
5. Why would it be impossible for Jesus Christ to come and establish His kingdom in the earth today?
6. Describe the appearance of the second coming of Christ as it will be seen by the world.
7. What will be the situation in the earth and in the heavens at the time of the second coming of Christ?
8. Why do all tribes of the earth mourn at the time of the second coming?
9. Who accompanies Christ in His second coming?
10. How can you account for the fact that the entire world will see the second coming?
11. To what place on earth will Christ return in His second coming, and what will occur when His feet touch the earth?
12. What is the first act of judgment of Christ upon His return?
13. What will Christ do in relation to Israel at His return?
14. What will Christ do in relation to the Gentiles at His return?
15. What contrast between the rapture and the second coming makes clear that these were two distinct events?
16. Name some of the important Scripture passages that relate to the rapture and to the second coming of Christ to the earth.
17. Why does literal interpretation of prophecy make it impossible to make the rapture of the church and Christ's coming to set up His kingdom the same event?

14

God the Holy Spirit:
His Personality

A. *The Importance of His Personality*

In teaching the fundamental truths as relating to the Holy Spirit, special emphasis should be made of the fact of His personality. This is because the Spirit does not now speak from Himself or of Himself; rather, He speaks whatsoever He hears (John 16:13; Acts 13:2), and He is said to come into the world to glorify Christ (John 16:14). In contrast to this, Scripture represents both the Father and the Son as speaking from Themselves; and this, not only with final authority and by the use of the personal pronoun *I*, but presenting them as being in immediate communion, cooperation, conversation — the one with the other. All this tends to make less real the personality of the Holy Spirit who does not speak from or of Himself. Accordingly, in the history of the church, the personality of the Spirit was for some centuries slighted; only after the doctrine of the Father and the Son was defined as in the Nicene Creed (A.D. 325) was the Spirit recognized as a personality in the creeds of the church.

As the orthodox doctrine was later defined, the scriptural

truth that the Godhead subsists or exists in three persons — the Father, the Son, and the Holy Spirit — became generally recognized. Scripture is entirely clear that the Holy Spirit is just as much a person as God the Father and God the Son, and yet, as seen in the study of the doctrine of the Trinity, the three persons form one God not three Gods.

B. The Personality of the Holy Spirit in Scriptures

1. *The Spirit is said to do that which is possible only for a person to do.*

(a) He reproves the world: "And when he is come, he will reprove the world of sin, and of righteousness, and of judgment" (John 16:8).

(b) He teaches: "He shall teach you all things" (John 14:26; note also Neh. 9:20; John 16:13-15; 1 John 2:27).

(c) The Spirit speaks: "And because ye are sons, God hath sent forth the Spirit of His Son into your hearts, crying, Abba, Father" (Gal. 4:6).

(d) The Spirit intercedes: "But the Spirit itself maketh intercession for us with groanings which cannot be uttered" (Rom. 8:26).

(e) The Spirit leads: "led of the Spirit" (Gal. 5:18; cp. Acts 8:29; 10:19; 13:2; 16:6-7; 20:23; Rom. 8:14).

(f) The Spirit appoints men to specific service: "The Holy Ghost said, Separate me Barnabas and Saul for the work whereunto I have called them" (Acts 13:2; cp. Acts 20:28).

(g) The Spirit is Himself subject to appointment (John 15:26).

(h) The Spirit ministers: He regenerates (John 3:6), He seals (Eph. 4:30), He baptizes (1 Cor. 12:13), He fills (Eph. 5:18).

2. *He is affected as a person by other beings.*

(a) The Father sends Him into the world (John 14:16, 26), and the Son sends Him into the world (John 16:7).

(b) Men may vex the Spirit (Isa. 63:10), they may grieve Him (Eph. 4:30), they may quench (resist) Him (1 Thess. 5:19), they may blaspheme Him (Matt. 12:31), they may lie to Him (Acts 5:3), they may disrespect Him (Heb. 10:29), they may speak against Him (Matt. 12:32).

3. *All Bible terms related to the Spirit imply His personality.*

(a) He is called "another Comforter" (Advocate), which indicates that He is as much a person as Christ (John 14:16-17; 26; 16:7; 1 John 2:1-2).

(b) He is called a Spirit and in the same personal sense as God is called a Spirit (John 4:24).

(c) The pronouns used of the Spirit imply His personality. In the Greek language the word "spirit" is a neuter noun which would naturally call for a neuter pronoun, and in a few instances the neuter pronoun is used (Rom. 8:16, 26); but often the masculine form of the pronoun is used, thus emphasizing the fact of the personality of the Spirit (John 14:16-17; 16:7-15).

C. As a Person of the Godhead the Holy Spirit Is Co-equal With the Father and the Son

1. *He is called God.* This fact will be seen by comparing Isaiah 6:8-9 with Acts 28:25-26; Jeremiah 31:31-34 with Hebrews 10:15-17. (Note also 2 Cor. 3:18 ASV, and Acts 5:3, 4 – "Why hath Satan filled thine heart to lie to the Holy Ghost? . . . thou hast not lied unto men, but unto God".) Though the judgments of God have fallen so drastically on some who have lied against the Spirit (Acts 5:3) and though men are evidently not permitted to swear in the name of the Holy Spirit and though He is called *The Holy Spirit,* it is certain that He is not more holy than the Father or the Son, absolute holiness being the primary attribute of the Triune God.

2. *He has the attributes of God* (Gen. 1:2; Job 26:13; 1 Cor. 2:9-11; Heb. 9:14).

3. *The Holy Spirit performs the works of God* (Job 33:4; Ps. 104:30; Luke 12:11-12; Acts 1:5; 20:28; 1 Cor. 6:11; 2:8-11; 2 Pet. 1:21).

4. *As indicated above, the use of the personal pronouns affirm His personality.*

5. *The Holy Spirit is presented in Scripture as a personal object of faith* (Ps. 51:11; Matt. 28:19; Acts 10:19-21). As an object of faith, He is also One to be obeyed. The believer in Christ, walking in fellowship with the Spirit, experiences His power, His guidance, His instruction, and His sufficiency, and confirms experientially the great doctrines concerning the personality of the Spirit which are revealed in Scripture.

Questions

1. Why is it necessary to emphasize the personality of the Holy Spirit?
2. What are some of the important works of the Spirit which demonstrate His personality?
3. To what extent does Scripture indicate that the Holy Spirit is affected as a person by other beings?
4. What biblical terms imply the personality of the Holy Spirit?
5. How does the fact that the Holy Spirit is called God demonstrate His equality with the Father and the Son?
6. What evidence supports the conclusion that the Holy Spirit has the attributes of God?
7. How do the works of the Holy Spirit demonstrate His deity?
8. How do the personal pronouns used of the Holy Spirit affirm His personality?
9. To what extent does Christian experience in which the Holy Spirit is the object of faith and obedience support His equality with the Father and the Son?

15

God the Holy Spirit: His Advent

The coming of the Spirit into the world on the day of Pentecost must be seen in relationship to His work in previous dispensations. In the Old Testament the Holy Spirit was in the world as the omnipresent God; yet He is said to come into the world on the day of Pentecost. During the present age He is said to remain in the world but will depart out of the world — in the same sense as He came on the day of Pentecost — when the rapture of the church occurs. In order to understand this truth of the Holy Spirit, various aspects of the Spirit's relationship to the world should be considered.

A. The Holy Spirit in the Old Testament

Throughout the extended period before the first coming of Christ, the Spirit was present in the world in the same sense in which He is present everywhere, and He worked in and through the people of God according to His divine will (Gen. 41:38; Exod. 31:3; 35:31; Num. 27:18; Job 33:4; Ps. 139:7; Hag. 2:4-5; Zech. 4:6). In the Old Testament the Spirit of God is

seen to have a relationship to the creation of the world. He had
a part in the revelation of divine truth to the saints and prophets.
He inspired the Scriptures which were written, and had a
ministry to the world in general in restraining sin, in enabling
believers for service, and in performing miracles. All these activities indicate that the Spirit was very active in the Old Testament; however, there is no evidence in the Old Testament that
the Holy Spirit indwelt every believer. As John 14:17 indicates
He was "with" them but not "in" them. Likewise there is no
mention of the sealing work of the Spirit or of the baptism of
the Holy Spirit prior to the day of Pentecost. Accordingly, it
may be anticipated that after Pentecost there would be a greater
work of the Spirit than in preceding ages.

B. The Holy Spirit During the Life of Christ on Earth

It is reasonable to suppose that the incarnate, active presence
of the Second Person of the Trinity in the world would affect
the ministries of the Spirit, and this we find to be true.

1. *In relation to Christ, the Spirit was the generating power
by which the God-man was formed in the virgin's womb.* The
Spirit is also seen descending, in the form of a dove, upon
Christ as the time of His baptism. And again, it is revealed that
it was only through the eternal Spirit that Christ offered Himself to God (Heb. 9:14).

2. *The relation of the Spirit to men during the earthly ministry of Christ was progressive.* Christ first gave assurance to His
disciples that they might receive the Spirit by asking (Luke
11:13). Though the Spirit had previously come upon men according to the sovereign will of God, His presence in the human
heart had never before been conditioned upon asking, and this
new privilege was never claimed at that time by any one, as far
as the record goes. At the close of His ministry and just before
His death, Christ said, "And I will pray the Father, and he shall
give you another Comforter, that he may abide with you forever; Even the Spirit of truth" (John 14:16-17). Likewise, after
His resurrection the Lord breathed on them and said, "Receive
ye the Holy Ghost" (John 20:22); but in spite of this temporary
gift of the Spirit they were to tarry in Jerusalem until they
should be endued with power permanently from on high (Luke
24:49; Acts 1:4).

C. The Coming of the Holy Spirit at Pentecost

As promised by the Father (John 14:16-17, 26) and by the Son (John 16:7), the Spirit — who as the Omnipresent One had always been in the world — came into the world on the day of Pentecost. The force of this seeming repetition of ideas is seen when it is understood that His coming on the day of Pentecost was that He might make His abode in the world. God the Father, though omnipresent (Eph. 4:6), is, as to His abode, "Our Father which art in heaven" (Matt. 6:9). Likewise God the Son, though omnipresent (Matt. 18:20; Col. 1:27) as to His abode now, is seated at the right hand of God (Heb. 1:3; 10:12). In like manner the Spirit, though omnipresent, is now as to His abode tabernacling here on the earth. The taking up of His abode on the earth was the sense in which the Spirit came on the day of Pentecost. His dwelling place was changed from heaven to earth. It was for this coming of the Spirit into the world that the disciples were told to wait. The new ministry of this age of grace could not begin apart from the coming of the Spirit.

In the chapters which follow, the work of the Spirit in the present age will be presented. The Spirit of God first of all has a ministry to the world as indicated in John 16:7-11. Here He is revealed as convicting the world of sin and of righteousness and of judgment. This work which prepares an individual to accept Christ intelligently is a special work of the Spirit, a work of grace, which enlightens the Satan-blinded mind of unbelieving men, in respect to three great doctrines.

1. *The unbeliever is made to understand that the sin of unbelief in Jesus Christ as his personal Savior is the one sin that stands between him and salvation.* It is not a question of his worthiness, his feelings, or any other factor. The sin of unbelief is the sin which prevents his salvation (John 3:18).

2. *The unbeliever is informed concerning the righteousness of God.* While on earth Christ was the living illustration of the righteousness of God; upon His departure the Spirit is sent to reveal the righteousness of God to the world. This includes the fact that God is a righteous God who demands much more than any man can do himself, and this eliminates any possibility of human works being the basis for salvation. More important, the Spirit of God reveals that there is a righteousness available by faith in Christ and that when one believes in Jesus Christ he

can be declared righteous, justified by faith, and accepted by his faith in Christ, who is righteous both in His person and in His work on the cross (Rom. 1:16-17; 3:22; 4:5).

3. *The fact is revealed that the prince of this world, that is, Satan himself, has been judged at the cross and is doomed to eternal punishment.* This reveals the fact that the work on the cross is finished, that judgment has taken place, that Satan has been defeated, and that salvation is available to those who put their trust in Christ. While it is not necessary for an unbeliever to understand completely all these facts in order to be saved, the Holy Spirit must reveal enough so that as he believes he intelligently receives Christ in His person and His work.

There is a sense in which this was partially true in ages past, as even in the Old Testament it was impossible for a person to believe and be saved without a work of the Spirit. However, in the present age, following the death and resurrection of Christ, these facts now become much more clear, and the work of the Spirit in revealing them to unbelievers is part of the important reason for His coming into the world's sphere and making it His residence.

In His coming to the world on the day of Pentecost, the work of the Spirit in the church took on many new aspects. These will be considered in later chapters. The Holy Spirit is said to regenerate every believer (John 3:3-7, 36). The Holy Spirit indwells every believer (John 7:37-39; Acts 11:15-17; Rom. 5:5; 8:9-11; 1 Cor. 6:19-20). As indwelling the believer, the Holy Spirit is our seal unto the day of redemption (Eph. 4:30). Further, every child of God is baptized into the body of Christ by the Spirit (1 Cor. 12:13). All these ministries apply equally to every true believer in this present age. In addition to these works that are related to the salvation of the believer, there is the possibility of the filling of the Spirit and of walking by the Spirit which opens the door to all the ministry of the Spirit to the believer in the present age. These great works of the Spirit are the key not only to salvation but to effective Christian living in the present age.

When the purpose of God in this age is brought to completion by the rapture of the church, the Holy Spirit will have accomplished the purpose of His special advent into the world and will depart from the world in the same sense that He came on the day of Pentecost. A parallel can be seen between the coming of Christ to the earth to accomplish His work and His departure into heaven. Like Christ, however, the Holy Spirit will continue to be omnipresent and will continue a work after the rapture similar to that which was true before the day of Pentecost.

The present age is, accordingly, in many respects the age of the Spirit, an age in which the Spirit of God is working in a special way to call out a company of believers from both Jew and Gentile to form the body of Christ. The Holy Spirit will continue to work after the rapture, as He also will in the kingdom age — which will have its own special characteristics and probably will include all the ministries of the Holy Spirit in the present age except that of the baptism of the Spirit. The coming of the Spirit should be regarded as an important event, essential to the work of God in the present age, even as the coming of Christ is essential to salvation and God's ultimate purpose to provide salvation for the whole world and especially fo. those who will believe.

Questions

1. In what sense was the Holy Spirit in the world before Pentecost?
2. What important works of the Holy Spirit are found in the Old Testament?
3. Distinguish the meaning of the Holy Spirit being "with" the Old Testament saints in contrast to the present age, when the Holy Spirit is "in" them.
4. How is the Holy Spirit related to the conception and birth of Christ?
5. What ministry did the Holy Spirit have in the period of the gospels?
6. Why did the disciples have to wait until Pentecost for the coming of the Spirit even though the Lord had breathed on them (John 20:22)?
7. In what sense did the promise of Christ of giving another Comforter who would abide with the disciples forever promise a new ministry of the Spirit?
8. In what sense did the Holy Spirit come on the day of Pentecost, and how does this relate to His omnipresence?
9. What three doctrines are taught by the Spirit in convicting the world?
10. In coming on the day of Pentecost, what important works of the Spirit are contemplated?
11. Where is the home of the Father and the Son during the present age?
12. Where is the home of the Holy Spirit during the present age?
13. What change in the ministry of the Spirit will take place at the time of the rapture?
14. Will the Holy Spirit continue to work in the earth after the rapture?
15. What may be expected of the ministry of the Spirit in the millennial kingdom?
16. How important is the ministry of the Spirit to the present purpose of God?

16

God the Holy Spirit: His Regeneration

As the Christian's life of faith begins with being born again, regeneration is one of the fundamental doctrines in relation to salvation. Accurate definition of this work of the Spirit and an understanding of its relation to the whole Christian life are important to effective evangelism as well as to spiritual maturity.

A. Regeneration Defined

In the Bible the word "regeneration" is found only twice. In Matthew 19:28 it is used of the renewal of the earth in the millennial kingdom and does not apply to the Christian's salvation. In Titus 3:5, however, the statement is made, "Not by works of righteousness which we have done, but according to His mercy He saved us, by the washing of regeneration, and renewing of the Holy Ghost." On the basis of this text, the word "regeneration" has been chosen by theologians to express the concept of new life, new birth, spiritual resurrection, the new creation, and, in general, a reference to the new supernatural life that believers receive as sons of God. In the history of the church, the term has not always had accurate usage, but properly understood, it means the origination of the eternal life which comes into the believer in Christ at the moment of faith, the instantaneous change from a state of spiritual death to a state of spiritual life.

B. Regeneration by the Holy Spirit

By its nature, regeneration is a work of God and aspects of its truth are stated in many passages (John 1:13; 3:3-7; 5:21; Rom. 6:13; 2 Cor. 5:17; Eph. 2:5, 10; 4:24; Titus 3:5; James 1:18; 1 Pet. 2:9). According to John 1:13, the regenerated one is "born, not of blood, nor of the will of the flesh, nor of the will of man, but of God." It is compared to spiritual resurrection in several passages (John 5:21; Rom. 6:13; Eph. 2:5). It is also compared to creation in that it is a creative act of God (2 Cor. 5:17; Eph. 2:10; 4:24).

All three persons of the Trinity are involved in the regeneration of the believer. The Father is related to regeneration in James 1:17-18. Jesus Christ is frequently revealed to be involved in regeneration (John 5:21; 2 Cor. 5:18; 1 John 5:12). It seems, however, that as in other works of God where all three persons are involved, the Holy Spirit is specifically the Regenerator as stated in John 3:3-7 and Titus 3:5. A parallel may be observed in the birth of Christ in which God became His Father, the life of Son was in Christ and yet He was conceived of the Holy Spirit.

C. Eternal Life Imparted by Regeneration

The central concept of regeneration is that a believer who formerly was spiritually dead now has received eternal life. Three figures are used to describe this. One is the idea of being born again, or the figure of rebirth. In Christ's conversation with Nicodemus He said, "Ye must be born again," or as sometimes translated, "Ye must be born from above." It is thus in contrast with human birth in John 1:13. In a second figure, that of spiritual resurrection, a believer in Christ is declared to be "alive from the dead" (Rom. 6:13). In Ephesians 2:5 it is stated that God, "even when we were dead in sins, hath quickened us together with Christ," literally, "made us alive together with

Christ." In the third figure, that of the new creation, the believer is exhorted to "put on the new man, which after God is created in righteousness and true holiness" (Eph. 4:24). In 2 Corinthians 5:17 the thought is made clear: "Therefore if any man be in Christ, he is a new creature: old things are past away; behold, all things are become new." All three figures speak of the new life which is received by faith in Christ.

From the nature of the act of new birth, spiritual resurrection, and creation, it is clear that regeneration is not accomplished by any good work of man. It is not an act of the human will in itself, and it is not produced by any ordinance of the church such as water baptism. It is entirely a supernatural act of God in response to the faith of man.

Likewise, regeneration should be distinguished from the experience which follows. Regeneration is instantaneous and is inseparable from salvation. A person genuinely saved will have a subsequent spiritual experience, but the experience is the evidence of regeneration, not the regeneration itself. In a sense it is possible to say that we experience the new birth, but what we mean is that we experience the results of the new birth.

D. The Results of Regeneration

In many respects, regeneration is the foundation upon which our total salvation is built. Without new life in Christ, there is no possibility of receiving the other aspects of salvation such as the indwelling of the Spirit, justification, or all the other subsequent results. There are some features, however, that are immediately evident in the fact of regeneration.

When a believer receives Christ by faith, he is born again and in the act of the new birth receives a new nature. This is what the Bible refers to as "the new man" (Eph. 4:24) which we are exhorted to "put on" in the sense that we should avail ourselves of its contribution to our new personality. Because of the new nature, a believer in Christ may often experience a drastic change in his life, in his attitude toward God, and in his capacity to have victory over sin. The new nature is patterned after the nature of God Himself and is somewhat different than the human nature of Adam before he sinned, which was entirely human even though sinless. The new nature has divine qualities and longs after the things of God. Although in itself it does not have the power to fulfill its desires apart from the Holy Spirit, it gives a new direction to the life and a new aspiration to attain the will of God.

While regeneration in itself is not an experience, the new life received in regeneration gives the believer new capacity for experience. Once he was blind, now he can see. Once he was dead, now he is alive to spiritual things. Once he was estranged from God and out of fellowship; now he has a basis for fellowship with God and can receive the ministry of the Holy Spirit. In proportion as the Christian yields himself to God and avails himself of God's provision, his experience will be a wonderful, supernatural demonstration of what God can do with a life that is yielded to Him.

Another important aspect of having eternal life is that it is the ground for eternal security. Although some have taught that eternal life can be lost and that a person once saved can be lost if he defects from the faith, the very nature of eternal life and the new birth forbids a reversal of this work of God. It is first of all a work of God, not of man, not dependent on any human worthiness. While faith is necessary, faith is not considered a good work which deserves salvation but rather is opening the channel through which God may work in the individual life. As natural birth cannot be reversed, so spiritual birth cannot be reversed; once effected, it assures the believer that God will always be his Heavenly Father.

In like manner, resurrection cannot be reversed, as we are raised to a new order of being by an act of God. The new birth as an act of creation is another evidence that once accomplished it continues forever. Man cannot uncreate himself. The doctrine of eternal security, accordingly, rests upon the question of whether salvation is a work of God or of man, whether it is entirely of grace or based on human merit. Although the new believer in Christ may fall short of what he ought to be as a child of God, just as in the case of human parentage, it does not alter the fact that he has received life which is eternal. It is also true that the eternal life which we have now is only partially expressed in spiritual experience. It will have its ultimate enjoyment in the presence of God in heaven.

Questions

1. What is meant by regeneration?
2. What important passages on regeneration are found in the New Testament, and what in general do they teach?
3. How are the three persons of the Trinity involved in the regeneration of the believer?
4. Describe regeneration as it is revealed in the figure of rebirth.
5. Why is the new birth called a spiritual resurrection?
6. How is the fact that a believer in Christ is a new creature a result of regeneration?
7. Why is it impossible for the human will in itself to produce new birth?
8. In what sense is regeneration not an experience?
9. How is experience related to regeneration?
10. How is the new nature a result of regeneration?
11. What new experiences will come to a regenerated believer?
12. How does regeneration relate to eternal security?

17

God the Holy Spirit:
His Indwelling and Sealing

A. A New Feature of the Present Age

Although the Spirit of God was with men in the Old Testament, the source of their new life, and the means of spiritual victory, there is no evidence that all believers in the Old Testament were indwelt by Him. This is made plain by the silence of the Old Testament on this doctrine and by the express teaching of Jesus Christ, contrasting the Old Testament situation with the present age in the words, "he dwelleth with you, and shall be in you" (John 14:17). The indwelling of the Spirit in every believer is a distinctive feature of the present age which will be repeated in the millennial kingdom but is found in no other period.

B. The Universal Indwelling of the Holy Spirit in Believers

Although Christians may vary greatly in spiritual power and in manifesting the fruit of the Spirit, Scripture teaches plainly that every Christian is indwelt by the Spirit of God since the day of Pentecost. Temporary delays in indwelling seen in a few instances in Acts (8:14-17; 19:1-6) were unusual instances, not normative, and due to the transitional character of the Book of Acts. The fact of indwelling is mentioned in so many passages in the Bible that it should not be questioned by anyone recognizing the authority of Scripture (John 7:37-39; Acts 11:17; Rom. 5:5; 8:9, 11; 1 Cor. 2:12; 6:19-20; 12:13; 2 Cor. 5:5; Gal. 3:2; 4:6; 1 John 3:24; 4:13). These passages make plain that prior to the day of Pentecost the Old Testament order — in which only some were indwelt — was in effect, but after Pentecost the normal work of the Spirit has been to indwell every Christian.

The universal indwelling of the Spirit is supported by Romans 8:9, stating that in the present age "if any man have not the Spirit of Christ, he is none of his." Likewise in Jude 19 unbelievers are described as "having not the Spirit." Even Christians who are living outside the will of God and are subject to God's chastisement nevertheless have bodies which are the temples of the Holy Spirit. Paul uses this argument in 1 Corinthians 6:19 to exhort the carnal Corinthians to avoid sin against God because their body is made holy by the presence of the Holy Spirit.

The Holy Spirit is also repeatedly declared to be a gift of God, and a gift by its nature is something made without merit on the part of the recipient (John 7:37-39; Acts 11:17; Rom. 5:5; 1 Cor. 2:12; 2 Cor. 5:5). Likewise, the high standard of life required of Christians who want to walk with the Lord presumes the indwelling presence of the Holy Spirit as providing the necessary divine enablement. Just as priests and kings were anointed and set apart to their sacred tasks, so the Christian is anointed by the Holy Spirit at the time of salvation and by the indwelling presence of the Holy Spirit set apart to his new life in Christ (2 Cor. 1:21; 1 John 2:20, 27). The anointing is universal, occurs at the moment of salvation, and doctrinally is the same as the indwelling of the Spirit. The teaching that one is anointed subsequent to salvation and that it is a second work of grace or possible only when filled with the Spirit is not the teaching of Scripture.

C. Problems in the Doctrine of Indwelling

The fact that every believer is indwelt by the Holy Spirit has sometimes been challenged on the basis of problem passages. On the basis of three passages in the Old Testament and the gospels (1 Sam. 16:14; Ps. 51:11; Luke 11:13), some have believed that one who possesses the Spirit can lose the Spirit of God. David's prayer (Ps. 51:11) that the Spirit of God would not be taken away from him as He was from Saul (1 Sam. 16:14) is based on the Old Testament order. Then it was not normal for everyone to be indwelt and, accordingly, that which was sovereignly given could be sovereignly taken away.

Three passages in Acts also seem to imply a problem in the universal indwelling of the Spirit. In Acts 5:32 the Holy Spirit is described as One "whom God hath given to them that obey him." The obedience here, however, is obedience to the gospel, as Scripture clearly indicates that some who are partially disobedient still possess the Spirit. The delay in administering the Spirit on the part of those who heard the gospel through Philip in Samaria was occasioned by the necessity of connecting this new work of the Spirit with that of the apostles in Jerusalem. Accordingly, the giving of the Spirit was delayed until they laid hands on them (Acts 8:17), but this was not the normal situation, as illustrated in the conversion of Cornelius, who received the Spirit without any such laying on of hands. The situation in Acts 19:1-6 seems to refer to those who had believed in John the Baptist but had never believed in Christ. They received the Spirit when Paul laid his hands on them, but this again is an abnormal rather than a normal situation and is never repeated. The anointing in 1 John 2:20 (referred to as "unction") and 1 John 2:27 if interpreted properly relates to the initial act of indwelling rather than to a subsequent work of the Spirit. In every instance of anointing in the New Testament, whether referring to the period after Pentecost or before, the anointing of the Spirit is an initial act (Luke 4:18; Acts 4:27; 10:38; 2 Cor. 1:21; 1 John 2:20, 27). Thus the difficulties in this doctrine are dissolved upon careful study of the passages in which the problems occur.

D. The Indwelling of the Holy Spirit Contrasted With Other Ministries

Because a number of works of the Spirit occur simultaneously at the time of the new birth of the believer, careful distinction should be made between these different undertakings of the

Spirit. The indwelling of the Spirit is, accordingly, not the same as the regeneration of the Spirit, although they occur at the same time. Likewise, regeneration and indwelling of the Holy Spirit are not the same as the baptism of the Spirit to be discussed next. The indwelling of the Spirit is not the same as the filling of the Spirit, as all Christians are indwelt but not all Christians are filled with the Spirit. Also, indwelling occurs once and for all, while the filling of the Spirit can occur many times in a Christian's experience. The indwelling of the Spirit is the same, however, as the anointing of the Spirit and the sealing of the Spirit.

The fact of the Spirit's indwelling or anointing is a characterizing feature of this age (John 14:17; Rom. 7:6; 8:9; 1 Cor. 6:19-20; 2 Cor. 1:21; 3:6; 1 John 2:20, 27). By the indwelling of the Spirit, the individual is sanctified or set apart for God. In the Old Testament the anointing oil typifies the present anointing by the Spirit, oil being one of the seven symbols of the Spirit.

1. Anything touched with the anointing oil was thereby sanctified (Exod. 40:9-15). In like manner, the Spirit now sanctifies (Rom. 15:16; 1 Cor. 6:11; 2 Thess. 2:13; 1 Pet. 1:2).

2. The prophet was sancified with oil (1 Kings 9:16), likewise Christ was a prophet by the Spirit (Isa. 61:1; Luke 4:18), and the believer is a witness by the Spirit (Acts 1:8).

3. The priest was sanctified with oil (Exod. 40:15), likewise Christ in His sacrifice by the Spirit (Heb. 9:14), and the believer by the Spirit (Rom. 8:26; 12:1; Eph. 5:18-20).

4. The king was sanctified with oil (1 Sam. 16:12-13), likewise Christ by the Spirit (Ps. 45:7), and by the Spirit the believer is to reign.

5. The anointing oil was for healing (Luke 10:34), suggesting the healing of the soul in salvation by the Spirit.

6. The oil made the face to shine, which was as the oil of gladness (Ps. 45:7), and fresh oil was required (Ps. 92:10). The fruit of the Spirit is joy (Gal. 5:22).

7. In the fittings for the tabernacle, oil for the lamps is specified (Exod. 25:6). The oil suggests the Spirit, the wick the believer as a channel, and the light the outshining of Christ. The wick must rest in the oil; so the believer must walk in the Spirit (Gal. 5:16). The wick must be free from obstruction; so the believer must not resist the Spirit (1 Thess. 5:19). The wick must be trimmed; so the believer must be cleansed by the confession of sin (1 John 1:9).

The holy anointing oil (Exod. 30:22-25) was composed of

four spices added to oil as a base. These spices represent peculiar virtues found in Christ. This compound thus symbolizes the Spirit taking up the very life and character of Christ and applying it to the believer. This oil could in no case be applied to human flesh (John 3:6; Gal. 5:17). It could not be imitated, which indicates that God cannot accept anything but the manifestation of the life which is Christ (Phil. 1:21). Every article of furnishing in the tabernacle must be anointed and thus set apart unto God, which suggests that the believer's dedication is to be complete (Rom. 12:1, 2).

E. The Sealing of the Spirit

The indwelling of the Holy Spirit is represented as God's seal in three passages in the New Testament (2 Cor. 1:22; Eph. 1:13; 4:30). In every important respect, the sealing of the Spirit is entirely a work of God. Christians are never exhorted to seek the sealing of the Spirit, as every Christian has already been sealed. The sealing of the Holy Spirit, therefore, is just as universal as the indwelling of the Holy Spirit and occurs at the time of salvation.

A misunderstanding has arisen from the King James Version in Ephesians 1:13, where it states, "After that ye believed, ye were sealed with that holy Spirit of promise." Literally translated, the passage should read, "Having believed, ye were sealed with the holy Spirit of promise." In other words, the believing and the receiving occurred at the same time. It is, therefore, neither a subsequent work of grace nor a reward for spirituality. The Ephesian Christians were exhorted, "Grieve not the holy Spirit of God, whereby ye were sealed unto the day of redemption" (Eph. 4:30). Even if they sin and grieve the Spirit, they nevertheless are sealed unto the day of redemption, that is, until the day of resurrection or translation, when they would receive new bodies and would no longer sin.

Like the indwelling of the Spirit, the sealing of the Spirit is not an experience but a fact to be accepted by faith. The sealing of the Spirit is a tremendously significant part of the Christian's salvation and indicates his security, his safety, and his ownership by God. In addition, it is the symbol of the finished transaction. The Christian is sealed until the day of the redemption of his body and his presentation in glory. Taken as a whole, the doctrine of the indwelling presence of the Holy Spirit as our seal brings great assurance and comfort to the heart of every believer who understands this great truth.

Questions

1. What evidence supports the conclusion that the indwelling of the Spirit in every believer is a distinctive feature of the present age?
2. What important passages in the New Testament unquestionably teach the universal indwelling of the Holy Spirit in believers?
3. Why is indwelling of the Holy Spirit necessary to the Christian's high standard of spiritual life?
4. How may the anointing of the Spirit be defined?
5. What problems in the doctrine of indwelling are raised by such passages as 1 Samuel 16:14; Psalm 51:11; Luke 11:13?
6. What is the explanation of Acts 5:32 in relation to the universal indwelling of the Holy Spirit?
7. Why was the giving of the Holy Spirit delayed according to Acts 8:17?
8. How can the problem of Acts 19:1-6 be explained in relation to the universal indwelling of the Spirit?
9. How can the indwelling of the Spirit be contrasted with regeneration?
10. How can the indwelling of the Holy Spirit be contrasted with the baptism of the Spirit?
11. How can the indwelling of the Holy Spirit be contrasted with the filling of the Holy Spirit?
12. How does the anointing oil used in the Old Testament typify the work of the Holy Spirit?
13. What is the significance of the four spices added to the holy anointing oil in the Old Testament?
14. What is the relationship between the indwelling and the sealing of the Spirit?
15. Explain the true meaning of Ephesians 1:13.
16. How does the sealing of the Spirit relate to the spiritual experience?
17. How does the sealing of the Spirit relate to eternal security?

18

God the Holy Spirit: His Baptism

A. The Meaning of the Baptism of the Holy Spirit

Probably no other doctrine of the Spirit has created more confusion than the baptism of the Spirit. Much of this stems from the fact the baptism of the Spirit began at the same time that other great works of the Spirit occurred, such as regeneration, indwelling, and sealing. Also, in some instances baptism of the Spirit and the filling of the Spirit occurred at the same time. This has led some expositors to make the two occurrences synonymous. The conflict in interpretation, however, is resolved if one carefully examines the Scripture relating to the baptism of the Spirit. In all, there are eleven specific references to Spirit baptism in the New Testament (Matt. 3:11; Mark 1:8; Luke 3:16; John 1:33; Acts 1:5; 11:16; Rom. 6:1-4; 1 Cor. 12:13; Gal. 3:27; Eph. 4:5; Col. 2:12).

B. The Baptism of the Holy Spirit Before Pentecost

In examining the references in the four gospels and in Acts 1:5, it becomes clear that the baptism of the Spirit is regarded in each instance as a future event which had never occurred previously. There is no mention of the baptism of the Spirit in the Old Testament, and the four gospels unite with Acts 1:5 in anticipating the baptism of the Spirit as a future event. In the gospels, the baptism of the Spirit is presented as a work which Christ will do by the Holy Spirit as His agent, as for instance, in Matthew 3:11 where John the Baptist predicts that Christ "shall baptize you with the Holy Ghost, and with fire." The reference to the baptism by fire seems to refer to the second coming of Christ and the judgments which will occur at that time and is also mentioned in Luke 3:16, but not in Mark 1:8 or John 1:33. Sometimes the agency of the Holy Spirit is expressed by the instrumental use of the Greek preposition *en* as in Matthew 3:11, Luke 3:16, and John 1:33. Whether or not the preposition is used, the thought is clear that Christ baptized by the Holy Spirit. Some have taken this as being different than the baptism of the Spirit as treated in Acts and the Epistles, but the preferable view is that the baptism of the Spirit is the same in the entire New Testament. The baptism is by the Holy Spirit in any case. The norm of the doctrine is expressed by Christ Himself in that He contrasted His baptism by John with the future baptism of believers by the Holy Spirit, which was to occur after His ascension. Christ said, "For John truly baptized with water; but ye shall be baptized with the Holy Ghost not many days hence" (Acts 1:5).

C. All Christians Baptized by the Spirit in the Present Age

Because of the confusion as to the nature and time of the baptism of the Spirit, it has not always been recognized that every Christian is baptized by the Spirit into the body of Christ at the moment of his salvation. This fact is brought out in the central passage on the baptism of the Spirit in the New Testament in 1 Corinthians 12:13. There it states, "For by one Spirit are we all baptized into one body, whether we be Jews or Gentiles, whether we be bond or free; and have been all made to drink into one Spirit." In this passage, the Greek preposition *en* is correctly translated "by" in what is called the instrumental use of this preposition. This instrumental use is illustrated by the same preposition in Luke 4:1 where Christ was said to be "led by the Spirit into the wilderness," and by the expression "by you" in 1 Corinthians 6:2, by the expression "by him" in Colossians 1:16, and by the phrase "by God the Father" in Jude 1. The allegation that the preposition is not used of persons in Scripture is wrong. Accordingly, while it is true, as 1 Corinthians 12:13 indicates, that by the baptism of the Spirit we enter into a new relationship to the Spirit, the thought is not so much that we are brought into the Spirit as that we are by the Spirit brought into the body of Christ.

The expression "we all" clearly refers to all Christians, not to all men, and it should not be limited to some particular group of Christians. The truth is rather that every Christian from the moment he is saved is baptized by the Spirit into the body of Christ. Thus Ephesians 4:5 refers to "one Lord, one faith, one baptism." While rites of water baptism vary, there is only one baptism of the Spirit. The universality of this ministry is also brought out by the fact that never in Scripture is the Christian exhorted to be baptized by the Spirit, whereas he is exhorted to be filled by the Spirit (Eph. 5:18).

D. The Baptism of the Spirit Into the Body of Christ

Two main results are accomplished by the baptism of the Holy Spirit. The first is, the believer is baptized or placed into the body of Christ; related to this is the second feature of baptism into Christ Himself. These two simultaneous results of the baptism of the Spirit are tremendously significant.

By Spirit baptism the believer is placed into the body of Christ in the living union of all true believers in the present age. Here baptism has its primary meaning of being placed in, initiated into, and given a new and abiding relationship. The baptism of the Spirit, accordingly, relates believers to all the great body of truth that is revealed in Scripture concerning the body of Christ.

The body of believers, thus formed by the baptism of the Spirit and increased as additional members are added, is mentioned frequently in Scripture (Acts 2:47; 1 Cor. 6:15; 12:12-14;

Eph. 2:16; 4:4-5, 16; 5:30-32; Col. 1:24; 2:19). Christ is the Head of this body and the One who directs its activities (1 Cor. 11:3; Eph. 1:22-23; 5:23-24; Col. 1:18). The body thus formed and directed by Christ is also nurtured and cared for by Christ (Eph. 5:29; Phil. 4:13; Col. 2:19). One of the works of Christ is that of sanctifying the body of Christ in preparation for its presentation in glory (Eph. 5:25-27).

As a member of the body of Christ, the believer is also given special gifts or functions in the body of Christ (Rom. 12:3-8; 1 Cor. 12:27-28; Eph. 4:7-16). Being placed into the body of Christ by the Holy Spirit not only ensures the unity of the body without regard to race, culture, or background, but also ensures that each believer has his particular place and function and opportunity to serve God within the framework of his own personality and gifts. The body as a whole is "fitly joined together" (Eph. 4:16); that is, although the members differ, the body as a whole is well planned and organized.

E. The Baptism of the Spirit Into Christ

In addition to his relationship to fellow believers in the body of Christ, one who is baptized by the Spirit has a new position in that he is declared to be in Christ. This was anticipated in the prediction of John 14:20, where Christ said the night before His crucifixion, "At that day ye shall know that I am in my Father, and ye in me, and I in you." The expression "ye in me" anticipated the future baptism of the Spirit.

Because the believer is in Christ, he is identified in what Christ did in His death, resurrection, and glorification. This is brought out in Romans 6:1-4, where it states that the believer is baptized into Jesus Christ and into His death, and if in His death, He is buried with Christ and raised with Christ. This has often been taken as representing the rite of water baptism, but in any case it also represents the work of the Holy Spirit without which the rite would be meaningless. A similar passage is found in Colossians 2:12. Our identification with Christ through the baptism of the Spirit is an important basis for all that God does for the believer in time and eternity.

Because a believer is in Christ, he also has the life of Christ which is shared by the head with the body. The relationship of Christ to the body as its Head also is related to the sovereign direction of Christ of His body just as the mind directs the body in the human body of believers.

F. Baptism of the Spirit Related to Spiritual Experience

In view of the fact that every Christian is baptized by the Spirit at the moment of salvation, it is clear that baptism is a work of God to be understood and received by faith. Although subsequent spiritual experience may confirm the baptism of the Spirit, the baptism is not in itself an experience. Baptism, because it is universal and related to our position in Christ, is an instantaneous act of God and is not a work to be sought subsequent to being born again.

Much confusion has been wrought by the assertion that Christians should seek the baptism of the Spirit especially as it was manifested in speaking in tongues in the early church. While on three instances in Acts (Chapters 2, 10, and 19) believers spoke in tongues at the time of their baptism by the Spirit, it is clear that this was unusual and related to the transitional character of the book. In all other instances where salvation took place, there is no mention of speaking in tongues as attending the baptism of the Spirit.

Further, it is quite clear that while all Christians are baptized by the Spirit, all Christians did not speak in tongues in the early church. The whole concept, therefore, of seeking baptism of the Spirit as a means to an unusual work of God in the life of a Christian is without scriptural foundation. Even the filling of the Spirit is not manifested in speaking in tongues, but rather in the fruit of the Spirit as mentioned in Galatians 5:22-23. The fact is that the Corinthian Christians spoke in tongues without being filled by the Spirit.

A similar error is sometimes advanced which claims that there are two baptisms of the Spirit, one in Acts 2 and the other in 1 Corinthians 12:13. A comparison of the conversion of Cornelius in Acts 10 — 11 with Acts 2 makes clear that what occurred to Cornelius, a Gentile, was exactly the same as what had occurred to the disciples on the day of Pentecost. Peter says in Acts 11:15-17, "And as I began to speak, the Holy Ghost fell on them, as on us at the beginning. Then remembered I the word of the Lord, how that he said, John indeed baptized with water; but ye shall be baptized with the Holy Ghost. Forasmuch then as

God gave them the like gift as he did unto us, who believed on the Lord Jesus Christ; what was I, that I could withstand God?" Inasmuch as the baptism of the Spirit places the believer into the body of Christ, it is the same work from Acts 2 throughout the present dispensation.

The baptism of the Holy Spirit is, therefore, important as being the work of the Spirit which places us in a new union with Christ and our fellow believers, a new position in Christ, and a new association in the intimacy of the body of Christ. It is the basis for justification and for all the work of God which ultimately presents the believer perfect in glory.

Questions

1. How would you distinguish the baptism of the Spirit from the work of the Spirit in regeneration, indwelling, and sealing?
2. How would you distinguish the baptism of the Spirit from the filling of the Spirit?
3. Why has there been confusion between the baptism of the Spirit and other works of the Spirit?
4. What is the significance of the fact that the baptism of the Spirit in the four gospels and in Acts 1 is mentioned as a future work?
5. What evidence may be advanced that all Christians are baptized by the Spirit in the present age?
6. Why are Christians never exhorted to be baptized by the Spirit?
7. What is the meaning of being baptized into the body of Christ?
8. How does the figure of the body of Christ indicate that Christ directs the church?
9. How does the figure of the body of Christ bring out special gifts given to individual believers?
10. What special truths are brought out by the baptism of the Spirit into Christ?
11. How does baptism into Christ relate to our identification with Him in His death, resurrection, and glorification?
12. How does baptism into Christ support the idea that we share eternal life?
13. Why is the baptism of the Spirit not in itself a spiritual experience?
14. Is it necessary to speak in tongues in order to be baptized by the Spirit?
15. Is it necessary to speak in tongues in order to be filled by the Spirit?
16. What is wrong with the teaching that the baptism of the Spirit in Acts 2 differs from the baptism of the Spirit in 1 Corinthians 12:13?
17. Summarize the importance of the baptism of the Spirit as a work relating to our salvation.

19

God the Holy Spirit: His Filling

A. *The Filling of the Holy Spirit Defined*

In contrast with the work of the Holy Spirit in salvation such as regeneration, indwelling, sealing, and baptism, the filling of the Spirit is related to Christian experience, power, and service. The works of the Spirit in relation to salvation are once and for all, but the filling of the Spirit is a repeated experience and is mentioned frequently in the Bible.

On a limited scale, the filling of the Spirit may be observed in certain individuals before Pentecost (Exod. 28:3; 31:3; 35:31; Luke 1:15, 41, 67; 4:1). Undoubtedly there were many other instances where the Spirit of God came upon individuals and empowered them for service. On the whole, however, relatively few were filled with the Spirit before the day of Pentecost, and the work of the Spirit seems to be related to the sovereign purpose of God to fulfill in the individual some special work. There is no indication that the filling of the Spirit was open before Pentecost to everyone who yielded his life to the Lord.

Beginning with the day of Pentecost, a new age dawned in which the Holy Spirit would work in every believer. Now everyone was indwelt by the Spirit and could be filled by the Spirit if he met the conditions. Numerous illustrations in the New Testament confirm this conclusion (Acts 2:4; 4:8, 31; 6:3, 5; 7:55; 9:17; 11:24; 13:9, 52; Eph. 5:18).

The filling of the Spirit may be defined as a spiritual state where the Holy Spirit is fulfilling all that He came to do in the heart and life of the individual believer. It is not a matter of acquiring more of the Spirit, but rather of the Spirit of God acquiring all of the individual. Instead of being an abnormal and unusual situation, as was true before Pentecost, in the present age to be filled with the Spirit is the normal, if not the usual, experience of a Christian. Every Christian is commanded to be filled with the Spirit (Eph. 5:18), and not to be filled with the Spirit is to be in a state of partial disobedience.

There is an observable difference in the character and quality of the daily life of Christians. Few can be characterized as being full of the Spirit. This lack, however, is not due to failure on the part of God to make provision, but rather failure on the part of the individual to appropriate and permit the Spirit of God to fill his life.

The state of being filled with the Spirit should be contrasted with spiritual maturity. A young Christian who has just been saved may be filled with the Spirit and manifest the power of the Holy Spirit in his life. Maturity, however, comes only through spiritual experiences which may extend over a lifetime and involve a growth in knowledge, a continued experience of being filled with the Spirit, and a maturity in judgment in spiritual things. Just as a newborn babe may be perfectly heathy, so a new Christian may be filled with the Spirit, but like a newborn babe only life and experience can bring out the full spiritual qualities which belong to maturity. This is why numerous passages in the Bible speak of growth. The wheat grows until the harvest (Matt. 13:30). God works in His church through gifted men with spiritual gifts to perfect the saints for the work of the ministry and to edify the body of Christ so that Christians may grow up in faith and knowledge and spiritual stature (Eph. 4:11-16). Peter speaks of newborn babes needing spiritual milk to grow (1 Pet. 2:2) and exhorts to "grow in grace, and in the knowledge of our Lord and Saviour Jesus Christ" (2 Pet. 3:18).

There is an obvious relationship between the filling of the Spirit and spiritual maturity, and a Chirstian filled with the Spirit will mature more rapidly than one who is not. The filling of the Spirit and the resulting spiritual maturity are the two most important factors in a Christian achieving the will of God for his life and fulfilling God's purpose in creating him unto good works (Eph. 2:10).

The filling of the Spirit is, accordingly, accomplished in every believer when he is fully yielded to the indwelling Holy Spirit, resulting in a spiritual condition in which the Holy Spirit controls and empowers the individual. While there may be degrees of manifestation of the filling of the Spirit and degrees of divine power, the central thought in the filling is that the Spirit of God is able to operate in and through the individual without hindrance, accomplishing God's perfect will for that person.

This concept of the filling of the Spirit is brought out in a number of references in the New Testament. It is preeminently illustrated in Jesus Christ who, according to Luke 4:1, was continually "full of the Holy Ghost." John the Baptist had the unusual experience of being filled with the Spirit from his mother's womb (Luke 1:15), and both his mother Elizabeth and his father Zacharias were temporarily filled with the Spirit (Luke 1:41, 67). These instances are still on the Old Testament pattern in which the filling of the Spirit is a sovereign work of God not available to every individual.

Beginning with the day of Pentecost, however, the entire company was filled with the Spirit. In the early church, the Spirit of God repeatedly filled those who sought to do the will of God, as in the case of Peter (Acts 4:8), the company of Christians who prayed for boldness and the power of God (Acts 4:31), and Paul after his conversion (Acts 9:17). Some are characterized as being in a continual state of being filled with the Spirit, as was illustrated in the first deacons (Acts 6:3) and Stephen the martyr (Acts 7:55) and Barnabas (Acts 11:24). Paul was repeatedly filled with the Spirit (Acts 13:9) and so were other disciples (Acts 13:52). In each case only Christians yielded to God were filled with the Spirit.

Old Testament believers were never commanded to be filled with the Spirit, although in some instances they were admonished, like Zerubbabel, that the work of the Lord is accomplished, "Not by might, nor by power, but by my spirit, saith the LORD of hosts" (Zech. 4:6). In the present age every Christian is commanded to be filled with the Spirit, as in Ephesians 5:18, "And be not drunk with wine, wherein is excess; but be filled with the Spirit." Being filled with the Spirit, like receiving salvation by faith, is not accomplished, however, by human effort; rather, it is by permitting God to accomplish this work in the life of the individual. It is clear from Scripture that a Christian may be genuinely saved without being filled with the Spirit, and the filling of the Spirit is therefore not a part of salvation itself. The filling of the Spirit also must be contrasted to the once-for-all work accomplished in the believer when he is saved. The filling of the Spirit, while it may occur at the time of salvation, occurs again and again in the life of a yielded Christian, and it should be the normal experience of Christians to have this constant infilling of the Spirit.

The fact that the filling of the Spirit is a repeated experience is brought out in the present tense of the command in Ephesians 5:18, "be filled with the Spirit." Literally translated, it is "keep on being filled with the Spirit." It is compared in the text to a state of intoxication in which wine affects the entire body, including both the mental activity of the mind and the physical activity of the body. The filling of the Spirit is, therefore, not a once-for-all experience. It is not properly named a second work of grace, as it occurs again and again. Undoubtedly the experience of being filled with the Spirit for the first time is a very dramatic one in the life of a Christian and may be a milestone which elevates Christian experience to a new plateau. Nevertheless, the Christian is dependent upon God for continuous filling of the Spirit, and no Christian can live on yesterday's spiritual power.

From the nature of the filling of the Spirit, it may be concluded that the wide difference in spiritual experience observed in Christians and the various degrees of conformity to the mind and will of God may be traced to the presence or absence of the filling of the Spirit. One desiring to do the will of God must accordingly enter fully into the privilege that God has given him in being indwelt by the Spirit and having the capacity to yield his life to the Spirit of God completely.

B. Conditions for the Filling of the Holy Spirit

Three simple commands have often been pointed out as being the conditions for being filled with the Spirit. In 1 Thessalonians 5:19 the command is given, "Quench not the spirit." In Ephesians 4:30 Christians are instructed, "And grieve not the holy Spirit of God, whereby ye are sealed unto the day of redemption." A third, more positive instruction is given in Galatians 5:16: "This

I say then, Walk in the Spirit, and ye shall not fulfill the lust of the flesh." Although other passages cast light upon these basic conditions for being filled with the Spirit, these three passages sum up the main idea.

1. *The command to "Quench not the Spirit," in 1 Thessalonians 5:19, although not explained in context, is obviously using the figure of fire as a symbol of the Holy Spirit.* Quenching the fire, as mentioned in Matthew 12:20 and Hebrews 11:34, illustrates what is meant. According to Ephesians 6:16, "the shield of faith" is "able to quench all the fiery darts of the wicked." Accordingly, quenching the Spirit is stifling or suppressing the Spirit and not allowing Him to accomplish His work .in the believer. It may be simply defined as saying No or being unwilling to let the Spirit have His way.

Rebellion against God was the original sin of Satan (Isa. 14:14), and when a believer says "I will" instead of saying, as Christ did in Gethsemane, "Not my will, but thine, be done" (Luke 22:42), he is quenching the Spirit.

In order to experience the fullness of the Spirit, it is necessary first for a Christian to surrender his life to the Lord. Christ observed that a man cannot serve two masters (Matt. 6:24), and Christians are constantly exhorted to yield themselves to God. In introducing the whole matter of achieving the will of God in the life of a Christian, Paul wrote in Romans 6:13, "Neither yield ye your members as instruments of unrighteousnes unto sin: but yield yourself unto God, as those that are alive from the dead, and your members as instruments of righteousness unto God." Here the option before every Christian is stated clearly: he can either yield himself to God or yield himself to sin.

A similar passage is found in Romans 12:1-2. In introducing the outworking of salvation and sanctification in the life of the believer, Paul urged the Romans, "I beseech you therefore, brethren, by the mercies of God, that ye present your bodies a living sacrifice, holy, acceptable unto God, which is your reasonable service. And be not conformed to this world: but be ye transformed by the renewing of your mind, that ye may prove what is that good, and acceptable, and perfect, will of God." In both Romans 6:13 and 12:1, the same Greek word is used. "To yield ourselves to God" is "to present ourselves to God." The tense of the verb is aorist, which means "to yield yourself to God once and for all." Accordingly, the experience of filling or being filled with the Spirit can only be achieved when a Christian takes the initial step of presenting his body a living sacrifice. A Christian has been prepared for this by salvation, which makes the sacrifice holy and acceptable unto God. It is reasonable of God to expect this in that Christ died for this individual.

In presenting his body, the Christian must face the fact that he should not conform outwardly to the world, but should be inwardly transformed by the Holy Spirit with the result that his mind is renewed to recognize true spiritual values. He is able to distinguish what is not the will of God from that which is the "good, and acceptable, and perfect, will of God" (Rom. 12:2).

Yieldedness is not in reference to some particular issue, but it is rather taking the will of God for one's life in every particular. It is, therefore, a matter of being willing to do anything that God wants the believer to do. It is making the will of God final in his life and being willing to do anything whenever, wherever, and however God may direct. The fact that the exhortation "Quench not the Spirit" is in the present tense indicates that this should be a continuous experience begun by the initial act of surrender.

A Christian who desires to be continually yielded to God finds that this yieldedness relates to several aspects. It is first of all a yieldedness to the Word of God in its exhortations and truth. The Holy Spirit is the supreme Teacher, and as truth becomes known, a believer must yield to the truth as he understands it. Refusal to submit to the Word of God renders the filling of the Spirit impossible.

Yieldedness also is related to guidance. In many cases the Word of God is not explicit as to decisions which a Christian faces. Here the believer must be guided by the principles of the Word of God, and the Spirit of God can give guidance on the basis of what the Scriptures reveal. Accordingly, obedience to the guidance of the Spirit is necessary to the filling of the Spirit (Rom. 8:14). In some cases the Spirit may command a Christian to do something and on other occasions may forbid him to follow a course of action. An illustration is the experience of Paul, who was forbidden to preach the Gospel in Asia and Bithynia early in his ministry and later was instructed to go to these very areas to preach (Acts 16:6-7; 19:10). The fullness of the Spirit involves following the guidance of the Lord.

A Christian must also be yielded to God's providential acts, which often bring in situations and experiences which are not desired by the individual. Accordingly, a believer must understand what it is to be submissive to the will of God even though it involves suffering and paths that in themselves are not pleasant.

The supreme illustration of what it means to be filled with the Spirit and yielded to God is Jesus Christ Himself. In Philippians 2:5-11 it is revealed that Jesus in coming to the earth and dying for the sins of the world was willing to be what God chose, willing to go where God chose, and willing to do what God chose. A believer who desires to be filled with the Spirit must have a similar attitude of yieldedness and obedience.

2. *In connection with the filling of the Spirit, a believer is also exhorted to "grieve not the Spirit"* (Eph. 4:30). Here it is presumed that sin has entered into the life of the Christian and unyieldedness has become a fact of his experience. In order to enter into a state of being filled with the Spirit, or to return to such a state, he is exhorted not to continue in his sin which grieves the Holy Spirit. When the Spirit of God is grieved in a believer, the fellowship, guidance, instruction, and power of the Spirit are hindered; the Holy Spirit, although indwelling, is not free to accomplish His work in the life of the believer.

Experience of the filling of the Spirit, may be affected by physical conditions. A Christian who is physically tired, hungry, or sick may not be experiencing the normal joy and peace which are fruit of the Spirit. The same apostle who speaks of being filled with the Spirit confesses in 2 Corinthians 1:8-9 that he was "pressed out of measure, above strength, insomuch that we despaired even of life." Accordingly, even a Christian filled with the Spirit may experience some inner turmoil. The greater the need in a believer's circumstances, however, the greater the need for the filling of the Spirit and yieldedness to the will of God that the power of the Spirit may be manifested in the individual life.

When a Christian becomes conscious of the fact that he has grieved the Holy Spirit, the remedy is to stop grieving the Spirit, as Ephesians 4:30 means literally translated. This can be accomplished by obeying 1 John 1:9, where the child of God is instructed, "If we confess our sins, he is faithful and just to forgive us our sins, and to cleanse us from all unrighteousness." This passage refers to a child of God who has sinned against his Heavenly Father. The way to restoration is open because the death of Christ is sufficient for all his sins (1 John 2:1-2).

Thus the way back into fellowship with God for a believer to confess his sins to God, recognizing anew the basis for forgiveness in the death of Christ, and desiring restoration to an intimate fellowship with God the Father as well as the Holy Spirit. It is not a question of justice at a court of law but rather a restored relationship between a father and a son who has strayed. The passage assures that God is faithful and just to forgive sin and remove it as a barrier to fellowship when a Christian sincerely confesses his wrongdoing to God. While in some instances confession of sin may require going to individuals who have been wronged and correcting difficulties, the main idea is establishing a new intimate relationship with God Himself.

In confessing his sins, the Christian may be assured that on the divine side the adjustment is immediate. Christ, as the believer's Intercessor and as the One who died on the cross, has already made all the necessary adjustments on the heavenly side. Restoration into fellowship is therefore subject only to the human adjustment of confession and yieldedness.

Scripture also warns a believer against the serious results of continually grieving the Spirit. This sometimes results in God's chastening the believer in order to restore him, as mentioned in Hebrews 12:5-6. The Christian is warned that if he does not judge himself God will need to step in with divine discipline (1 Cor. 11:31-32). In any case, there is immediate loss when a Christian is walking out of fellowship with God, and there is the constant danger of severe judgment from God as a faithful father deals with his erring child.

3. *Walking by the Spirit is a positive command, in contrast to the previous commands which are negative.* Walking by the Spirit (Gal. 5:16) is a command to appropriate the power and blessing that is provided by the indwelling Spirit. Walking by the Spirit is a command in the present tense, that is, a Christian should keep on walking by the Spirit.

The Christian's standard of spiritual life is high, and he is unable to fulfill the will of God apart from God's power. Accordingly, the provision of the indwelling Spirit makes it possible for the Christian to be walking by the power and guidance of the indwelling Spirit.

Walking by the Spirit is an act of faith. It is depending upon the Spirit to do what only the Spirit can do. The high standards of the present age — where we are commanded to love as Christ loves (John 13:34; 15:12) and where every thought is commanded to be brought into obedience to Christ (2 Cor. 10:5) — are impossible apart from the power of the Spirit. Likewise, the other manifestations of spiritual life — such as the fruit of the Spirit (Gal. 5:22-23) and such commands as "Rejoice evermore. Pray without ceasing" (1 Thess. 5:16-17), and "In every thing give thanks: for this is the will of God in Christ Jesus concerning you" (1 Thess. 5:18) — are impossible unless one is walking by the Spirit.

Attaining a high standard of spiritual life is all the more difficult because the Christian is living in a sinful world and is under constant evil influence (John 17:15; Rom. 12:2; 2 Cor. 6:14; Gal. 6:14; 1 John 2:15). Likewise, the Christian is opposed by the power of Satan and is engaged in ceaseless warfare with this enemy of God (2 Cor. 4:4; 11:14; Eph. 6:12).

In addition to conflict with the world system and with Satan, the Christian has an enemy within, his old sin nature which desires to draw him back to the life of obedience to the sinful flesh (Rom. 5:21; 6:6; 1 Cor. 5:5; 2 Cor. 7:1; 10:2-3; Gal. 5:16-24; 6:8; Eph. 2:3). Because the sin nature is constantly at war with the new nature in the Christian, only continued dependence upon the Spirit of God can bring victory. This is why although some have erroneously concluded that a Christian can reach sinless perfection, there is the need for constantly walking by the Spirit that this power may achieve the will of God in the life of a believer. Ultimate perfection of body and spirit awaits the believer in heaven, but until death or translation spiritual warfare continues unabated.

All of these truths emphasize the importance of appropriating the Spirit by walking in His power and guidance and letting the Spirit have control and direction of a Christian's life.

C. The Results of the Filling of the Spirit

Impressive results come when one is yielded to God and filled with the Spirit.

1. *A Christian walking in the power of the Spirit experiences a progressive sanctification, a holiness of life in which the fruit of the Spirit* (Gal. 5:22-23) *are fulfilled.* This is the supreme manifestation of the power of the Spirit and is the earthly preparation for the time when the believer in heaven will be completely in the image of Christ.

2. *One of the important ministries of the Spirit is that of teaching the believer spiritual truth.* Only by the guidance and illumination of the Spirit can a believer understand the infinite

truth of the Word of God. As the Spirit of God is necessary in revealing the truth concerning salvation (John 16:7-11) before a person can be saved, so the Spirit of God also guides the Christian into all truth (John 16:12-14). The deep things of God, truth that can be understood only by a Spirit-taught man, are revealed to one who is walking by the Spirit (1 Cor. 2:9 – 3:2).

3. *The Holy Spirit is able to guide a Christian and apply the general truths of the Word of God to the particular situation of the Christian.* This is what is meant in Romans 12:2 by proving "what is that good, and acceptable, and perfect, will of God." Like the servant of Abraham of old, a Christian can experience the statement, "I being in the way, the Lord led me" (Gen. 24:27). Such guidance is the normal experience of Christians who are in proper relationship to the Spirit of God (Rom. 8:14; Gal. 5:18).

4. *Assurance of salvation is another important result of communion with the Spirit.* According to Romans 8:16, "The Spirit itself beareth witness with our spirit, that we are the children of God" (cf. Gal. 4:6; 1 John 3:24; 4:13). It is as normal for a Christian to have assurance of his salvation as it is for an individual to know that he is physically alive.

5. *All worship and love of God are possible only as one is really walking by the Spirit.* In the context of the exhortation of Ephesians 5:18, the verses which follow describe the normal life of worship and fellowship with God. A person out of fellowship cannot truly worship God even though he attends church services in lovely cathedrals and goes through the ritual of worship. Worship is a matter of the heart, and as Christ has told the Samaritan woman, "God is a Spirit: and they that worship him must worship him in spirit and in truth" (John 4:24).

6. *One of the most important aspects of a believer's life is his prayer fellowship with the Lord.* Here again the Spirit of God must guide and direct if prayer is to be intelligent. Here also the Word of God must be understood if prayer is to be according to the Word of God: True praise and thanksgiving are impossible apart from the enablement of the Spirit. In addition to the prayer of the believer himself, Romans 8:26 reveals that the Spirit intercedes for the believer. An effective prayer life, accordingly, depends upon walking by the Spirit.

7. *In addition to all the spiritual qualities already mentioned, the whole life of a believer's service and the exercise of his natural and spiritual gifts are dependent upon the power of the*

Spirit. Christ referred to this in John 7:38-39, where He described the work of the Spirit as a river of living water flowing from the heart of man. Accordingly, a Christian may have great spiritual gifts and not use them because he is not walking in the power of the Spirit. By contrast, others with relatively few spiritual gifts can be greatly used of God because they are walking in the power of the Spirit. The teaching of Scripture on the filling of the Spirit is, therefore, one of the most important lines of truth which a Christian should comprehend, apply, and appropriate.

Questions

1. How would you contrast the filling of the Spirit with the work of the Holy Spirit in salvation?
2. What instances of the filling of the Spirit may be observed before the day of Pentecost?
3. Was the filling of the Spirit open to any and all yielded to God before Pentecost?
4. How did the coming of the Spirit on the day of Pentecost change the possibility of being filled by the Spirit?
5. Define the filling of the Spirit.
6. Contrast being filled with the Spirit with spiritual maturity.
7. Can any Christian be filled with the Spirit?
8. What is the relationship between filling of the Spirit and spiritual maturity?
9. In what sense are there degrees of manifestation of the filling of the Spirit?
10. What outstanding illustrations of being filled with the Spirit are found in the Book of Acts?
11. What is the significance of the comparison of being filled with wine and being filled with the Spirit?
12. Why is it inaccurate to refer to the filling of the Spirit as a second work of grace?
13. What is meant by the command "Quench not the Spirit"?
14. Why is yielding to God necessary to be filled with the Spirit?
15. Contrast the initial step of presenting one's body as a living sacrifice with the life of continuous yieldedness.
16. Name the various aspects of a Christian's yieldedness to God.
17. In what sense is Christ the supreme example of yieldedness to God?
18. What is the meaning of the command "Grieve not the Spirit"?
19. How does a Christian's circumstances affect his experience of being filled with the Spirit?
20. What is the remedy for grieving the Spirit?
21. Why may a Christian confess his sin in confidence that he will be forgiven?

22. What are some of the serious results of continuing in a state of grieving the Spirit?
23. Define what is meant by walking by the Spirit.
24. How does a Christian's high standard of spiritual life make walking by the Spirit necessary?
25. Why is walking by the Spirit necessary in light of the fact that Christians live in a sinful world?
26. Why is walking by the Spirit necessary in view of the Christian's sin nature?
27. Why does the need of walking by the Spirit demonstrate that it is impossible for a Christian to reach sinless perfection in this life?
28. Name and define briefly seven results of the filling of the Spirit.
29. Summarize the important reasons for a Christian being filled by the Spirit.

20

The Dispensations

A. The Meaning of Dispensations

In the study of Scripture, it is important to understand that scriptural revelation falls into well-defined periods. These are clearly separated, and the recognition of these divisions and their divine purposes constitute one of the important factors in true interpretation of the Scriptures. These divisions are termed "dispensations," and in successive periods of time different dispensations may be observed.

A dispensation can be defined as a stage in the progressive revelation of God constituting a distinctive stewardship or rule of life. Although the concept of a dispensation and an age in the Bible is not precisely the same, it is obvious that each age has its dispensation. Ages are often mentioned in the Bible (Eph. 2:7; 3:5, 9; Heb. 1:2). Ages are also distinguished in the Bible (John 1:17; cf. Matt. 5:21-22; 2 Cor. 3:11; Heb. 7:11-12).

It is probable that the recognition of the dispensations sheds more light on the whole message of the Bible than any other aspect of biblical study. Often the first clear understanding of the dispensations and God's revealed purposes in them results in the beginning of useful Bible knowledge and in the fostering of a personal interest in the Bible itself. Man's relation to God is not the same in every age. It has been necessary to bring fallen man into divine testing. This, in part, is God's purpose in the ages, and the result of the testings is in every case an unquestionable demonstration of the utter failure and sinfulness of man. In the end, every mouth will have been stopped because every assumption of the human heart will be revealed as foolish and wicked by centuries of experience.

Each dispensation, therefore, begins with man being divinely placed in a new position of privilege and responsibility, and each closes with the failure of man resulting in righteous judgments from God. While there are certain abiding facts such as the holy character of God which are of necessity the same in every age, there are varying instructions and responsibilities which are, as to their application, limited to a given period.

In this connection the Bible student must recognize the difference between a primary and a secondary application of the Word of God. Only those portions of the Scriptures which are directly addressed to the child of God under grace are to be given a personal or primary application. All such instructions he is expected to perform in detail. In secondary applications it should be observed that, while there are spiritual lessons to be drawn from every portion of the Bible, it does not follow that the Christian is appointed by God to conform to those governing principles which were the will of God for people of other dispensations. The child of God under grace is not situated as was Adam, or Abraham, or the Israelites when under the law; nor is he called upon to follow that peculiar manner of life which according to Scripture will be required of men when the King shall have returned and set up His kingdom on the earth.

Since the child of God depends wholly on the instructions contained in the Bible for his direction in daily life, and since the principles obtaining in the various dispensations are so diverse and even at times contradictory, it is important that he recognize those portions of the Scriptures which directly apply to him if he is to realize the will of God and the glory of God. In considering the whole testimony of the Bible it is almost as important for the believer who would do the will of God to recognize that which does not concern him as it is for him to recognize that which does concern him. It is obvious that, apart from the knowledge of dispensational truth, the believer will not be intelligently adjusted to the present purpose and will of God in the world. Such knowledge alone will save him from assuming the hopeless legality of the dispensation that is past or from undertaking the impossible world transforming program belonging to the dispensation which is to come.

Because of imperfect translations, some important truth is hidden to the one who reads only the English text of the Bible. This is illustrated by the fact that the Greek word *aion*, which means an age, or dispensation, is forty times translated by the English word "world." Thus, when it states in Matthew 13:49, "So shall it be at the end of the world," there is reference not to the end of the material earth, which in due time must come (Isa. 66:22; 2 Pet. 3:7; Rev. 20:11), but rather to the end of this age. The end of the world is not drawing near, but the end of the age is. According to Scripture, there are in all seven major dispensations, and it is evident that we are now living in the extreme end of the sixth. The kingdom age of a thousand years (Rev. 20:4, 6) is yet to come.

A dispensation is normally marked off by a new divine appointment and responsibilities with which it begins and by divine judgment with which it ends. Seven dispensations are commonly recognized in Scripture: (1) innocence, (2) conscience, (3) government, (4) promise, (5) law, (6) grace, (7) millennial kingdom.

In studying the seven dispensations, certain principles are essential to understanding this teaching. Dispensationalism is derived from normal, or literal, interpretation of the Bible. It is impossible to interpret the Bible in its normal, literal sense without realizing that there are different ages and different dispensations. A second principle is that of progressive revelation, that is, the fact recognized by practically all students of Scripture, that revelation is given by stages. Third, all expositors of the Bible will need to recognize that later revelation to some extent supersedes earlier revelation with a resulting change in rules of life in which earlier requirements may be changed or withdrawn and new requirements added. For instance, while God commanded Moses to kill a man for gathering sticks on Saturday (Num. 15:32-36), no one would apply this command today because we live in a different dispensation.

Although seven dispensations are frequently distinguished in Scripture, three are more important than the others, namely, the dispensation of law, governing Israel in the Old Testament from the time of Moses; the dispensation of grace, the present age; and the future dispensation of the millennial kingdom.

B. Dispensation of Innocence: Age of Liberty

This dispensation began with the creation of man (Gen. 1:26-27) and continues until Genesis 3:6. In this dispensation man was given the human responsibility of being fruitful, subduing the earth, having dominion over animals, using vegetables for food, and caring for the Garden of Eden (Gen. 1:28-29; 2:15).

One prohibition was given, that is, man was instructed not to eat of the tree of knowledge of good and evil (Gen. 2:17). Although man was given a blessed estate, a perfect body, mind and nature, and everything needed for enjoyment of life, Eve succumbed to temptation and ate the forbidden fruit and Adam joined her in her act of disobedience (Gen. 3:1-6). As a result, divine judgment came, spiritual death, knowledge of sin, fear of God, and loss of fellowship.

Even in these circumstances, God introduced the principle of grace with a promise of the Redeemer (Gen. 3:15), provided coats of skin, typical of provision of redemption (Gen. 3:21). They were driven out of the garden, but were allowed to live out their natural lives (Gen. 3:23-24), and with God's judgment upon them a new dispensation began.

In the dispensation of innocence God revealed the failure of man, gave the promise of a coming Redeemer, revealed His sovereignty in judging His creatures, and introduced the principle of grace.

C. Dispensation of Conscience: Age of Human Determination

This dispensation beginning in Genesis 3:7 and extending to Genesis 8:19 brought new responsibilities upon man, stated in the so-called covenant with Adam and Eve. A curse was placed upon Satan (Gen. 3:14-15), but a curse also fell upon Adam and Eve (Gen. 3:16-19). Although no detailed code of morals is revealed as given to man at this time, he was required to live according to his conscience and in keeping with such knowledge of God as was given to him.

Under conscience, however, man continued to fail just as he has failed ever since. Conscience could convict, but it could not bring victory (John 8:9; Rom. 2:15; 1 Cor. 8:7; 1 Tim. 4:2). Adam's children had his sin nature manifested in Cain's refusal to bring a blood offering (Gen. 4:7) and the consequent murder of Abel by Cain (Gen. 4:8). The resulting civilization of Cain was sinful (Gen. 4:16-24), and physical death became common (Gen. 5:5-31). The wickedness of the human heart reached such a stage that judgment again was necessary (Gen. 6:5, 11-13). Judgment was manifested on Cain (Gen. 4:10-15) and on mankind in general in death (Gen. 5). Finally God had to bring upon the earth the universal flood (Gen. 7:21-24).

In this period, however, there was divine grace also manifested, as some were saved like Enoch (Gen. 5:24), and Noah's family was saved by the ark (Gen. 6:8-10; Heb. 11:7). The dispensation ended with the flood in which only Noah's family was saved.

The purpose of God in this dispensation was to demonstrate again man's failure under the new situation in which he operated under conscience. However, in this period God preserves the line of the future Redeemer, demonstrated His sovereignty in judging the world by the flood, and manifested His grace to Noah and his family.

D. Dispensation of Human Government: Covenant With Noah

This dispensation covers the period from Genesis 8:20 through 11:9. To Noah God gave an unconditional covenant (Gen. 8:20 — 9:17) in which He promised no further destruction by a flood (Gen. 8:21; 9:11). God promised that seasons in the course of nature would not change (Gen. 8:22) and gave man the renewed command to multiply (Gen. 9:1) and to continue his dominion over animals (Gen. 9:2); eating of flesh was now allowed even though blood was forbidden (Gen. 9:4). Most important was the establishment of the essence of government in which man was given the right to kill murderers (Gen. 9:5-6).

In this covenant, as in the others, there is human failure as indicated in Noah's drunkenness (Gen. 9:21) and Ham's irreverence (Gen. 9:22). It is a period of moral and religious deterioration (Gen. 11:1-4). Human government, like conscience, failed to curb man's sin, and the Tower of Babel was the result (Gen. 11:4). God's judgment was to confound their speech (Gen. 11:5-7), and man's civilization was scattered (Gen. 11:8-9).

In this period, however, grace was evident as the godly remnant was preserved and Abram selected (Gen. 11:10 — 12:3).

Also, the seed of the woman was preserved and God's sovereignty was manifested. The dispensation ended with the judgment of the Tower of Babel and preparations for the next dispensation.

It is important to note that both conscience and human government continue in later dispensations. Only Abram and his seed come under the dispensation of promise. In general, the dispensation of human government revealed the failure of man under this new rule of life, revealed the selective judgment of God, and continued to manifest divine grace.

E. Dispensation of Promise: Covenant With Abraham

This covenant beginning in Genesis 11:10 extended through Exodus 19:2. In it the human responsibility was given to trust in the promises of God revealed to Abraham. The content of their divine revelation included the promise to Abraham (Gen. 12:1-2; 13:16; 15:5; 17:6); the promise to Israel, Abraham's seed, that they would be a great nation and channel of the fulfillment of God's promise (Gen. 12:2-3; 13:16; 15:5, 18-21; 17:7-8; 28:13-14; Josh. 1:2-4); and a promise of blessing to the entire earth through Abraham (Gen. 12:3). The principle was also laid down that God would bless those who bless Abraham and curse those who curse Abraham's seed.

Abrahamic covenant is one of the important covenants of the Bible and includes the provision that Israel be a nation forever, have title to the land forever, be blessed in spiritual things, be under divine protection, and have the special sign of circumcision (Gen. 17:13-14). The covenant was both gracious in principle and unconditional as it did not depend upon human faithfulness but upon the faithfulness of God. Only partially fulfilled in Abraham's lifetime, the blessings and promises of the Abrahamic covenant continue in their fulfillment to the end of human history. Some of the immediate blessings of the covenant for any particular generation were conditioned on obedience, but the covenant itself was declared to be an everlasting covenant (Gen. 17:7, 13, 19; 1 Chron. 16:16-17; Ps. 105:10). The covenant with Abraham was directed primarily to Abraham and his descendants as far as dispensational responsibility is concerned. The world as a whole continued under human government and conscience as its primary responsibility.

Under the Abrahamic covenant, however, there was a constant

pattern of failure which was manifested in the delay in going to the Promised Land (Gen. 11:31); in Abraham in becoming the father of Ishmael (Gen. 16:1-16); and in going down into Egypt (Gen. 12:10 – 13:1). It is evident, however, that Abraham grew in faith and grace and ultimately was willing even to sacrifice his son Isaac in obedience to God (Gen. 22).

Following Abraham, Isaac failed, living as close to Egypt as he could without violating God's command (Gen. 26:6-16). Jacob likewise failed, in not believing the promise made to his mother at his birth (Gen. 25:23; 28:13-15, 20); he was guilty of lying, deceit, and bargaining (Gen. 27:1-29) and eventually moved out of the land to Egypt to avoid the famine (Gen. 46:1-4).

In Egypt, Israel also failed God in their complaining and lack of faith (Exod. 2:23; 4:1-10; 5:21; 14:10-12; 15:24), in their desire to go back to Egypt (Exod. 14:11-12), and in their constant murmuring (Exod. 15:24; 16:2; Num. 14:2; 16:11, 41; Josh. 9:18). Their failure is evident both at the time of the giving of the law and subsequently in their failure to trust the promises of God at Kadesh-barnea (Num. 14). The failure under the period when the Abrahamic promise was especially their responsibility resulted in their temporary loss of the land, their bondage in Egypt, and their wilderness wanderings before reentering the land. Their failure set the stage for the bringing in of the Mosaic law.

In the dispensation of promise, there was much divine grace illustrated in God's constant care of His people, their deliverance from Egypt, and the institution of the Passover feast. The dispensation of promise ends at the time of the giving of the law (Exod. 19) but ends only in the sense of being the principle or main test of responsibility. The dispensation of promise continues to the end of history, and many of its promises are still in force as an object of faith and hope. The promises to Abraham are the basis for the later dispensations of grace and of the kingdom. To some extent the promises never end and are fulfilled in the eternal state.

The dispensation of promise established clearly the principle of divine sovereignty, provided a channel of special divine revelation to the nation of Israel, continued provision of divine redemption and blessing, revealed the grace of God, and promised a witness to the world. Like the other dispensations, however, it ended in failure as far as bringing conformity to the will of God, and it laid the ground work for bringing in the law as a schoolmaster to bring believers to Christ (Gal. 3:24).

F. The Dispensation of the Law

The dispensation of the law begins in Exodus 19:3 and extends throughout the whole period up to the day of Pentecost in Acts 2, although the law ended in one sense at the cross. Certain portions like the gospel of John and selected passages in the other gospels anticipated the present age of grace, however.

The Mosaic law was directed to Israel alone, and Gentiles were not judged by its standards. The law contained a detailed system of works including three major divisions: the commandments (the express will of God, Exod. 20:1-26); the judgments (the social and civil life of Israel, (Exod. 21:1 − 24:11); and the ordinances (the religious life of Israel, Exod. 24:12 − 31:18). The sacrificial and priestly system which was included was both gracious and legal. Government in this dispensation was a theocracy, a government by God through His prophets, priests, and (later) kings. The Mosaic covenant was also a temporary covenant, in force only until Christ should come (Gal. 3:24-25). The nature of the dispensation was conditional, that is, blessing was conditioned on obedience.

For the first time in history, Scripture revealed a complete and detailed religious system under the law, provided a ground for cleansing and forgiveness, worship, and prayer, and offered a future hope.

Under the law there was continual failure. This is especially evident in the period of judges, but continued after the death of Solomon and the division of the kingdom of Israel into two kingdoms. There were periods when the law was completely forgotten and ignored, and idolatry reigned supreme. The New Testament continues the record of failure, culminating in the rejection and crucifixion of Christ, who in His life perfectly kept the law.

Many judgments were inflicted during the dispensation of the law as described in Deuteronomy 28:1 − 30:20. The major judgments were the Assyrian and Babylonian captivities from which they returned in due time. The judgments on Israel also came after the close of the dispensation and included the destruction of Jerusalem in A.D. 70 and the worldwide dispersion of Israel. Another time of Jacob's trouble, the great tribulation, is still ahead (Jer. 30:1-11; Dan. 12:1; Matt. 24:22).

Under the law, however, divine grace was also administered in that a sacrificial system was provided as a way of restoration for sinning Israel, and the longsuffering God is manifested in the provision of prophets, judges, and kings, and in the preservation of the nation. At various times, genuine repentance of Israel was accepted by God, and throughout this period the Old Testament was written. The crowning blessing was the coming of Christ as the Messiah of Israel, whom the nation as a whole rejected.

In one sense the dispensation of the law ended at the cross (Rom. 10:4; 2 Cor. 3:11-14; Gal. 3:19, 25). But in another sense it was not concluded until the day of Pentecost, when the dispensation of grace began. Although the law ended as a specific rule of life, it continues to be a revelation of the righteousness of God and can be studied with profit by Christians in determining the holy character of God. The moral principles underlying the law continue, since God does not change; but believers today are not obligated to keep the details of the law, as the dispensation has changed and the rule of life given Israel is not the rule of life for the church. Although many applications of the law may be made, a strict interpretation relates the Mosaic law to Israel only.

The purpose of the law was to provide a righteous rule of life and to bring sin into condemnation. Israel's experience under the law demonstrated that moral, civic, and religious law cannot save or sanctify. The law was never intended to provide for man's salvation, while in force or later, and by its nature was weak in that it could not justify (Rom. 3:20; Gal. 2:16); it could not sanctify or perfect (Heb. 7:18-19); was limited in its force and duration (Gal. 3:19); could not regenerate (Gal. 3:21-22); and could only bring sin out into the open (Rom. 7:5-9; 8:3; 1 Cor. 15:56). The law made it possible for God to demonstrate that everyone was guilty and every mouth stopped (Rom. 3:19), and made the need of Christ evident (Rom. 7:7-25; Gal. 3:21-27).

G. Dispensation of Grace

The dispensation of grace begins properly at Acts 2 and continues throughout the New Testament, culminating with the rapture of the church. Some teachings concerning the dispensation of grace were introduced earlier, as in John 13 – 17. Scriptures involved in this dispensation extend from Acts 1 through Revelation 3.

The dispensation of grace was directed to the church alone, as the world as a whole continues under conscience and human government. In it salvation is clearly revealed to be by faith alone, which was always true but is now more evident (Rom. 1:16; 3:22-28; 4:16; 5:15-19). The high standards of grace elevate this dispensation above all previous rules of life (John 13:34-35; Rom. 12:1-2; Phil. 2:5; Col. 1:10-14; 3:1; 1 Thess. 5:23).

Under grace, however, failure also was evident as grace produced neither worldwide acceptance of Christ nor a triumphant church. Scripture in fact predicted that there would be apostasy within the professing church (1 Tim. 4:1-3; 2 Tim. 3:1-13; 2 Pet. 2 – 3; Jude). Although God is fulfilling His purpose in calling out a people to His name from Jew and Gentile, the professing but unsaved portion of the church left behind at the Rapture will be judged in the period between the Rapture and Christ's coming to set up His kingdom (Matt. 24:1-26; Rev. 6-19). The true church will be judged in heaven at the judgment seat of Christ (2 Cor. 5:10-11).

In this present age, divine grace is especially evident in the coming of Christ (John 1:17), in the salvation of the believer and our standing before God (Rom. 3:24; 5:1-2, 15-21; Gal. 1:1 – 2:21; Eph. 2:4-10), and in the nature of grace as a rule of life (Gal. 3:1 – 5:26).

The dispensation of grace ends with the rapture of the church, which will be followed by judgment on the professing church (Rev. 17:16). The age of grace is a different dispensation in that it concerns the church comprising Jewish and Gentile believers. By contrast, the law of Israel was for Israel only, human government was for the entire world, and conscience extends to all people. In the present dispensation, the Mosaic law is completely canceled as to immediate application, but continues to testify to the holiness of God and provides many spiritual lessons by application. Although all dispensations contain a gracious element, the dispensation of grace is the supreme manifestation both in the fullness of salvation received and in the rule of life.

H. Dispensation of the Kingdom

The dispensation of the kingdom begins with the second coming of Christ (Matt. 24; Rev. 19) and is preceded by a period of time including the Tribulation, which to some extent is a transitional period. Scriptures which apply are all passages on the future kingdom, whether in the Old or New Testament (major Scriptures being Ps. 72; Isa. 2:1-5; 9:6-7; 11; Jer. 33:14-17; Dan. 2:44-45; 7:9-14, 18, 27; Hos. 3:4-5; Zech. 14:9; Luke 1:31-33; Rev. 19 — 20). In the kingdom, the human responsibility will be to obey the king who will rule with a rod of iron (Isa. 11:3-5; Rev. 19:15). The kingdom will be theocratic, that is, a rule of God, and there will be a renewed sacrificial system and priesthood (Isa. 66:21-23; Ezek. 40 — 48). An unusual feature of this period is that Satan will be bound and demons rendered inactive (Rev. 20:1-3, 7). The kingdom, however, will also be a period of failure (Isa. 65:20; Zech. 14:16-19), and there will be rebellion at its close (Rev. 20:7-9).

The divine judgment which follows includes destruction of the rebels by fire (Rev. 20:9) and destruction of the old earth and heaven by fire (2 Pet. 3:7, 10-12).

In the millennial kingdom, divine grace is also revealed in fulfillment of the new covenant (Jer. 31:31-34), in salvation (Isa. 12), in physical and temporal prosperity (Isa. 35), in abundance of revelation (Jer. 31:33-34), forgiveness of sin (Jer. 31:34), and in the regathering of Israel (Isa. 11:11-12; Jer. 30:1-11; Ezek. 39:25-29). The millennial kingdom ends with the destruction of the earth and heaven by fire and is followed by the eternal state (Rev. 21 — 22).

The dispensation of the kingdom differs from all preceding dispensations in that it is the final form of moral testing. The advantages of the dispensation include a perfect government, the immediate glorious presence of Christ, universal knowledge of God and the terms of salvation, and Satan rendered inactive. In many respects the dispensation of the kingdom is climactic and brings to consummation God's dealings with man.

In the dispensations God has demonstrated every possible means of dealing with man. In every dispensation man fails and only God's grace is sufficient. In the dispensations is fulfilled God's purpose to manifest His glory, both in the natural world and in human history. Throughout eternity no one can raise a question as to whether God could have given man another chance to attain salvation or holiness by his own ability. A knowledge of the dispensations is, accordingly, the key to understanding God's purpose in history and the unfolding of the Scripture which records God's dealings with man and His divine revelation concerning Himself.

Questions

1. How important is the doctrine of dispensations?
2. How may a dispensation be defined?
3. Contrast a dispensation and an age in the Bible.
4. What, in general, characterizes the beginning and the end of each dispensation?
5. How can primary and secondary application of the Word of God be distinguished?
6. How does dispensational interpretation offer an explanation of scriptural instructions that seem contradictory?
7. What seven dispensations are commonly recognized in Scripture?
8. How does normal, or literal, interpretation relate to dispensationalism?
9. How does progressive revelation relate to dispensationalism?
10. How does dispensationalism explain changes in rules of life?
11. Which dispensations are most important?
12. What was the requirement of man under the dispensation of innocence?
13. How was grace shown in the dispensation of innocence?
14. Summarize the revelation of God in the dispensation of innocence.
15. To what extent did the dispensation of conscience reveal human failure?
16. How was grace shown in the dispensation of conscience?
17. What were some of the outstanding results of the dispensation of conscience?
18. What was the requirement of man under the dispensation of human government?
19. To what extent did man fail under human government?
20. To what extent was grace shown in the human government?
21. What did the dispensation of human government reveal?
22. In what senses do the dispensations of conscience and human government continue today?
23. What was provided in the dispensation of promise, and what was required of man in regard to it?
24. Explain how the dispensation of promise did not extend to the entire race.
25. Describe human failure under the dispensation of promise.
26. How was divine grace shown in the dispensation of promise?
27. Who was placed under the dispensation of the law?
28. Name the major divisions of the law.

29. How complete was the law as a detailed religious system?
30. Describe, in general, the failure of Israel under the law.
31. To what extent was grace shown under the law?
32. When did the law end?
33. Describe the extent and the limitation of the purpose of the law.
34. To whom was the dispensation of grace directed?
35. Characterize the standards of grace as a rule of life.
36. To what extent was there failure under the dispensation of grace?
37. What ends the dispensation of grace?
38. Contrast the dispensation of grace with the dispensation of law.
39. When does the dispensation of the kingdom begin?
40. Name some of the important Scripture passages relating to the kingdom.
41. What are some of the unusual features of the dispensation of the kingdom?
42. Describe the failure and judgment at the end of the dispensation of the kingdom.
43. What was revealed in the millennial kingdom concerning grace?
44. How does the dispensation of the kingdom differ from all preceding dispensations?
45. Why was the dispensation of the kingdom a fitting climax to the program of God?

21

The Covenants

The Bible discloses the fact that human history is the fulfillment
of an eternal purpose of God. God's eternal plan is revealed in
Scripture and centers in solemn covenants or promises which
God has made. At least eight biblical covenants are recorded,
and they incorporate the most important facts relating to God's
plan and purpose in the world. Most of these covenants are in
the form of a declaration of divine purpose which will certainly
be fulfilled. In addition to the biblical covenants, theologians
have advanced three theological covenants especially relating to
the salvation of man.

A. *The Theological Covenants*

In defining the eternal purpose of God, theologians have advanced the theory that it is God's central purpose to save the
elect, those chosen for salvation from eternity past. Accordingly,
they view history as primarily the outworking of God's plan of
salvation. In developing this doctrine, they have expounded
three basic theological covenants.

1. *A covenant of works is said to have been made with Adam.* The provision of the covenant was that if Adam obeyed God, he would be rendered secure in his spiritual state and would receive eternal life. It is claimed that this covenant is supported by the warning concerning the tree of knowledge of good and evil, that "in the day that thou eatest thereof thou shalt surely die" (Gen. 2:17). It is inferred that if he did not eat of the tree, he would not die, and like the holy angels he would be confirmed in his holy estate. This covenant is based almost entirely on inference and is not called a covenant in the Bible, and for this reason is rejected by many students of Scripture as having an insufficient ground.

2. *Another covenant is suggested and named the covenant of redemption in which the teaching is advanced that a covenant was made between God the Father and God the Son in relation to the salvation of man in eternity past.* In this covenant, the Son of God undertook to provide the redemption for the salvation of those who believe, and God promised to accept His sacrifice.

This covenant has more support in Scripture than the covenant of works in that the Bible clearly declares that God's plan of salvation is eternal, and in that plan Christ had to die as a sacrifice for sin and God had to accept that sacrifice as a sufficient basis for saving those who believed in Christ. According to Ephesians 1:4, "He hath chosen us in him before the foundation of the world, that we should be holy and without blame before him in love." Also, in reference to our position in Christ, it is stated in Ephesians 1:11, "In whom also we have obtained an inheritance, being predestinated according to the purpose of him who worketh all things after the counsel of his own will."

From these and other Scriptures, it is clear that God's purpose in salvation is eternal. That a formal covenant was entered into between God the Father and God the Son is inferred from the fact that God's purpose is also a promise.

3. *Still another approach is to regard eternal purpose of God in salvation as a covenant of grace.* In this point of view, Christ is regarded as the Mediator of the covenant and as the representative of those who put their trust in Him. Individuals meet the conditions of this covenant when they place faith in Jesus Christ as Savior. Although this covenant also is an inference from the eternal plan of salvation, it tends to emphasize the gracious character of God's salvation. The covenant of redemption and the covenant of grace, accordingly, have some

scriptural basis and are more acceptable to most students of the Bible than the concept of the covenant of works, which has no scriptural support.

A problem has arisen, however, in that those who are adherents of these theological covenants often make the plan of God for salvation His primary purpose in human history. Thus they tend to ignore the particulars of the plan of God for Israel, the plan of God for the church, and the plan of God for the nation. While it is true that God's plan of salvation is an important aspect of His eternal purpose, it is not the total of God's plan. A better view is that God's plan for history is to reveal His glory, and He does this not only by saving men but by fulfilling His purpose and revealing Himself through His dealings with Israel, with the church, and with the nations. Accordingly, it is preferable to view history through the eight biblical covenants which reveal the essential purposes of God throughout human history and include God's plan of salvation. Those who emphasize the theological covenants are often termed "covenant theologians," whereas those who emphasize the biblical covenants are called "dispensationalists," because the biblical covenants reveal the distinctions in the various stages in human history which are revealed in the dispensations.

B. *The Biblical Covenants*

The covenants of God contained in Scripture fall into two classes, those that are conditional and those that are unconditional. A conditional covenant is one in which God's action is in response to some action on the part of those to whom the covenant is addressed. A conditional covenant guarantees that God will do His part with absolute certainty when the human requirements are met, but if man fails, God is not obligated to fulfill His covenant.

An unconditional covenant, while it may include certain human contingencies, is a declaration of the certain purpose of God, and the promises of an unconditional covenant will certainly be fulfilled in God's time and way. Of the eight biblical covenants, only the Edenic and Mosaic were conditional. However, even under unconditional covenants, there is a conditional element as it applies to certain individuals. An unconditional covenant is distinguished from a conditional covenant by the fact that its ultimate fulfillment is promised by God and depends upon God's power and sovereignty.

1. *The Edenic covenant was the first covenant that God made with man* (Gen. 1:26-31; 2:16-17), and it was a conditional covenant with Adam in which life and blessing or death and cursing were made to depend on the faithfulness of Adam. The Edenic covenant included giving Adam the responsibility of being father of the human race, subduing the earth, having dominion over animals, caring for the garden, and not eating of the tree of knowledge of good and evil. Because Adam and Eve failed and disobeyed by eating the forbidden fruit, the penalty of death for disobedience was imposed. Adam and Eve died spiritually immediately and needed to be born again in order to be saved. Later they also died physically. Their sin plunged the whole human race into its pattern of sin and death.

2. *The Adamic covenant was made with man after the Fall* (Gen. 3:16-19). This is an unconditional covenant in which God declares to man what his lot in life will be because of his sin. There is no appeal allowed, nor is any human responsibility involved.

The covenant as a whole provides important features which condition human life from this point on. Included in the covenant is the fact that the serpent used of Satan is cursed (Gen. 3:14; Rom. 16:20; 2 Cor. 11:3, 14; Rev. 12:9); the promise of a Redeemer is given (Gen. 3:15), which promise is ultimately fulfilled in Christ; the place of women is detailed as being subject to multiplied conception, to sorrow and pain in motherhood, and to the headship of man (Gen. 1:26-27; 1 Cor. 11:7-9; Eph. 5:22-25; 1 Tim. 2:11-14). Man will henceforth earn his bread by the sweat of his brow (cp. Gen. 2:15 with 3:17-19); man's life will be one of sorrow and ultimate death (Gen. 3:19; Eph. 2:5). To a large extent, man continues from this point on to operate under the Adamic covenant.

3. *The Noahic covenant was made with Noah and his sons* (Gen. 9:1-18). This covenant, while repeating some of the features of the Adamic covenant, introduced a new principle of human government as a means to curb sin. Like the Adamic covenant it was unconditional, and it revealed God's purpose for the race subsequent to Noah.

Provisions of the covenant included the establishment of the principle of human government in that capital punishment was provided for those who took another man's life. The normal order of nature was reaffirmed (Gen. 8:22; 9:2), and man was given permission to eat the flesh of animals (Gen. 9:3-4) instead of living only on vegetables, as he seems to have done before the flood.

The covenant with Noah included prophecy concerning the descendants of his three sons (Gen. 9:25-27) and designated Shem as the one through whom the godly line leading to the Messiah would come. The dominance of Gentile nations in world history is implied in the prophecy concerning Japheth. Just as the Adamic covenant introduced the dispensation of conscience, so the Noahic covenant introduced the dispensation of human government.

4. *The Abrahamic covenant* (Gen. 12:1-4; 13:14-17; 15:1-7; 17:1-8) *is one of the great revelations of God concerning future history, and in it profound promises were given along three lines.* First of all, promises were given to Abraham that he would have numerous posterity (Gen. 17:16), that he would have much personal blessing (Gen. 13:14-15, 17; 15:6, 18; 24:34-35; John 8:56), that his name would be great (Gen. 12:2), and that he personally would be a blessing (Gen. 12:2).

Second, through Abraham the promise was made that a great nation would emerge (Gen. 12:2). In the purpose of God, this had reference primarily to Israel and the descendants of Jacob, who formed the twelve tribes of Israel. To this nation was given the promise of the land (Gen. 12:7; 13:15; 15:18-21; 17:7-8).

A third major area of the covenant was the promise that through Abraham blessing would come to the entire world (Gen. 12:3). This was to be fulfilled in that Israel was to be the special channel of God's divine revelation, the source of the prophets who would reveal God, and would provide the human writers of Scripture. Supremely, the blessing to the nations would be provided through Jesus Christ, who would be a descendant of Abraham. Because of Israel's special relationship to God, God pronounced a solemn curse on those who would curse Israel and a blessing upon those who would bless Israel (Gen. 12:3).

The covenant with Abraham, like the Adamic and Noahic covenants, is unconditional. While any particular generation of Israel could enjoy its provisions only if they were obedient and could, for instance, be led off into captivity if they were disobedient, the ultimate purpose of God to bless Israel, to reveal Himself through Israel, to provide redemption through Israel, and to bring Israel into the Promised Land is absolutely certain because it depends upon God's sovereign power and will rather than man's. In spite of Israel's many failures in the Old Testament, God did reveal Himself to them and caused the Scriptures to be written, and ultimately Christ was born, lived, and died, and rose again exactly as the Word of God had anticipated. In spite of human failure, the purposes of God are certain of fulfillment.

5. *The Mosaic covenant was given through Moses for the children of Israel while they were journeying from Egypt to the Promised Land* (Exod. 20:1 – 31:18).

As contained in Exodus and amplified in many other portions of Scripture, God gave to Moses the law which was to govern his relationship to the people of Israel. The approximately six hundred specific commands are classified into three major divisions, (a) the commandments, containing the express will of God (Exod. 20:1-26), (b) the judgments, relating to the social and civic life of Israel (Exod. 21:1 – 24:11), and (c) the ordinances (Exod. 24:12 – 31:18).

The Mosaic law was a conditional covenant and embodied the principle that if Israel was obedient, God would bless them, but if Israel was disobedient, God would curse them and discipline them. This is brought out especially in Deuteronomy 28. Although it was anticipated that Israel would fail, God promised that He would not forsake His people (Jer. 30:11). The Mosaic covenant was also a temporary one and would terminate at the cross of Christ. Although containing gracious elements, it was basically a covenant of works.

6. *The Palestinian covenant* (Deut. 30:1-10) *was an unconditional covenant regarding Israel's final possession of the land.* This covenant illustrates how a covenant basically unconditional and sure in its fulfillment nonetheless has conditional elements for any particular generation. The promise given to Abraham in Genesis 12:7 and subsequently reaffirmed throughout the Old Testament was that Abraham's seed would possess the land. Nevertheless, because of disobedience and failure, Jacob and his descendants lived in Egypt hundreds of years before the Exodus. In keeping with the purpose of God, however, they returned and possessed at least a portion of the land. Later, because of disobedience and disregard of the law of God, they were led off into the Assyrian and Babylonian captivities. Again, in the grace of God, they were allowed to return after seventy years of the Babylonian captivity and repossessed the land until Jerusalem was destroyed in A.D. 70. Israel is promised, however, that in spite of all her failures, she will ultimately be returned

to the land, live in safety and blessing there, and never be scattered again (Ezek. 39:25-29; Amos 9:14-15).

The present return of Israel to the land is, therefore, highly significant because it fulfills the first phase of the return of Israel necessary for setting the stage for the endtime. Israel's return will be made complete to the last man after Jesus Christ returns and sets up His kingdom (Ezek. 39:25-29). While any one generation might be driven out of the land because of disobedience, the ultimate purpose of God to bring His people into their promised land is unconditional and certain of fulfillment.

The Palestinian covenant, accordingly, includes Israel's dispersion for unbelief and disobedience (Gen. 15:13; Deut. 28:63-68), times of repentance and restoration (Deut. 30:2), the regathering of Israel (Deut. 30:3; Jer. 23:8; 30:3; 31:8; Ezek. 39:25-29; Amos 9:9-15; Acts 15:14-17), Israel's restoration to the land (Isa. 11:11-12; Jer. 23:3-8; Ezek. 37:21-25; Amos 9:9-15), their spiritual conversion and national restoration (Hos. 2:14-16; Rom. 11:26-27), their ultimate safety and prosperity as a nation (Amos 9:11-15), and divine judgment of their oppressors (Isa. 14:1-2; Joel 3:1-8; Matt. 25:31-46).

7. *The Davidic covenant* (2 Sam. 7:4-16; 1 Chron. 17:3-15) *was an unconditional covenant in which God promised David an unending royal lineage, a throne, and a kingdom, all of them forever.* In the declaration of this covenant, Jehovah reserves the right to interrupt the actual reign of David's sons if chastisement is required (2 Sam. 7:14-15); Ps. 89:20-37); but the perpetuity of the covenant cannot be broken.

As the Abrahamic covenant guaranteed to Israel an everlasting entity as a nation (Jer. 31:36) and an everlasting possession of the land (Gen. 13:15; 1 Chron. 16:15-18; Ps. 105:9-11), so the Davidic covenant guarantees to them an everlasting throne (2 Sam. 7:16; Ps. 89:36), an everlasting King (Jer. 33:21), and an everlasting kingdom (Dan. 7:14). From the day that the covenant was made and confirmed by Jehovah's oath (Acts 2:30) to the birth of Christ, David did not lack for a son to sit on his throne (Jer. 33:21); and Christ the eternal Son of God and Son of David, being the rightful heir to that throne and the One who will yet sit on that throne (Luke 1:31-33), completes the fulfillment of this promise to David that a son would sit on his throne forever.

The Davidic covenant is most important as assuring the millennial kingdom in which Christ will reign on earth. Resurrected David will reign under Christ as a prince over the house of Israel (Jer. 23:5-6; Ezek. 34:23-24; 37:24). The Davidic covenant is not fulfilled by Christ reigning on His throne in heaven, as David has never and never will sit upon the Father's throne. It is rather an earthly kingdom and an earthly throne (Matt. 25:31). The Davidic covenant is, accordingly, the key to God's prophetic program yet to be fulfilled.

8. *The new covenant prophesied in the Old Testament and to have its primary fulfillment in the millennial kingdom is also an unconditional covenant* (Jer. 31:31-33). As described by Jeremiah, it is a covenant made "with the house of Israel, and with the house of Judah" (v. 31). It is a new covenant in contrast with the Mosaic covenant which was broken by Israel (v. 32).

In the covenant God promises, "After those days, saith the LORD, I will put my law in their inward parts, and write it in their hearts; and will be their God, and they shall be my people (v. 33). Because of this intimate and personal revelation of God and His will to His people, it goes on in Jeremiah 31:34 to state, "And they shall teach no more every man his neighbor, and every man his brother, saying, Know the LORD: for they shall all know me, from the least of them unto the greatest of them, saith the LORD: for I will forgive their iniquity, and I will remember their sin no more."

This passage anticipates the ideal circumstances of the millennial kingdom where Christ is to be reigning, and all will know the facts about Jesus Christ. It will not be necessary, accordingly, for a person to evangelize his neighbor, for the facts about the Lord will be universally known. It will also be a period in which God will forgive Israel's sin and bless them abundantly. It should be clear from this description of the covenant promise as given in Jeremiah that this is not being fulfilled today, since the church has been instructed to go into all the world and preach the Gospel because of almost universal ignorance of the truth.

Because the New Testament, however, also relates the church to a new covenant, some have taught that the church fulfills the covenant given to Israel. Those who do not believe in a future millennial kingdom and a restoration of Israel, therefore, find complete fulfillment now in the church, spiritualizing the provisions of the covenant and making Israel and the church one and the same. Others who recognize Israel's future restoration and the millennial kingdom consider the New Testament references to the new covenant either to be an application of the general truths of the future covenant with Israel to the church, or to distinguish two new covenants (one for Israel as given in Jeremiah and the second, a new covenant given through Jesus Christ in the present age of grace providing salvation for the church). Actually the new covenant, whether for Israel or for the church, stems from the death of Christ and His shed blood.

The new covenant guarantees all that God proposes to do for men on the ground of the blood of His Son. This may be seen in two aspects:

(a) That He will save, preserve, and present in heaven conformed to His Son, all who have believed on Christ. The fact that it is necessary to believe on Christ in order to be saved does not form a condition in this covenant. Believing is not a part of the covenant, but rather is the ground of admission into its eternal blessings. The covenant is not related to the unsaved, but it is made with those who believe, and it promises the faithfulness of God in their behalf. "He which hath begun a good work in you will perform it until the day of Jesus Christ" (Phil. 1:6) and every other promise concerning the saving and keeping power of God are part of this covenant in grace.

There is no salvation contemplated for man in this age that does not guarantee perfect preservation here and a final presentation of the saved one in glory. There may be an issue between the Father and His child as to the daily life, and as in the case of David's sins, the Christian's sin may call for the chastening hand of God; but those questions which enter into the daily life of the believer are never made to *condition* the promise of God concerning the eternal salvation of those whom He has received in grace.

There are those who emphasize the importance and power of the human will and who contend that both salvation and safekeeping must be made *conditional* on the cooperation of the human will. This may seem reasonable to the human mind; but it is not according to the revelation given in Scripture.

In every case God has declared *unconditionally* what He will do for all those who put their trust in Him (John 5:24; 6:37; 10:28). This is a very great undertaking which must of necessity involve the absolute control of the very thoughts and intents of the heart; but it is no more unreasonable than that God should declare to Noah that his seed would follow the absolute channels which he had decreed, or that he should declare to Abra-

ham that He would make of him a great nation and that of his
seed Christ should be born.

In every case it is the manifestation of sovereign authority
and power. It is evident that God has given latitude for the
exercise of the human will. He appeals to the wills of men, and
men who are saved are conscious that both their salvation and
their service are according to their own deepest choice. We are
told that God controls the will of man (John 6:44; Phil.
2:13) and at the same time appeals to and conditions His blessing on
the will of man (John 5:40; 7:17; Rom. 12:1; 1 John 1:9).

Scripture gives unquestionable emphasis to the sovereignty of
God. God has perfectly determined what will be, and His determined purpose will be realized; for it is impossible that God
should ever be either surprised or disappointed. So, also, there
is equal emphasis in Scripture upon the fact that lying between
these two undiminished aspects of His sovereignty — His eternal
purpose and its perfect realization — He has permitted sufficient latitude for some exercise of the human will. In so doing,
His determined ends are in no way jeopardized. One aspect of
this truth without the other will lead, in the one case, to fatalism,
wherein there is no place for petition in prayer, no motive for
the wooing of God's love, no ground for condemnation, no occasion for evangelistic appeal, and no meaning to very much
Scripture; in the other case it will lead to the dethroning of God.
It is reasonable to believe that the human will may be under
the control of God; but most unreasonable to believe that the
sovereignty of God is under the control of the human will.
Those who believe are saved and safe forever because it is according to the *unconditional* covenant of God.

(b) The future salvation of Israel is promised under the *unconditional* new covenant (Isa. 27:9; Ezek. 37:23; Rom. 11:26-
27). This salvation will be accomplished only on the ground of
the shed blood of Christ. Through the sacrifice of Christ, God
is as free to save a nation as He is free to save an individual.
Israel is represented by Christ as a treasure hid in the field.
The field is the world. It was Christ, we believe, who sold
all that He had that He might purchase the field and possess
the treasure (Matt. 13:44).

In contemplating the eight covenants, too much emphasis
cannot be placed on the fact of the sovereignty of God as it is
related to those covenants which are *unconditional*, in contrast
with the absolute failure of man as it is revealed in the out-
working of those covenants which are *conditional*. Whatever

God undertakes *unconditionally* will be completed in all the perfection of His own infinite being.

Questions

1. According to the theological covenants, what is God's central purpose and how does it affect history?
2. What is the covenant of works, and what is its scriptural basis?
3. What is the covenant of redemption, and what is its scriptural basis?
4. What is the covenant of grace, and what is its scriptural basis?
5. What is the problem raised by the theoligical covenants in relationship to the plan of God for Israel, for the church, and for the nations?
6. Why is it preferable to view history through the eight covenants rather than from the viewpoint of the theological covenants.
7. Distinguish the conditional covenants from the unconditional covenants.
8. What was the Edenic covenant, and what was the result of failure under it?
9. What was the Adamic covenant, and to what extent does it condition life today?
10. What were the important provisions of the Noahic covenant, and to what extent does it continue today?
11. What promises were given Abraham in the Abrahamic covenant?
12. What promises were given concerning the nation Israel in the Abrahamic covenant?
13. What promises were given to the entire world in the Abrahamic covenant?
14. In what sense was the covenant with Abraham unconditional?
15. To what extent was the Mosaic covenant conditional and temporary?
16. To what extent was the Palestinian covenant unconditional?
17. How do you explain the Assyrian and Babylonian captivities and Israel's worldwide dispersion in view of the unconditional character of the Palestinian covenant?
18. How would you summarize the overall provisions of the Palestinian covenant in relation to Israel's disobedience, regathering, restoration, and ultimate safety in prosperity as a nation?
19. What was promised unconditionally in the Davidic covenant?
20. How does the Davidic covenant relate to the future millennial kingdom?
21. According to the Old Testament, what was provided in the new covenant for Israel?
22. When will the new covenant be fulfilled for Israel?

23. Why have some taught that the new covenant has a present application, and how can this be explained?
24. How does the new covenant relate to the security of the believer's salvation?
25. How does the new covenant relate to the sovereignty of God?
26. How does the new covenant relate to the future salvation of Israel?

22

The Angels

A. *The Nature of Angels*

According to Scripture, long before the creation of man God created an innumerable company of beings described as angels. Like men, they have personality and are capable of great intelligence and moral responsibility. The word "angel" means messenger and, while referring to a special class of beings, the term is sometimes employed of others who are messengers — such as the angels of the seven churches of Asia (Rev. 2 – 3) who seem to be men (Rev. 1:20; 2:1, 8, 12, 18; 3:1, 7, 14) – and the term is sometimes used of ordinary human messengers (Luke 7:24; James 2:25). The term is also used of the spirits of men who have died (Matt. 18:10; Acts 12:15), but when so used it should not be concluded that angels are departed spirits of men or that men at death become angels. It is rather that the term "messenger" is a general term. In like manner the term "angel" is used of the Angel of Jehovah, referring to appearances of Christ in the Old Testament in the form of an angel and as a messenger from God to men (Gen. 16:1-13); 21:17-19; 22:11-16).

When not used in reference to men or God Himself, the term is used of a distinct order of beings who, like man, have moral responsibility and who are servants of God in the moral sphere. Like man, angels continue forever and are distinct from all other created beings. They form a prominent part of God's program for the ages and are mentioned over a hundred times in the Old Testament and even more frequently in the New Testament.

Angels apparently were all created simultaneously and were innumerable in number (Heb. 2:22; Rev. 5:11). They have all the essential elements of personality including intelligence, moral will, and sensibility or emotion and, accordingly, are able to render intelligent worship of God (Ps. 148:2). They are also held responsible for the quality of their service and their moral choices.

Their natures do not include bodies unless they are bodies of a spiritual order (1 Cor. 15:44), although they may be seen at times in bodies and appear as men (Matt. 28:3; Rev. 15:6; 18:1). They do not experience increase in number through birth nor do they experience physical death or cessation of existence. Thus, while they are similar to man in personality, they differ from man in many important particulars.

B. The Unfallen Angels

Angels generally fall into two major classifications: (1) the unfallen angels, (2) the fallen angels. The first classification are those who have remained holy throughout their existence and thus accordingly are called "holy angels" (Matt. 25:31). In Scripture, generally, when angels are referred to, the unfallen angels are in view. By contrast, fallen angels are those who have not maintained their holiness.

Unfallen angels fall into special classes, and certain individuals are mentioned.

1. *Michael the archangel is the head of all the holy angels and his name means "who is like unto God"* (Dan. 10:21; 12:1; 1 Thess. 4:16; Jude 9; Rev. 12:7-10).

2. *Gabriel is one of the principal messengers of God, his name meaning "hero of God."* He was entrusted with important messages such as those delivered to Daniel (Dan. 8:16; 9:21), the message to Zacharias (Luke 1:18-19), and the message to the Virgin Mary (Luke 1:26-38).

3. *Most angels are not given individual names but are described as elect angels* (1 Tim. 5:21). This introduces the interesting thought that like saved men who are declared to be chosen or elected, the holy angels likewise were divinely appointed.

4. *The expressions "principalities" and "powers" seem to be used of all angels whether fallen or unfallen* (Luke 21:26; Rom. 8:38; Eph. 1:21; 3:10; Col. 1:16; 2:10, 15; 1 Pet. 3:22). There is unceasing warfare between the holy angels and the fallen angels for control of men in history.

5. *Some angels are designated "cherubims," living creatures who defend God's holiness from any defilement of sin* (Gen. 3:24; Exod. 25:18, 20; Ezek. 1:1-18). Satan, the head of fallen angels, was originally created holy for this purpose also (Ezek. 28:14). Angelic figures in the form of cherubim were made of gold overlooking the mercy seat of the ark and the Holy of Holies in both the Tabernacle and the Temple.

6. *Seraphim are mentioned only once in the Bible — in Isaiah 6:2-7.* They are described as having three pairs of wings, apparently have the function of praising God and being God's messengers to earth, and are especially concerned with the holiness of God.

7. *The term "angel of Jehovah" is found frequently in the Old Testament to refer to appearances of Christ in the form of an angel.* The title belongs only to God and is used in connection with the divine manifestations in the earth, and therefore it is in no way to be included in the angelic hosts (Gen. 18:1 — 19:29; 22:11, 12; 31:11-13; 32:24-32; 48:15, 16; Josh. 5:13-15; Judg. 13:19-22; 2 Kings 19:35; 1 Chron. 21:12-30; Ps. 34:7). The strongest contrast between Christ, who is the Angel of Jehovah, and the angelic beings is presented in Hebrews 1:4-14.

C. The Fallen Angels

In contrast with the unfallen angels, an innumerable company of angels is described as fallen from their first estate. Led by Satan, who originally was a holy angel, an innumerable company of angels defected, rebelled against God, and became sinful in their nature and work.

The fallen angels have been divided into two classes: (1) those who are free, and (2) those who are bound. Of the fallen angels, Satan alone is given particular mention in Scripture.

It is probable that when Satan fell (John 8:44) he drew after him a multitude of lesser beings. Of these, some are reserved in chains unto judgment (1 Cor. 6:3; 2 Pet. 2:4; Jude 6); the remainder are free and are the demons, or devils, to whom reference is constantly made throughout the New Testament (Mark 5:9, 15; Luke 8:30; 1 Tim. 4:1). They are Satan's servants in all his undertakings and share his doom (Matt. 25:41; Rev. 20:10).

D. The Ministry of Holy Angels

Most of the references to angels in Scripture refer to their ministries, which cover a wide field of achievement. Primarily they are given to worshiping God and, according to Revelation 4:8, at least some of them "rest not day and night, saying, Holy, holy, holy, Lord God Almighty, which was, and is, and is to come." Frequent other allusions to this are found in Scripture (Ps. 103:20; Isa. 6:3). In general, the ministry of unfallen angels extended to many different forms of service for God.

1. *They were present at creation* (Job 38:7), at the giving *of the law* (Acts 7:53; Gal. 3:19; Heb. 2:2; Rev. 22:16), *at the birth of Christ* (Luke 2:13), *at His temptation* (Matt. 4:11), in *the garden* (Luke 22:43), *at the Resurrection* (Matt. 28:2), *at the Ascension* (Acts 1:10), *and they will yet appear at the second coming of Christ* (Matt. 24:31; 25:31; 2 Thess. 1:7).

2. *The angels are ministering spirits sent forth to minister to those who shall be heirs of salvation* (Heb. 1:14; Ps. 34:7; 91:11). Though we have been given no communication or fellowship with the angels, yet we should recognize the fact of their ministry, which is constant and effective.

3. *The angels are spectators and witnesses of the things of earth* (Ps. 103:20; Luke 12:8, 9; 15:10; 1 Cor. 11:10; 1 Tim. 3:16; 1 Pet. 1:12; Rev. 14:10).

4. *Lazarus was carried by the angels to Abraham's bosom* (Luke 16:22).

5. *In addition to their ministries in history, angels are seen as included in the company descending from heaven to earth at the second coming and are also seen in the eternal state in the New Jerusalem* (Heb. 12:22-24; Rev. 19:14; 21:12). Apparently the holy angels will be judged and rewarded at the end of the millennium and the introduction of the eternal estate at the

same time that fallen angels are judged and cast into the lake of fire.

6. *The ministry of angels throughout Scripture is an important doctrine and essential to understanding God's providential and sovereign direction of His creation throughout history.*

Questions

1. How did angels originate?
2. How are angels like men?
3. How is the word "angel" used of beings other than angels themselves, and how is this derived from the meaning of the name?
4. How frequently do angels appear in Scripture, and how do you explain their appearance as men?
5. Into what two major classifications can angels be placed, and what is the nature of each?
6. What unfallen angels are named in the Bible, and what do they do?
7. What is the meaning of the terms "elect angels," "principalities," and "powers" as relating to angels?
8. What are the cherubims, and what do they do?
9. How are seraphim described in the Bible, and what is their function?
10. What is the meaning of the term "angel of Jehovah" in the Old Testament, and why is this not a reference to angels?
11. Into what two classifications can fallen angels be placed, and what are their respective functions according to Scripture?
12. Describe some of the important ministries of holy angels in Scripture.
13. How are angels related to God's providential sovereign direction of His creation?
14. What part do angels have in the second coming of Christ and the eternal state?

23

Satan: His Personality and Power

Satan was originally created as the highest being above all the moral creatures of God, although an inmeasurable gulf exists between him and the uncreated, self-existent, and eternal persons of the Godhead. As will be presented in the next chapter, Satan, although originally a holy angel, fell from his holy estate and became the enemy of God and the leader of other fallen angels.

A. The Personality of Satan

Since he does not appear in corporeal form, Satan's personality, like that of the Godhead and like all the angelic host, must be accepted upon the evidence set forth in Scripture. Considering this evidence, it is revealed:

1. *Satan was created as a person.* The fact of the creation of all things that are in heaven and in earth, "visible and invisible, whether they be thrones, or dominions, or principalities, or powers," and the fact that these were created by Christ and for Christ, are stated in Colossians 1:16. The time of the creation

of the angelic host is not stated beyond the fact that their creation probably preceded all material things and was itself preceded by that eternity of existence on the part of the Godhead, which existence is declared in John 1:1-2.

Among all the heavenly host, Satan's creation alone is mentioned in particular. This fact suggests the supreme place which Satan holds in relation to all the invisible creatures of God.

In Ezekiel 28:11-19 there is recorded a lamentation addressed to "the king of Tyrus," and while this may have had some partial and immediate application to a king of Tyre, it is evident that the supreme one among all the creatures of God is in view; for the one here addressed was said to be the "sum" of wisdom and perfect in beauty. He had been in "Eden the garden of God" (v. 13, probably the primal Eden of God's original creation, rather than the Eden of Genesis 3), and by divine design was created and anointed as a covering cherub over the holy mountain of God (v. 14), which in biblical imagery represents the throne or center of God's governing power. No king of Tyrus could fit this description. In fact, this description could apply to none other than Satan as he existed before his sin and fall.

2. *Satan exercises all the functions of a person.* Of many Scriptures which set forth the personality of Satan, the following may be noted:

a. Isaiah 14:12-17. Contemplating Satan as having completed his course and having been judged finally at the end of time, the prophet addresses him in this passage under the heavenly title of "Lucifer, son of the morning" and sees him as fallen from his primal estate and glory. He who "didst weaken the nations" (v. 12) is also guilty of opposing his own will against the will of God in five particulars; in this passage, as in Ezekiel 28:15, his sin is said to be a secret purpose hid within his own heart which God discovered and disclosed (cf. 1 Tim. 3:6).

b. Genesis 3:1-15. By the events recorded in this passage, Satan gains the title of "Serpent," for through the serpent he appeared to Adam and Eve. Every word here spoken and Satan's design revealed are evidence of Satan's personality (cf. 2 Cor. 11:3, 13-15; Rev. 12:9; 20:2).

c. Job 1:6-12; 2:1-13. Revelations peculiar to these texts are that Satan has access to God (cf. Luke 22:31; Rev. 12:10) as well as to men (Eph. 6:10-12; 1 Pet. 5:8), and that he exhibits every feature of a true personality.

d. Luke 4:1-13. Again the personality of Satan is revealed

when in the wilderness he comes into conflict with the Son of
God — the last Adam. He who purposed to become like the
Most High (Isa. 14:14), and who recommended this purpose
to the first man and woman (Gen. 3:5), is now seen offering all
his earthly possessions to Christ if only He will worship him.
This proffered authority and power which Christ refused will
yet be received and administered by the Man of Sin (2 Thess.
2:8-10; 1 John 4:3).

e. Ephesians 6:10-12. The strategies and warfare of Satan
against the children of God as declared in this passage are
proof positive of the personality of Satan. There is no mention
in Scripture of a warfare by Satan against the unregenerate:
they are his own and therefore under his authority (John 8:44;
Eph. 2:2; 1 John 5:19).

B. The Power of Satan

Though morally fallen and now judged in the Cross (John
12:31; 16:11; Col. 2:15), Satan has not lost his position, and he
has lost but little of his power. His power both as to personal
strength and authority is disclosed in two forms.

1. *His personal strength cannot be estimated.* According to
Satan's own declaration, which Christ did not deny, he has
power over the kingdoms of this world, which kingdoms he said
were delivered unto him, and which power he bestows on whom
he will (Luke 4:6). It is said of him that he had the power of
death (Heb. 2:14), but that power has been surrendered to
Christ (Rev. 1:18). Satan had the power over sickness in the
case of Job (Job 2:7), and was able to sift Peter as wheat in a
sieve (Luke 22:31; 1 Cor. 5:5). Likewise, Satan is said to have
weakened the nations, to have made the earth to tremble, to
have shaken kingdoms, to have made the earth a wilderness,
destroying the cities thereof, and not to have opened the house
of his prisoners (Isa. 14:12-17). Against the power of Satan
even Michael the archangel dare not contend (Jude 9); but
there is victory for the child of God through the power of the
Spirit and the blood of Christ (Eph. 6:10-12; 1 John 4:4; Rev.
12:11). Satan's power and authority are exercised always and
only within the permissive will of God.

2. *Satan is aided by demons.* Satan's power is increased by
the innumerable host of demons who do his will and serve him.
Though he is not omnipresent, omnipotent, or omniscient,

through the wicked spirits he is in touch with the whole world.

Demons play an important part in Satan's control of the earth and make Satan's power everywhere present (Mark 5:9). They are capable of indwelling and controlling animals as well as men (Mark 5:2-5, 11-13) and apparently desire to be possessed of physical bodies (Matt. 12:43-44; Mark 5:10-12).

Sometimes demons merely influence men and in other cases actually possess them so that men's physical bodies as well as their speech are controlled by the demons (Matt. 4:24; 8:16, 28, 33; 9:32; 12:22; Mark 1:32; 5:15-16, 18; Luke 8:36; Acts 8:7; 16:16). Like Satan, they are totally evil and malicious and affect those they control in this way (Matt. 8:28; 10:1; Mark 1:23; 5:3-5; 9:17-26; Luke 6:18; 9:39-42). In numerous cases they show that they know Jesus Christ to be God (Matt. 8:28-32; Mark 1:23-24; Acts 19:15; James 2:19).

Like Satan, demons are fully aware that they are destined for eternal punishment (Matt. 8:29; Luke 8:31). They are capable of bringing on physical disorders (Matt. 12:22; 17:15-18; Luke 13:16) as well as insanity (Mark 5:2-13). While mental disorders may be due to physical causes, unquestionably some forms of insanity are due to demon control. Demon influence may lead to false religion, asceticism, and unbelief (1 Tim. 4:1-3).

The fact of the influence of demons on Christians is evident (Eph. 6:12; 1 Tim. 4:1-3). There seems to be a difference between the power and influence of demons over unsaved people and those who are born again, due to the fact that a Christian is indwelt by the Holy Spirit. While demons may possess an unsaved person and may oppress a saved person, there is a difference in the duration and power of demonic influence over those who are born again. The work of Satan as a whole would be impossible if it were not for the innumerable demons who carry out his wishes, and an unseen warfare of tremendous proportion is going on continuously between the holy angels and demons.

Questions

1. What place did Satan originally have in God's creation?
2. What is some of the evidence that Satan was created as a person, and what qualities did he possess before he fell?
3. How does Satan exercise the function of a person? Illustrate this from his dealings with Adam and Eve, Job, and Christ.
4. How is the personality of Satan revealed in his conflict with Christians?
5. Summarize the evidence of the great power of Satan.
6. How do demons aid Satan?
7. Illustrate the extent of the demonic influence on men and to what extent man can be controlled by demons.
8. How are demons related to physical and mental disorders of men?
9. How can demonic influence be related to false religion and religious practices?
10. What difference seems to exist between the power and influence of demons over unsaved people as contrasted with those who are saved?
11. How does the indwelling Holy Spirit aid a Christian in his conflict with Satan and demons?

24

Satan: His Work and Destiny

A. False Concepts About Satan

Two errors regarding Satan are current, and since he alone is benefited by them it is reasonable to conclude that he is the author of them.

1. *Many believe that Satan does not really exist and that the supposed person of Satan is no more than an evil principle, or influence, which is in man and in the world.* This conception is proved to be wrong by the fact that there is the same abundant evidence that Satan is a person as there is that Christ is a person. Scripture, which alone is authoritative on these matters, treats one to be a person as much as the other, and if the personality of Christ is accepted on the testimony of the Bible, the personality of Satan must also be accepted on the same testimony.

2. *Likewise, others believe the error that Satan is the direct cause of sin in every person.* This impression is not true (a) because Satan is not aiming to promote sin in the world. He did not purpose to be a fiend, but rather to be "like the most High" (Isa. 14:14); he is not aiming to destroy so much as he is to

construct and to realize his own ambition for authority over this world-system with its culture, morality, and religion (2 Cor. 11:13-15). The impression that Satan is the direct cause of sin is not true (b) because human sin is said to come directly from the fallen human heart (Gen. 6:5; Mark 7:18-23; James 1:13-16).

B. *The Work of Satan*

Isaiah 14:12-17 is only one of the many passages bearing on the work of Satan. This passage reveals Satan's original and supreme purpose. He would ascend into heaven, exalt his throne above the stars of God, and be like the most High. To this end he will use his unmeasured wisdom and power; he will weaken the nations, make the earth to tremble, make the world as a wilderness, destroy the cities thereof, and refuse to release his prisoners. Though every phrase of this passage is a startling disclosure, two in particular may be noted.

1. *The expression "I will be like the most High"* (v. 14) *indicates the supreme motive that guides all his activities after the fall.* It was this purpose which in all seriousness he recommended to Adam and Eve (Gen. 3:5), and they, by adopting Satan's ideal, became self-centered, self-sufficient, and independent of God. This attitude on the part of Adam and Eve became their very nature and has been transmitted to all their posterity to the extent that their posterity are called the "children of wrath" (Eph. 2:3; 5:6; Rom. 1:18), they must be born again (John 3:3), and when saved, have a struggle to be yielded wholly to the will of God. Again, Satan's desire to be "like the most High" is seen in his passion to be worshiped by Christ (Luke 4:5-7). When the Man of Sin enters the holy place and is worshiped as God (2 Thess. 2:3, 4; Dan. 9:27; Matt. 24:15; Rev. 13:4-8) for a brief moment, Satan's supreme desire will be realized under the permissive will of God.

2. *The expression that He "opened not the house of his prisoners"* (Isa. 14:17) *seems to refer to Satan's present power over unsaved people as well as his incapacity to help them in their eternal judgment.* The entire prophecy from which this phrase is taken concerns the work of Satan as it will have been completed in the day of his final judgment. Doubtless there is a larger fulfillment yet future; however, we know that Satan is now doing all in his power to keep the unsaved from being delivered from the power of darkness and translated into the

kingdom of God's dear Son (Col. 1:13). Satan is the one who energizes the children of disobedience (Eph. 2:2), blinds the minds of the unsaved lest the light of the Gospel reach them (2 Cor. 4:3, 4), and holds the unconscious world in his arms (1 John 5:19, NASB).

It is also revealed that Satan in his warfare will counterfeit the things of God, which undertaking will likewise be in accord with his purpose to be "like the most High." He will promote extensive religious systems (1 Tim. 4:1-3; 2 Cor. 11:13-15). In this connection it should be observed that Satan can promote forms of religion which are based on selected Bible texts, which elevate Christ as the leader, and which incorporate every phase of the Christian faith except one – the doctrine of salvation by grace alone on the ground of the shed blood of Christ. Such satanic delusions are now in the world and multitudes are being deceived by them. Such false systems are always to be tested by the attitude they take toward the saving grace of God through the efficacious blood of Christ (Rev. 12:11).

Satan's enmity is evidently against God alone. He is in no way at enmity with the unsaved, and when he aims his "fiery darts" at the children of God, he attacks them only because of the fact that they are indwelt by the divine nature, and through them he is enabled to secure a thrust at God.

Likewise, the attack against the children of God is not in the sphere of "flesh and blood," but in the sphere of their heavenly association with Christ. That is, the believer may not be drawn away into immorality, but he may utterly fail in prayer, in testimony, and in spiritual victory. Such failure, it should be seen, is as much defeat and dishonor in the sight of God as those sins which are freely condemned by the world.

C. The Destiny of Satan

As the Word of God is explicit regarding the origin of Satan, so it is explicit regarding his career and destiny. Five progressive judgments of Satan are to be distinguished.

1. *Satan's moral fall, with its necessary separation from God, is clearly indicated, although the time in the dateless past is not disclosed* (Ezek. 28:15; 1 Tim. 3:6). It is evident, however, that he did not lose his heavenly position, the larger portion of his power, or his access to God.

2. *A perfect judgment of Satan has been secured through*

the Cross (John 12:31; 16:11; Col. 2:14, 15), *but the execution of that sentence is yet future.* This sentence with its execution was predicted in the Garden of Eden (Gen. 3:15).

3. *Satan will be cast out of heaven.* In the midst of the coming Tribulation and as a result of a war in heaven, Satan will be cast out of heaven and be limited to the earth. He will then act in great wrath, knowing that he has but a short time to continue (Rev. 12:7-12. Note also, Isa. 14:12; Luke 10:18).

4. *Satan will be confined to the abyss.* For the thousand-year reign of Christ upon the earth, Satan will be sealed in the abyss, after which he must be loosed for a "little season" (Rev. 20:1-3, 7). The purpose of putting him in the abyss is to make it impossible for him to be active and to continue deceiving the nations.

5. *Satan's final doom will come at the close of the millennium.* Having promoted an open rebellion against God during the "little season," Satan is then cast into the lake of fire to be tormented day and night forever (Rev. 20:10).

Questions

1. What evidence supports the conclusion that Satan actually exists as a person and is much more than simply an evil principle or influence?
2. What is wrong with the teaching that Satan directly causes sin in every person?
3. What is revealed in Isaiah 14 concerning Satan's original purpose in rebelling against God?
4. How did Satan's original purpose govern the temptation of Adam and Eve?
5. How did Satan's purpose relate to his desire to be worshiped by Christ?
6. When will Satan for a brief time realize his purpose to be worshiped as God?
7. What in general is Satan doing to those who are unsaved?
8. To what extent does Satan counterfeit the things of God?
9. What is Satan's objective in attacking a child of God?
10. Describe the five progressive judgments of Satan.

25

Man: His Creation

A. Man as a Created Being

Discovering himself in the midst of a wonderful universe and being the highest order of its physical creatures, man would naturally seek to understand his own origin as well as the origin of all existing things. Because nature does not reveal the creation of man and tradition would not be a reliable source of information, it is reasonable to expect that God would reveal the essential facts about man's creation in the Bible. In the early chapters of Genesis and elsewhere in the Bible, the creation of man is clearly taught in Scripture.

Because the origin of man is a natural subject for human inquiry and speculation, those who have tried to answer the question apart from Scripture have made numerous attempts to explain the origin of man. These conflicting accounts demonstrate that man has no certain information about his origin apart from what the Bible can give, and only in Scripture can one expect to find a complete and accurate account.

One of the most common views which have arisen in contradiction to the doctrine of the creation of man revealed in the

Bible is the theory of evolution. This theory is that somehow there came into existence a living cell and from this living cell man evolved by a process of natural selection. Evolution attempts to explain all the complicated forms of life in the world by this natural process.

According to the theory of evolution, all plants, animals, and man were formed by a process of small changes accomplished by mutations which are supposed to explain all species. However, mutations are almost invariably harmful rather than beneficial, and no series of mutations have ever been observed to be beneficial or to have produced a new species. Accordingly, while the biblical record recognizes that there can be variations within a species, it declares that God created animals "after their kind" (Gen. 1:21, 24, 25).

In contrast with animals, man was made in the image and likeness of God (1:26-27). Although most adherents to evolution admit that it is only a theory and fossils reveal no systematic evolution from lower forms of life to higher forms of life, evolution is about the only explanation that natural man has been able to offer in contradiction to the Bible's doctrine of creation; it is clearly based on a naturalistic concept rather than a supernatural origin for man.

In like manner, the theory of so-called theistic evolution — that God used evolution as a method — depends for its support upon a denial of the literal meaning of the creation narratives in the Bible.

The doctrine of man's creation is clearly taught in Scripture (Gen. 1:1–2:25; John 1:3; Col. 1:16; Heb. 11:3). The first chapter of Genesis alone refers to God as the Creator about seventeen times, and about fifty other references may be found in the Bible. Some directly teach creation, and other passages imply that God is the Creator of Adam and Eve (Exod. 20:11; Ps. 8:3-6; Matt. 19:4-5; Mark 10:6-7; Luke 3:38; Rom. 5:12-21; 1 Cor. 11:9; 15:22,45; 1 Tim. 2:13-14). The very concept of creation is that God created the world out of nothing, as no previous existence is mentioned in Genesis 1:1.

As presented in Genesis, man is the crowning work of God in creation, and the entire work of creation is declared to have taken place in six days. Among those who accept the Bible as the inspired work of God, different explanations have been given of these creative days. Some regard the narrative of Genesis 1 as a re-creation following an early creation which was judged and destroyed in connection with the fall of Satan and the fallen angels. This would account for the evidence that the inorganic world was in existence long before the creation described in the six days of Genesis 1-2.

Some regard the six days as periods of time, longer or shorter than twenty-four hours, because the word "day" is sometimes used for long periods such as in the expression "the day of the Lord." Others insist, however, that because numerals are used with the word "day" that it must apply to a day of twenty-four hours. In this case it is assumed that God created the world with apparent age as He did, for instance, in the creation of man himself and in the case of animals.

Others point, however, to the suggestion that a time process was involved longer than twenty-four hours because of such expressions as in Genesis 1:11, where the fruit tree is pictured as growing out of the earth. While God could create a full-grown fruit tree, the fact that it is said to grow implies a longer period than twenty-four hours. While even evangelicals have differed on the precise interpretation of the process of creation, most interpreters who hold to the inspiration and inerrancy of the Bible attribute the present existence of animals and man to the immediate creation of God, and there is no evidence in Scripture of evolutionary development of species by natural laws.

B. The Nature of Man

According to the testimony of Scripture, man in his present human form was created by God as the conclusion and consummation of all creation. Of man it is said that he was made in the image and likeness of God (Gen. 1:26) and that God breathed into him the breath of life (Gen. 2:7). These distinctions classify man above all other forms of life which are upon the earth and indicate that man is a moral creature with intellect, capacity for feeling, and a will.

Speaking generally, man's creation included that which was material ("the dust") and immaterial ("the breath of life"). This twofold distinction is referred to as "outward man" and "inward man" (2 Cor. 4:16); "the earthen vessel" and "this treasure" (2 Cor. 4:7). While the soul and spirit of man are represented as continuing forever, the body returns to the dust from which it was formed, and the spirit goes to God who gave it (Eccl. 12:7). Accordingly, people can kill the body but not kill the soul (Matt. 10:28).

When considering the immaterial part of man, Scripture sometimes uses various terms interchangeably (cp. Gen. 41:8 with Ps. 42:6; Matt. 20:28 with 27:50; John 12:27 with 13:21; Heb. 12:23 with Rev. 6:9), even applying these terms to God (Isa. 42:1; Jer. 9:9; Heb. 10:38) and to animals (Eccl. 3:21; Rev. 16:3). Sometimes the spirit and soul of man are distinguished (1 Thess. 5:23; Heb. 4:12).

Although the highest functions of the immaterial part of man are sometimes attributed to the spirit and sometimes to the soul (Mark 8:36-37; 12:30; Luke 1:46; Heb. 6:18-19; James 1:21), the spirit is usually mentioned in Scriptures as that part of man which is capable of contemplating God, and the soul is that part of man which is related to self and the various functions of the intellect, sensibilities, and will of man.

Other terms, however, are also used of man's immaterial nature such as the heart (Exod. 7:23; Ps. 37:4; Rom. 9:2; 10:9-10; Eph. 3:17; Heb. 4:7). Another term used is that of the mind of man, either in reference to the sinfulness of the mind of the unsaved man (Rom. 1:28; 2 Cor. 4:4; Eph. 4:17-18; Titus 1:15), or to the renewed mind which a Christian possesses (Matt. 22:37; Rom. 12:2; 1 Cor. 14:15; Eph. 5:17). Other expressions such as "will" and "conscience" also refer to the immaterial part of man.

Because of the variety of terms which sometimes are used in the similar sense and sometimes in contrast to each other, many have considered the division of man into material and immaterial as the basic division; but even here expressions like "soul" and "spirit" are sometimes used of the whole man including his body.

Immaterial origin of man's nature is held by some pagan religions to be preexistent, that is, to have existed eternally and only becoming incarnated at the beginning of human existence; this is not supported by Scripture. Another view offered by some evangelical theologians is that the soul is created by God at the beginning of individual human existence; this theory has difficulty in accounting for the sinfulness of man. Probably the best view, known as the traducian theory, is that the soul and the spirit was propagated by natural generation, and for this reason man receives a sinful soul and spirit because his parents are sinful.

The human body of man is the abode of man's soul and spirit until he dies. Although it decays upon death, it is subject to resurrection. This is true both for the saved and for the unsaved although the resurrections are different. Sometimes the body is referred to as "flesh" (Col. 2:1, 5) and is used of the body of Christ (1 Tim. 3:16; 1 Pet. 3:18). Other times it refers to the sin nature which includes the soul aud spirit, as in Paul's statement that he had "crucified the flesh" (Gal. 5:24). Accordingly, flesh should not be considered synonymous with the body in all passages, as it may denote the whole, unregenerate man.

The bodies of saved persons are declared to be "temples" (John 2:21; 1 Cor. 6:19; Phil. 1:20), although at the same time their bodies are considered "earthern vessels" (2 Cor. 4:7), "vile" bodies (Phil. 3:21), bodies to be mortified (Rom. 8:13; Col. 3:5), and bodies which have to be kept under and brought into subjection (1 Cor. 9:27). The bodies of the saved will be transformed, sanctified, saved, and redeemed and finally glorified forever at the coming of Christ for His church (Rom. 8:11, 17-18, 23; 1 Cor. 6:13-20; Phil. 3:20-21). Jesus Christ possessed a perfect human body before His death, and after His resurrection had a body of flesh and bone that is the pattern of the believer's resurrection body. The term "body" is also used as a figure of the church as the body of Christ and of which Christ is the head.

Questions

1. Does man have any certain knowledge concerning his origin apart from the Bible?
2. How does the theory of evolution explain the origin of man?
3. What is theistic evolution?
4. How does man differ from animals, and how does this enter into the problem of his origin?
5. How much evidence is there in Scripture for the creation of man?
6. What are the various explanations of the scriptural description of man as being created in six days?
7. Why do you believe that the scriptural explanation of the origin of man by creation is superior to the evolutionary theory?
8. What is meant by the statement that man is made in the image and likeness of God?
9. What is the meaning of "spirit" and "soul" as used of man?
10. What other terms are used of man's immaterial nature besides soul and spirit?
11. Discuss other views of the origin of man's nature such as being preexistent, or being created as each individual is born.
12. What is the traducian theory of the origin of the soul and spirit of man, and why is it probably superior to any other view?
13. What is the meaning of "flesh" in the Bible, and in what ways is the term used?
14. In what sense is the body of a saved person a temple?
15. What is the prospect of the body of a saved person being transformed and glorified?

26

Man: His Fall

The problem of how sin entered the universe is a question which every system of thought encounters. Only the Bible, however, provides a reasonable explanation. As seen in the previous study on angels, sin first entered the universe in the rebellion of some of the holy angels led by Satan, which occurred long before man was created. The early chapters of Genesis record the fall into sin by Adam and Eve. The various interpretations of this record either take it as a literal event explaining the sinfulness of the human race or attempt to explain it away as unhistorical or a myth. The orthodox interpretation, however, is that the event took place exactly as recorded in Scripture, and this is the way it is treated in the rest of the Bible.

The fall of man into sin may be considered from three aspects: (1) Adam before the fall, (2) Adam after the fall, and (3) the effect upon the human race of Adam's fall.

A. Adam Before the Fall

In words of charming simplicity, the Bible introduces Adam as

the first man and Eve as the woman whom God provided to be
his helpmate. Together they constituted the human race and,
before the fall, were free from sin. When both Adam and Eve
sinned against God, sin entered the human race and this is referred to in the Bible as the fall of man.

Scripture does not indicate the length of time the first man
and the first woman remained in an unfallen state, but they
were unfallen long enough to become accustomed to the situation in which they were placed, to name the animals, and to
experience the blessing of fellowship with God. As to the object
of creation, Adam and Eve like all the works of God were "very
good" (Gen. 1:31), that is, they were pleasing to their Creator.
Their spiritual state was one of innocence, that is, freedom from
sin; but their character was short of holiness, such as is seen
as an attribute of God which is a positive term, making it impossible for God to sin.

Man, because he was made in the image of God, possessed a
complete personality and the capacity to make moral decisions.
In contrast with God who cannot sin, both men and angels
could sin. As seen in the earlier study of angels, Satan sinned
(Isa. 14:12-14; Ezek. 28:15), and the angels who joined Satan
in sinning are described as those who "kept not their first estate"
(Jude 6). Because of the fact that Satan and the fallen angels
sinned first, man did not originate sin, but became a sinner
due to satanic influence (Gen. 3:4-7).

The account of how Adam and Eve sinned is revealed in
Genesis 3:1-6. According to this record, Satan appeared in the
form of a serpent, a creature which at that time was a very
beautiful and attractive animal. God had given to Adam and
Eve only one prohibition as far as the scriptural record is concerned — they should not eat of the tree of knowledge of good
and evil. According to Genesis 2:17, God said, "But of the tree
of knowledge of good and evil, thou shalt not eat of it: for in
the day that thou eatest thereof thou shalt surely die." This relatively simple prohibition was a test case to see whether Adam
or Eve would obey God.

In his conversation with Eve, Satan introduced this prohibition
saying to Eve, "Yea, hath God said, Ye shall not eat of every
tree of the garden?" (Gen. 3:1). The implication was that God
was holding something back that was good and was being un-
necessarily severe in His prohibition. Eve replied to the serpent, "We may eat of the fruit of the trees of the garden: But
of the fruit of the tree which is in the midst of the garden, God

hath said, Ye shall not eat of it, neither shall ye touch it, lest ye die" (Gen. 3:2-3).

Eve in her reply fell into Satan's trap by leaving out the word "freely" in God's permission to eat of the trees of the garden, and she left out also the word "surely" in God's warning. The natural tendency of man to minimize God's goodness and to magnify His strictness are familiar characteristics of human experience ever since. Satan immediately seized upon the omission of the word "surely" in regard to the penalty and said to the woman, "Ye shall not surely die: For God doth know that in the day that ye eat thereof, then your eyes shall be opened, and ye shall be as gods, knowing good and evil" (Gen. 3:4-5).

In his conversation with the woman, Satan is revealed as the arch deceiver. The certainty of the punishment is directly challenged, and the Word of God expressly denied. That through eating the fruit their eyes would be opened to know good and evil was true, but what Satan did not reveal was that they would have the power to know good and evil without the power to do the good.

According to Genesis 3:6, the fall of Adam and Eve into sin is recorded, "And when the woman saw that the tree was good for food, and that it was pleasant to the eyes, and a tree to be desired to make one wise, she took of the fruit thereof, and did eat, and gave unto her husband with her; and he did eat." Whether Satan pointed this out to the woman or whether she came to those conclusions herself, Scripture does not say.

The familiar pattern, however, of temptation along three lines indicated in 1 John 2:16 is seen here: the fact that the fruit was good for food appealed to the "lust of the flesh"; the fact that it was "pleasant to the eyes" appealed to "the lust of the eyes"; and the power of the fruit of the tree to make them wise appealed to "the pride of life." A similar pattern of temptation was followed by Satan in the temptation of Christ (Matt. 4:1-11; Mark 1:12-13; Luke 4:1-13). Eve was deceived into partaking of the fruit, and Adam followed her example although he was not deceived (1 Tim. 2:14).

B. Adam After the Fall

When Adam and Eve sinned they lost their blessed estate in which both had been created, and they became subject to certain far-reaching changes.

1. *They became subject to both spiritual and physical death.*
God had said, "In the day that thou eatest thereof thou shalt
surely die" (Gen. 2:17); and this divine declaration was fulfilled. Adam and Eve passed immediately into a state of spiritual
death, meaning that spiritually they were separated from God.
Their fall into sin also introduced into their bodies the process
of age and decay, and in due time they also suffered the penalty
of physical death, which separates the soul from the body.

2. *God's judgment also fell upon Satan, and the serpent was
condemned to crawl on the ground* (Gen. 3:14). The warfare
between God and Satan is described in Genesis 3:15 as it relates
to the human race, and God said, "I will put enmity between
thee and the woman, and between thy seed and her seed; it shall
bruise thy head, and thou shalt bruise his heel." This refers to
the conflict between Christ and Satan, in which Christ died on
the cross but could not be held by death, as anticipated in the
expression, "Thou shalt bruise his heel." Satan's ultimate defeat,
however, is indicated in the fact that the seed of the woman
"shall bruise thy head," that is, inflict a deadly and permanent
wound. The seed of the woman refers to Jesus Christ, who in
His death and resurrection conquered Satan.

3. *A special judgment also fell on Eve, who would experience
pain in giving birth to children and would be required to submit
to her husband* (Gen. 3:16). The fact of death would necessitate
multiplied births.

4. *A special curse fell on Adam, and he was assigned to the
hard labor of bringing forth from the soil, now cursed with
thorns and thistles, the necessary food for his continued existence.* Creation itself would, accordingly, be changed by man's
sin (Rom. 8:22). Later Scripture indicates how the effects of sin
would be partially alleviated by salvation in the case of man and
by partial lifting of the curse in the future millennial kingdom.
Adam and Eve after the fall, however, were driven out of the
garden and began to experience the sorrow and struggle which
have characterized the human race ever since.

C. *The Effect Upon the Race of Adam's Sin*

The immediate effect of sin on Adam and Eve was that they died
spiritually and became subject to spiritual death. Their nature
now was depraved and, henceforth, the human race would ex-

perience the slavery of sin. In addition to the change of the fate of man and the change of his environment, Scripture also reveals a profound doctrine of imputation, setting forth the truth that God now charged Adam with sin and, subsequently, charged his descendants with the responsibility of Adam's first sin.

Three imputations are set forth in Scripture: (1) The sin of Adam is imputed to his posterity (Rom. 5:12-14); (2) the sin of man is imputed to Christ (2 Cor. 5:21); and (3) the righteousness of God is imputed to those who believe (Gen. 15:6; Ps. 32:2; Rom. 3:22; 4:3, 8,21-25; 2 Cor. 5:21; Philem. 17, 18).

It is obvious that there was a judicial transfer of the sin of man to Christ the Sin-Bearer. Jehovah has laid on Him the iniquity of us all (Isa. 53:5; John 1:29; 1 Pet. 2:24; 3:18). So, in the same way, there is a judicial transfer of the righteousness of God to the believer (2 Cor. 5:21); for there could be no other grounds of justification or acceptance with God. This imputation belongs to the new relationship within the new creation. Being joined to the Lord by the baptism of the Spirit (1 Cor. 6:17; 12:13; 2 Cor. 5:17; Gal. 3:27) and vitally related to Christ as a member in His body (Eph. 5:30), it follows that every virtue of Christ is extended to those who have become an organic part of Him. The believer is "in Christ" and thus partakes of all that Christ is.

In like manner, the facts of the old creation are actually transferred to those who by natural generation are "in Adam." They become possessed of the Adamic nature and themselves are said to have sinned in Adam. This is as real in constituting a sufficient ground for divine judgment as the imputation of the righteousness of God in Christ is a sufficient ground for justification; the result is the divine judgment upon the race whether or not they have sinned as Adam did.

Although men contend, as they do, that they are not responsible for Adam's sin, the divine revelation stands that because of the far-reaching effect of representation of Adam as the federal head of the race, Adam's one, initial sin is immediately and directly imputed to each member of the race with the unvarying sentence of death resting upon all (Rom. 5:12-14). Likewise, by the fall of Adam the effect of the one, initial sin is transmitted in the form of a sinful nature immediately, or by inheritance, from father to son throughout all generations. The effect of the fall is universal; so, also, the offer of divine grace.

Men do not now fall by their first sin; they are born fallen sons of Adam. They do not become sinful by sinning, but they sin because by nature they are sinful. No child needs to be taught to sin, but every child must be encouraged to be good.

It should be observed that, though the fall of Adam rests upon the race, there is evident divine provision for infants and all who are irresponsible.

The holy judgments of God must rest upon all men outside of Christ, (1) because of imputed sin, (2) because of an inherited sin nature, (3) because they are under sin, and (4) because of their own personal sins. Though these holy judgments of God cannot be diminished, the sinner may be saved from them through Christ. This is the good news of the Gospel.

The penalties resting on the old creation are (1) physical death, which is separation of the soul from the body; (2) spiritual death, which (like Adam's) is the present estate of the lost and is the separation of the soul from God (Eph. 2:1; 4:18, 19); and (3) the second death, which is the eternal separation of the soul from God and banishment from His presence forever (Rev. 2:11; 20:6, 14; 21:8).

Questions

1. How does the Bible explain the origin of sin in the universe and in the human race?
2. What was the state of man before he sinned?
3. How did Satan tempt Eve?
4. How did Eve misstate God's prohibition?
5. How did Satan lie to Eve and expressly deny the word of God?
6. How did Satan misrepresent the desirability of the power to know good and evil?
7. How does 1 John 2:16 indicate three lines of temptation?
8. What was the effect on Adam and Eve after they sinned?
9. What was the effect upon Satan and the serpent after Adam and Eve sinned?
10. What was the effect upon Adam and Eve's descendants because Adam had sinned?
11. State the three imputations set forth in Scripture.
12. Why is it true that man does not become sinful by sinning?
13. Why do God's holy judgments rest upon men outside of Christ?
14. What is the penalty resting on the old creation?
15. Why is salvation in Christ the only hope for man in his fallen estate?

27

Sin: Its Character
and Universality

A. Human Speculation on Sin

Because sin is a dominant fact of human experience as well as a
major theme of the Bible, it has been the subject of endless discussion. Those who reject scriptural revelation have frequently
provided inadequate concepts of sin. A familiar feature of the
nonbiblical approach is to regard sin as to some extent an
illusion, that is, that sin is just a misconception based upon a
false theory that there is right and wrong in the world. This
theory, of course, fails to face the facts of life and the evils
of sin, and denies the existence of a moral God and moral
principles.

Another ancient approach to the problem of sin regards it
as an inherent principle, the opposite of what God is, and related to the physical world. This is found in oriental philosophy
as well as in Greek Gnosticism and is the background both for
asceticism, the denial of the desires of the body, and its opposite,
Epicureanism, advocating indulgence of the body. The effect,
however, is to deny that man really sins and is accountable to
God. A common, although inadequate, concept is that sin is

just selfishness. While sin is often selfish, this concept does not cover all cases, for man sometimes sins against himself.

All these theories fall short of the biblical standard and are a rejection of the biblical revelation of the character and universality of sin.

B. The Biblical Doctrine of Sin

The teaching of Scripture is that sin is any want of conformity to the character of God, whether it be an act, disposition, or state. Various sins are defined in the Word of God as illustrated, for instance, in the Ten Commandments which God gave to Israel (Exod. 20:3-17). Sin is sin because it is different from what God is and God is eternally holy. Sin is always against God (Ps. 51:4; Luke 15:18), even though it may be directed against human beings. A person who sins is, accordingly, unlike God and subject to God's judgment. The doctrine of sin is presented in the Bible in four aspects.

1. *Personal sin* (Rom. 3:23) *is the form of sin which includes everything in the daily life which is against or fails to conform to the character of God.* Men are frequently conscious of their personal sins, and personal sins may take a variety of form. Generally speaking, personal sin relates to some particular command of God in Scripture. It includes the aspect of rebellion or disobedience. Although at least eight important words are used for sin in the Old Testament and as many as twelve in the New Testament, the basic idea is lack of conformity to God's character and will by acts either of omission or commission. The essential idea is that man comes short, he misses the mark, and he fails to attain the standard of God's own character of holiness.

2. *The sin nature of man* (Rom. 5:19; Eph. 2:3) *is another major aspect of sin as revealed in the Bible.* Adam's own initial sin caused him to fall, and in the fall he became an entirely different being, depraved and degenerate, and only capable of begetting posterity like his fallen self. Therefore, every child of Adam is born with the Adamic nature, is ever and always prone to sin, and, though this nature was judged by Christ on the cross (Rom. 6:10), it remains a vitally active force in every Christian's life. It is never said to be removed or eradicated in this life, but for the Christian there is overcoming power provided through the indwelling Spirit (Rom. 8:4; Gal. 5:16-17).

Many biblical passages allude to this important subject. According to Ephesians 2:3, all men "were by nature the children of wrath," and man's whole nature is depraved. The concept of total depravity is not that every man is as evil as he possibly could be but rather that man, throughout his nature, is corrupted by sin (Rom. 1:18 – 3:20). Accordingly, man in his will (Rom. 1:28), his conscience (1 Tim. 4:2), and his intellect (Rom. 1:28; 2 Cor. 4:4) is corrupted and depraved, and his heart and understanding are blinded (Eph. 4:18).

As seen in previous study, the reason why men have a sin nature is that it is transmitted to them from their parents. No child ever born in the world has been free from his sin nature except in the unique case of the birth of Christ. Men do not sin and become sinners; it is rather that men sin because they have a sin nature. The remedy for this as well as for personal sin is, of course, the redemption which is provided in salvation in Christ.

3. *Sin is also presented in Scripture as imputed or reckoned to our account* (Rom. 5:12-18). As revealed in connection with the fall of man in the preceding chapter, there are three major imputations set forth in the Scriptures: (a) the imputation of Adam's sin to the race, on which fact the doctrine of original sin is based; (b) the imputation of the sin of man to Christ, on which fact the doctrine of salvation is based; and (c) the imputation of the righteousness of God to those who believe on Christ, on which fact the doctrine of justification is based.

Imputation may be either (a) actual, or (b) judicial. Actual imputation is the reckoning to one of that which is antecedently his own. Although God might righteously do this, yet because of the reconciling work of Christ God is not now imputing to man the sin which is antecedently his own (2 Cor. 5:19).

Judicial imputation is the reckoning to one of that which is not antecedently his own (Philem. 18). Though there has been disagreement as to whether the imputation of Adam's sin to each member of the race is *actual* or *judicial,* Romans 5:12 clearly states that the imputation is *actual,* since in the federal-head representation, Adam's posterity sinned when he sinned.

The next two verses (Rom. 5:13-14) are written to prove that this is not a reference to personal sins (cf. Heb. 7:9-10). However, Romans 5:17-18 implies that his imputation is also judicial, as it is stated that by one man's sin judgment came upon all men. Only the one initial sin of Adam is in question. Its effect is death — both to Adam and directly from Adam to each member of the race. The divinely provided cure for imputed sin is the gift of God, which is eternal life through Jesus Christ.

4. *The resulting judicial state of sin for the entire human race is also presented in Scripture.* By divine reckoning the whole world, including Jew and Gentile, is now "under sin" (Rom. 3:9; 11:32; Gal. 3:22). To be *under sin* is to be divinely reckoned to be without merit which might contribute toward salvation. Since salvation is by grace alone and grace excludes all human merit, God has decreed all, as regards their salvation, to be "under sin," or without merit. This estate under sin is remedied only when the individual, through riches of grace, is reckoned to stand in the merit of Christ.

Taken as a whole, the Bible clearly indicates the devastating effects of sin upon man and the hopelessness of man solving his own sin problem. The proper understanding of the doctrine of sin is essential to undertanding God's remedy for it.

Questions

1. What are some inadequate concepts of sin which are sometimes advanced?
2. How does the Bible, in general, define sin?
3. What sins are specifically mentioned in the Ten Commandments?
4. Why is sin always a sin against God?
5. What four aspects of sin are presented in the Bible?
6. What is meant by personal sin?
7. What does the Bible teach about the sin nature of man?
8. To what extent is man depraved?
9. How do you account for the fact that all children are born sinners?
10. What are the three major imputations?
11. What is meant by actual imputation?
12. What is meant by judicial imputation?
13. Is there scriptural evidence that the whole world is in a judicial state of sin?
14. Why is a proper understanding of the doctrine of sin important to understanding the doctrine of salvation?

28

Salvation From the Penalty of Sin

A. *The Meaning of Salvation*

The divine revelation concerning salvation should be mastered by every child of God, (1) since personal salvation depends on it, (2) it is the one message which God has committed to the believer to proclaim to the world, and (3) it alone discloses the full measure of God's love.

According to its largest meaning as used in Scripture, the word "salvation" represents the whole work of God by which He rescues man from the eternal ruin and doom of sin and bestows on him the riches of His grace, including eternal life now and eternal glory in heaven. "Salvation is of the Lord" (Jonah 2:9). Therefore it is in every aspect a work of God in behalf of man and is in no sense a work of man in behalf of God.

Certain details of this divine undertaking have varied from age to age. We are assured that, beginning with Adam and continuing to Christ, those individuals who put their trust in God were spiritually reborn and made heirs of heaven's glory. Likewise, the nation Israel will yet be spiritually born in a day at the time of the Lord's return (Isa. 66:8).

181

It is also said of the multitudes of both Jews and Gentiles who are to live on the earth during the coming kingdom that all shall know the Lord from the least unto the greatest (Jer. 31:34). However, the salvation which is offered to men in the present age is not only more fully revealed in the Bible as to its details, but it far exceeds every other saving work of God in the marvels which it accomplishes; for, as offered in the present age, salvation includes every phase of the gracious work of God such as the indwelling, sealing, and baptism of the Spirit.

B. Salvation as God's Remedy for Sin

While in the biblical doctrine of sin there are certain distinctions, two universal facts should first be noted:

1. *Sin is always equally sinful whether it be committed by the heathen or the civilized, the unregenerate or the regenerate.* The question of many stripes or few is taken into consideration in the judgments to be imposed upon the sinner (Luke 12:47-48); but any sin in itself is unvarying sinful because it outrages the holiness of God.

2. *Sin can be cured only on the ground of the shed blood of the Son of God.* This was as true of those who anticipated the death of Christ by animal sacrifices as it is now of those who look back to that death by faith. Divine forgiveness has never been a mere act of leniency in remitting the penalty of sin. If the penalty is remitted, it is because a substitute has met the holy demands against the sinner. In the old order it was only after the priest had offered the atoning blood sacrifice which anticipated the death of Christ that the sinner was forgiven (Lev. 4:20, 26, 31, 35; 5:10, 13, 16, 18; 6:7; 19:22; Num. 15:25, 26, 28). Likewise, after Christ has died the same truth applies, as stated in the passage, "In whom we have redemption through his blood, even the forgiveness of sins" (Col. 1:14; cf. Eph. 1:7).

The substitutionary work of Christ upon the cross is infinitely perfect in its sufficiency. Therefore the sinner who trusts in Christ not only is forgiven, but he is even justified forever (Rom. 3:24). God has never treated sin lightly. Forgiveness may impose no burden on the sinner, but he is forgiven and justified only because the undiminished divine penalty has been borne by Christ (1 Pet. 2:24; 3:18).

C. Salvation Before and After the Cross

1. *The divine method of dealing with sin before the cross is said to have been by atonement, which word, in its biblical use, means simply "to cover."* The blood of bulls and goats could not, and did not, take away sin (Heb. 10:4). The offering of sacrificial blood indicated on the part of the sinner the acknowledgment of the just penalty of death (Lev. 1:4), and, on the part of God, the sacrifice anticipated the efficacious blood of Christ. By symbolizing the shed blood of Christ, the atoning blood of the sacrifices served *to cover* sin until that day when Christ would deal in finality with the sin of the world.

Two New Testament passages throw light upon the meaning of the Old Testament word "atonement," or "covering."

a. In Romans 3:25 the word "remission" has the meaning of "passing over," and in this connection it is stated that when Christ died He proved God to have been righteous in passing over the sins which were committed before the cross and for which the atoning blood of the sacrifices had been shed. God had promised a sufficient Lamb and had forgiven sin on the strength of that promise. Therefore, by the death of Christ, God was proven to have been righteous in all that He had promised.

b. In Acts 17:30 it is stated that, before the cross, God "winked at" sin. This word should be translated "overlooked."

2. *The divine method of dealing with sin since the cross is stated in Romans 3:26. Christ has died.* No longer is the value of His sacrifice a matter of expectation to be taken as a promise and symbolized by the blood of animals; the blood of Christ has been shed, and now all that can be asked of any person, regardless of his degree of guilt, is that he *believe* in the work which, in infinite grace, has been accomplished for him. This passage declares that Christ upon the cross so answered the divine judgment against every sinner that God can remain just, or uncompromised in His holiness, when at the same time and apart from all penalties, He justifies the sinner who does no more than *believe in Jesus.*

The word "atonement," which occurs properly only in the Old Testament, indicated the "passing over," "overlooking," and "covering" of sin; but Christ in dealing with sin on the cross did not pass it over or cover it. Of His sufficient sacrifice it is said: "Behold the Lamb of God, which taketh away the sin of the world" (John 1:29; cf. Col. 2:14; Heb. 10:4; 1 John 3:5). "Who his own self bare our sins in his own body on the tree" (1 Pet. 2:24). There was no temporizing or partial dealing with sin at the cross. This great issue between God and man was there dealt with in a manner which is satisfying even to the infinite holiness of God, and the only question that remains is whether man is satisfied with the sacrifice which satisfies God. To accept the work of Christ for us is to believe upon the Savior to the saving of the soul.

D. The Three Tenses of Salvation

1. *The past tense of salvation is revealed in certain passages which, when speaking of salvation, refer to it as being wholly past, or completed for the one who has believed* (Luke 7:50; 1 Cor. 1:18; 2 Cor. 2:15; Eph. 2:5, 8). So perfect is this divine work that the saved one is said to be safe forever (John 5:24; 10:28, 29; Rom. 8:1).

2. *The present tense of salvation, which will be the theme of the next chapter, has to do with present salvation from the reigning power of sin* (Rom. 6:14; 8:2; 2 Cor. 3:18; Gal. 2:19-20; Phil. 1:19; 2:12-13; 2 Thess. 2:13).

3. *The future tense of salvation contemplates that the believer will yet be saved into full conformity to Christ* (Rom. 8:29; 13:11; 1 Pet. 1:5; 1 John 3:2). The fact that some aspects of salvation are yet to be accomplished for the one who believes does not imply that there is ground for doubt as to its ultimate completion; for it is nowhere taught that any feature of salvation depends upon the faithfulness of man. God is faithful and, having begun a good work, will perform it until the day of Jesus Christ (Phil. 1:6).

E. Salvation as the Finished Work of Christ

When comtemplating the work of God for lost men, it is important to distinguish between the finished work of Christ for all, which is completed to infinite perfection, and the saving work of God which is wrought for and in the individual at the moment he believes on Christ.

"It is finished" is the last recorded word of Christ before His death (John 19:30). It is evident that He was not referring to

His own life, His service, or His suffering; but rather to a special work which His Father had given Him to do, which did not even begin until He was on the cross and which was completed when He died. This was distinctly a work for the whole world (John 3:16; Heb. 2:9) and, in a provisionary sense, provided redemption (1 Tim. 2:6), reconciliation (2 Cor. 5:19), and propitiation (1 John 2:2) for every man.

The fact that Christ died does not save men, but it provides a sufficient ground upon which God in full harmony with His holiness is free to save even the chief of sinners. This is the good news which the Christian is appointed to proclaim to all the world. The blood of God's only and well-beloved Son was the most precious thing before His eyes, yet it was paid to ransom the sinner. The offense of sin had separated the sinner from God, yet God provided His own Lamb to bear away the sin forever. The holy judgments of God were against the sinner because of his sin, yet Christ became the propitiation for the sin of the whole world.

The fact that all this is already finished constitutes a message which the sinner is asked to believe as the testimony of God. One can scarcely be said to have believed who, having heard this message, has not experienced a sense of relief that the sin problem has thus been solved, and responded with a sense of gratitude to God for this priceless blessing.

F. Salvation as the Saving Work of God

The saving work of God which is accomplished the moment one believes includes various phases of God's gracious work: redemption, reconciliation, propitiation, forgiveness, regeneration, imputation, justification, sanctification, perfection, glorification. By it we are made fit to be partakers of the inheritance of saints (Col. 1:12), made accepted in the Beloved (Eph. 1:6), made the righteousness of God (2 Cor. 5:21), made near to God (Eph. 2:13), made sons of God (John 1:12), made citizens of heaven (Phil. 3:20), made a new creation (2 Cor. 5:17), made members of the family and household of God (Eph. 2:19; 3:15), and made complete in Christ (Col. 2:10). The child of God has been delivered from the power of darkness and translated into the kingdom of God's dear Son (Col. 1:13), and he now possesses every spiritual blessing (Eph. 1:3).

Among the stupendous works of God just mentioned, the guilt and penalty of sin are seen to have been removed; for it is said of the saved one that he both is forgiven all trespasses and is justified forever. God could not forgive and justify apart from the cross of Christ; but since Christ has died, God is able to save to the uttermost all who come to Him by Christ Jesus.

G. Salvation as Related to the Sin of the Saved

1. *The forgiveness of sin is accomplished for the sinner when he believes upon Christ and is a part of his salvation.* Many things which constitute salvation are wrought of God at the moment one believes; but forgiveness is never received by the unsaved apart from the whole work of saving grace or the ground of believing on Christ as Savior.

2. *In the divine dealing with the sins of the Christian, it is the sin question alone that is in view, and the Christian's sin is forgiven, not on the ground of believing unto salvation, but on the ground of confessing the sin* (1 John 1:9).

The effect of the Christian's sin, among other things, is the loss of fellowship with the Father and the Son and the grieving of the indwelling Spirit. The child of God who has sinned will be restored to fellowship, joy, blessing, and power when he confesses his sin.

While the effect of sin upon the believer is the loss of blessing, which may be renewed by confession, the effect of the believer's sin upon God is a far more serious matter. But for the value of the shed blood of Christ and the present advocacy of Christ in heaven (Rom. 8:34; Heb. 9:24; 1 John 3:1-2), sin would separate Christians from God forever. However, we are assured that the blood is efficacious (1 John 2:2) and the Advocate's cause is righteous (1 John 2:1). The sinning saint is not lost because of his sin since, even while sinning, he has an Advocate with the Father. This truth, which alone forms the basis on which any Christian has ever been kept saved for a moment, so far from encouraging Christians to sin, is presented in Scripture to the end that the Christian "sin not," or "be not sinning" (1 John 2:1). Beholding the Savior advocating for us in heaven must cause us to hesitate before yielding to temptation.

H. Salvation Conditioned Upon Faith Alone

In the New Testament in about 115 passages, the salvation of a sinner is declared to depend only upon *believing* and in about 35 passages to depend on *faith,* which is a synonym for believing. By believing an individual wills to trust Christ. It is an act of the whole man, not just his intellect or his emotion. While intellectual assent is not of real faith, and merely a stirring of the emotions is short of faith, believing is a definite act in which the individual wills to receive Christ by faith.

Scripture everywhere harmonizes with this overwhelming body of truth. God alone can save a soul, and God can save only through the sacrifice of His Son. Man can sustain no other relation to salvation than to believe God's message to the extent of turning from self-works to depend only on the work of God through Christ. Believing is the opposite of doing anything; it is trusting another instead. Therefore Scripture is violated and the whole doctrine of grace confused when salvation is made to depend on anything other than *believing.* The divine message is not "believe and pray," "believe and confess sin," "believe and confess Christ," "believe and be baptized," "believe and repent," or "believe and make restitution." These six added subjects are mentioned in Scripture, and there they have their full intended meaning; but if they were as essential to salvation as believing they would never be omitted from any passage wherein the way to be saved is stated (note John 1:12; 3:16, 36; 5:24; 6:29; 20:31; Acts 16:31; Rom. 1:16; 3:22; 4:5, 24; 5:1; 10:4; Gal. 3:22). Salvation is only through Christ, and men are therefore saved when they receive Him as their Savior.

Questions

1. Why should a child of God master the doctrine of salvation?
2. What is included in salvation in its largest dimension?
3. To what extent is salvation the same in every age, and to what extent is the present age more inclusive?
4. What two universal facts are brought out in Scripture concerning the relationship of salvation to sin?
5. How did God deal with sin in connection with salvation in the Old Testament?
6. How does God's dealing with sin after the cross differ from the Old Testament method?
7. What is brought out in the passages that deal with salvation in the past tense?
8. How is salvation revealed as a present work of God?
9. What is contemplated when salvation is regarded as future?
10. Distinguish between the finished work of Christ and the saving work of God as it applies to the individual when he believes.
11. Why is it true that the fact that Christ died does not save all men?
12. What may be expected as a response on the part of a believer when he is saved?
13. Name some of the important phases of God's gracious work in saving men as embodied in important doctrinal words.
14. What are some of the aspects of the work of God accomplished when an individual is saved?
15. How is salvation related to forgiveness of sin?
16. In dealing with the sins of Christians, what is involved in their forgiveness?
17. If a Christian fails to confess sin, what does he lose?
18. Why does not the doctrine of Christ serving as our Advocate in heaven tend to make Christians careless in sinning?
19. Discuss the scriptural evidence that salvation is conditioned upon faith alone.
20. Why is intellectual assent insufficient evidence of real faith?
21. Why is emotional response to the Gospel in itself insufficient to save?
22. Why is faith an act of the whole man — intellect, feelings, and will?
23. What is the error of attaching certain works to believing?
24. Discuss the fact that works are a result of believing unto salvation not a condition of salvation.
25. Summarize what a man must do to be saved.

29

Salvation From the Power of Sin

A. Deliverance From Sin for Christians Only

Since salvation from the power of sin is God's gracious provision for those whom He has already saved from the guilt and penalty of sin, this doctrine in its application is limited to Christians. Though saved and safe in Christ, Christians still have the disposition to sin, and do sin. To these facts both Scripture and human experience give aboundant proof. Based upon the fact that Christians sin, the New Testament proceeds to explain the divinely provided way of deliverence.

Supposing that a Christian would neither sin nor be disposed to sin, many young believers are confused and alarmed — even doubting their own salvation — when they discover the reigning power of sin in their lives. Well may they be alarmed at sin, for it outrages the holiness of God; but in place of doubt as to salvation or yielding to the practice of sin, they should learn God's gracious provisions whereby there is deliverance.

189

Next to the way of salvation, there is no more important theme to be mastered by the human mind than the divine plan whereby a Christian may live to the glory of God. Ignorance and error may result in tragic spiritual failure. As in the preaching of the Gospel, there is great need for accuracy in the statement of the scriptural doctrine of salvation from the power of sin.

B. The Problem of Sin in the Life of a Christian

Having received the divine nature (2 Pet. 1:4) while still retaining the old nature, every child of God possesses two natures; one is incapable of sinning, and the other is incapable of holiness. The old nature, sometimes called "sin" (meaning the source of sin) and "old man," is a part of the flesh; for, in scriptural usage, the term "flesh," when used in a moral sense, refers to the spirit and soul as well as the body — especially of the unregenerate man. Therefore, the Apostle Paul states, "For I know that in me (that is, in my flesh,) dwelleth no good thing" (Rom. 7:18). On the other hand, when considering the imparted divine nature, the Apostle John writes, "Whosoever is born of God doth not commit [practice] sin; for his seed remaineth in him: and he cannot sin, because he is born of God" (1 John 3:9). This passage teaches that *every* Christian, being born of God, does not practice sin, or keep on sinning. (The verb is in the present tense implying continuous action.) However, it should be observed that it is this same epistle which warns every child of God against professing that he has no sin nature (1:8), or that he has not sinned (1:10).

These two sources of action in the believer are again considered in Galatians 5:17, where both the Holy Spirit and the flesh are seen constantly to be active and in unceasing conflict: "For the flesh lusteth against the Spirit, and the Spirit against the flesh: and these are contrary the one to the other." The apostle is not writing here of the carnal Christian, but of the most spiritual, even of the one who is not fulfilling the lust of the flesh (5:16). In such a one this conflict exists, and though he is delivered from the lust of the flesh, it is because he is walking in dependence upon the Spirit.

C. Law as a Rule of Life

In understanding God's program for deliverance from the power of sin, it is important to distinguish between law and grace as rules of life. The word "law" is used in many different senses in Scripture. Sometimes it is used as a rule of life. When used in this way, the word has various meanings.

1. *The Ten Commandments, which were written by the finger of God on tables of stone* (Exod. 31:18).

2. *The whole system of government for Israel when in the land which included the commandments* (Exod. 20:1-26), *the judgments* (Exod. 21:1 – 24:11), *and the ordinances* (Exod. 24:12 – 31:18).

3. *The governing principles of the yet future kingdom of the Messiah in the earth, which are said to be the fulfilling of the Law and the Prophets* (Matt. 5:1 – 7:29; note 5:17-18; 7:12).

4. *Any aspect of the revealed will of God for men* (Rom. 7:22, 25; 8:4).

5. *Any rule of conduct prescribed by men for their own government* (Matt. 20:15; Luke 20:22; 2 Tim. 2:5). The word "law" is also used a few times of a force in operation (Rom. 7:21; 8:2).

6. *In the Old Testament especially, law is also presented as a conditional covenant of works.* Under this conception of the law, its scope is extended beyond the actual writings of the Mosaic system and the kingdom law, and it includes any human action which is attempted (whether in conformity to a precept of the Scriptures or not) with a view to securing favor with God. The law formula is "If you will do good, I will bless you." Thus the highest ideal of heavenly conduct — if undertaken with a view to securing favor with God instead of being undertaken because one has already secured favor through Christ — becomes purely legal in its character.

7. *Law is also introduced as a principle of dependence on the flesh.* The law provided no enablement for its observance. No more was expected or secured in return from its commands than the natural man in his environment could provide. Therefore, whatever is undertaken in the energy of the flesh is legal in its nature, whether it be the whole revealed will of God, the actual written commandments contained in the law, the exhortations of grace, or any spiritual activity whatsoever.

D. Grace as a Rule of Life

For the child of God under grace, every aspect of the law is now done away (John 1:16, 17; Rom. 6:14; 7:1-6; 2 Cor. 3:1-18; Gal. 3:19-25; Eph. 2:15; Col. 2:14).

1. *The legal commands of the Mosaic system and the commands which are to govern in the kingdom are not now the guiding principles of the Christian.* They have been superseded by a new and gracious rule of conduct which includes in itself all that is vital in the law, but restates it under the peculiar order and character of grace.

2. *The child of God under grace has been delivered from the burden of a covenant of works.* He is not now striving to be accepted, but rather is free to live as one who is accepted in Christ (Eph. 1:6).

3. *The child of God is not now called upon to live by the energy of his own flesh.* He has been delivered from this feature of the law and may live in the power of the indwelling Spirit. Since the written law was addressed to Israel, she alone could be delivered from the written commandments of Moses by the death of Christ. However, both Jew and Gentile were delivered by that death from the hopeless principle of human merit and from the useless struggle of the flesh.

4. *In contrast with law, the word "grace" refers to the unmerited favor which represents the divine method of dealing with man that was introduced with Adam.* Under grace, God does not treat men as they deserve, but He treats them in infinite mercy and grace without reference to their desserts. This He is free to do on the ground that the righteous punishment for sin, which His holiness would otherwise impose upon sinners as their just dessert, was borne for the sinner by the Son of God.

Although the people of Israel experienced the grace of God in many ways, as a rule of life they passed from a grace relationship to God to a law relationship to God. When they accepted the law as recorded in Exodus 19:3-25, they foolishly presumed that they would be able to keep the law of God through ignorance of their need of grace as the only possible basis of being accepted before God. The experience of Israel under the law, accordingly, demonstrates to all men the impossibility of being delivered from the power of sin by the law of principle.

5. *In contrast with law, grace is revealed in three different aspects:* (a) salvation by grace, (b) safekeeping through grace, and (c) grace as a rule of life for the saved.

a. God saves sinners by grace, and there is no other way of salvation offered to men (Acts 4:12). Saving grace is the limitless, unrestrained love of God for the lost acting in compliance with the exact and unchangeable demands of His own righteousness through the sacrificial death of Christ. Grace is more than love; it is love set free and made to be a triumphant victor over the righteous judgments of God against the sinner.

When He saves a sinner by grace, it is necessary that God shall deal with every sin, for they would otherwise demand judgment and thus hinder His grace. This He has wrought in the death of His Son. It is also necessary that every obligation shall be canceled, and to this end salvation has been made an absolute gift from God (John 10:28; Rom. 6:23; Eph. 2:8). Likewise, it is necessary that every human merit shall be set aside, lest the thing which God accomplishes be in any measure based on the merit of men and not on His sovereign grace alone (Rom. 3:9; 11:32; Gal. 3:22). Since every human element is excluded, the gospel of grace is the proclamation of the mighty, redeeming, transforming grace of God, which offers eternal life and eternal glory to all who will believe.

b. The divine program of safekeeping through grace demonstrates that through grace alone God keeps those who are saved. Having provided a way whereby He can act in freedom from His own righteous demands against sin, having disposed of every human obligation for payment, and having set aside eternally every human merit, God has only to continue the exercise of grace toward the saved one to secure his safekeeping forever. This He does, and the child of God is said to stand in grace (Rom. 5:2; 1 Pet. 5:12).

c. God provides also a rule of life for the saved based on the grace principle. God teaches those who are saved and kept how they should live in grace and how they may live to His eternal glory. As the law provided a complete rule of conduct for Israel, so God has provided a complete rule of conduct for the Christian. Since all rules of life which are presented in the Bible are complete in themselves, it is not necessary that they be combined. Therefore the child of God is not under law as a rule of life, but he is under the counsels of grace. What he does under grace is not done to secure the favor of God, but it is done because he is already accepted in the Beloved. It is not undertaken in the energy of the flesh, but it is the outliving and manifestation of the power of the indwelling Spirit. It is a life which is lived on the principle of faith: "The just shall live by faith."

These principles are stated in portions of the gospels and the epistles.

E. The Only Way of Victory

Various teachings are suggested which attempt to secure deliverance for the Christian from the power of sin.

1. *It is claimed that the Christian will be compelled to live to the glory of God if he observes sufficient rules.* This law principle is doomed to fail because it depends upon the very flesh from which deliverance is sought (Rom. 6:14).

2. *It is widely claimed that the Christian may seek and secure the eradication of the old nature, being thus permanently free from the power of sin.* There are objections to this theory.

a. There is no Scripture upon which the theory of eradication may be based.

b. The old nature is a part of the flesh and will naturally be dealt with as God deals with the flesh. The flesh is one of the Christian's mighty foes — the world, the flesh, and the devil. God does not eradicate the world, or the flesh, or the devil; but He provides victory over these by His spirit (Gal. 5:16; 1 John 4:4; 5:4). In like manner, He provides victory over the old nature by the Spirit (Rom. 6:14; 8:2).

c. No actual human experience confirms the theory of eradication, and were that theory true, parents of this class would give birth to unfallen children.

d. Likewise, when this theory is accepted, there remains no place for, and no meaning to, the ministry of the indwelling Spirit. On the contrary, the most spiritual Christians are warned concerning the necessity of walking by the Spirit, reckoning, yielding, not letting sin reign, putting off, mortifying, and abiding.

3. *Some Christians suppose that, apart from the Spirit and simply because they are saved, they can live to the glory of God.* In Romans 7:15 — 8:4 the apostle records his own experience with this theory. He states that he knew what was good, but he did not know how to perform what he knew (7:18). He therefore concluded that (a) at his best he was always defeated because of an ever-present law of sin in his members warring against his mind (7:23); (b) such an estate is wretched (7:24); (c) though he was saved, the law of the Spirit of life in Christ Jesus made him free, and not his own works (8:2); (d) the whole

will of God is fulfilled *in* the believer, but never fulfilled *by* the beliver (8:4).

In Romans 7:25 it is stated that deliverance from the power of sin is *through* — not *by* — Jesus Christ our Lord. Since a problem related to the holiness of God is involved, deliverance can only be *through* Jesus Christ. The Holy Spirit could not take control of an unjudged fallen nature; but it is stated in Romans 6:1-10 that the believer's fallen nature has been judged by co-crucifixion, co-death, and co-burial with Christ, making it morally possible for the indwelling Holy Spirit to give victory. Under these provisions, the believer may walk in the power of a new life principle which is by dependence upon the Spirit alone, and he should reckon himself to be dead indeed unto sin (6:4, 11). Thus it is that deliverance is *by* the Spirit *through* Christ.

F. *Victory by the Holy Spirit*

As brought out in the previous studies in the doctrine of the Holy Spirit, a Christian can be delivered from the power of sin by the Holy Spirit. "If by means of the Spirit ye are walking, ye shall not fulfil the lust of the flesh" (Gal. 5:16, lit.). Salvation from the power of sin, like salvation from the penalty of sin, is of God and depends, on the human side, upon an *attitude* of faith — as salvation from the penalty of sin depends on an *act* of faith. The justified one shall live by faith — faith which depends on the power of another — and the justified one will never know a time in this life when he will need to depend less on the Spirit.

There are three reasons for a life of dependence on the indwelling Spirit.

1. *Under the teachings of grace, a believer faces an impossible heavenly standard of life.* Being a citizen of heaven (Phil. 3:20), a member of the body of Christ (Eph. 5:30), and of the household and family of God (Eph. 2:19; 3:15), the child of God is called upon to act in accordance with his heavenly position. Since this is a superhuman manner of life (John 13:34; 2 Cor. 10:5; Eph. 4:1-3, 30; 5:20; 1 Thess. 5:16-17; 1 Pet. 2:9), he must depend upon the indwelling Spirit (Rom. 8:4).

2. *The Christian faces Satan — the world-ruling foe.* Because of this, he must be "strong in the Lord" (Eph. 6:10-12; 1 John 4:4; Jude 9).

3. *The Christian possesses the old nature which he is powerless to control.*

Scriptural revelation, accordingly, reveals not only that God saves from the guilt of sin, but is also able to deliver from the power of sin. Ultimately, when the Christian stands complete in heaven, he will be delivered from the presence of sin.

Questions

1. Why is deliverance from sin for Christians only?
2. To what extent is sin a problem for Christians?
3. What evidence is given in Scripture that a Christian has two natures?
4. How does the Holy Spirit relate to the old nature?
5. What are some of the senses in which the word "law" is used in the Bible?
6. To what extent is law lacking in providing enablement for its observants?
7. Why is the Christian not under the Mosaic system of law?
8. Why is a Christian not striving to be accepted by God?
9. Why should a child of God not attempt to live by the energy of his own flesh?
10. Compare Israel's relationship to grace as a rule of life with the church's relationship to grace as a rule of life.
11. To what extent is grace revealed in "salvation by grace", and what is involved on God's part?
12. How is grace related to the safekeeping of a believer?
13. How is grace a complete rule of life?
14. Why is the law principle doomed to failure?
15. What objections may be raised to the theory that the old nature can be eradicated?
16. Why is it an error to conclude that just because one is saved he can easily lead a Christian life?
17. By what means is deliverance from the power of sin made possible, and how is this related to Jesus Christ, and how to the Holy Spirit?
18. How is salvation from the power of sin dependent upon faith?
19. How does the impossible heavenly standard of life for a believer make necessary a life of dependeance on the indwelling Spirit?
20. How does the power of Satan relate to a believer's need of deliverance?
21. How does the power of the old nature require deliverance?
22. Contrast the present extent of deliverance from sin with that which will exist in heaven.

30

Four Aspects of Righteousness

A vital difference between God and man which Scripture emphasizes is that God is righteous (1 John 1:5), while the fundamental charge against man as recorded in Romans 3:10 is that "there is none righteous, no, not one." So also, one of the glories of divine grace is the fact that a perfect righteousness, likened to a spotless wedding garment, has been provided and is freely bestowed upon all who believe (Rom. 3:22).

The Scriptures distinguish four aspects of righteousness.

A. God Is Righteous

This righteousness of God is unchanging and unchangeable (Rom. 3:25-26). He is infinitely righteous in His own being and infinitely righteous in all His ways.

God is righteous in His being. It is impossible for Him to deviate from His righteousness by so much as the "shadow of turning" (James 1:17). He cannot look on sin with the least degree of allowance. Therefore, since all men are sinners both by nature and by practice, the divine judgment has come upon

197

all men unto condemnation. The acceptance of this truth is vital to any right understanding of the gospel of divine grace.

God is righteous in His ways. It must also be recognized that God is incapable of slighting sin or merely forgiving sin in leniency. The triumph of the Gospel is not in the belittling of sin on the part of God; it is rather in the fact that all those judgments which infinite righteousness must of necessity impose upon the sinner have been borne in substitution by God's provided Lamb, and that this is a plan of God's own devising which according to His own standards of righteousness is sufficient for all who believe. By this plan God can satisfy His love in saving the sinner without infringing upon His own unchangeable righteousness; and the sinner, utterly hopeless in himself, can pass from all condemnation (John 3:18; 5:24; Rom. 8:1; 1 Cor. 11:32).

It is not unusual for men to conceive of God as a righteous being; but they often fail to recognize the fact that, when He undertakes to save the sinful, the righteousness of God is not and cannot be diminished.

B. The Self-Righteousness of Man

In complete accord with the revelation that God is supremely righteous, there is the corresponding revelation that, in the sight of God, the righteousness of man (Rom. 10:3) is as "filthy rags" (Isa. 64:6). Though the sinful estate of man is constantly declared throughout Scripture, there is no description more complete and final than is found in Romans 3:9-18, and it should be noted that this, like all other estimates of sin which are recorded in the Bible, is a description of sin as God sees it. Men have erected legitimate standards for the family, for society, and for the state; but these are no part of the basis upon which man must stand and by which he must be judged before God. In their relation to God, men are not wise when thus comparing themselves with themselves (2 Cor. 10:12). For not merely those who are condemned by society are lost, but those who are condemned by the unalterable righteousness of God (Rom. 3:23). There is therefore no hope for any individual outside the provisions of God's grace; for none can enter heaven's glory who are not as acceptable to God as Christ is. For this need of man God has made abundant provision.

C. The Imputed Righteousness of God

As brought out in previous discussion of the doctrine of imputation, the important revelation of the imputed righteousness of God (Rom. 3:22) is essential to understanding both the principles upon which God condemns the sinner and the principles on which God saves the Christian. Although the doctrine is difficult to understand, it is important to understand this as a major aspect of God's revelation.

1. *The fact of imputation is brought out in the imputing of Adam's sin to the human race with the effect that all men are considered sinners by God* (Rom. 5:12-21). This is further developed in the fact that the sin of man was imputed to Christ when He became the sin offering for the whole world (2 Cor. 5:14, 21; Heb. 2:9; 1 John 2:2). So also, the righteousness of God is imputed to all who believe, so that they may stand before God in all the perfection of Christ. By this divine provision those who are saved are said to have been "made" the righteousness of God (1 Cor. 1:30; 2 Cor. 5:21). Since it is the righteousness of God and not of man, and since it is said to be apart from all self works or deeds of law observance (Rom. 3:21), obviously this imputed righteousness is not something accomplished by man. Being the righteousness of God, it is not increased by the goodness of the one to whom it is imputed, nor is it decreased by his badness.

2. *The results of imputation are seen in that the righteousness of God is imputed to the believer on the basis of the fact that the believer is, through the baptism of the Spirit, in Christ.* Through that vital union to Christ by the Spirit, the believer becomes related to Christ as a member in His body (1 Cor. 12:13) and as a branch in the True Vine (John 15:1, 5). Because of the reality of this union, God sees the believer as a living part of His own Son. He therefore loves him as He loves His Son (John 17:23), He accepts him as He accepts His own Son (Eph. 1:6; 1 Pet. 2:5), and He accounts him to be what His own Son is — the righteousness of God (Rom. 3:22; 1 Cor. 1:30; 2 Cor. 5:21). Christ is the righteousness of God, therefore those who are saved are *made* the righteousness of God by being *in Him* (2 Cor. 5:21). They are complete in Him (Col. 2:10) and perfected forever (Heb. 10:10, 14).

3. *Many biblical illustrations of imputation are given in Scripture.* Garments of skin which necessitated the shedding of blood were divinely provided for Adam and Eve (Gen. 3:21).

A righteous standing was imputed to Abraham because he *believed* God (Gen. 15:6; Rom. 4:9-22; James 2:23), and as the priests of old were clothed with righteousness (Ps. 132:9), so the believer is robed in the wedding garment of the righteousness of God and in that garment he will appear in glory (Rev. 19:8).

The attitude of the Apostle Paul toward Philemon is an illustration both of imputed merit and imputed demerit. Speaking of the slave Onesimus, the apostle said: "If thou count me therefore a partner, receive him as myself [the imputation of merit]. If he hath wronged thee, or oweth thee ought, put that on mine account [the imputation of demerit]" (Philem. 17-18; note also Job 29:14; Isa. 11:5; 59:17; 61:10).

4. *Imputation affects the standing and not the state.* There is, then, a righteousness from God, apart from all human works, which is *unto* and *upon* all who believe (Rom. 3:22). It is the eternal standing of all who are saved. In their daily life, or state, they are far from perfect, and in this aspect of their relation to God they are "to grow in grace, and in the knowledge of our Lord and Saviour Jesus Christ" (2 Pet. 3:18).

5. *Imputed righteousness is the ground of justification.* According to the New Testament usage, the words "righteousness" and "justify" are from the same root. God declares the one justified forever whom He sees *in Christ.* It is an equitable decree since the justified one is clothed in the righteousness of God. Justification is not a fiction or a state of feeling; it is rather an immutable reckoning in the mind of God. Like imputed righteousness, justification is by faith (Rom. 5:1), through grace (Titus 3:4-7), and made possible through the death and resurrection of Christ (Rom. 3:24; 4:25). It is abiding and unchangeable since it rests only on the merit of the eternal Son of God.

Justification is more than forgiveness, since forgiveness is the cancellation of sin while justification is the imputing of righteousness. Forgiveness is negative (the removal of condemnation), while justification is positive (the bestowing of the merit and standing of Christ).

James, writing of a justification by works (2:14-26), has in view the believer's standing before men; Paul writing of justification by faith (Rom. 5:1), has in view the believer's standing before God. Abraham was justified before men in that he proved his faith by his works (James 2:21); likewise he was justified by faith before God on the ground of imputed righteousness (James 2:23).

D. Righteousness Imparted by the Spirit

When filled with the Spirit, the child of God will produce the righteous works (Rom. 8:4) of the "fruit of the Spirit" (Gal. 5:22-23) and will manifest the gifts for service which are by the Spirit (1 Cor. 12:7). These results are distinctly said to be due to the immediate working of the Spirit in and through the believer. Reference is made, therefore, to a manner of life which is in one way produced *by* the believer; it is rather a manner of life which is produced *through* him by the Spirit. To those who "walk not after the flesh, but after the Spirit," the righteousness of the law, which in this case means no less than the realization of the whole will of God for the believer, is fulfilled *in* them.

It could never be fulfilled *by* them. When thus wrought by the Spirit, it is none other than a life which is the imparted righteousness of God.

Questions

1. How are God and man distinguished as to righteousness?
2. What are the four aspects of righteousness revealed in Scripture?
3. In what different ways is God completely righteous?
4. To what extent is man self-righteous, and why is this insufficient?
5. Why is the imputed righteousness of God necessary for man?
6. What are the results of imputation of righteousness to man?
7. Give some biblical illustrations of imputation.
8. How does imputation affect standing and state before God?
9. How does imputed righteousness relate to justification?
10. Contrast justification and forgiveness.
11. What is the difference between justification by works and justification by faith?
12. To what extent is righteousness imparted by the Spirit?

31

Sanctification

A. *Importance of Correct Interpretation*

The doctrine of sanctification suffers misunderstanding despite the fact that the Bible provides extensive revelation on this important theme. In light of the history of the doctrine, it is important to observe three laws of interpretation.

1. *The right understanding of the doctrine of sanctification depends upon the consideration of all Scripture bearing on this theme.* The body of Scripture presenting this doctrine is much more extensive than appears to the one who reads only the English text; for the same root Hebrew and Greek words which are translated "sanctify," with their various forms, are also translated by two other English words, "holy" and "saint," with their various forms. Therefore, if we would discover the full scope of this doctrine from the Scriptures, we must go beyond the passages in which the one English word "sanctify" is used and include as well the passages wherein the words "holy" and "saint" are used.

Leviticus 21:8 illustrates the similarity of meaning between the words "sanctify" and " holy" as used in the Bible. Speaking of the priest, God said, "Thou shalt sanctify him therefore; for he offereth the bread of thy God: he shall be holy unto thee: for I the LORD, which sanctify you, am holy." Here the root word used four times is twice translated "sanctify" and twice translated "holy."

2. *The doctrine of sanctification cannot be interpreted by experience.* Only one aspect of sanctification out of three deals with the problems of human experience in daily life. Therefore an analysis of some personal experience must not be substituted for the teaching of the Word of God. Even if sanctification were limited to the field of human experience, there would never be an experience that could be proven to be its perfect example, nor would any human statement of that experience exactly describe the full measure of the divine reality. It is the function of the Bible to interpret experience, rather than the function of experience to interpret the Bible. Every experience which is wrought of God will be found to be according to Scripture.

3. *The doctrine of sanctification must be rightly related to every other Bible doctrine.* Disproportionate emphasis on any one doctrine, or the habit of seeing all truth in the light of one line of Bible teaching, leads to serious error. The doctrine of sanctification, like all other doctrines of the Scriptures, represents and defines an exact field within the purpose of God, and since it aims at definite ends, it suffers as much from overstatement as from understatement.

B. *The Meaning of Words Related to Sanctification*

1. *"Sanctify" in its various forms is used 106 times in the Old Testament and 31 times in the New Testament and means to "set apart," or the state of being set apart.* It indicates classification in matters of position and relationship. The basis of the classification is usually that the sanctified person or thing has been set apart, or separated from others in position and relationship before God, from that which is unholy. This is the general meaning of the word.

2. *"Holy" in its various forms is used about 400 times in the Old Testament and about 12 times of believers in the New Testament and refers to the state of being set apart, or being separate, from that which is unholy.* Christ was "holy, harmless,

undefiled, and separate from sinners." Thus was He sanctified. So, also, there are certain things which the words "holy" and "sanctify," in their biblical use, do not imply.

a. Sinless perfection is not necessarily implied, for Scripture speaks of a "holy nation," "holy priests," "holy prophets," "holy apostles," "holy men," "holy women," "holy brethren," "holy mountain," and "holy temple." None of these were sinless before God. They were holy according to some particular standard or issue that constituted the basis of their separation from others. Even the Corinthian Christians who were utterly at fault were said to be sanctified. Many inanimate things were sanctified, and these could not even be related to the question of sin.

b. The word does not necessarily imply finality. All these people just named were repeatedly called to higher degrees of holiness. They were set apart again and again. People, or things, became holy as they were set apart for some holy purpose. Thus they were sanctified.

3. *"Saint" is used of Israel about fifty times and of believers about sixty-two times, is applied only to human persons, and relates only to their position in the reckoning of God.* It is never associated with their own quality of daily life. They are saints because they are particularly classified and set apart in the plan and purpose of God. Being sanctified they are saints.

In several epistles, according to the Authorized Version (Rom. 1:7; 1 Cor. 1:2), believers are addressed as those who are "called to be saints." This is most misleading; the words "to be" should be omitted. Christians are saints by their present calling from God. The passages do not anticipate a time when they will be saints. They are already sanctified, set apart, classified, "holy brethren," who therefore are saints.

Sainthood is not subject to progression. Every born-again person is as much a saint the moment he is saved as he ever will be in time or eternity. The whole church which is His body is a called-out, separate people; they are the saints of this dispensation. According to certain usages of these words, they are all sanctified. They are all holy. Because they do not know their position in Christ, many Christians do not believe they are saints. The Spirit has chosen to give us the title of "saints" more than any other but one. Believers are called "brethren" 184 times, "saints" 62 times, and "Christians" but 3 times.

C. The Means of Sanctification

1. *Because of infinite holiness, God Himself — Father, Son, and Spirit — is eternally sanctified.* He is classified, set apart, and separate from sin. He is holy. The Spirit is called the Holy Spirit. He is sanctified (Lev. 21:8; John 17:19).

2. *God — Father, Son, and Spirit — are said to sanctify persons.*

 a. The Father sanctifies (1 Thess. 5:23).

 b. The Son sanctifies (Eph. 5:26; Heb. 2:11; 9:12, 14; 13:12).

 c. The Spirit sanctifies (Rom. 15:16; 2 Thess. 2:13).

 d. God the Father sanctified the Son (John 10:36).

 e. God sanctified the priests and the people of Israel (Exod. 29:44; 31:13).

 f. Our sanctification is the will of God (1 Thess. 4:3).

 g. Our sanctification from God is: by our union with Christ (1 Cor. 1:2, 30); by the Word of God (John 17:17; cf. 1 Tim. 4:5); by the blood of Christ (Heb. 9:13; 13:12); by the body of Christ (Heb. 10:10); by the Spirit (1 Pet. 1:2); by our own choice (Heb. 12:14; 2 Tim. 2:21, 22); by faith (Acts 26:18).

3. *God sanctified days, places, and things* (Gen. 2:3; Exod. 29:43).

4. *Man may sanctify God.* This he may do by setting God apart in his own thought as holy. "Hallowed be thy name" (Matt. 6:9). "But sanctify the Lord God in your hearts" (1 Pet. 3:15).

5. *Man may sanctify himself.* Many times God called upon Israel to sanctify themselves. He exhorts us, "Be ye holy, for I am holy." Also, "If a man therefore purge himself from these [vessels of dishonor and by departing from iniquity], he shall be a vessel unto honour, sanctified, and meet for the master's use" (2 Tim. 2:21). Self-sanctification can only be realized by the divinely provided means. Christians are asked to present their bodies a living sacrifice, holy, and acceptable unto God (Rom. 12:1). They are to "come out from among them" and be separate (2 Cor. 6:17). Having these promises, they are to cleanse themselves "from all filthiness of the flesh and spirit, perfecting holiness [sanctification] in the fear of God" (2 Cor. 7:1). "This I say then, Walk in the Spirit, and ye shall not fulfil the lust of the flesh" (Gal. 5:16).

6. *Man may sanctify persons and things.* "For the unbelieving husband is sanctified by the wife, and the unbelieving wife is sanctified by the husband: else were your children unclean; but now are they holy [sanctified]" (1 Cor. 7:14). Moses sanctified

the people (Exod. 19:14). "So they sanctified the house of the LORD" (2 Chron. 29:17).

7. *One thing may sanctify another thing.* "For whether is greater, the gold, or the temple that sanctifieth the gold?" "For whether is greater, the gift, or the altar that sancifieth the gift?" (Matt. 23:17, 19).

From this limited consideration of Scripture on the subject of sanctification and holiness, it is evident that the root meaning of the word is to set apart unto a holy purpose. The thing set apart is sometimes cleansed and sometimes it is not. Sometimes it can itself partake of the character of holiness and sometimes, as in the case of an inanimate thing, it cannot. Yet a thing which of itself can be neither holy nor unholy is just as much sanctified when set apart unto God as is the person whose moral character is subject to transformation. It is also evident that where these moral qualities exist, cleansing and purification are sometimes required in sanctification; but not always (1 Cor. 7:14).

D. Three Major Aspects of Sanctification

Although the Old Testament has an extensive revelation of the doctrine of sanctification, especially as related to the law of Moses and Israel, the New Testament provides a clearer picture of the major aspects of sanctification. The New Testament doctrine falls into three divisions: (1) positional sanctification, (2) experiential sanctification, (3) ultimate sanctification.

1. *Positional sanctification is a sanctification, holiness, and sainthood which is accomplished by the operation of God through the body and shed blood of our Lord Jesus Christ.* Believers have been redeemed and cleansed in His precious blood, forgiven all trespasses, made righteous through our new headship in Him, justified, and purified. They are the sons of God. All of this indicates a distinct classification and separation, deep and eternal, through the saving grace of Christ. It is based on facts of position which are true of every Christian. Hence every believer is now said to be *positionally* sanctified, holy, and is therefore a saint before God. This position bears no relationship to the believer's daily life more than that it should inspire him to holy living. The Christian's position in Christ is, according to Scripture, the greatest incentive to holiness of life.

The great doctrinal epistles observe this order. They first state the marvels of saving grace and then conclude with an appeal for a life corresponding to the divinely wrought position (cf. Rom. 12:1; Eph. 4:1; Col. 3:1). We are not now accepted in ourselves: we are accepted in the Beloved. We are not now righteous in ourselves: He has been made unto us righteousness. We are not now redeemed in ourselves: He has been made unto us redemption. We are not now positionally sanctified by our daily walk: He has been *made* unto us sanctification. Positional sanctification is as perfect as He is perfect. As much as He is set apart, we who are in Him are set apart.

Positional sanctification is as complete for the weakest saint as it is for the strongest. It depends only on his union and position in Christ. All believers are classified as "the saints." So, also, they are classified as "the sanctified" (note Acts 20:32; 1 Cor. 1:2; 6:11; Heb. 10:10, 14; Jude 1). The proof that imperfect believers are nevertheless positionally sanctified, and are therefore saints, is found in 1 Corinthians. Corinthian Christians were unholy in life (1 Cor. 5:1-2; 6:1-8), but they are twice said to have been sanctified (1 Cor. 1:2; 6:11).

By their position, then, Christians are rightly called "holy brethren" and "saints." They have been "sanctified through the offering of the body of Jesus Christ once for all" (Heb. 10:10), and are "new men" who are "created in righteousness and true holiness" (Eph. 4:24). Positional sanctification and positional holiness are "true" sanctification and holiness. In his position in Christ, the Christian stands righteous and accepted before God forever. Compared to this, no other aspect of this truth can have an equal recognition. But let no person conclude that he is holy or sanctified in life because he is now said to be holy or sanctified in position.

While all believers are sanctified positionally, there is never a reference in any Scripture to their daily lives. The daily-life aspect of sanctification and holiness will be found in another and entirely different body of truth which may be termed experiential sanctification.

2. *Experiential sanctification is the second major aspect of the doctrine in the New Testament and relates to sanctification as experienced by the believer.* As positional sanctification is absolutely dissociated from the daily life, so experiential sanctification is absolutely dissociated from the position in Christ. Experiential sanctification may depend (a) on some degree of yieldedness to God, (b) on some degree of separation from sin,

or (c) on some degree of Christian growth to which the believer has already attained.

a. Experiential sanctification is the result of yieldedness to God. Complete self-dedication to God is our reasonable service: "That ye present your bodies a living sacrifice, holy, acceptable unto God, which is your reasonable service" (Rom. 12:1). By so doing the Christian is classfied and set apart unto God by his own choice. This is self-determined separation unto God and is an important aspect of experiential sanctification. "But now being made free from sin, and become servants to God, ye have your fruit unto holiness" (Rom. 6:22).

Sanctification cannot be experienced as a matter of feeling or emotion any more than justification or forgiveness. A person may be at peace and be full of joy because he *believes* he is set apart unto God. So also, by yielding unto God, a new infilling of the Spirit may be made possible which will result in a blessedness in life hitherto unknown. This might be either sudden or gradual. In any case it is not the sanctification that is experienced: it is the blessing of the Spirit made possible through sanctification or a more complete separation unto God.

b. Experiential sanctification is the result of freedom from sin. The Bible takes full account of the sins of Christians. It does not teach that only sinless people are saved or kept saved; on the contrary, there is faithful consideration of, and full provision made for, the sins of saints. These provisions are both preventive and curative.

There are three divine provisions for the prevention of sin in the Christian: (1) the Word of God with its clear instructions (Ps. 119:11), (2) the present interceding, shepherding ministry of Christ in heaven (Rom. 8:34; Heb. 7:25; cf. Luke 22:31-32; John 17:1-26), and (3) the enabling power of the indwelling Spirit (Gal. 5:16; Rom. 8:4). However, should the Christian sin, there is the divinely provided cure, which is the present advocacy of Christ in heaven by which He pleads His own sufficient, sacrificial death. By this means alone imperfect believers are kept saved.

The divine prevention of sin is imperative in the case of every child of God, since as long as he is in this body he retains a fallen nature which is ever prone to sin (Rom. 7:21; 2 Cor. 4:7; 1 John 1:8). Scripture promises no eradication of this nature, but there is a moment-by-moment victory promised through the power of the Spirit (Gal. 5:16-23). This victory will be realized just so long as it is claimed by faith and the conditions for a Spirit-filled life are met.

The sin nature itself is never said to have died. It was crucified, dead, and buried with Christ; but since this was accomplished two thousand years ago, the reference is to a divine judgment against the nature which was gained by Christ when He "died unto sin." There is no Bible teaching to the effect that some Christians have died to sin and some have not. The passages include *all* saved persons (Gal. 5:24; Col. 3:3). All believers have died unto sin in Christ's death; but not all believers have claimed the riches which were provided for them by that death. We are not asked to die experimentally, or to enact His death; we are asked to "reckon" ourselves to be dead indeed unto sin. This is the human responsibility (Rom. 6:1-14).

Every victory over sin is itself a separation unto God and is therefore a sanctification. Such victory should ever be increasing as the believer comes to know his own helplessness and the marvels of divine power.

c. Experiential sanctification is related to Christian growth. Christians are immature in wisdom, knowledge, experience, and grace. In all these things they are appointed to grow, and their growth should be manifest. They are to "grow in grace, and in the knowledge of our Lord and Saviour Jesus Christ" (2 Pet. 3:18). Beholding the glory of the Lord as in a glass, they are "changed into the same image from glory to glory, even as by the Spirit of the Lord" (2 Cor. 3:18). This transformation will have the effect of setting them more and more apart. They will, to that extent, be more sanctified.

A Christian may be "blameless," though it could not be truthfully said of him that he is "faultless." The child laboring to form his first letters in a copybook may be blameless in the work he does; but the work is not faultless. We may be walking in the full measure of our understanding today, yet we know that we are not now living in the added light and experience that will be ours tomorrow. There is perfection within imperfection. We who are so incomplete, so immature, so given to sin, may "abide in him."

3. *Ultimate sanctification is that aspect which is related to our final perfection, and will be ours in the glory.* By His grace and transforming power He will have so changed us — spirit, soul, and body — that we will be "like him," and "conformed to his image." He will then present us "faultless" before the presence of His glory. His bride will be free from every "spot and

wrinkle." It therefore is fitting for us to "abstain from every appearance of evil. And the very God of peace sanctify you wholly; and I pray God your whole spirit and soul and body be preserved blameless unto the coming of our Lord Jesus Christ" (1 Thess. 5:22-23).

Questions

1. Why is it unnecessary to have misunderstanding concerning the doctrine of sanctification?
2. What is the basic meaning of, and what words are used for, sanctification in Scripture?
3. What are the dangers of interpreting the doctrine of sanctification by experience?
4. How can the doctrine of sanctification be properly related to other biblical doctrines?
5. To what extent is sanctification in its various forms mentioned in the Bible?
6. Does sanctification imply sinless perfection or finality of sanctification?
7. To what extent is sanctification related to quality of daily life?
8. Why is sainthood not subject to progression?
9. To what extent is God the Father, Son, and Spirit said to sanctify persons?
10. To what extent does God sanctify days, places, and things?
11. In what sense may a man sanctify God?
12. In what sense may a man sanctify himself?
13. Is it possible for man to sanctify persons and things?
14. How can one thing sanctify another thing?
15. How does sanctification in its various usages relate to cleansing of an object?
16. What are the three major aspects of sanctification?
17. How is positional sanctification effected?
18. What is the relationship between positional sanctification and holy living in the doctrinal epistles?
19. To what extent is positional sanctification immediately complete for every child of God?
20. How does experiential sanctification differ from positional sanctification?
21. Upon what factors does experiential sanctification depend?
22. How does yieldedness to God relate to experiential sanctification?
23. How is experiential sanctification related to feeling or emotion?
24. How is experiential sanctification related to freedom from sin?
25. What three divine provisions are made by God for the prevention of sin in the Christian?

26. Contrast the divine method of deliverance from sin with the suggested method of eradication of the believer's sin nature.

27. Is it true that some Christians have died to sin and others have not?

28. What is meant by the command to "reckon" ourselves to be dead unto sin?

29. How is experiential sanctification related to Christian growth?

30. What is the difference between a Christian being "blameless" and being "faultless"?

31. Contrast our present experiential sanctification with our ultimate sanctification in heaven.

32. Contrast the believer's present position and state spiritually with his position and state in heaven.

32

Assurance of Salvation

A. The Importance of Assurance

In Christian experience, assurance that one is saved by faith in Christ is essential to the whole program of growth in grace and in the knowledge of Christ. Assurance is a matter of experience and relates to personal confidence in present salvation. It should not be confused with the doctrine of eternal security, which will be discussed in the next chapter. Eternal security is a question of fact, while assurance is a matter of what one believes at a given time concerning his personal salvation.

Assurance of salvation depends upon three major aspects of experience: (1) understanding of the completeness of the salvation provided in Jesus Christ; (2) the confirming testimony of Christian experience; (3) acceptance by faith of biblical promises of salvation.

B. Understanding the Nature of Salvation

Essential to any real assurance of salvation is a clear understanding of what was accomplished by Jesus Christ in His death on the cross. Salvation is not a work of man for God, but a work of God for man; it depends completely upon divine grace without respect to human merit. One who understands that Jesus Christ died for him and provided a complete salvation which is offered to anyone who sincerely believes in Christ can, accordingly, have assurance of his salvation just as soon as he meets the condition of trusting in Christ as his Savior. In many cases, lack of assurance is due to incomplete understanding of the nature of salvation. Once it is understood that salvation is a gift which cannot be earned, cannot be obtained by human effort, and cannot be deserved, and is available as a gift of God to all who will receive it by faith, a proper basis for assurance of salvation is provided, and the question resolves itself into the issue of whether one has really trusted in Christ. This question can be answered by the confirmations that are found in Christian experience of a person who has received salvation.

Among the various divine accomplishments which together constitute the salvation of a soul, the importation of a new life from God is, in the Bible, given the supreme emphasis. Upwards of eighty-five New Testament passages attest this feature of saving grace. Consideration of these passages discloses the fact that this imparted life is the *gift* of God to all those who believe on Christ (John 10:28; Rom. 6:23); it is *from* Christ (John 14:6); it *is* Christ indwelling the believer in the sense that eternal life is inseparable from Him (Col. 1:27; 1 John 5:11, 12), and therefore is as eternal as He is eternal.

C. The Confirming Testimony of Christian Experience

On the basis of the fact that Christ indwells him, the believer is appointed to judge himself as to whether he is in the faith (2 Cor. 13:5); for it is reasonable to expect that the heart wherein Christ dwells will, under normal conditions, be aware of that wonderful presence. However, the Christian is not left to his own misguided feelings and imagination as to the precise manner in which the indwelling Christ will be manifested, as it is clearly defined in Scripture. For the Christian who is subject to the Word of God, this particular revelation serves a twofold purpose: it protects against the assumption that fleshly emotionalism is of God — a belief far too prevalent at the present time — and it sets a standard of spiritual reality toward which all who are saved should ceaselessly strive.

It is obvious that an unsaved person, be he ever so faithful in outward conformity to religious practice, will never manifest the life which is Christ. In like manner, the carnal Christian is abnormal to the extent that he can in no way with accuracy prove his salvation by his experience. Although eternal life in itself is unlimited, all normal Christian experience is limited by that which is carnal (1 Cor. 3:1-4).

A carnal Christian is as perfectly saved as the spiritual Christian; for no experience or merit or service can form any part of the grounds of salvation. Though but a baby, he is, nevertheless, *in Christ* (1 Cor. 3:1). His obligation toward God is not to exercise saving faith, but rather to adjust to the mind and will of God. It is of fundamental importance to understand that a normal Christian experience is realized only by those who are Spirit-filled.

The new life in Christ which results from being saved by faith issues in certain major manifestations.

1. *The knowledge that God is our Heavenly Father is one of the precious experiences which belong to one who has put his trust in Christ.* In Matthew 11:27 it is declared that no one knows the Father except the Son and he to whom the Son will reveal Him. It is one thing to know about God, an experience possible for the unregenerate, but quite another thing to know God, which can be realized only as the Son reveals Him, "And this is life eternal, that they might know thee the only true God" (John 17:3). Fellowship with the Father and with the Son is known only by those who "walk in the light" (1 John 1:7). A normal Christian experience includes, therefore, a personal appreciation of the fatherhood of God.

2. *A new reality in prayer is another confirming experience which leads to assurance.* Prayer assumes a very large place in the experience of the spiritual Christian. It becomes increasingly his most vital resource. By the indwelling Spirit the believer offers praise and thanksgiving (Eph. 5:18-19), and by the Spirit he is enabled to pray according to the will of God (Rom. 8:26-27; Jude 20). It is reasonable to believe, also, that since Christ's ministry both on earth and in heaven was and is so much one of prayer, the one in whom He dwells will normally be moved to prayer.

3. *A new ability to understand Scripture is another important experience related to salvation.* According to the promise of

Christ, the child of God will understand through the Spirit the things of Christ, the things of the Father, and things to come (John 16:12-15). On the Emmaus road Christ opened Scripture to His hearers (Luke 24:32) and opened their hearts to Scripture as well (Luke 24:45). Such an experience, though so wonderful, is not designed alone for favored Christians; it is the normal experience of all who are right with God (1 John 2:27), since it is a natural manifestation of the indwelling Christ.

4. *A new sense of the sinfulness of sin is the normal experience of one who is saved.* As water removes that which is foreign and unclean (Ezek. 36:25; John 3:5; Titus 3:5-6; 1 Pet. 3:21; 1 John 5:6-8), so the Word of God displaces all human conceptions and implants those ideals which are of God (Ps. 119:11), and by the action of the Word of God as applied by the Spirit the divine estimate of sin displaces the human estimate. It is impossible that the sinless Christ, who sweat drops of blood on becoming a sin offering, should not, when free to manifest His presence, create a new sense of the corrupting nature of sin in the one in whom He dwells.

5. *A new love is realized for the unsaved.* The fact that Christ has died for all men (2 Cor. 5:14-15, 19) is the grounds upon which the Apostle Paul could say, "Henceforth know we no man after the flesh" (2 Cor. 5:16). Apart from all earthly distinctions, men were seen by his spiritual eyes only as souls for whom Christ had died. Likewise, for the lost Paul ceased not to pray (Rom. 10:1) and to strive (Rom. 15:20), and for them he was willing to be "accursed from Christ" (Rom. 9:1-3). As a result of the divine presence in the heart this divine compassion should be experienced by every Spirit-filled believer (Rom. 5:5; Gal. 5:22).

6. *A new love is experienced also for the saved.* In 1 John 3:14, love for the brethren is made an absolute test of personal salvation. This is reasonable, since by the regenerating work of the Spirit the believer is brought into a new kinship in the household and family of God, wherein alone the true fatherhood of God and brotherhood of man exist. The fact that the same divine presence indwells two individuals relates them vitally and anticipates a corresponding bond of devotion. The Christian's love one for the other is therefore made the insignia of true discipleship (John 13:34-35), and this affection is the normal experience of all who are born of God.

7. A supreme basis for salvation is the manifestation of the character of Christ in the believer. His resulting subjective

experiences which are due to the unhindered divine Presence in the heart are indicated in nine words: "Love, joy, peace, long-suffering, gentleness, goodness, faith, meekness, temperance" (Gal. 5:22-23), and each word represents a flood tide of reality on the plane of the limitless character of God.

This is the life which Christ lived (John 13:34; 14:27; 15:11), it is the life which is Christlike (Phil. 2:5-7), and it is the life which is Christ (Phil. 1:21). Since these graces are wrought by the Spirit who indwells every believer, this experience is provided for all.

8. *The combined experiences of the Christian life bring a consciousness of salvation through faith in Christ.* Saving faith in Christ is a definite experience. The Apostle Paul related of himself, "I know whom I have believed" (2 Tim. 1:12). A personal reliance upon a Savior is so definite an act of the will and attitude of the mind that one could hardly be deceived regarding it. But it is the purpose of God that the normal Christian be assured in his own heart that he is accepted of God. To the spiritual Christian, the Spirit bears witness that he is a son of God (Rom. 8:16). Similarly, having trusted in Christ, the believer will have no more the *consciousness* of condemnation because of sin (John 3:18; 5:24; Rom. 8:1; Heb. 10:2). This does not imply that the Christian will not be conscious of the sin which he commits; it rather has to do with a consciousness of an eternal acceptance with God through Christ (Eph. 1:6; Col. 2:13), which is the portion of all who believe.

In concluding the enumeration of the essential elements of a true Christian experience, it should again be stated that mere fleshly emotionalism is excluded, and that the experience of the believer will be normal only as he is "walking in the light" (1 John 1:7).

D. Accepting the Veracity of the Promises of the Bible

1. *Confidence that the Bible is true and that its promises of salvation will be certainly fulfilled is essential to assurance of salvation.* Above and beyond all that the believer may experience — which experience is too often indefinite because of carnality — there is given the abiding evidence of the dependable Word of God. In addressing believers the Apostle John states, "These things have I written unto you that believe on the name

of the Son of God; that ye may know that ye have eternal life" (1 John 5:13). By this passage assurance is given to every believer, carnal and spiritual alike, that they may *know* they have eternal life. This assurance is made to rest, not on a changeable experience, but upon the things which are written in the unchangeable Word of God (Ps. 119:89, 160; Matt. 5:18; 24:35; 1 Pet. 1:23, 25).

The written promises of God are like a title deed (John 3:16, 36; 5:24; 6:37; Acts 16:31; Rom. 1:16; 3:22, 26; 10:13), thus challenge confidence. These promises of salvation form the unconditional covenant of God under grace and call for no human merit, nor are they proven to be true through any human experience. These mighty realities are to be reckoned as accomplished on no other ground than the veracity of God.

2. *Doubting whether one has really committed himself to faith in Christ and the promises of God is destructive to the Christian faith.* Multitudes are in no way certain that they ever have had a personal transaction with Christ regarding their own salvation. While it is nonessential that one should know the day and the hour of his decision, it is imperative that he know that he is *now* trusting Christ without reference to the time it began. The apostle states that he is persuaded that God is able to keep (lit., "guard his deposit") that which he had committed unto Him (2 Tim. 1:12).

Obviously the cure for any uncertainty as to one's acceptance of Christ is to receive Christ *now*, reckoning that no self-merit or religious works are of value — Christ alone can save. One lacking assurance that he has actually committed himself by faith to God for the salvation which only God can supply should remedy this lack by taking the definite step of faith. This is an act of the will, although it may be accompanied by emotion and necessarily requires some understanding of the doctrine of salvation. Many have been helped by the simple prayer, "Lord, if I have never put my trust in you before, I do it now." No true assurance of salvation can be experienced unless there is a definite act of receiving Christ by faith as Savior.

3. *Doubting the faithfulness of God is also fatal to any true experience of assurance.* Some lack assurance of their own salvation because they are not sure that God has actually received them and saved them. This state of mind is usually caused by looking for a change in their feelings rather than looking to the faithfulness of Christ. Feelings and experiences have their place; but, as stated before, the final evidence of personal salva-

tion, which is unchanged by these, is the truthfulness of God. What He has said, He will do, and it is not pious or commendable for a person to distrust his salvation after having definitely cast himself upon Christ.

4. *Assurance of salvation, accordingly, depends upon understanding the nature of God's complete salvation for those who put their trust in Christ.* Confirmation may also be found in part in Christian experience, and normally there is some change in life on the part of a person who has trusted Christ as his Savior. It is most essential that he realize that assurance of salvation depends upon the certainty of the promises of God and the certainty that the individual has committed himself by faith to Jesus Christ in keeping with these promises. One who has made this commitment can rely upon the faithfulness of God, who cannot lie to keep His promises and to save the believer by divine power and grace.

Questions

1. How would you distinguish the doctrine of assurance from the doctrine of eternal security?
2. Why is assurance of salvation important?
3. How is assurance related to understanding the meaning of the death of Christ?
4. How is assurance related to knowledge that salvation is a gift?
5. How is assurance related to knowledge that salvation is by grace alone?
6. Is it reasonable to assume that a Christian will know that he is saved?
7. To what extent will a carnal Christian be subject to loss of assurance of his salvation?
8. How does assurance relate to knowledge that God is our Heavenly Father?
9. How does reality in prayer constitute a confirming experience of salvation?
10. Relate the ability to understand Scripture to assurance of salvation.
11. To what extent does a sense of the sinfulness of sin relate to assurance of salvation?
12. How does a love for the unsaved constitute a basis for assurance of salvation?
13. How does love for one's fellow Christian give assurance of salvation?
14. Relate the fruit of the Spirit to assurance of salvation.
15. How does a definite placing of faith in Christ assist in the matter of assurance of salvation?
16. How does accepting the promises of salvation in the Bible relate to assurance of salvation?
17. Is it necessary to know the exact time when a believer trusted in Christ for the first time?
18. Is it important that one know that he is trusting in Christ now as his Savior?
19. If there is lack of assurance of salvation, what should an individual do?
20. How does assurance of salvation relate to confidence in the faithfulness of God?

33

Security of Salvation

While most believers in Christ accept the doctrine that they can have assurance of salvation at any given moment in their experience, the question is often raised, "Can a person once saved become lost again?" Since the fear of losing salvation could seriously affect a believer's peace of mind, and because his future is so vital, this question is a most important aspect of the doctrine of salvation.

The claim that one who is once saved may be lost again is based on certain biblical passages which seem to raise questions concerning the continuance of salvation. In the history of the church, there have been opposing systems of interpretation known as Calvinism, in support of eternal security, and Arminianism, in opposition to eternal security (each named after its foremost apologist, John Calvin or Jacob Arminius).

A. Arminian View of Security

As many as eighty-five passages are listed by those holding the Arminian view as establishing the doctrine of conditional security. Among these, the more important passages are as follows: Matthew 5:13; 6:23; 7:16-19; 13:1-8; 18:23-35; 24:4-5, 11-13, 23-26; 25:1-13; Luke 8:11-15; 11:24-28; Luke 12:42-46; John 6:66-71; 8:31-32, 51; 13:8; 15:1-6; Acts 5:32; 11:21-23; 13:43; 14:21-22; Romans 6:11-23; 8:12-17; 11:20-22; 14:15-23; 1 Corinthians 9:23-27; 10:1-21; 11:29-32; 15:1-2; 2 Corinthians 1:24; 11:2-4; 12:21 — 13:5; Galatians 2:12-16; 3:4 — 4:1; 5:1-4; 6:7-9; Colossians 1:21-23; 2:4-8, 18-19; 1 Thessalonians 3:5; 1 Timothy 1:3-7, 18-20; 2:11-15; 4:1-16; 5:5-15; 6:9-12, 17-21; 2 Timothy 2:11-18, 22-26; 3:13-15; Hebrews 2:1-3; 3:6-19; 4:1-16; 5:8-9; 6:4-20; 10:19-39; 11:13-16; 12:1-17, 25-29; 13:7-17; James 1:12-26; 2:14-26; 4:4-10; 5:19-20; 1 Peter 5:9, 13; 2 Peter 1:5-11; 2:1-22; 3:16-17; 1 John 1:5 — 3:11; 5:4-16; 2 John 6-9; Jude 5-12, 20-21; Revelation 2:7, 10-11, 17-26; 3:4-5, 8-22; 12:11; 17:14; 21:7-8; 22:18-19.

A study of these passages involves a number of important questions.

1. *Probably the most important question facing the interpreter of the Bible on the subject is the question of who is a true believer.* Many who oppose the doctrine of eternal security do so on the ground that it is possible for a person to have intellectual faith without actually being saved. Adherents to eternal security agree that a person can experience a superficial conversion or outward change in his life, may go through the outer motions of accepting Christ such as joining a church or being baptized, and even experience a measure of change in his life pattern, yet still be short of real salvation in Christ.

While it is impossible to lay down binding rules on how to distinguish one who is saved from one who is not saved, obviously in the mind of God there is no question. An individual believer must first of all make sure that he has really received Christ as Savior. It is helpful in this regard to understand that receiving Christ is an act of the will which may involve some knowledge of the way of salvation and may be expressed emotionally to some extent, but the fundamental question is, "Have I really received Jesus Christ by faith as my personal Savior?" Until this question is honestly faced, there can, of course, be no ground for eternal security and no real assurance of salvation. Many who deny eternal security are merely saying that superficial faith is not enough to save. Adherents to eternal security agree on this point. The question properly stated is whether one who is actually saved and has received eternal life can lose that which God has done in saving him from sin.

2. *Many of the passages quoted by those who oppose eternal security deal with human works or the evidence of salvation.* One who is truly saved should manifest his new life in Christ in both his character and his works. However, judging a person by works can be deceiving, as sometimes those who are not Christians can conform relatively to the morality of a Christian life, while those who are genuine Christians sometimes can lapse into carnality and sin where they become indistinguishable from those who are unsaved. All agree that mere moral reformation such as is mentioned in Luke 11:24-26 is not genuine salvation, and reversion back to the former life does not correspond to losing salvation.

Several passages also bear on the important fact that Christian profession is justified by its fruit. Salvation which is of God will, under ordinary conditions, prove itself to be such by its fruit (John 8:31; 15:6; 1 Cor. 15:1-2; Heb. 3:6-14; James 2:14-26; 2 Pet. 1:10; 1 John 3:10). However, not all Christians at all times manifest the fruits of salvation. Accordingly, all passages which deal with the evidences of salvation in works do not necessarily affect the doctrine of the security of the believer, as the question is one of fact, that is, whether God Himself considers a person saved.

3. *Many passages quoted in support of the insecurity of believers are in the form of warnings against superficial belief in Christ.* Jews in the New Testament are warned that since their sacrifices have ceased they must turn to Christ or be lost (Heb. 10:26). In like manner, unsaved Jews as well as Gentiles are warned against "falling away" from the illuminating, converting work of the Spirit (Heb. 6:4-9). Unspiritual Jews are warned that they will not be received into the coming kingdom (Matt. 25:1-13). Gentiles, a group as opposed to Israel as a group, are warned concerning the danger of their losing, through unbelief, their place of blessing which they have in the present age (Rom. 11:21).

4. *Some passages deal with the matter of reward rather than the question of salvation.* One who is saved and safe in Christ may lose his reward (1 Cor. 3:15; Col. 1:21-23) and be disapproved concerning his service for Christ (1 Cor. 9:27).

5. *A genuine Christian may also lose his fellowship with God because of sin (1 John 1:6) and be deprived of some of the present benefits of being saved such as having the fruit of the Spirit (Gal. 5:22-23) and enjoying the satisfaction of effective service for Christ.*

6. *A true believer because of his waywardness may be chastened or disciplined just as a child is disciplined by his father* (John 15:2; 1 Cor. 11:29-32; 1 John 5:16), *and this may be even to the point of taking away his physical life.* This chastening, however, is not an evidence of lack of salvation but, on the contrary, the evidence that he is a child of God who is being dealt with by his heavenly Father.

7. *According to Scripture, it is also possible for a believer to be "fallen from grace"* (Gal. 5:1-4). This properly interpreted does not refer to a Christian's losing salvation, but rather falling from a standard of grace in his life and losing the true liberty which he has in Christ by returning to the bondage of legalism. His fall is from a standard of life, not from a work of salvation.

8. *Much of the difficulty relates to passages which are cited out of context, especially passages that relate to another dispensation.* The Old Testament does not give a clear view of eternal security, although it may be assumed on the basis of New Testament teaching that an Old Testament saint who was truly born again was just as safe as a believer in the present age. However, passages which relate to a past or future dispensation must be interpreted in their context, such as Ezekiel 33:7-8; and major passages such as Deuteronomy 28 dealing with the blessings and curses on Israel for obedience or disobedience to the law. Other passages refer to false and unregenerate teachers of the last days (1 Tim. 4:1-2; 2 Pet. 2:1-22; Jude 17-19), which are people who, although having a Christian profession, have never really been saved.

9. *A number of passages offered in support of insecurity are simply misinterpreted, like Matthew 24:13:* "He that shall endure unto the end, the same shall be saved." This refers not to salvation from the guilt or power of sin but deliverance from enemies and persecution. The verse refers to those who survive the Tribulation and are rescued by Jesus Christ at His second coming. Scripture clearly teaches that many true believers will die as martyrs before Christ's second coming and do not endure, or survive, until Christ returns (Rev. 7:14). This passage illustrates how verses may be misapplied to the question of security or insecurity.

10. *The ultimate answer to the insecurity or security of the believer rests on the question of who does the work of salvation.* The concept that a believer who is once truly saved is always saved is based on the principle that salvation is the work of God not resting on any merit in the believer and not sustained

by any effort of the believer. If man does the saving, it is insecure. If it is a work of God, it is secure.

The solid scriptural basis for believing that a person once saved is always saved is supported by at least twelve important arguments. Four of these works relate to the Father, four to the Son, and four to the Holy Spirit.

B. The Work of the Father in Salvation

1. *Scripture reveals the sovereign promise of God which is unconditional and which promises eternal salvation to everyone who believes in Christ* (John 3:16; 5:24; 6:37). Obviously what God promises He is able to do, and His unchangeable will is revealed in Romans 8:29-30.

2. *The infinite power of God is able to save and keep eternally* (John 10:29; Rom. 4:21; 8:31, 38-39; 14:4; Eph. 1:19-21; 3:20; Phil. 3:21; 2 Tim. 1:12; Heb. 7:25; Jude 24). God clearly not only has the fidelity to fulfil His promise but the power to accomplish anything He wills to do. Scripture reveals that He wills the salvation of those who believe in Christ.

3. *The infinite love of God not only accounts for God's eternal purpose but assures that His purpose will be fulfilled* (John 3:16; Rom. 5:7-10; Eph. 1:4). In Romans 5:8-11 the love of God for those who are saved is said to be greater than His love for those who are unsaved, and this assures their eternal security. The argument is simple: if He loved men enough to give His Son to die for them when they were "sinners" and "enemies," He will love them "much more" when through redeeming grace they are justified in His sight and reconciled to Him.

The surpassing love of God for those whom He has redeemed at such infinite cost is sufficient assurance that He will never allow them to be plucked out of His hand until every resource of His infinite power has been exhausted (John 10:28-29); and, of course, the infinite power of God can never be exhausted. The promise of the Father, the infinite power of the Father, and the infinite love of the Father make it impossible for one who has once committed himself to God the Father by faith in Jesus Christ ever to lose the salvation which God has wrought in his life.

4. *The righteousness of God also assures the eternal security of those who have trusted in Christ because the demands of*

God's righteousness have been completely met by the death of Christ in that He died for the sins of the whole world (1 John 2:2). God in forgiving sin and promising eternal salvation is acting on perfectly righteous grounds. God in saving the sinner is not doing so on the ground of leniency and is perfectly righteous in forgiving sin, not only for those in the Old Testament who lived before the cross of Christ but for all who live after the cross of Christ (Rom. 3:25-26). Accordingly, the eternal security of the believer cannot be challenged without challenging the righteousness of God. Thus His faithfulness to His promises, His infinite power, His infinite love, and His infinite righteousness combine to give the believer absolute security in his salvation.

C. The Work of the Son

1. *The substitutionary death of Jesus Christ on the cross is the absolute guarantee of the believer's security.* The death of Christ is the sufficient answer to the condemning power of sin (Rom. 8:34). When it is claimed that the saved one might be lost again, that claim is usually based on the fact of possible sin. Such an assumption of necessity proceeds on the supposition that Christ has not borne *all* the sins the believer will ever commit, and that God, having saved a soul, might be disappointed and surprised by unexpected, subsequent sin. On the contrary, the omniscience of God is perfect. He foreknows every sin or secret thought that will ever darken the life of His child, and for those sins the sufficient, sacrificial blood of Christ has been shed and by that blood God has been propitiated (1 John 2:2).

Because of that blood which avails for the sins of both saved and unsaved, God is as free to *continue* His saving grace toward the meritless as He is to save them at all. He keeps them forever; not for their sakes alone, but to satisfy His own love and manifest His own grace (Rom. 5:8; Eph. 2:7-10). It is because of the fact that salvation and safekeeping depend only on the sacrifice and merit of the Son of God that all condemnation is forever removed (John 3:18; 5:24; Rom. 8:1; 1 Cor. 11:31-32).

2. *The resurrection of Christ as God's seal upon the death of Christ secures the resurrection and the life for the believers* (John 3:16; 10:28; Eph. 2:6). Two vital facts connected with the resurrection of Christ make the eternal security of the be-

liever sure. The gift of God is eternal life (Rom. 6:23), and this life is the resurrection life of Christ (Col. 2:12; 3:1). This life is eternal as Christ is eternal and is just as incapable of dissolution or destruction as Christ is incapable of dissolution or destruction. In the resurrection of Christ through baptism of the Spirit and receiving eternal life, a child of God is also made a part of the new creation. As a sovereign object of God's creative work, the creature cannot reverse the creation process, and because he is in Christ as the Last Adam he cannot fall because Christ could not fall. While failures in the Christian life and experience are all too evident, these do not affect the position of the believer in Christ which is holy because of the grace of God and the death and resurrection of Christ.

3. *The work of Christ as our advocate in heaven also assures our eternal security* (Rom. 8:34; Heb. 9:24; 1 John 2:1). In His work as the advocate or legal representative of the believer, Christ pleads the sufficiency of His work on the cross as a basis both for propitiation, or satisfaction of all God's demands on the sinner, and as affecting reconciliation, or the reconciliation of the sinner to God through Christ. Since the work of Christ is perfect, the true believer can rest in the security of the perfection of the work of Christ presented as it is by Jesus Christ as the believer's representative in heaven.

4. *The Work of Christ as our intercessor supplements and confirms His work as our advocate* (John 17:1-26; Rom. 8:34; Heb. 7:23-25). The present ministry of Christ in glory has to do with the eternal security of those on earth who are saved. Christ both intercedes and serves as our advocate. As intercessor, He has in view the weakness, ignorance, and immaturity of the believer — things concerning which there is no guilt. In this ministry Christ not only prays for His own who are in the world and at every point of their need (Luke 22:31-32; John 17:9, 15, 20; Rom. 8:34), but on the grounds of His own sufficiency in His unchanging priesthood, He guarantees that they will be kept saved forever (John 14:19; Rom. 5:10; Heb. 7:25).

Taken as a whole, the work of Christ in His death, resurrection, advocacy, and intercession provides absolute security for the one who is thus represented by Christ both on the cross and in heaven. If salvation is a work of God for man rather than a work of man for God, its outcome is certain and sure and the promise of John 5:24 that the believer "shall not come into condemnation" will certainly be fulfilled.

D. The Work of the Holy Spirit

1. *The work of regeneration or new birth in which the believer partakes of the divine nature is an irreversible process and the work of God* (John 1:13; 3:3-6; Titus 3:4-6; 1 Pet. 1:23; 2 Pet. 1:4; 1 John 3:9). Just as there is no reversal of the creation process, there can be no reversing of the new birth process. If this is accomplished by God and not by man and is entirely on the principle of grace, there is no just ground or reason why it should not continue forever.

2. *The indwelling presence of the Spirit in the present age is a permanent possession of the believer* (John 7:37-39; Rom. 5:5; 8:9; 1 Cor. 2:12; 6:19; 1 John 2:27). In ages preceding the day of Pentecost not all true believers were indwelt by the Spirit even though they were secure in their salvation; yet in the present age the fact that the body of a believer, even though sinful and corrupt, is the temple of God is another confirming evidence of the unswerving purpose of God to finish what He has begun in saving the believer. While the Spirit may be grieved by unconfessed sin (Eph. 4:30) and may be quenched in the sense that He is resisted (1 Thess. 5:19), it is never intimated that these acts cause a Christian to lose his salvation. It is rather that the very fact of his salvation and the continued presence of the Holy Spirit in his heart is made the grounds for an appeal to return to a walk and fellowship in conformity to the will of God.

3. *The work of the Spirit in baptism by which the believer is joined to Christ and to the body of Christ eternally is another evidence for security.* By the Spirit's ministry in baptizing, the believer is joined to that body of which Christ is the Head (1 Cor. 6:17; 12:13; Gal. 3:27) and he is therefore said to be *in Christ.* To be *in Christ* constitutes a union which is both vital and abiding. In that union, old things — as to position and relationship which might be the ground of condemnation — are passed away, and all positions and relationships have become new and are of God (2 Cor. 5:17, 18). Being accepted for ever "in the beloved," the child of God is as secure as the One in whom he is and in whom he stands.

4. *The presence of the Holy Spirit in the believer is said to be the seal of God which will endure until the day of redemption, the day of the translation or resurrection of the believer* (2 Cor. 1:22; Eph. 1:13-14; 4:30). Since this sealing of the Holy Spirit is a work of God and signifies the safety and security of

the one thus sealed until God completes His purpose to present the believer faultless in heaven, it is another evidence that a believer once saved is always saved.

Taken as a whole, the eternal security of the believer rests upon the nature of salvation. It is a work of God, not a work of man. It rests on the power and faithfulness of God not on strength or faithfulness of man. If salvation were by works or if salvation were a reward for faith as a good work, it is understandable how a man's security might be in question. Because it rests instead upon grace and the promises and works of God, the believer can be assured of his security and, with Paul, "confident of this very thing, that he which hath begun a good work in you will perform it until the day of Jesus Christ" (Phil. 1:6).

It may be concluded, then, from this extensive body of truth that the eternal purpose of God which is for the preservation of His own can never be defeated. To this end He has met every possible hindrance. Sin which might otherwise separate has been borne by a Substitute who, in order that the believer may be kept, pleads the efficacy of His death before the throne of God. The believer's will is held under divine control (Phil. 2:13), and every testing is tempered by the infinite grace and wisdom of God (1 Cor. 10:13).

It cannot be too strongly emphasized that while in this chapter salvation and safekeeping have been treated as separate divine undertakings as an adaptation to the usual ways of speaking, the Bible recognizes no such distinction. According to Scripture, there is no salvation purposed, offered, or undertaken under grace which is not infinitely perfect and that does not abide forever.

Questions

1. Why is the matter of eternal security important to a believer?
2. What are the opposing positions of Calvinism and Arminianism on the matter of eternal security?
3. Approximately how many passages are listed by Arminians as teaching the doctrine of conditional security?
4. In approaching these many passages, what is the most important question?
5. On what can all parties agree on the matter of security?
6. Is there any question in the mind of God as to who is saved?
7. Is it true that superficial faith is not enough to save?

8. How do you evaluate the many passages quoted in opposition to eternal security which deal with human works as an evidence of salvation?
9. Are warnings against superficial belief in Christ to be regarded as warnings of the possibility of losing salvation?
10. Is it possible for a Christian to lose his reward in heaven and still be saved?
11. Is it possible for a genuine Christian to lose fellowship with God and still be saved?
12 Is it possible for a true believer to be chastened or disciplined and still be saved?
13. How do you explain the expression "fallen from grace" as relating to a Christian's salvation?
14. Why is there difficulty in passages from the Old Testament on the matter of eternal security?
15. How do you explain Matthew 24:13?
16. Why does insecurity or security depend on the question of who does the work of salvation?
17. What four works of the Father in salvation support eternal security?
18. Why do the works of God the Father in themselves assure eternal security?
19. What four works of the Son of God support the doctrine of eternal security?
20. How is the death of Christ related to eternal security?
21. How is the resurrection of Christ related to eternal security?
22. How are the works of Christ as our advocate and intercessor related to eternal security?
23. What are the four works of the Holy Spirit related to eternal security?
24. Is the new birth a reversible process?
25. Is there any record of anyone being born again more than once?
26. How does the permanent indwelling presence of the Spirit relate to eternal security?
27. Can a believer in the present age lose the Spirit?
28. What is accomplished by the work of the Spirit in baptism relating to security?
29. How is the promise of the Holy Spirit as a seal unto the day of redemption a promise of security?
30. Summarize the reasons why eternal security rests upon the nature of salvation as a work of God.
31. How does the nature of salvation include the aspect of a believer's safekeeping?

34

Divine Election

A. Election Defined

Scripture reveals God as an absolute sovereign who by His own will has chosen to create the universe and to direct its history according to a foreordained plan. That God should be sovereign and should be able to execute such programs as He may be pleased to determine is in keeping with the concept of an infinite, omnipotent God. Human comprehension of such a program, however, presents innumerable problems and, in particular, how man can operate freely and responsibly in a programed universe.

Systems of human thought have tended to go either to one extreme where God's sovereign purpose is made absolute or to another extreme of magnifying the freedom of man until God is no longer in control. In attempting to resolve such a difficult problem, the only solution is to appeal to divine revelation and attempt to interpret human experience on the basis of what the Bible teaches.

In Scripture, God's sovereign purpose extends to individuals as well to nations. Israel is referred to an an elect nation (Isa.

45:4; 65:9, 22). The term "elect" is frequently applied to individuals who are chosen to salvation (Matt. 24:22, 24, 31; Mark 13:20, 22, 27; Luke 18:7; Rom. 8:33; Col. 3:12; 1 Tim. 5:21; 2 Tim. 2:10; Titus 1:1; 1 Pet. 1:2; 5:13; 2 John 1, 13). The same expression is used of Christ (Isa. 42:1; 1 Pet. 2:6). In addition to the word "elect," the fact of election is also mentioned (Rom. 9:11; 11:5, 7, 28; 1 Thess. 1:4; 2 Pet. 1:10). The thought in election is that the one or group mentioned is chosen for a divine purpose, usually related to salvation.

A synonym for the word "election" is the word "chosen." It is applied to Israel (Isa. 44:1), to the church (Eph. 1:4; 2 Thess. 2:13; 1 Pet. 2:9), and also to the apostles (John 6:70; 13:18; Acts 1:2).

A number of expressions are related to the concept of election or being chosen, such as foreordination (1 Pet. 1:20) and predestination (Rom. 8:29, 30; Eph. 1:5, 11). The thought is to determine beforehand, as in Acts 4:28, or to ordain beforehand, as in Jude 4 and Ephesians 2:10. Also, there is frequent reference to this concept in the Bible, where the word "determine" is used, as in 2 Chronicles 25:16; Isaiah 19:17; Luke 22:22; Acts 17:26. The thought in all of these terms is that God's choice precedes the act and is determined by His sovereign will.

Election, foreordination, and predestination are according to God's divine purpose (Eph. 1:9; 3:11), and are also related in Scripture to God's foreknowledge (Acts 2:23; Rom. 8:29; 11:2; 1 Pet. 1:2). Still another term used is the word "call," as in Romans 8:30 and many other passages (1 Cor. 1:9; 7:18, 20, 21, 22, 24; 15:9; Gal. 5:13; Eph. 4:1, 4; Col. 3:15; 1 Tim. 6:12; Heb. 5:4; 9:15; 1 Pet. 2:21; 3:9; 1 John 3:1). In John 12:32 our Lord referred to calling as a drawing of men to God (cf. John 6:44). All of these passages imply that a sovereign God is carrying out His purpose; in His purpose certain individuals are chosen to salvation, and certain nations, especially Israel, are chosen to fulfill a special divine purpose.

B. The Fact of Divine Election

Although the doctrine of election is beyond human comprehension, it is clearly a doctrine of Scripture. By divine election God has chosen certain individuals to salvation and predestined them to be conformed to the character of His Son Jesus Christ (Rom. 16:13; Eph. 1:4-5; 2 Thess. 2:13; 1 Pet. 1:2). It is clear that the choice originates in God and that this choice is part of God's eternal plan.

Divine election is not an act of God in time, but rather a part of His eternal purpose. This is brought out in numerous passages such as Ephesians 1:4 which states, "According as he hath chosen us in Him before the foundation of the world, that we should be holy and without blame before Him in love." According to 2 Timothy 1:9 our election is "according to his own purpose and grace, which was given us in Christ Jesus before the world began." Because God's plan is eternal, election as an essential part of it must also be eternal.

One of the knotty problems in the doctrine of election is the relationship of election to foreknowledge. One form of interpretation which tends to soften the concept of election builds on the idea that God foreknew those who would receive Christ, and on the basis of this foreknowledge elected them to salvation. This concept, however, has inherent problems as it seems to make God subject to a plan in which He is not sovereign. While election and foreknowledge are coextensive, foreknowledge in itself would not be determinative.

Although theologians have wrestled with these problems and often have failed to come up with satisfactory conclusions, one possible solution is to recognize to begin with that God is omniscient, that is, He had knowledge of all possible plans for the universe. Out of all the possible plans with their infinite number of variations, God chose a plan. Having chosen a plan and knowing all its details, God could then foreknow those who would be saved or elected and also all the facts that relate to their salvation.

The immediate problem that faces the interpreter, however, is that of human freedom. It seems evident from experience as well as from Scripture that man has choices. How can one avoid a fatalistic system where everything is predetermined and no moral choices are left? Is human responsibility just a mockery or is it real? These are the problems which face the interpreter of Scripture on this difficult doctrine.

While theologians have never been able to resolve completely the problem of divine election as related to human choices and moral responsibility on the part of man, the answer seems to be that in choosing a plan God chose the plan as a whole, not piecemeal. He knew in advance, before the choice of a plan, who in this plan would be saved and who would not be saved. By faith we must assume that God chose the best possible plan, and that if a better plan could have been put into operation God would have chosen it. The plan included much that God would do Himself, such as creation and the establishment of natural law. It included what God sovereignly chose to do Himself, such as to reveal Himself through the prophets and influence men in their choices even though they still are responsible for the choices they make.

In other words, the plan included giving man some freedom of choice for which he would be held responsible. The fact that God knew under each plan what each man would do does not mean that God forced man to do something against his will and then punish him for it.

In the notable instance of the crucifixion of Christ, on which the whole plan of God hinged, Pilate freely made a choice to crucify Christ and was held responsible for it. Judas Iscariot freely determined to betray Christ and was held responsible for it. Yet the choices of both Pilate and Judas were essentially God's program and were sure long before they made them.

Accordingly, while there are problems in human comprehension, the best solution is to accept what the Bible teaches whether or not we can understand it completely. Sometimes better translations are helpful, as in 1 Peter 1:1-2 where in the Authorized Version it is declared that Christians are "elect according to the foreknowledge of God the Father" which makes election subject to the foreknowledge of God. The word "elect," however, properly belongs to the word "strangers" in verse 1 and teaches not the logical order of election in relation to foreknowledge but the fact that they are coextensive.

Some help can be found in the fact that the whole process of the divine purpose, election, and foreknowledge are all eternal. All man can do is attempt to set up a logical relationship, but all of these were always true in the mind of God, and God did not arrive at His decisions after long pondering the difficulties of each plan. In other words, there never was another plan, and thus all aspects of the eternal purpose of God are equally timeless.

It must be concluded, then, that election and its kindred terms are clearly taught in the Bible, that it involves some being chosen to salvation with others being nonelect or passed by. Election is eternal and not an act of God in time. In election God does not adjust to foreknowledge, although election may be seen to proceed from omniscience of God. While there are serious problems in human comprehension of this doctrine, one should submit to divine revelation even if he cannot completely understand it.

C. Defense of the Doctrine of Election

Although some theologians have attempted to explain away the doctrine of election and to resolve the problem, in effect, by denying what the Scriptures teach, the arguments against divine election are usually based upon misunderstanding. As often stated, election is represented as asserting that God is arbitrary. This, of course, arises from unbelief. God is sovereign, but His sovereignty is always wise, holy, good and loving.

Another objection is often raised that this makes God unjust, as some are not included in His purpose of salvation. Here it should be observed that God is not obligated to save any and those whom He does save will to believe. While the working of God in the actual salvation of an individual is inscrutable — as there is obviously an act of divine grace when a person believes in Christ and is saved — the Bible clearly commands man to believe (Acts 16:31). No one is saved against his will, and no one disbelieves against his will.

A very common objection to this doctrine is that it discourages missionary effort to bring the Gospel to the lost and discourages those who desire to be saved. The answer, of course, is that God has included in His plan that the Gospel should be preached to every creature, and God desires the salvation of all (2 Pet. 3:9). However, in setting up a moral universe in which men have a choice to believe or not to believe, it is inevitable that some will not be saved.

Still another objection is that if some are elected to salvation and others are elected to not being saved, they are hopeless in their lost estate. Scripture clearly emphasizes that some are elected to salvation, and the unsaved are destined for their lot, not because men who desired salvation were unable to secure it, but always on the ground that those who are unsaved chose to be unsaved. Gods' mercy is shown in His longsuffering, as in Romans 9:21-22 and 2 Peter 3:9. No one will ever be able to stand before God and say, "I wanted to be saved but was unable to do so because I was not elected."

While the greatest of scholars as well as ordinary students of Scripture will continue to struggle with this difficult doctrine, the fact of divine election is clearly presented in the

Bible, and those who are saved, though they were unconscious of the doctrine at the time they accepted Christ, can glory in the fact that they were in God's plan from eternity past and that their salvation is a supreme illustration of the grace of God. A God who is sovereign and eternal would logically have a planned program. On the basis of scriptural revelation, a believer in Christ can only conclude that God's plan is holy, wise and good, that God is a longsuffering God, and that He is concerned over the lost estate of those who refuse the salvation for which Christ died.

Questions

1. Why is it reasonable to assume God has a sovereign plan for the universe?
2. To what two extremes have human thought tended to go in regard to God's sovereign purpose?
3. How can it be demonstrated that God's sovereign purpose extends both to individuals and to nations as well as to other groups?
4. What are the various terms used to express the idea of election?
5. What is the central idea of all the terms used relating to election?
6. What is accomplished by divine election?
7. What evidence supports the idea that divine election was from eternity past?
8. How is election related to foreknowledge?
9. How can the problem of the relationship between human freedom and divine election be solved?
10. Explain how in the plan of God human freedom is included.
11. Explain how the crucifixion of Christ is an outstanding illustration of both freedom and the eternal plan of God.
12. Why should an individual accept the doctrine of election even if he does not understand it?
13. How can the objections to election which allege that God is arbitrary and unjust be answered?
14. How would you answer the objections that the doctrine of election discourages missionary effort?
15. Why was it necessary in the plan of God for some to be unsaved?
16. Does the doctrine of election give unsaved people an excuse for being unsaved?
17. Is there evidence that God's plan is holy, wise and good, and that God is longsuffering and is actually concerned over the lost estate of those who refuse salvation?

35

The Church: Her Members

A. The Church as the Present Purpose of God

The church in the New Testament is revealed to be the central purpose of God in the present age. In contrast with God's purposes for individuals and nations of the Old Testament and a larger purpose for the nation of Israel, the church is revealed to be the company of believers formed of both Jew and Gentile who are called out of the world and joined together in one living union by the baptism of the Spirit.

In general, the concept of the church falls into two major categories. The principle emphasis in the New Testament is on the church as an organism, a living union of all true believers in Christ. This is the distinctive truth that is presented beginning with the day of Pentecost, with the advent of the Spirit, and concluding with the coming of Christ for His church, in which the church will be caught up out of the world and taken to heaven.

Another concept, however, is that of the local church or the organized church. This is a company of professing believers in any one locality or a group of such local assemblies (1 Cor. 1:2; Gal. 1:2; Phil. 1:1).

The word "church" is a translation of a Greek word "ekklesia" and is frequently used of any assembly or congregation of people whether gathered for religious or for political purposes. The word actually means "called out ones." In early Greece, cities were often ruled by pure democracy in which every citizen in the town would gather together to act upon matters of mutual interest. As they would be called out from their ordinary occupations to an assembly where they could vote, the word came to mean the result of being called out, or those who were thus assembled.

This word is found frequently in the Septuagint, a Greek translation of the Old Testament, to denote various assemblies in the Old Testament. It is used in a similar sense in such passages as Acts 7:38 and Acts 19:32, where the word is used simply of a crowd that had gathered. When used of the church as the body of Christ, however, it becomes a technical word referring to those called out of the world and joined together with a living union in Christ. This concept is not found in the Old Testament even though Israel sometimes was gathered together for religious purposes. The term when used of the saved applies specifically to the company of those who are saved in the present age whether on earth or in heaven.

B. The Church: A New Testament Revelation

Because the concept of a church formed of Jews and Gentiles alike — all of whom are saved and joined together by eternal life — is not found in the Old Testament, only the New Testament gives the divine revelation on this important subject. In the plan of God it was necessary for Christ to come first, to die on the cross, to be raised from the dead, and to ascend into heaven. With the advent of the Spirit on the day of Pentecost, however, it was possible for God to fulfill His purpose of having a special company of believers disregarding the distinction between Israel and the Gentiles and having their own place in the eternal purpose of God.

According to Acts 2, as confirmed by the experience of Cornelius in Acts 10, believers in Christ were baptized by the Spirit (1 Cor. 12:13) and became members one of another with the advent of the Holy Spirit. From Pentecost on, as each believer became saved he became a member of the body of Christ, as was previously discussed in the doctrine of the baptism of the Spirit. Once the church is complete and caught up in the Rapture into heaven, the divine purpose will return to the normal distinction between Jew and Gentiles who are saved in the period of trial following the Rapture and also in the millennial kingdom.

C. The Jew, the Gentile, and the Church of God

In the present age, the Bible recognizes three major divisions of the human family — the Jew, the Gentile, and the church of God (1 Cor. 10:32). Observing these distinctions are most important to understanding God's present purpose.

1. *The Jews, or the children of Israel, are that nation which sprang from Abraham in the line of Isaac and Jacob, and who, according to divine purpose and promise, are the chosen earthly people of God.* This nation has been miraculously preserved to the present time and, according to prophecy, will yet be the dominant, glorified people of the earth in the coming kingdom age (Isa. 62:1-12).

The eternal promises of Jehovah to this people cannot be altered. These promises include a national entity (Jer. 31:36), a land (Gen. 13:15), a throne (2 Sam. 7:13), a king (Jer. 33:20-21), and a kingdom (2 Sam. 7:16). In the faithfulness of God, their promises, which are primarily earthly in character, have been fulfilled to the present hour and will be fulfilled to all eternity; for each of these covenants is said to be everlasting in duration.

Four words describe the out-working of the divine purpose in this people — "chosen," "scattered," "gathered," "blessed." It is obvious that they were chosen and are now scattered among all the nations of the earth. They will yet be gathered and blessed. The peculiar ministry of this people is stated in Romans 9:4-5 (cf. Gen. 12:3).

2. *The Gentiles are that vast unnumbered company, excluding the Israelites, who have lived on the earth from Adam until now.* Apart from certain individuals, there is no record that during the period from Adam to Christ God sustained any special relation or extended any immediate promises to them.

However, the prophecies of the Old Testament predict great earthly blessings to come upon the Gentiles in the yet future kingdom on the earth, and in the present age they partake alike with the Jews in the privileges of the Gospel.

3. *The church of God refers, not to the membership of organized churches, but to the whole company of the redeemed who will have been saved in the present age.* They are a distinct people because (a) all individuals in that company being born again enter the kingdom of God (John 3:5) and are destined to be conformed to the image of Christ (Rom. 8:29); (b) they are no longer in Adam partaking of the ruin of the old creation (2 Cor. 5:17), but are in Christ partaking in the new creation of all that Christ is in His resurrection life and glory (Eph. 1:3; Col. 2:10); (c) in the sight of God, their nationality is changed, for they have come upon new ground where there is neither Jew or Gentile, but Christ is all in all (Col. 3:11); (d) they are now citizens of heaven (Phil. 3:20; Col. 3:3), and all their promises, their possessions, and their position are heavenly (2 Cor. 5:17-18). By so much this heavenly people are distinguished from all other people of the earth.

D. The Church Formed From Both Jews and Gentiles

The respective earthly positions of the Jews and the Gentiles have already been pointed out. To this it should be added that God, during the present age and for the purposes of grace, has placed both Jews and Gentiles upon a common ground (Rom. 3:9). They are now said to be "under sin," which means that they are now shut up to salvation by grace alone.

At the death of Christ the change in the divine program from the recognition of a favored nation to an appeal to individuals, Jews and Gentiles alike, was most difficult for the Jew to understand. He did not understand that his covenants were set aside for a time, but not abrogated. The nation's struggles with this problem are recorded in the Book of Acts.

The Jew is unadjusted to this age-program to the present time, and it is predicted of him that he will remain blinded in part until the church is called out (Rom. 11:25), after which the Deliverer will come out of Zion and will turn away ungodliness from Jacob. This, it is stated, is God's covenant with them

when He will take away their sins (Rom. 11:26-27). Nevertheless, through the preaching of the Gospel both Jews and Gentiles are now being saved and the church is being completed.
The apostle directed that the Gospel should first be preached
to the Jew (Rom. 1:16), and his own ministry was ordered according to this program (Acts 17:1-3).

As has been suggested, two revelations were given to the
Apostle Paul: one, of the gospel of the grace of God — probably
while in Arabia at the beginning of his ministry (Gal. 1:11-12);
and the other, of the church which is the body of Christ — probably while in prison (Eph. 3:3-6). The vital feature of the
second revelation is that out of the two sources — Jews and
Gentiles — God is now forming one new body (Eph. 2:15). This
was a mystery, or hitherto unrevealed divine secret. That God
had purposes for Israel, or for the Gentiles, was no secret since
it is the theme of Old Testament prophecy; but the secret "hid
in God" was the making of a new heavenly order of beings
from both Jews and Gentiles.

E. Church Membership

The answer to the question, "Could a person be saved and not
be a church member?" depends upon the meaning which is
given the word "church." It is obviously true that a person may
be a Christian and not be a member of a local organized church.
In fact, all should be saved before they join a church; and, if
saved, it is normal for the individual to choose the fellowship of
the people of God in one form or another.

On the other hand, it is impossible to be saved and not be a
member of the church which is Christ's own body; for a part
of the divine work in salvation is the uniting of the saved one
to Christ by baptism with the Holy Spirit (1 Cor. 12:13). As
used in connection with the work of the Spirit, "baptize" is a
word of discriminating meaning which reaches far beyond the
limits of the outward ordinance of water baptism and represents that ministry of the Spirit for the believer which is more
far-reaching in its effects than any other divine undertaking
in salvation. It is not surprising that Satan has undertaken to
distort the plain meaning of the baptism with the Spirit and
the divine ministry it represents; for only on the ground of this
ministry can we understand the riches of divine grace or enter
into the celestial joy, with its impulse to a holy life, which these
riches impart.

On the earth, the church is seen to be a pilgrim band of witnesses. They are not of this world even as Christ is not of this world (John 17:16), and as the Father has sent the Son into the world, so has the Son sent these witnesses into the world. As to what they really are through riches of grace, "it doth not yet appear" (see Col. 3:4; 1 John 3:2). Being the heavenly people in contrast with Israel the earthly people, the church — glorified in the realization of her divine purpose — is seen in heaven where she appears as the bride of the Lamb, co-reigning with the King, and partaker forever in the glory of the eternal Son of God.

Questions

1. How does the purpose of God for the church contrast with the purposes of God for individuals and nations in the Old Testament?
2. What are the two major categories of the concept of the church?
3. What is the original meaning of the word "church"?
4. How is the word "church" used in the Old Testament, and how does this differ from its use in regard to the church which is the body of Christ?
5. What was necessary in the plan of God before the advent of the Spirit on the day of Pentecost?
6. How does the baptism of the Holy Spirit relate to the church?
7. Name the three major divisions of the human family in the present age, and define each.
8. What are some of the eternal promises which God has given to Israel?
9. What promises has God given the Gentiles?
10. In what sense is the church a distinct company of people?
11. On what common ground has God placed Jew and Gentile in the present age?
12. What has happened to Israel's covenants during the present age?
13. How is Israel characterized according to Romans 11:25 during the present age?
14. What will happen to Israel after the rapture of the church?
15. Name and define the two major revelations given to the Apostle Paul.
16. How does the salvation of an individual relate to his being a member of a church?
17. Is it possible to be saved and not a member of the church as the body of Christ?
18. What is the destiny of the church after the present age?

36

The Church:
Her Purpose and Commission

By means of the church in the present age, God is now making known His wisdom and manifesting His grace to the angelic host (Eph. 3:10). In heaven the church will eternally be the illustration of what the grace of God can do (Eph. 2:7). Strictly speaking, however, the divine commission of the church is given to individual believers rather than to the corporate body. Christ as the Head of the church is able to direct each believer in the paths of the Lord's will in keeping with His personal gifts and the plan of God for the individual life. All of this, however, is in harmony with God's general purpose for the church in the present age. In the church corporately, God is fulfilling a present divine purpose which is unfolding exactly as prophesied in the Scriptures.

A. *The Present Divine Purpose in the World*

The present divine purpose of this age is not the conversion of the world, but rather the calling out from the world those who will believe in Christ to form the body of Christ which is the church. It is true that the world will be converted, and there is yet to be a kingdom of righteousness in the earth; but according to the Bible, that day of a transformed earth, far from being the result of Christian service, is said to follow rather than precede the return of Christ, and is said to be made possible only by His personal presence and immediate power.

It is *after* the smiting of the Stone — a symbol of the return of Christ — that the God of heaven sets up an everlasting kingdom in the earth (Dan. 2:44-45). It is *after* the Lord returns and sits on the throne of His glory that He directs the sheep on His right hand to enter the earthly kingdom prepared for them (Matt. 25:31-34). In like manner, it is *after* He is seen descending from heaven that Christ reigns a thousand years on the earth (Rev. 19:11 — 20:9; cf. Acts 15:13-19; 1 Cor. 15:20-25).

When anticipating the peculiar features of this age (Matt. 13:1-50), the Lord made mention of three major characteristics: (1) Israel's place in the world would be as a treasure hid in the field (Matt. 13:44); (2) evil would continue to the end of the age (Matt. 13:4, 25, 33, 48); and (3) the children of the kingdom — who are likened to wheat, to a pearl of great cost, and to good fish — shall be gathered out (Matt. 13:30, 45, 46, 48).

Of these three characteristics of the age, it is disclosed that the last, or the gathering out of the children of the kingdom, constitutes the supreme purpose of God in this age. In accordance with this, it is stated in Romans 11:25 that Israel's present blindness is only "until" the completion of the church (note Eph. 1:22-23), the end of the age of special Gentile blessing.

Likewise, the mystery of iniquity," or evil in the present age, is declared to continue, though restrained, until the Restrainer — the Spirit of God — is taken out of the way (2 Thess. 2:7). As the Spirit will depart only when He has completed the calling out of the church, the immediate purpose of God is not the correction of the evil in the world, but the out-calling of all who will believe. Israel's covenants will yet be fulfilled (Rom. 11:27), and evil will be banished from the earth (Rev. 21:1); but the present purpose of God, for which all else evidently awaits, is the completion of the church.

In Acts 15:13-19 the substance of James's address at the conclusion of the first council of the church in Jerusalem is given. The occasion of this council was to determine this same question as to the present purpose of God. The early church comprised largely Jews, and these were confused with regard to their own national position in the light of the fact that the new gospel was flowing out to Gentiles. James states that, according to Peter's experience in the house of Cornelius the Gentile, God is first visiting Gentiles to take out of them a people for His name. "After this," James continues, the Lord will return and then will fulfill all His purposes for Israel and the Gentiles.

The practical bearing of all this upon the subject of this study is that, in the present age, never is the individual believer (much less the church) appointed of God to a world-improvement program; but the believer is called to be a witness in all the world to Christ and His saving grace, and through this ministry of gospel preaching the Spirit of God will accomplish the supreme divine purpose in the age.

B. The Formation of the Church

Christ prophesied that He would *build* His church (Matt. 16:18), and the Apostle Paul likened the church to a structure of living stones growing "unto an holy temple in the Lord" and "builded together for an habitation of God through the Spirit" (Eph. 2:21-22). Likewise, the believer's ministry of soul-winning and edification of the body of Christ continues, not forever, but "till we all come in the unity of the faith, and of the knowledge of the Son of God, unto a perfect man, unto the measure of the stature of the fulness of Christ" (Eph. 4:13). The "stature of the fulness of Christ" does not refer to the development of Christlike men, but rather to the development of the body of Christ to its completion (Eph. 1:22-23). The same aspect of truth is restated in Ephesians 4:16, where the members of the body, like living cells in the human body, are represented as being unceasingly active in soul-winning and are thereby making "increase of the body."

C. The Believer's Commission

Christ gave a prediction that the seed-sowing which is to characterize the present age would result in but a fourth portion becoming "wheat" (Matt. 13:1-23). Nevertheless, though the preaching of the gospel relates to death as well as to life (2 Cor. 2:16), the child of God is commissioned to be instant in season and out of season in his efforts to win the lost. He is appointed to go into all the world and preach the Gospel to every creature (Mark 16:15), knowing that faith cometh by hearing, and hearing by the Word of God (Rom. 10:17). It is also stated in 2 Corinthians 5:19 that God who was in Christ, reconciling the world unto Himself, has committed to us the word of reconciliation. "Now then we are ambassadors for Christ, as though God did beseech you by us: we pray you in Christ's stead, be ye reconciled to God" (2 Cor. 5:20).

This ministry rests upon every believer alike and may be exercised in many ways.

1. *The Gospel may be presented to the unsaved through sacrificial gifts.* Evidently there are many earnest believers who would rejoice to win a soul for Christ who have not awakened to the effectiveness of giving their substance to this end. The messenger cannot go except he be sent, but the one who sends him is a partner in the service and has taken stock which will pay eternal dividends.

2. *The Gospel may be presented to the unsaved in answer to prayer.* He who has said "If ye shall ask any thing in my name, I will do it" (John 14:14) will certainly thrust laborers into the harvest in answer to prayer. It is easily proven that there is no more fruitful ministry possible to the child of God than prayer; yet how very few seem to realize that souls are saved through that service.

3. *The Gospel may be presented to the unsaved by word of mouth.* Since all are commissioned to this task, there are certain imperative conditions to be observed: (a) the messenger must be willing to be placed where the Spirit wills; (b) the messenger should be instructed as to the precise truths which constitute the gospel of grace which he is appointed to declare; (c) the messenger must be Spirit-filled, else he will lack that impelling passion for the lost which alone prompts one to fearless and tireless soul-winning service. "After that the Holy Ghost is come upon you," Christ said, ". . . ye shall be witnesses unto me" (Acts 1:8). Apart from this filling, there will be no disposition to witness. But, being filled, there is no staying the outflow of divine compassion (Acts 4:20).

4. *The Gospel may be also presented by various mechanical means such as literature, the radio, television, and sacred music.*

Regardless of means, the truth must be presented in such a way that the Holy Spirit can use it.

5. *Undoubtedly, God uses many other means to promote the Gospel such as educational institutions where men are trained to preach, missionary aviation which serves to transport men who are carrying the Gospel, and the printed page.* Although every Christian may not be equally effectual in preaching the Gospel directly, every Christian bears a portion of the responsibility of seeing to it that the Gospel is preached to every creature.

Questions

1. How is the church related to manifesting the grace of God?
2. Who directs each believer in the path of the Lord's will?
3. Contrast the purpose of God in the present age with His purpose in the millennial kingdom.
4. What is necessary before the world can be converted?
5. Name the three major characteristics which form the peculiar features of this age according to Matthew 13.
6. What will be some of the immediate results for Israel and the world when God's present purpose for the church is completed at the Rapture?
7. According to Acts 15, what is the order of God's program for blessing on Gentiles and blessing on the Jews?
8. Describe God's present purpose in building His church.
9. What is the believer's present commission?
10. Name the various ways by which a believer can exercise his privilege of extending the Gospel to the world.
11. What are some of the basic conditions for being an effective messenger of the Gospel?
12. In what sense is every Christian responsible for preaching the Gospel to every creature?

37

The Church:
Her Service and Stewardship

A. Her Service Toward God

Service is any work performed for the benefit of another. When this theme is traced through the Bible, a series of similiarities and contrasts between the Old and New Testaments will be observed. Almost every doctrine of the New Testament is anticipated in the Old, and almost every doctrine of the Old Testament is incomplete until perfected in the New. The theme of service is no exception; its study will prove to be largely a recognition of the Old Testament type with the New Testament antitype.

Service which God appoints, whether of the Old or New Testament order, is committed primarily to a divinely fitted priesthood. In the Old Testament order the priesthood was a hierarchy over the nation, and in their service they were under the authority of the high priest. In the New Testament order every believer is a priest unto God (1 Pet. 2:5-9; Rev. 1:6). The whole ministering company of New Testament priests is under the authority of Christ, who is the true High Priest, of whom all other high priests were but types. Therefore, according to the New Testament order, service is committed to all believers alike and on the ground of their priestly relation to God. In their priestly ministry, the priests of the New Testament, like the priests of the Old Testament, were appointed to serve both God and man.

As there was no evangel to be preached to the nations of the earth, service in the period covered by the Old Testament consisted only of the performance by the priests of the divinely appointed ritual in the Tabernacle or Temple. In contrast with this, the New Testament priestly ministry is much broader in its scope, including not only a service to God and fellow-believers, but to all men everywhere.

1. *The service of sacrifice is strikingly similar in both the Old and New Testaments.* The Old Testament priest was sanctified or set apart both by the fact that he was born into the priestly family of Levi and by the fact that he, with due ceremony, was inducted into the priestly office, which appointment continued so long as he lived. Likewise, at the beginning of his ministry he was ceremonially cleansed by a once-for-all bathing (Exod. 29:4).

In fulfilling the antitype, the believer priest is wholly and once for all cleansed at the moment he is saved (Col. 2:13; Titus 3:5) and, by virtue of his salvation, is set apart unto God. So also, he is set apart by the new birth into the family of God. In addition to all this, it is peculiarly required of the New Testament priest that he *willingly* dedicate himself to God.

Concerning his self-dedication we read: "I beseech you therefore, brethren, by the mercies of God, that ye present your bodies a living sacrifice, holy, acceptable unto God, which is your reasonable service" (Rom. 12:1). The phrase, "the mercies of God," refers to the great facts of salvation which have been set forth in the preceding chapters of the Book of Romans, into which mercies every believer enters the moment he is saved; while the presentation of the body as a living sacrifice is the self-dedication to the will of God of all that the believer is and has. That which is thus yielded God accepts and places where He wills in the field of service (Eph. 2:10).

According to Scripture, this divine act of accepting and placing is consecration. Therefore, the believer priest may *dedicate himself*, but never *consecrates* himself, to God. In connection with the divine act of consecration, it should be observed that the present work of Christ as High Priest — receiving, directing, and administering the service of believers — fulfills what was typified by the ministry of the Old Testament priest in the consecration of the sons of Levi.

Having yielded to God and being no longer conformed to this world, the believer-priest will experience a transformed life by the power of the indwelling Spirit, and by that power he will make full proof of "what is that good, and acceptable, and perfect, will of God" (Rom. 12:2).

According to the New Testament order, priestly service in sacrifice toward God is fourfold: (a) the dedication of self which is declared to be a "reasonable service" (Rom. 12:1), or more literally, a "spiritual worship." As Christ Himself was both the Sacrificer and the Sacrifice, so the believer may glorify God by the offering of his whole body as a living sacrifice to God; (b) the sacrifice of the lips which is the voice of praise and is to be offered continually (Heb. 13:15); (c) the sacrifice of substance (Phil. 4:18); (d) the sacrifice of good works (Heb. 13:16).

Referring to the cleansing of the priests, it should be noted again that the Old Testament priest upon entering his holy office was once-for-all cleansed by a *whole* bathing, which was administered by another (Exod. 29:4); afterward, however, though thus wholly bathed, he was required to be cleansed repeatedly by a *partial* bathing at the brazen laver, and this before undertaking any priestly service. In fulfilling the typical significance of this, the New Testament priest, though wholly cleansed and forgiven when saved, is at all times required to confess every known sin in order that he may be cleansed and qualified for fellowship with God (1 John 1:9). As the appointment of the Old Testament priest was for life, so the New Testament priest is a priest unto God forever.

2. *The service of worship, which will be presented at length in a later chapter, may here be considered as part of the service of every believer-priest in the present age, just as it was also a part of the worship and service of every priest in the Old Testament.* As the furnishings of the holy place symbolized the worship of the priest in the Old Testament order, and every feature and furnishing of that place spoke of Christ, so the believer's worship is by and through Christ alone.

Again, in service unto God, the believer's worship may be the offering of oneself to God (Rom. 12:1), the ascribing of praise and thanksgiving to God from the heart (Heb. 13:15), or the sacrificial gifts that are offered to Him.

In connection with the worship of the Old Testament priests, there were two prohibitions recorded, and these also have typical meaning. No "strange" incense was to be borne (Exod. 30:9) — which speaks typically of mere formality in service toward God; and no "strange" fire was allowed (Lev. 10:1) — which symbolizes the substitution of fleshly emotions in our service for true devotion to Christ by the Spirit, or the love of lesser things to the exclusion of the love for Christ (1 Cor. 1:11-13; Col. 2:8, 16-19).

3. *The service of intercession, also to be considered in a later chapter, is an important function of the believer-priest.* As the prophet is God's representative to the people, so the priest is the people's representative to God. As the priesthood is a divine appointment, the necessary access to God is always provided; however, no priest of the old dispensation was permitted to enter the holy of holies other than the high priest, and he but once a year on the ground of sacrificial blood (Heb. 9:7).

In this dispensation Christ as High Priest has through His own blood now entered into the heavenly sanctuary (Heb. 4:14-16; 9:24; 10:19-22) and is interceding for His own who are in the world (Rom. 8:34; Heb. 7:25). When Christ died, the veil of the temple was rent — which signifies that the way into the holiest is now open, not to the world, but to all who come unto God on the ground of the shed blood of Christ (Heb. 10:19-22).

Having unhindered access to God because of the blood of Christ, the New Testament priest is thus privileged to minister in intercession (Rom. 8:26-27; Heb. 10:19-22; 1 Tim. 2:1; Col. 4:12).

B. Service Toward Man

There is a divine arrangement in the order of the truth as found in Romans 12:1-8. Here, as in all Scripture, Christian service is not mentioned until the great issues of dedication and consecration are presented. Immediately following the message concerning these fundamental issues, the subject of divinely bestowed gifts for service is introduced, and in this connection it is important to observe the wide difference between the biblical use of the word "gift" and that meaning given to it in common speech. A gift is generally understood to refer to some native ability, received by birth, enabling one to do special things. According to the scriptural use of the word, a gift is a ministry of the indwelling Spirit. It is the Spirit performing a service and using the believer as an instrument. In no sense is it something which is wrought by the believer alone, or even by the believer when assisted by the Spirit. Christian service is said to be a "manifestation of the Spirit" (1 Cor. 12:7), just as Christian character is a "fruit of the Spirit" (Gal. 5:22-23).

Though every believer possesses some divinely bestowed gift (1 Cor. 12:7; Eph. 4:7), there is a diversity of gifts (Rom. 12:6; 1 Cor. 12:4-11; Eph. 4:11). Christians are not all appointed to do the same thing. In this there is a contrast with the priestly office in which *all* believers sacrifice, worship, and intercede. Though certain representative gifts which are general are named in Scripture (Rom. 12:6-8; 1 Cor. 12:8-11; Eph. 4:11) and though some of these have evidently ceased (1 Cor. 13:8), it is probable that the ministry of the Spirit through the believers is as varied as the circumstances in which they are called to serve.

Gifts are bestowed that the servant of God may be "profitable" (1 Cor. 12:7), and it is therefore implied that service which is wrought in the energy of the flesh is not profitable. The Spirit's manifestation in the exercise of a gift is as "rivers of living water" (John 7:37-39) and is the realization of those "good works, which God hath before ordained that we should walk in them" (Eph. 2:10).

Without being urged, Spirit-filled believers are constantly active in the exercise of their gifts. Carnal believers, though possessing a gift, are not active in its exercise, nor do they respond to human exhortations. However, when they become adjusted to God by confession of sin, yieldedness of life, and a walk in dependence on the indwelling Spirit, immediately they are Spirit-filled and as a result they *desire* to do the will of God and by His sufficient power working in them become profitable in that service to which they have been before ordained of God. Christians are not Spirit-filled because they are active in service; they are active in service because they are Spirit-filled. Likewise, it is sometimes the will of God that all activity cease and that the weary servant rest. It was Christ who said, "Come ye apart . . . and rest."

C. Her Stewardship

The Christian's responsibility in stewardship may be considered under three phases: (1) earning money, (2) possessing money,

(3) giving money. Since money earned by toil is human life in concrete form, and since money however gained is a vital factor in both spiritual and material progress, the child of God must face his responsibility as a steward for which he will be judged at the judgment seat of Christ (Rom. 14:10-12). Too often money is acquired, held, or given by the child of God without due recognition of that fundamental relationship which he sustains to God.

1. *The earning of money for a Christian must be in a manner worthy of a Christian's relationship to God.* As the command admonishes us, "whatsoever ye do, do all to the glory of God" (1 Cor. 10:31). It is divinely arranged that all shall engage in toil (Gen. 3:19; 2 Thess. 3:10), and the Christian is not excepted. However, to the spiritual, instructed believer, labor is more than merely earning a living; it is doing the will of God. Every employment, be it ever so menial, should be accepted by the child of God as a specific appointment from God, and to be done *for* Him, else not done at all.

The incidental fact that God is pleased to give His child food and raiment through daily labor should not obscure the greater truth that God in infinite love is committed to the care of His children, and this without reference to their earning power (Phil. 4:19; Heb. 13:5). The saying "God provides for those only who cannot provide for themselves" is untrue. He cares for His own at all times, since all that they have is from Him (1 Sam. 2:7).

In relationships among men there are agreements and salaries to be recognized, for "the labourer is worthy of his hire" (Luke 10:7); but in relation to his Father, the Christian's highest ideal concerning his toil is that whatever he does, he does at the appointment of his Father, for His sake, and as an expression of devotion to Him. Likewise, whatever is received is not *earned,* but is rather the expression of the Father's loving care. Such an attitude is not sentimental or impractical; it is the only basis upon which the believer can sanctify all his toil by doing it for the glory of God, or be able to "rejoice evermore" (1 Thess. 5:16) in the midst of the burdens of life.

2. *The possessing of money becomes a great responsibility for any sincere Christian.* In view of the appalling need on every hand and the unmeasured good that money may accomplish, every spiritual Christian must face the practical question relative to retaining property in his own possession. It is doubtless often the will of God that property shall be kept in store; but the yielded Christian will not *assume* this. His property should be

held only as God directs, and it should be subject to His control. The motives which actuate men both rich and poor – the desire to be rich (1 Tim. 6:8-9, 17-18; James 1:11; Heb. 13:5; Phil. 4:11), the desire to provide against a day of need (Matt. 6:25-34), and the desire to provide for others – are commendable only as they fulfill the specifically revealed will of God in each individual's life.

3. *The giving of money which a Christian has earned becomes an important aspect of any believer's service for God.* Self and money are alike the roots of much evil, and in the dispensing of money, as in its acquisition and possession, the Christian is expected to stand upon a grace relationship to God. This relationship presupposes that he has first given himself to God in unqualified dedication (2 Cor. 8:5); and a true dedication of self to God includes all that one is and has (1 Cor. 6:20; 7:23; 1 Pet. 1:18-19) – his life, his time, his strength, his ability, his ideals, and his property.

In matters pertaining to the giving of money, the grace principle involves the believer's recognition of God's sovereign authority over all that the Christian is and has, and contrasts with the Old Testament legal system of tithing which was in force as a part of the law until the law was done away with (John 1:16-17; Rom. 6:14; 7:1-6; 2 Cor. 3:1-18; Gal. 3:19-25; 5:18; Eph. 2:15; Col. 2:14). Though certain principles of the law were carried forward and restated under grace, tithing, like sabbath observance, is never imposed on the believer in this dispensation. Since the Lord's Day superseded the legal sabbath and is adapted to the principles of grace as the sabbath could not be, so tithing has been superseded by a new system of giving which is adapted to the teachings of grace as tithing could not be.

Christian giving under grace, as illustrated in the experience of the saints at Corinth, is summarized in 2 Corinthians 8:1 – 9:15. In this passage we discover

(a) Christ was their pattern. The Lord's giving of Himself (2 Cor. 8:9) is the pattern of all giving under grace. He did not give a tenth; He gave all.

(b) Their giving was even out of great poverty. A striking combination of phrases is employed to describe what the Corinthians experienced in their giving (2 Cor. 8:2): "in a great trial of affliction," "the abundance of their joy," "their deep poverty abounded," "the riches of their liberality." Likewise, concerning liberality in spite of great poverty, it should be remembered that "the widow's mite" (Luke 21:1-4), which drew the commendation of the Lord Jesus, was not a part, but "all that she had."

(c) Their giving was not by commandment, nor of necessity. Under the law, a tenth was *commanded* and its payment was a *necessity;* under grace, God is not seeking the gift, but an expression of devotion from the giver. Under grace no law is imposed, and no proportion to be given is stipulated; and, while it is true that God works in the yielded heart both to will and to do His good pleasure (Phil. 2:13), He finds pleasure only in that gift which is given cheerfully, or more literally, "hilariously" (2 Cor. 9:7).

If a law existed stipulating the amount to be given, there are those, doubtless, who would seek to fulfill it, even against their own wishes. Thus their gift would be made "grudgingly" and "of necessity." If it be said that to support the work of the Gospel we must have money whether given hilariously or not, it may also be said that it is not *the amount* which is given, but rather the divine blessing upon the gift that accomplishes the desired end.

Christ fed five thousand from five loaves and two fishes. There is abundant evidence to prove that wherever the children of God have fulfilled their privilege in giving under grace, their liberality has resulted in "all sufficiency in all things" which has made them "abound to every good work," for God is able to make even the grace of giving to "abound" to every believer (2 Cor. 9:8).

(d) The early Christians, first of all, gave themselves. Acceptable giving is preceded by a complete giving of oneself (2 Cor. 8:5). This suggests the important truth that giving under grace, like giving under the law, is limited to a certain class of people. Tithing was never imposed by God on any other than the nation Israel. So, Christian giving is limited to believers and is most acceptable when given by believers who have yielded their lives to God.

(e) Christians in the early church also gave systematically. Like tithing, there is suggested systematic regularity in giving under grace. "Upon the first day of the week let every one of you lay by him in store, as God hath prospered him" (1 Cor. 16:2). This injunction is addressed to "every man" (every Christian man), and thus excuses none; and giving is to be from that which is already "in store."

(f) God sustains the giver. God will sustain grace-giving with limitless temporal resources (2 Cor. 9:8-10; Luke 6:38). In this connection it may be seen that those who give as much as a tenth are usually prospered in temporal things; but since the believer can have no relation to the law (Gal. 5:1), it is evident that this prosperity is the fulfillment of the promise under grace, rather than the fulfillment of promises under the law. No blessings are thus dependent on the exact tithing.

The blessings are bestowed because a heart has expressed itself through a gift. It is manifest that no gift will be made to God from the heart which He will not graciously acknowledge. There is no opportunity here for designing people to become rich. The giving must be from the *heart,* and God's response will be according to His perfect will for His child. He may respond by bestowing spiritual riches, or in temporal blessings as He shall choose.

(g) True riches are from God. The Corinthian Christians were made rich with heavenly riches. There is such a thing as being rich in this world's goods and yet not rich toward God (Luke 12:21). All such are invited to buy of Him that gold which is tried in the fire (Rev. 3:18). Through the absolute' poverty of Christ in His death, all may be made rich (2 Cor. 8:9). It is possible to be rich in faith (James 2:5) and rich in good works (1 Tim. 6:18); but in Christ Jesus the believer receives "the riches of his grace" (Eph. 1:7), and "the riches of his glory" (Eph. 3:16).

Questions

1. To whom is divine service primarily committed?
2. Contrast the Old Testament and the New Testament priesthoods in the character of their service.
3. To what extent was the service of sacrifice similar in both Testaments?
4. In what way in particular is the New Testament priest expected to dedicate himself to God willingly?
5. What is the difference between dedication and consecration?
6. What may the believer priest in the New Testament experience if yielded to God?
7. Name the fourfold sacrifices of the New Testament priest.
8. Contrast the ceremony of bathing the Old Testament priest and the partial bathing at the brazen laver.
9. How does the cleansing of the Old Testament priest anticipate the cleansing of the New Testament priest?
10. How is the priest related to worship?
11. What prohibitions were given concerning worship in the Old Testament, and how do these apply to the New Testament priest?
12. Compare the work of the high priest in the Old Testament with that of the other priests.
13. Compare the work of Christ as our High Priest and our work as priests.
14. How does the diversity of gifts relate to the service of a New Testament priest?
15. How is the exercise of a spiritual gift affected by carnality?
16. What are the three phases of a Christian's stewardship?
17. How does the earning of money relate to a Christian's walk with God?
18. How does the possessing of money become a responsibility for every sincere Christian?
19. How does the giving of money by a Christian reflect his grace relationship to God?
20. In what sense is Christ our pattern in giving?
21. How is giving related to poverty?
22. How is giving related to commandment or necessity?
23. How is giving related to giving ourselves first?
24. How is giving to be achieved systematically?
25. How does God sustain the giver?
26. Contrast earthly riches and heavenly riches.

38

The Church:
Her Worship in
Prayer and Thanksgiving

As brought out in Romans 12:1-2 and Hebrews 13:15-16, a Christian as a believer-priest is occupied with four sacrifices: (1) the sacrifice of his body (Rom. 12:1-2); (2) the sacrifice of praise (Heb. 13:15); (3) the sacrifice of good works (Heb. 13:16); and (4) the sacrifice of stewardship or sharing as brought out in the expression "to communicate forget not" (Heb. 13:16). God is well pleased with such sacrifices (Heb. 13:16). Having dealt with the sacrifice of good works and stewardship of material possessions in previous discussion, we may now consider the work of the believer-priest in his prayer and praise to God which forms the essential of worship.

In the present age, worship is not a matter of form and circumstance, but as Christ said to the Samaritan woman, "God is a Spirit: and they that worship him must worship him in spirit and in truth" (John 4:24). Accordingly, worship is not confined to sacred services in great cathedrals, but is the adoration of the heart of the Christian as he expresses his praise and intercession to his Heavenly Father in the name of Christ. Prayer and praise are the principal elements of worship and are acts of direct communion of men with God. The study of the doctrine of prayer and praise in the Old and New Testaments reveals a progressive revelation and increasing privilege.

A. Prayer Before the First Advent of Christ

Though individual and private prayer was offered by godly men in all the ages, it is evident that prayer, in the main, was offered by the patriarch in behalf of his household (Job 1:5) and, during the period between Moses and Christ, by the priests and rulers in behalf of the people. Throughout these centuries the ground of prayer consisted in pleading the covenants of Jehovah (1 Kings 8:22-26; Neh. 9:32; Dan. 9:4) and His holy character (Gen. 18:25; Exod. 32:11-14), and it followed the shedding of sacrificial blood (Heb. 9:7).

B. Prayer in Expectation of the Kingdom

The Messianic claim of Christ and the acceptance of the kingdom at His hand were rejected by the nation Israel; but during the early days of His preaching, and when the kingdom was being offered to Israel, He taught His disciples to pray for the kingdom to be set up in the earth.

The familiar Lord's Prayer is stated in Matthew 6:9-13 and includes the petition "thy kingdom come" (Matt. 6:10). This prayer has primarily in view the realization of the kingdom on earth in the millennium when Christ would reign supreme on earth. The doxology as contained in Matthew 6:13 concludes, "for thine is the kingdom, and the power, and the glory, for ever. Amen." This doxology is not found in many ancient manuscripts of the gospel of Matthew and is omitted in the parallel account in Luke 11:2-4. Accordingly, many believe it was added by those who copied Scripture as a suitable way to conclude the prayer. Whether originally in Matthew or not, it correctly states the doctrine of the future kingdom.

Because the Lord's Prayer also includes other items that are suitable for all ages and circumstances — such as the adoration of the Father, petition for daily bread, and for deliverance from temptation — it has often been taken as a model prayer. It is doubtful, however, whether this was the intention of Christ. The real "Lord's Prayer" is found in John 17, where our Lord interceded for His church in the full recognition of God's purpose for the church in the present age.

Some have held that the Lord's Prayer in Matthew is improperly used in the present age, and yet its many timeless characteristics and its simplicity have endeared it to many believers; moreover, it is not improper for those living today to anticipate in prayer the coming of the millennial kingdom. However, it must be clearly understood that this kingdom will not come by human effort before the second coming of Christ, as some have taught, but awaits the glorious return of Christ who by His power and might will set up His kingdom on earth.

C. The Prayer of Christ

In John 17 the true "Lord's Prayer" is presented and reveals the utmost freedom in communion between the Father and the Son. In this chapter Christ is exercising His office as High Priest, and the theme of His prayer is the need of believers on earth in the coming age following Pentecost.

While on earth prior to His death, Christ spent long seasons in prayer (Matt. 14:23), even all night (Luke 6:12), and it is probable that the form of His prayer was the same familiar communion with His Father found in John 17. The prayer of Christ does not seem to depend upon the promises or covenants, but rather rests in His own person and priestly work of sacrifice. The prayer of Christ especially in John 17 is, accordingly, a revelation of the intercessory work of Christ at the right hand of the Father which continues throughout the present dispensation.

D. Prayer Under the Relationship of Grace

Prayer is not the same throughout all ages, but like all other human responsibilities, it is adapted to the various dispensations. With the great advance in the revelation provided in the New Testament, prayer takes on the new status of prayer in the name of Christ in the full revelation of His sacrifice on the cross.

Among the seven outstanding features of the believer's life under grace which Christ mentioned in the Upper Room and in Gethsemane (John 13:1 — 17:26), prayer is included. The teaching of Christ on this most vital theme is given in three passages (John 14:12-14; 15:7; 16:23-24). According to this word of Christ, the present possibility of prayer under grace is lifted out of earthly limitations into the sphere of the infinite relationships which obtain in the new creation. This form of prayer may be considered under four aspects.

1. *The function of prayer includes not only praise but the believer presenting his own needs to the Lord and interceding on behalf of others.* Rationalism teaches that prayer is unreasonable because an omniscient God would already know what is required better than the man who prays. God, nevertheless, has sovereignly ordained prayer as a means to accomplishing His will in the world and has instructed those who believe in Him to present their petitions. The importance of prayer is revealed in John 14:13-14 wherein Christ promised to do whatever they would ask in His name. Accordingly, God has elevated the importance of prayer to the point where to a large degree God has conditioned His own action on the faithful prayer of the believer.

This responsibility in partnership has been established. It is no longer a question of reasonableness; it is a question of adjustment. It is probable that we cannot know all that is involved, but we do know that in the ministry of prayer the child of God is brought into vital partnership in the work of God in a manner in which he could not otherwise partake. Since the Christian may share in the glory that follows, he is given this opportunity of sharing in the achievement. This responsibility in partnership is not extended to the believer as a special concession; it is the normal function of one for whom the sacrificial blood has been shed (Heb. 10:19-20), and who has been vitally joined to Christ in the New Creation. It is not unreasonable that one who is a living part of Christ (Eph. 5:30) should share both in His service and in His glory.

It should be noted that it is in connection with this announcement of the new office of prayer as a partnership in achievement that Christ stated, "Greater works than these shall he [the believer] do" (John 14:12), which word is immediately followed by the assurance that He alone undertakes to respond to this ministry of prayer. So vital is this blending of endeavor between prayer and that which is divinely wrought in its answer that the believer is said by Christ to be the *doer* of the "greater works."

2. *The privilege of praying in the name of the Lord Jesus Christ, which under grace is extended to every child of God, lends to prayer a characteristic which lifts it to an infinite degree above every other form of prayer that ever was or will be.* Likewise, the present form of prayer supersedes all preceding privileges; for when Christ said, "Hitherto have ye asked nothing in my name" (John 16:24), He dismissed every other ground of prayer that had existed.

We may be sure that the name of the Lord Jesus Christ commands the attention of the Father and that the Father will not only listen when that name is used, but will be inclined to do whatsoever is asked to be done for the sake of His beloved Son. The name of Christ is equivalent to the person of Christ, and the name is not given to believers merely as something with which to conjure. Praying in the name of Christ means recognition of oneself as a living part of Christ in the New Creation and therefore limits the subjects of prayer to those projects which are in direct line with the purposes and glory of Christ. It is praying a prayer which Christ might pray. Since prayer in the name of Christ is like signing His name to our petition, it is reasonable that prayer in His name should be thus limited.

Having pointed out that sometimes spiritual poverty is due to the fact that we "ask not," James goes on to state that "Ye ask, and receive not, because ye ask amiss, that ye may consume it upon your lusts" (James 4:2-3). Prayer thus may become an appeal either for the things of self or for the things of Christ. The believer, having been saved from self and vitally united to Christ (2 Cor. 5:17-18; Col. 3:3), is no longer concerned with self. This is not to say that the believer's best interests are abandoned; but it is to say that these interests are now looked upon as belonging to the new sphere wherein "Christ is all in all." Being in Christ, it is normal for us to pray in His name and abnormal to pray for the mere desires of self which are apart from the glory of Christ.

Since prayer is possible only on the ground of the shed blood and by virtue of the believer's vital union with Christ, the prayer of the unsaved cannot be accepted by God.

3. *The scope of prayer under grace is stated in the one word "whatsoever"; but not without its reasonable limitations.* It is *whatsoever* ye ask in the name, according to the purposes and glory, of Christ. Before true prayer can be offered, the heart

must be conformed to the mind of Christ. Thus it is said, "If ye abide in me, and my words abide in you, ye shall ask what ye will" (John 15:7), and this is true; for under such heart adjustment the child of God will ask only for those things which are in the sphere of God's will.

Under grace, there is perfect liberty of action given to the one in whom God is working both to will and to do of His good pleasure (Phil. 2:13). Likewise, there is unlimited freedom of petition to the one who prays in the will of God. To the Spirit-filled believer it is said: "Likewise the Spirit also helpeth our infirmities: for we know not what we should pray for as we ought: but the Spirit itself maketh intercession for us with groanings which cannot be uttered. And he that searcheth the hearts knoweth what is the mind of the Spirit, because he maketh intercession for the saints according to the will of God" (Rom. 8:26-27). The scope of prayer under grace is not narrow; it is as infinite as the eternal interests of the One in whose name we are privileged to pray.

4. *The practice of prayer should be given careful attention by every faithful believer.* It is most important that believers observe regular times of prayer. They should avoid any irreverent use of prayer or useless repetitions as characterize the heathen world and follow the divine order prescribed for prayer under grace. This is stated in the words, "In that day ye shall ask me nothing. Verily, verily, I say unto you, Whatsoever ye shall ask the Father in my name, he will give it you" (John 16:23), and prayer is to be "in the Holy Spirit" (Jude 20).

This order is not arbitrarily imposed. However, to pray to Christ is to abandon His mediation by praying *to* Him, rather than *through* Him, thereby sacrificing the most vital feature of prayer under grace — prayer in His name. To pray to the Spirit of God is to pray *to* Him, rather than *by* Him, and implies that we are to that degree depending on our own sufficiency.

It may be concluded then, that prayer under grace is to be offered to the Father, in the name of the Son, and in the power of the Holy Spirit.

E. The Prayer of Thanksgiving

True thanksgiving is the voluntary expression of heartfelt gratitude for benefit received. Its effectiveness depends upon its sincerity, as its intensity depends upon the value which is placed upon the benefit received (2 Cor. 9:11). Thanksgiving is peculiarly personal. There are obligations belonging to us which may be assumed by another; but no one can offer for us our word of thanksgiving (Lev. 22:29).

Thanksgiving is in no way a payment for the benefit received; it is rather a gracious acknowledgement of the fact that the one who had received the benefit is indebted to the giver. Since no payment can be made to God for His unmeasured and uncounted benefits, the obligation to be thankful to Him is stated throughout Scriptures, and all thanksgiving is closely related to worship and praise.

Under the old order, the spiritual relationships to God were expressed in material ways. Among these, provision was made for the offering, or sacrifice, of thanksgiving (Lev. 7:12, 13, 15; Pss. 107:22; 116:17). Similarly, in this age it is the privilege of the believer to make sacrificial offerings of thanksgiving to God. However, if while offering the sacrificial gift of thanksgiving the motive should include the thought of compensation, the essential value of thanksgiving is destroyed.

The subject of prayer is mentioned many times in the Old Testament and frequently in the Psalms. In the Old Testament explicit direction is given for the thanksgiving offerings (Lev. 7:12-15), and praise and thanksgiving were especially emphasized in the revival under Nehemiah (Neh. 12:24-40). Likewise, the prophetic message of the Old Testament anticipates thanksgiving as a special feature of worship in the coming kingdom (Isa. 51:3; Jer. 30:19). So also, there is ceaseless thanksgiving in heaven (Rev. 4:9; 7:12; 11:17).

An important feature of Old Testament thanksgiving is the appreciation of the Person of God apart from all His benefits (Pss. 30:4; 95:2; 97:12; 100:1-5; 119:62). Though so constantly neglected, this theme of thanksgiving is most important and such praise is reasonable and fitting. "It is a good thing to give thanks unto the LORD" (Ps. 92:1).

In the New Testament the theme of thanksgiving is mentioned about forty-five times, and this form of praise is offered for both temporal and spiritual blessings. Christ's unfailing practice of giving thanks for food (Matt. 15:36; 26:27; Mark 8:6; 14:23; Luke 22:17, 19; John 6:23; 1 Cor. 11:24) should prove an effectual example to all believers. The Apostle Paul was also faithful in this particular (Acts 27:35; Rom. 14:6; 1 Tim. 4:3-4).

Thanksgiving on the part of the Apostle Paul is worthy of close attention. He uses the phrase "thanks be unto God" in connection with Christ as the "unspeakable gift" (2 Cor. 9:15), concerning the victory over the grave which is secured by the resurrection (1 Cor. 15:57), and because of the present triumph which is ours through Christ (2 Cor. 2:14). His thanksgiving to God for believers (1 Thess. 1:2; 3:9), for Titus in particular (2 Cor. 8:16), and his exhortation that thanks be given for all men (1 Tim. 2:1) are likewise object lessons to all the children of God.

Two important features of thanksgiving according to the New Testament should be noted.

1. *Thanksgiving should be prayer without ceasing.* Since the adorable Person of God is unchanged and His benefits never cease, and since the abundant grace of God will redound to the glory of God through the thanksgiving of many (2 Cor. 4:15), it is reasonable that thanksgiving be given to Him without ceasing. Of this form of praise we read: "By him therefore let us offer the sacrifice of praise to God continually, that is, the fruit of our lips giving thanks to his name" (Heb. 13:15; cf. Eph. 1:16; 5:20; Col. 1:3; 4:2). This feature of thanksgiving is also emphasized in the Old Testament (Pss. 30:12; 79:13; 107:22; 116:17).

2. *Thanksgiving should be offered for all things as stated in Ephesians 5:20:* "Giving thanks always for all things unto God and the Father in the name of our Lord Jesus Christ." A similar command is found in 1 Thessalonians 5:18: "In every thing give thanks: for this is the will of God in Christ Jesus concerning you" (cf. Phil. 4:6; Col. 2:7; 3:17).

Giving thanks *always* for *all* things is far removed from giving thanks *sometimes* for *some* things. However, having accepted the truth that *all* things work together for good to them who love God, it is fitting that thanks be rendered to God for *all* things. Such God-honoring praise can be offered only by those who are saved and who are Spirit-filled (Eph. 5:18-20). Daniel gave thanks to God in the fact of the sentence of death (Dan. 6:10), and Jonah gave thanks to God from the belly of the great fish and from the depths of the sea (Jonah 2:9).

The common sin of ingratitude toward God is illustrated by one of the events recorded in the ministry of Christ. Ten lepers were cleansed, but only one returned to give thanks, and he was a Samaritan (Luke 17:11-19). It should be noted here that ingratitude is a sin, being included as one of the sins of the "last days" (2 Tim. 3:2).

It is probable that there is true sincerity on the part of many unsaved who try to be thankful to God for temporal benefits; but their utter failure to appreciate the gift of His Son leaves them most unthankful in His sight.

It should be remembered that Thanksgiving Day was established in this country by believers and for believers and in recognition of the fact that the Christ-rejecting sinner cannot give acceptable praise unto God.

Questions

1. What are the four sacrifices of the believer-priest?
2. What importance would you attach to the fact that praise is one of these four sacrifices?
3. How is worship related to form and circumstances?
4. What characterized prayer before the first coming of Christ?
5. What was the purpose of the Lord's Prayer as stated in Matthew 6:9-13?
6. In what sense is it proper for us to pray for the kingdom to come?
7. Why should John 17 be regarded as the true "Lord's Prayer"?
8. What do we learn in Scripture concerning the prayer life of Christ, and how does John 17 indicate the form of His petitions?
9. Why under the present dispensation of grace does the function of prayer include intercession, in view of God's omniscience?
10. What assurance does the believer have that God will undertake in answer to prayer?
11. What is meant by praying in the name of the Lord Jesus Christ, and how does this give us assurance?
12. What are the twin dangers pointed out by James in relation to prayer?
13. What is the unlimited scope of prayer under grace?
14. How does the Spirit relate to our petitions?
15. What are the dangers on the one hand of irregular prayer time and on the other hand of useless repetitions?
16. Why should prayer under grace be offered to the Father in the name of the Son and in the power of the Holy Spirit?
17. Why is thanksgiving to God a personal matter?
18. In what sense is thanksgiving a sacrifice?
19. How does thanksgiving relate to the person of God as in contrast with His works?
20. What are some of the outstanding illustrations of thanksgiving in the New Testament?
21. What two important features of thanksgiving are noted in the New Testament?
22. Why is failure to give thanksgiving a sin?
23. Why is thanksgiving properly offered only by believers?

39

The Church:
Her Organization and Ordinances

A. Church Government

The church, as the body of Christ, includes every Christian joined to Christ as the head of the body by the baptism of the Spirit. The church as an organism is ordered on the same principle as the human body, for each part relates to each other part and the whole body relates to the head directing the body. The body of Christ essentially needs no organization, as its relationship is spiritual and supernatural.

In the local church, however, in biblical times as well as today, some church organization seems to be necessary in practice. Three forms of church government are found in the history of the church, each having its roots in apostolic times.

1. *The episcopalian form of government recognizes a bishop, or church leader by some other designation, who has power by virtue of his office of directing the local church.* This has developed into an extensive organization such as is true in the Roman Catholic Church or a more simple system as found in the Episcopalian Church or the Methodist Episcopal body, where bishops are appointed to supervise the activities of the churches in a given area.

2. *A representative form of government recognizes the authority of duly appointed representatives of local churches, usually grouped geographically, and is illustrated in the Reformed and Presbyterian churches.* Often representatives of a local group (presbytery) of churches come under the supervision and direction of a larger body, or synod, and in turn the synod comes under the larger body of a general assembly. While rules and extent of power vary, the idea is that duly appointed representatives constitute the authority of the church.

3. *The congregational form of government is where the seat of authority is in the local congregation, and important matters are decided by the congregation without respect to authority of other churches or officials.* Illustrating this form of government are Congregational churches (United Church of Christ), the Disciples churches, and Baptist churches. While local churches may be subject in some degree to higher bodies, committees, or officials, the concept of a congregational church is that a local congregation determines its own affairs, elects and ordains its own ministers, and directs the use of its own treasury.

In the early church all three forms of government are in evidence to some extent. Many of the early churches recognize the apostles as having primary authority. This seems to have passed, however, with the first generation of Christians. Representative government is illustrated in the council at Jerusalem in Acts 15, wherein the apostles and elders in Jerusalem were considered authoritative on the doctrinal questions which the churches raised. Strictly speaking, however, they were neither elected nor representatives of the church in the modern sense. As churches matured and no longer needed apostolic supervision, the government of the churches seems to have passed to each local church itself. This seems to have been true of the seven churches of Asia mentioned in Revelation 2 – 3 which were subject to no human authority although remaining under the authority of Christ Himself. It is questionable whether Scripture authorizes the extensive and complicated government sometimes appearing in the modern church, and a return to biblical simplicity would seem in order.

B. The Order of the Church

The concept of church order relates to those who have authority in the local church and provide leadership for it. The local church in the New Testament included those designated as bishops and elders who were the responsible leaders of the local church. It is probable that the bishops and elders were the same people although the titles were slightly different in meaning.

The concept of elder in the New Testament was probably derived from the elders who exercised authority over Israel (Matt. 16:21; 26:47, 57; Acts 4:5, 23) and indicated a person who was mature in judgment and worthy of an authoritative position. Hence, an elder was one who had the personal qualifications for leadership, while the term "bishop" or "overseer" described the office or function of the person. A bishop was always an elder, but an elder might not be a bishop under certain circumstances — that is, he might have the qualities without the office. Normally the terms seem to have been used in identical sense in the early church (Titus 1:5, 7).

In apostolic times bishops and elders in the local church were plural although some may have provided more leadership than others. Bishops and elders were charged with certain responsibilities such as ruling the church (1 Tim. 3:4-5; 5:17), they were to protect the church from moral or theological error (Titus 1:9), and they were to superintend or oversee the church as a shepherd would his flock (John 21:16; Acts 20:28; Heb. 13:17; 1 Pet. 5:2). Although they were appointed by the apostles, in the early church it seems that as these churches matured appointment was by the church itself, and such appointment was a recognition of their spiritual qualities which qualified them for places of leadership (Acts 14:23; 20:28; Titus 1:5; 1 Pet. 5:2).

In contrast with elders and bishops, others were designated deacons. In the early church they concerned themselves with charity for the needy and ministering in physical things, although they could also have spiritual gifts (Acts 6:1-6; 1 Tim. 3:8-13). Like the elders they were set aside to their office by the apostles (Acts 6:6; 13:3; 2 Tim. 1:6) or may have been appointed by the elders (1 Tim. 4:14) in the early church. As in the case of elders and bishops, distinction must be made between the office of being a deacon and the ministry which a deacon might perform. Philip is an illustration of one who held the office of a deacon, but who by spiritual gift was an evangelist (Acts 6:5; 21:8).

In the church today, some churches tend to recognize a single pastor as the elder and other officials who assist him in spiritual matters as deacons. This does not seem, however, to be based on biblical practice.

C. The Ordinances of the Church

Most Protestant churches recognize only two ordinances, baptism and the Lord's Supper. Exceptions to this may be found in certain bodies who recognize footwashing, as illustrated in Christ's washing the disciples' feet (John 13), as another ordinance. The Roman Catholic Church adds a number of ordinances. Only baptism and the celebration of the Lord's Supper are almost universally recognized.

1. *The ordinance of water baptism, in the history of the church, has been the subject of countless controversies and has resulted in major divisions in the organized church.* In general, the arguments have been over two major problems: (1) whether water baptism is merely a ritual or actually bestows some supernatural benefit on the recipient; (2) the question of mode, whether baptism is only by immersion or can also be administered by affusion, referring to baptism by sprinkling or pouring water upon the one being baptized.

Those who hold that water baptism is a ritual believe that it represents spiritual truth, but in itself does not bestow any supernatural grace or life upon the recipient. The concept that baptism is a ritual is the better interpretation. Those who hold that water baptism actually administers some special grace vary considerably in the extent of such benefit to the person being baptized. Some believe in baptismal regeneration, that is, that water baptism affects the new birth of the believer, and others held merely that it provides grace or an inclination to faith and obedience to the Gospel. Those who oppose the idea of baptism as only a *ritual* refer to water baptism as *real* baptism inseparably related to the baptism of the Spirit and the new birth of the believer.

A second problem arises in connection with the mode of baptism. Here the controversy seems to revolve around the question as to whether the ordinance uses the word "baptize" as used in its primary or secondary sense. The primary meaning of "baptize" is "to immerse" or "place in" a body such as water. The Greek word meaning "to dip" is never used of water baptism. Accordingly, some argue that baptism is used in a secondary sense of *initiation* in which one passes from a former relationship into a new relationship.

Christ referred to His sufferings in death as a baptism (Matt. 20:22-23), and the Israelites who passed through the Red Sea without the water touching them were declared to be baptized in the cloud and in the sea (1 Cor. 10:2). Hence it is argued that physical immersion into water is not necessary for scriptural baptism.

In the history of the church there arose the practice of pouring water over the one baptized, in fulfillment of the symbol of the outpouring of the Spirit in salvation, or applying water in less quantity, often referred to as "sprinkling." Endless arguments have characterized the history of the doctrine. In some cases, as in the instance of Christ being baptized, the implication seems to be that He was immersed. In other instances, as in the baptism of the Philippian jailer (Acts 16:33), it is held that it is extremely unlikely that the jailer and his household would have been immersed in the darkness of the early morning, and baptism would normally have been by pouring while still in the house.

Because baptism by immersion is recognized by all as constituting ritual baptism, the tendency has been in many evangelical churches to follow this mode rather than to debate whether affusion is a legitimate mode of baptism. Undoubtedly, undue importance has been attached to the mode of baptism, since the more important question is whether the individual is born again and baptized by the Spirit into the body of Christ. Arguments for and against various definitions of both the meaning and mode of baptism can be found in standard Bible dictionaries.

Still another problem raised in the matter of baptism as a ritual is the question of infant baptism as opposed to believers' baptism. Relatively little evidence is found in the Bible for infant baptism. Its adherents usually regard infant baptism as the contemporary expression of setting aside an infant to God much as circumcision was in the nation Israel. Although households were baptized, as in Acts 16, with presumably some children included, there is no clear case of infant baptism in the Bible. Accordingly, most evangelicals prefer a service of infant dedication, with water baptism reserved for recognition of true faith in Christ on the part of those of sufficient age to make such an intelligent decision.

Infant baptism when practiced can be no more than an expression of the faith and hope of the parents that their child will ultimately be saved. Baptism of adults should in every case follow evidence of true faith in Christ. Although mode of baptism is not necessarily tied to the question of infant baptism, infants, generally speaking, are baptized by affusion rather than immersion, and those who accept only immersion as a mode of baptism generally also recognize only believer's baptism following faith in Christ.

Regardless of mode of baptism, the ultimate meaning is that the believer is separated from what he was without Christ to what he is in Christ, partaking as he does in the benefits of the death and resurrection of Christ. The early church consistently observed the rite of baptism, and practically all branches of the church observe water baptism in some form today.

2. *The ordinance of the Lord's Supper was instituted on the night before the crucifixion of Christ as a symbolic presentation of the believer's participation in the benefits of His death.* As such, it superseded the Passover, which the Jews have celebrated ever since their deliverance from Egypt.

In instructing His disciples to eat the bread, according to the exposition given in 1 Corinthians 11:23-29, Christ told them that the bread represented His body which would be sacrificed for them. They were to observe this ritual during His absence in remembrance of Christ. The cup of wine was declared by Christ to be the new covenant in His blood; in drinking from the cup they would remember Christ especially in His death. They were to observe this. celebration until His return.

Endless controversies in the history of the church have characterized the various views of the Lord's Supper. In general, three principal points of view have been advanced. The Roman Catholic Church has upheld the doctrine of transubstantiation, that is, that the bread and the wine are changed into the body and blood of Christ and the one who partakes of them is literally partaking of Christ's body and blood even though his senses may recognize the elements as still being bread and wine. A second view is offered by the Lutheran Church and is sometimes called "consubstantiation," although the term is not usually accepted by the Lutherans. This view holds that while the bread remains bread and the wine remains wine, the presence of the body of Christ is in both elements, and thus one partakes of Christ's body in observing the Lord's Supper.

A third view offered by Zwingli is called the memorial view and holds that observing the Lord's Supper is a memorial to His death with no supernatural change in the elements. A variation of this was held by John Calvin, who held that Christ was spiritually in the elements.

The Scriptures seem to support the memorial view, and rather than the elements containing or symbolizing the presence of

272 MAJOR BIBLE THEMES

Christ, they are instead a recognition of His absence. As part of this, the Lord's Supper is to be observed "till he come."

A fitting observance of the Lord's Supper needs to take into consideration the careful instructions of the Apostle Paul in 1 Corinthians 1:27-29. Observance of the Lord's Supper must be with due reverence and self-examination. One who partakes of the celebration in an unworthy or careless manner brings condemnation upon himself. Paul states, "But let a man examine himself, and so let him eat of that bread, and drink of that cup" (1 Cor. 11:28).

The Lord's Supper has been rightly regarded by many Christians as a sacred time of commemoration of the death of Christ and all its meaning for the individual Christian. As indicated by Paul, it is a time of heart-searching, a time of confession of sin, and a time of restoration. It is also a reminder of the wonderful benefits which have come to every Christian through the death of Christ.

As the Lord's Supper points back to the historic fact of the first coming of Christ and His death on the cross, so it also points ahead to His coming again when observance of the Lord's Supper will cease. While the frequency of observance is not clearly given in the Scriptures, it seems probable that the early Christians practiced it frequently, perhaps as often as each week, as they gathered on the first day to celebrate the resurrection of Christ. In any case, observance of the Lord's Supper should not be infrequent, but in proper and respectful obedience to the command of Christ to do this until He comes.

Questions

1. Contrast the concepts of the church as an organism and the church as an organization.
2. What are the three forms of church government found in the history of the church?
3. What are the essential features of the episcopalian form of government?
4. What are the characteristics of representative form of government, and how is this illustrated in some denominations today?
5. What are the characteristics of congregational form of government, and how is this illustrated in churches today?
6. To what extent was the episcopalian form of government found in the early church?
7. How is representative government illustrated in the early church?

8. How is congregational government recognized in the early church?
9. According to Scripture, what are bishops and elders, and how are they to be distinguished?
10. What were the responsibilities of a bishop?
11. What was the office of a deacon, and what responsibilities were given to deacons?
12. What are the principal ordinances of the church?
13. What additions to the usual two ordinances are found in the church today?
14. What is meant by water baptism when it is considered a ritual?
15. What is the meaning of water baptism when it is considered to have actual spiritual benefit?
16. What are the different views of mode of baptism?
17. How does mode relate to primary and secondary meanings of the word "to baptize"?
18. What illustrations are found in the New Testament of baptism in the secondary sense?
19. What instance is cited in support of immersion?
20. What instance is cited in support of affusion, that is, either sprinkling or pouring?
21. How important is the mode of baptism?
22. Why do some hold to infant baptism?
23. Why do some oppose infant baptism as a teaching of Scripture?
24. If infant baptism is practiced, what is the limitation on its meaning?
25. What is the ultimate meaning of baptism regardless of mode?
26. When was the Lord's Supper initiated?
27. What instructions did Christ give His disciples as to the meaning of the bread and the wine?
28. What three principal points of view have been advanced about the Lord's Supper?
29. What is held by the doctrine of transubstantiation, and who advances this viewpoint?
30. What viewpoint is usually offered by the Lutheran Church?
31. What is the memorial view as held by Zwingli, and what variation of it was held by John Calvin?
32. What view of the Lord's Supper seems to have the most scriptural support?
33. What preparation should be made by one partaking of the Lord's Supper?
34. Describe the twofold meaning of the Lord's Supper as it alludes to history and prophecy.

40

The Church:
The Body and Bride of
Christ and Her Reward

A. *The Seven Figures of Christ and His Church*

In the Scripture, seven figures are used to reveal the relationship between Christ and His church.

1. *The Shepherd and the sheep anticipated in the Twenty-Third Psalm are used in John 10, where Christ is the Shepherd and those who believe in Him are His sheep.* According to this passage (a) Christ came by the door, that is, through the appointed lineage of David; (b) He is the true Shepherd who is followed by the true sheep; (c) Christ is also the Door of the sheep, the Door of entrance into salvation as well as the Door which provides security (John 10:28-29); (d) life and food are provided for the sheep by the Shepherd; (e) in contrast, other shepherds are merely hirelings who would not give their lives for the sheep; (f) there is a fellowship between the sheep and the Shepherd — just as the Father knows the Son and the Son knows the Father, so the sheep know the Shepherd; (g) although Israel belonged to a different fold in the Old

Testament, in the present age there is one fold and one Shepherd in which Jew and Gentile alike have salvation (John 10:16); (h) As the Shepherd, Christ not only lays down His life for His sheep but ever lives to intercede for them and provide for them the spiritual life and food they need (Heb. 7:25). According to Psalm 23:1, "The LORD is my shepherd; I shall not want."

2. *Christ is the True Vine, and believers are the branches.* Although Israel was related to God in the figure of a vine in the Old Testament, Christ is the True Vine and believers are the branches, according to John 15. The figure speaks of both the union with Christ and communion with Christ. Believers are exhorted to abide in this unbroken fellowship with Christ (15:10), and the results of abiding are cleansing or pruning (v. 2), effectual prayer (v. 7), celestial joy (v. 11), and eternal truth (v. 16). The central truth of the vine and the branches is that the believer cannot enjoy his Christian life or be fruitful in his service apart from a living connection with Christ the true Vine.

3. *Christ is the Cornerstone, and the church comprises the stones of the building.* In contrast with the Old Testament, in which Israel had a temple (Exod. 25:8), the church is a temple (Eph. 2:21). In the figure Christ is pictured as the Chief Cornerstone and individual believers as stones of the building (Eph. 2:19-22). It is God's present purpose to build His church (Matt. 16:18). In the construction of the church as a building, each stone is a living stone because it partakes of the divine nature (1 Pet. 2:5); Christ is the Chief Cornerstone and Foundation (1 Cor. 3:11; Eph. 2:20-22; 1 Pet. 2:6); and the building as a whole becomes "an habitation of God through the Spirit" (Eph. 2:22). In the figure of the building, the dependence of each believer upon Christ as the Foundation and Chief Cornerstone is evident, and the stones of the building likewise reveal interdependence of believers, with the building as a whole the temple of God through the Spirit.

4. *Christ is pictured in the New Testament as our High Priest with the believers as believer-priests.* As pointed out in previous studies, the believer-priest has a fourfold sacrifice: (a) he offers a service of sacrifice, presenting himself once for all to God (Rom. 12:1-2); (b) he offers a service of worship, in giving praise and thanksgiving to God (Heb. 13:15), including a service of intercession, or prayer on behalf of his own needs and others' (Rom. 8:26-27; Col. 4:12; 1 Tim. 2:1; Heb. 10:19-22). As our High Priest, Christ enters into heaven through His blood

shed on Calvary (Heb. 4:14-16; 9:24; 10:19-22) and now intercedes for us (Rom. 8:34; Heb. 7:25).

As members of the royal priesthood, it is important for us to note that believers also offer (c) the sacrifice of good works and (d) the sacrifice of their substance in addition to offering their bodies as a living sacrifice (Heb. 13:16).

5. *Christ as the Head and the church as the body of Christ revealing the present purpose of God.* This figure will be given separate and extended consideration later in this chapter.

6. *Christ as the Last Adam and the church as the new creation is a figure in which Christ, as the Resurrected One, replaces Adam, the head of the old order, and becomes head of the new creatures in Christ.* The figure is based on the certainty of the resurrection of Christ and the significance that in His resurrection Christ established a new order. The believer is seen to be in Christ by baptism of the Spirit, in contrast with being in Adam. In his new position in Christ he shares all that Christ did on his behalf by way of providing both righteousness and new life in Christ. Because Christ is the Head of a new creation, it requires a new commemorative day, the first day of the week, in contrast with the Sabbath, which belonged to the old order.

7. *Christ as the Bridegroom and the church as the bride is the figure that is prophetic of both present and future relationships between Christ and His church.* In contrast with Israel presented in the Old Testament as an unfaithful wife of Jehovah, the church is revealed in the New Testament to be a virgin bride waiting the coming of her Bridegroom. This will be the subject of an extended discussion later in this chapter. Just as the church as the body of Christ is the most important figure revealing the present purpose of God, so the church as the bride is the most important figure revealing the future relationship of the church to Christ.

B. The Church as the Body of Christ

Previous discussion of the baptism of the Holy Spirit brought out the New Testament revelation of the church joined together and formed into the body of Christ by the baptism of the Spirit, as declared in 1 Corinthians 12:13: "For by one Spirit are we all baptized into one body, whether we be Jews or Gentiles, whether we be bond or free; and have been all made to drink into one Spirit." Three major truths are presented in this figure: (1) the church is a self-developing body; (2) members of the body are given special gifts and are appointed to special service; (3) the body is a living union or an organism.

1. *As a self-developing body, the church is presented in Ephesians 4:11-16 as comprising individuals who have spiritual gifts.* Hence some are apostles, others are prophets, evangelists, or pastors and teachers. The central truth is that believers are not only exhorted to serve God in various capacities, but they are equipped to do a particular work to which God has called them. A believer fulfills his proper service when he fulfills the particular role in the body of Christ which is assigned to him and shares in perfecting the body of Christ (Eph. 4:13).

2. *Members of the body of Christ are appointed to a specific service in keeping with their gifts.* Just as in the human body different members have different functions, so it is in the body of Christ. It is most important that each believer examine himself soberly to see what gifts God has given him and then use these gifts to the glory of God. Important gifts are mentioned in Romans 12:3-8 and 1 Corinthians 12:28. Every believer has some gifts, and believers may have more than one. The spiritual gifts, while sometimes related to natural abilities, are not to be confused with them. For instance, while a person may have the gift of teaching naturally, only God can give the gift of teaching spiritual things.

Spiritual gifts are not secured by seeking, but rather by the Holy Spirit apportioning gifts "to every man severally as he will" (1 Cor. 12:11). In the apostolic church some gifts were given which continue throughout the present age; others were sign gifts which apparently ceased after the first generation of Christians. Every gift, however, is subject to regulation by the Word of God, is not a proper basis for pride, and is a great responsibility for which each believer will have to give an account.

While local churches may develop extensive organizations, the work of God is done primarily through the church as an organism, directed by Christ the Head in keeping with the capacities of each individual member. While it is not uncommon for a believer in Christ to be required to do some things in areas where he may not be especially gifted, obviously his highest function is to perform the task for which he has been placed in the body of Christ. As he presents his body to the Lord as a living sacrifice, he can know God's perfect will (Rom. 12:1-2).

3. *The body is a living organism united eternally in Christ.* The unity of the body comprising both Jews and Gentiles and

people of various races and cultures is set forth in Ephesians 1:23; 2:15-16; 3:6; 4:12-16; 5:30. The church as the body of Christ has a marvelous unity in which the division between Jew and Gentile is ignored, and Gentiles and Jews have equal privilege and grace. The body of Christ contrasts sharply with the relationship of God to Israel and Gentiles in the Old Testament and is a unique situation limited to the present age. Members of the body, according to Ephesians 3, share in the wonderful truth hidden from Old Testament prophets but revealed in the New that Gentiles are fellowheirs and of the same body, partakers of the same promise in Christ by the Gospel as the Jews (Eph. 3:6). The unity of the body emphasized in Ephesians 4:4-7 is an eternal unity which is the basis of Christian fellowship and service in the present age and the ground for eternal fellowship in the ages to come.

C. Christ as the Bridegroom and the Church as the Bride

Of the seven figures of Christ and the church, only the figure of the Bridegroom and the bride has prophetic significance. In contrast with Israel, who is the unfaithful wife of Jehovah, the church is pictured in the New Testament as the virgin bride awaiting the coming of her Bridegroom (2 Cor. 11:2). Christ as the Bridegroom is introduced as early as John 3:29 by John the Baptist.

The major revelation, however, is given in Ephesians 5:25-33 to illustrate the proper relationship between husbands and wives in Christ. Here the threefold work of Christ is revealed: (a) in His death, "Christ also loved the church, and gave himself for it" (v. 25); (b) Christ is engaged in the present work "that he might sanctify and cleanse it with the washing of water by the word" (v. 26); (c) "that he might present it to himself a glorious church, not having spot, or wrinkle, or any such thing; but that it should be holy and without blemish" (v. 27). In dying on the cross Christ fulfilled the oriental symbolism of paying the dowry or necessary price to secure His wife. In the present age, by the washing of water, the application of the Word of God, and sanctification to the believer, Christ is preparing and cleansing His bride for her future relationship. At the end of the age at the rapture of the church, the Bridegroom will come for His bride and take her to heaven. There He will present her as the church which reflects His own glory, perfect, without blemish, spot, or wrinkle, a holy bride suitable for a holy Bridegroom. The wedding feast which follows, probably fulfilled in the spiritual fellowship of the millennial kingdom, is one in which all other saints join in celebrating the marriage of Christ and His church. This marriage feast is announced in Revelation 19:7-8 at the very time that Christ is about to come to earth to set up His kingdom.

The love of Christ for His church revealed in this figure is an outstanding demonstration of the love of God. Five characteristics of divine love may be mentioned.

1. *The eternal duration of the love of God stems from the fact that "God is love"* (1 John 4:8). He has not attained to love by self-effort or cultivation, nor does He hold love as a detached possession which might be abandoned at will. Love is a vital part of His being. It began when He began. If His love were to cease, a very essential part of the person of God would cease. He is what He is, to a large degree, because of His love. The love of God can know no change. To Israel He said, "I have loved thee with an everlasting love" (Jer. 31:3); and of Christ it is written, "Having loved his own which were in the world, he loved them unto the end" (lit., "without end"; John 13:1; cf. 15:9). In God's love toward an individual there is neither fluctuation nor cessation.

2. *The love of God is the motivation for His ceaseless activity.* Though the love of God was once and for all manifested in the sacrifice of His well-beloved Son (Rom. 5:8; 1 John 3:16), what was manifested in a moment of time is, nevertheless, the revelation of the eternal attitude of God toward men. Could we have gazed into the heart of God before the creation of the material universe we would have seen every provision then made for His Lamb to be slain for the sin of the world (Rev. 5:6). Could we now gaze into the heart of God we would see the same undiminished compassion for the lost that was expressed in the death of His Son. The momentary death of Christ was not a spasm in the divine affection; it is the announcement to a lost world of the fact of God's eternal, unchangeable love.

3. *The love of God has transparent purity.* Concerning this aspect of the love of God no human words avail. There is no selfishness in divine love; God has never sought benefits for Himself. He receives nothing; He bestows everything. Peter exhorts believers to love with a pure heart fervently (1 Pet. 1:22); but how very few love God for what He is in Himself apart

from all His benefits! How different it is with God's love! Judging by ourselves, we are sure He needs our money, our service, or our influence. He needs nothing from us; but He needs *us*, and only because His infinite love cannot be satisfied apart from us. The title "Beloved" when addressed to believers is most expressive; for, in their relation to God, their highest function is to *be loved*.

4. *The love of God has limitless intensity.* The most costly thing in the universe is the blood of God's only Son; yet God so loved the world that He gave His only begotten Son. The sacrifice of His Son for men when they were "sinners" and "enemies" seems to reach to the outmost bounds of infinity; however, we are told of a "much more" love even than this. It is God's love for those who have been reconciled and justified through Christ's death (Rom. 5:8-10) — indeed, nothing "shall be able to separate us from the love of God, which is in Christ Jesus our Lord" (Rom. 8:39).

5. *The love of God has inexhaustible benevolence.* There is no hope for this world apart from the marvelous fact that God loves even sinners. But divine love is not passive. Moved to an infinite degree by His love, God acted in behalf of those whom He otherwise would have had to banish from His presence forever. God could not ignore the just condemnation of the sinner which His own holiness imposed; but He could take upon Himself the curse which belonged to the sinner — "Greater love hath no man than this, that a man lay down his life for his friends" (John 15:13) — and this He did in order that, without violating His own holiness, He might be free to save the guilty (Rom. 3:26). Being free through the substitutionary death of Christ, God knows no limitations and does not cease working until, to His own satisfaction, He places the justly doomed sinner in heaven's highest glory, even conformed to the image of Christ.

Saving grace is more than love; it is God's love set absolutely free and made to triumph over His righteous judgments against the sinner. "By grace are ye saved through faith" (Eph. 2:8; cf. 2:4; Titus 3:4-5).

There is also in God a perfect hatred for sin which, like a counterpart of His love, prompts Him to save the sinner from his doom. In like manner, this same hatred for sin, combined with His love, makes of God a Father who chastens His child. "As many as I love, I rebuke and chasten" (Rev. 3:19), and "Whom the Lord loveth he chasteneth" (Heb. 12:6).

Because of his living union with Christ (1 Cor. 6:17), the

believer is loved by the Father even as Christ is loved (John 17:23), and this infinite love is never decreased even in the hour of correction or trial.

In addition to these direct manifestations of the love of God, many indirect manifestations can be cited. There is little reference in the New Testament to human love; its emphasis falls rather upon the imparted divine love which is experienced only by the Spirit-filled believer. The message of Romans 5:5 is that the love of God gushes forth from the Spirit who is given unto us. Since this divine love is "the fruit of the Spirit" (Gal. 5:22), He is its source. Thus passing through the believer's heart, the divine love is indirectly manifested. 1 John emphasizes the truth that, if born of God, we will love as God loves; and 1 Corinthians 13 is a description of the superhuman character of that love. There is no ecstasy in this life comparable to experiencing the unhindered outflow of the love of God.

It should be observed that love *for* God is not under consideration; rather it is the love which is God's own. Concerning this love, certain things should be noted:

It is experienced in answer to the prayer of Christ (John 17:26). God loves the lost world (John 3:16; Eph. 2:4), and as certainly He abhors the world-system which is evil (1 John 2:15-17). God loves those whom He has redeemed (John 13:34-35; 15:12-14; Rom. 5:8; Eph. 5:25; 1 John 3:16; 4:12). God loves the nation Israel (Jer. 31:3). God loves those who have wandered from Him (Luke 15:4, 20). God's love is eternal (John 13:1). God's love is sacrificial, even giving His own Son (1 John 3:16; 2 Cor. 8:9; Eph. 5:2). In the mystery of this imparted divine compassion, the Apostle Paul was willing to be accursed from Christ for his brethren — his kinsmen after the flesh (Rom. 9:1-3).

The exercise of divine love is the first commandment of Christ under grace (John 13:34-35; 15:12-14) and should be the outstanding characteristic of every Christian (Gal. 5:13; Eph. 4:2, 15; 5:2; Col. 2:2; 1 Thess. 3:12; 4:9). The imparted love of God cannot be cultivated, nor can it be produced by the flesh. It is the normal experience of those who, having met the simple conditions, are filled with the Spirit (Gal. 5:22).

D. The Bride Adorned and Rewarded

Among the many judgments of Scripture, one of the most important is the judgment seat of Christ where the church is judged and rewarded. With reference to sin, Scripture teaches that the child of God under grace shall not come into judgment (John 3:18; 5:24; 6:37; Rom. 5:1; 8:1; 1 Cor. 11:32); in his standing before God, and on the ground that the penalty for all sin — past, present, and future (Col. 2:13) — has been borne by Christ as the perfect Substitute, the believer is not only placed beyond condemnation, but being in Christ is accepted in the perfection of Christ (1 Cor. 1:30; Eph. 1:6; Col. 2:10; Heb. 10:14) and loved of God as Christ is loved (John 17:23). But with reference to his daily life and service for God, the Christian must give an account before the judgment seat of Christ (Rom. 14:10; 2 Cor. 5:10; Eph. 6:8), which judgment will occur at the coming of Christ to receive His own (1 Cor. 4:5; 2 Tim. 4:8; Rev. 22:12; cf. Matt. 16:27; Luke 14:14).

When standing before the great white throne for their final judgment, the unsaved are to be judged "according to their works" (Rev. 20:11-15). It is not the purpose of this judgment to determine whether those standing there are saved or lost; it rather determines the *degree* of penalty which, because of their evil works, shall rest upon those who are lost. Likewise, the saved, when standing before the judgment seat of Christ at His coming, are judged according to their works, and this judgment does not determine whether they are saved or lost; rather, it determines the reward or loss of reward for service which will be due each individual believer. Those who stand before the judgment seat of Christ will not only be saved and safe, but will already have been taken into heaven: not on the ground of their merit or works, but on the ground of divine grace made possible through the saviorhood of Christ. Under grace the character of the believer's life and service does not, and cannot, in any way condition his eternal salvation, and so the life and service of the believer becomes a separate and unrelated issue to be judged by Christ — whose we are and whom we serve.

When gathered before "the throne of his glory," there is also to be a reckoning of reward on the basis of merit for both Israel and the nations, but apart from the issues of personal salvation (Matt. 25:31; cf. Matt. 6:2-6; 24:45-46; 25:1-46).

There are three major figures used in the Scriptures to reveal the nature of the believer's rewards at the judgment seat of Christ.

1. *The figure of stewardship is brought out in Romans 14:10-12.* Here in connection with the judgment of other he

lievers, the exhortation is given, "But why dost thou judge thy brother? or why does thou set at naught thy brother? for we shall all stand before the judgment seat of Christ. For it is written, As I live, saith the Lord, every knee shall bow to me, and every tongue shall confess to God. So then every one of us shall give account of himself to God."

In this passage we are exhorted not to try to evaluate the quality of a fellow Christian's works. This does not mean that sin should not be judged and rebuked, but it refers rather to the value or quality of his life. Too often Christians indulge in criticism of others in order that their own lives may appear better in their own sight. In other words, they "set at nought" their brother in an effort to exalt themselves.

Revealed in this passage is the fact that every Christian will have to render account to God. The figure is that of a steward or a trustee. Everything a Christian has in life — whether it is intellectual capacity, natural gifts, physical health, spiritual gifts, or wealth — is a gift of God to him. The more entrusted to him, the more for which he will have to give an account. As brought out in 1 Corinthians 6:19-20, "Ye are not your own . . . ye are bought with a price." As stewards of all that God has given to us we will give an account at the judgment seat of Christ and will not be held responsible for that which was given to others, but will be held responsible only for what has been given to us. The key to the judgment is not success or public acclaim, but rather faithfulness in using what God has committed to us.

2. *In 1 Corinthians 3:9-15 the believer's life is viewed as a building built upon Christ as the Foundation.* In determining the force of this passage, it should be observed: (a) Only those who are saved are in view. The personal pronouns "we" and "ye" include all who are saved and exclude all who are not saved; likewise, the word "man" refers only to the one who is building on the Rock Christ Jesus.

(b) Having presented to the Corinthians the Gospel by which they were saved — which salvation provides the Rock on which the saved one stands — the Apostle Paul likens himself to a wise master-builder who has laid the foundation; but in strong contrast with this, he indicates that each believer for himself is building the superstructure upon the one Foundation which is provided through the grace of God.

The appeal, therefore, is to each one to take heed how he builds thereon. This is not a reference to so-called "character building," which finds no basis in those passages addressed to the saints of this dispensation; their character is said to be "the fruit of the Spirit" (Gal. 5:22-23) and is realized not by fleshly effort, but when walking by means of the Spirit (Gal. 5:16). The believer is represented as building a superstructure of service, or works, which is to be tested by fire — possibly by the eyes of fire of the Lord before whom he will stand (Rev. 1:14).

(c) The "work" which the Christian is building upon Christ Jesus may be of wood, hay, or stubble, which fire destroys; or it may be of gold, silver, and precious stone which fire does not destroy and which, as in the case of gold and silver, is purified by it.

(d) To the one whose "work" shall abide which he hath built on Christ, a reward shall be given; but the one whose "work" shall be burned shall suffer loss: not of his salvation which is secured through the finished work of Christ, but of his reward. Even when passing through the fire which is to test every Christian's work and even when suffering the loss of his reward, he himself shall be saved.

3. *In 1 Corinthians 9:16-27 and especially in verses 24-27, the figure of a race and winning the prize is used to reveal the quality of Christian life and service.* Having reference to his own service in preaching the Gospel, the apostle inquires, "What is my reward then?" The true answer to this question most naturally depends upon the nature and quality of the service he has rendered to God. The apostle therefore proceeds to recount his own faithfulness in works (vv. 18-23); no one will deny the truthfulness of his report. He then likens Christian service to a race in which all believers are running, and as in a foot race only one receives the prize — and that through a superior effort.

Similarly, in Christian service the believer should exert all his strength that he may obtain his full reward — run, as it were, to surpass all others. Again, as the athlete is temperate in all things that he may obtain a corruptible crown, so the Christian should be temperate in all things that he may obtain an incorruptible crown. The apostle's self-control is seen in the fact that he kept his own body under subjection lest through some unworthy and half-hearted service for others he himself should be disapproved. The word here translated "castaway" is *adokimos*, which is the negative form of *dokimos*; as *dokimos* is translated "approved" (Rom. 14:18; 16:10; 1 Cor. 11:19; 2 Cor. 10:18; 2 Tim. 2:15), so *adokimos* should be translated "disapproved." Since the apostle's salvation was in no way in question, he was not afraid he would be dismissed from God forever; but he did fear being disapproved in the sphere of his service.

The Christian's reward is sometimes mentioned as a "prize" (1 Cor. 9:24), and sometimes as a "crown" (1 Cor. 9:25; Phil. 4:1; 1 Thess. 2:19; 2 Tim. 4:8; James 1:12; 1 Pet. 5:4; Rev. 2:10; 3:11). These crowns may be classified under five divisions representing five distinct forms of Christian service and suffering, and the child of God is also warned lest he lose his reward (Col. 2:18; 2 John 8; Rev. 3:11).

The doctrine of rewards is the necessary counterpart to the doctrine of salvation by grace. Since God does not and cannot reckon the believer's merit or works to the account of his salvation, it is required that the believer's good works shall be divinely acknowledged. The saved one owes nothing to God in payment for salvation which is bestowed as a gift; but he does owe God a life of undivided devotion, and for this life of devotion there is promised a reward in heaven.

Although the rewards of the believer are symbolized by crowns, according to Revelation 4:10 crowns as a symbol of reward will be cast at the feet of the Savior in heaven. What then will be the reward for faithful service on the part of the individual believer?

The probability is that faithful service on earth will be rewarded by a privileged place of service in heaven. According to Revelation 22:3: "His servants shall serve him." Believers will find their highest fulfillment in loving service for the Savior who loved them and gave Himself for them. In the illustration of the talents used by Christ in Matthew 25:14-30, the man receiving five talents and the man receiving two talents (both of whom doubled what they had been given by their lord) were told, "Thou hast been faithful over a few things, I will make thee ruler over many things: enter thou into the joy of thy lord" (Matt. 25:21, 23). While this judgment does not seem to deal directly with the church, the principle may apply to all believers of all ages who are rewarded in eternity. Faithfulness in our service here will result in privileged service in eternity.

The central passage on the judgment seat of Christ, 2 Corinthians 5:10-11, reveals that the judgment seat of Christ is one where good works are distinguished from bad works, and on the basis of good works the believer is rewarded. As previously brought out, it is not a matter of sin being judged, because the believer is already justified. It is not a matter of sanctification such as is experienced in present chastisement for failure to confess sin (1 Cor. 11:31-32; 1 John 1:9), because the believer is already perfect in the presence of God.

The only remaining issue, then, is the quality of the believer's life and the works that God counts good in contrast with works that are worthless. The solemn fact that every believer must someday stand before God to give an account for his life should encourage present faithfulness and proper evaluation and priorities of life based on the question of how it will be evaluated in eternity.

Questions

1. Name the seven figures that are used of Christ and His church.
2. What are some of the important truths taught by the figure of the Shepherd and the sheep?
3. Explain how the figure of Christ as the True Vine and believers as branches speaks of union, communion, and fruitfulness.
4. What is the main thought in the figure of the church as a building of which Christ is the Cornerstone?
5. What are the principal functions of a believer as a priest?
6. What truth is brought out by the figure of Christ as the Last Adam and the church as a new creation?
7. Of what is the figure of Christ as the Bridegroom and the church as a bride prophetic?
8. What are the three major truths presented in the figure of the church as the body of Christ?
9. How do spiritual gifts determine an individual's particular service for God?
10. What is brought out by the concept of the church as a living organism?
11. What is the threefold work of Christ under the figure of a Bridegroom?
12. Develop, in particular, what Christ is doing at the present time for His bride.
13. Name the five characteristics of divine love revealed in Christ's love for His church.
14. In view of the love of Christ for His church, what is revealed about the love of the Father for believers?
15. In view of God's love for the church, what is revealed concerning our love?
16. In connection with the judgment of the child of God, why will a believer never be condemned for his sins?
17. What is the main purpose of the judgment of Christians at the judgment seat of Christ?
18. How does the judgment of Christians contrast with the judgment at the great white throne?
19. How does the figure of stewardship illustrate the nature of the judgment of Christians?
20. How does a building built upon Christ as the Foundation illustrate the judgment of the believer?
21. How does the figure of winning a race relate to the judgment seat of Christ?
22. What is the nature of the believer's reward?
23. How important is the judgment seat of Christ, and how does it relate to evaluating our present lives?

41

The Sabbath and the Lord's Day

A. The Sabbath in the Old Testament

Beginning with His own work in creation, God has chosen to sanctify, or set apart, one-seventh of all time. To Israel He prescribed the seventh day as a day of rest; the seventh, or sabbatic year in which the land was to rest (Exod. 23:10-11; Lev. 25:2-7); and the fiftieth year as a year of jubilee in recognition of seven times seven years. In various details both the sabbatic year and the year of jubilee were typically prophetic of the kingdom age, which is the seventh and last of the dispensations and which is characterized by the enjoyment of a sabbatic rest for all creation. Though in the present age the day to be celebrated is divinely changed from the seventh to the first day of the week because of the new creation's beginning, the same proportion in the division of time — one day in seven — is perpetuated.

The word "sabbath" means cessation, or perfect rest, from activity. Apart from the continual burnt offerings and feasts, the day was in no sense one of worship or service.

In view of the widespread confusion which exists regarding

the Sabbath, and especially in view of the effort which is made to recognize it as in force in this present age, it is imperative that the precise teachings of Scripture concerning the Sabbath be carefully weighed.

A degree of clarity is gained when the Sabbath is considered in its relation to various periods of time:

In the period from Adam to Moses it is recorded that God rested at the close of His six creative days (Gen. 2:2-3; Exod. 20:10-11; Heb. 4:4). But there is no intimation in the Word of God that man was appointed to observe, or ever did observe, a Sabbath until Israel came out of Egypt.

The Book of Job discloses the religious life and experience of the patriarchs, and though their various responsibilities to God are there discussed, there is no reference to a Sabbath-day obligation. On the other hand, it is distinctly stated that the giving of the Sabbath to Israel by the hand of Moses was the beginning of Sabbath observance among men (Exod. 16:29; Neh. 9:14; Ezek. 20:12).

Likewise, it is evident from the records of the first imposition of the Sabbath (Exod. 16:1-35) that on the particular day which was one week, or seven days, previous to the first recorded Sabbath, the children of Israel took a Sabbath-breaking journey of many miles from Elim to the wilderness of Sin. There they murmured against Jehovah, and on that day the supply of food from heaven began which was to be gathered for six days, but was not to be gathered on the seventh day. It is evident, therefore, that the day of their journey which would have been a Sabbath was not observed as a Sabbath.

In the period from Moses to Christ, the Sabbath was rightfully in force. It was embedded in the law (Exod. 20:10-11), and the divine cure for its nonobservance was likewise provided in the law of the offerings. In this connection, it is important to observe that the Sabbath was never imposed on the Gentiles, but was peculiarly a sign between Jehovah and Israel (Exod. 31:12-17). Among Israel's sins, her failure to keep the Sabbath and to give the land its rest are especially emphasized.

In the midst of this period of the law, Hosea predicted that, as a part of the judgments which were to come upon Israel, her Sabbaths would cease (Hos. 2:11). This prophecy must at some time be fulfilled, for the mouth of the Lord has spoken it.

As the preceding age continued to the death of Christ, His earth-life and ministry were under the law. For this reason He

290 MAJOR BIBLE THEMES

is seen as keeping the law, expounding the law, and applying the law. Finding the Sabbath law obscured by the traditions and teachings of men, He pointed out that the Sabbath was given as a benefit to man, and man was not to be made a sacrifice for the Sabbath (Mark 2:27). Christ was faithful to the whole Mosaic system, which included the Sabbath, because that system was in force during His earth-life; but that obvious fact is no basis for the claim that a Christian who is under grace and living in another dispensation is appointed to follow Christ in His Sabbath observance.

B. The Sabbath in the Present Church Age

Following the resurrection of Christ, there is no record in the New Testament that the Sabbath was observed by any believer, even in error. Doubtless the multitude of Judaized Christians did observe the Sabbath; but no record of such observance was permitted to appear in the Word of God. In like manner, following the resurrection of Christ, there is no injunction given to Jew, Gentile, or Christian to observe the Sabbath, nor is Sabbath-breaking once mentioned among the numerous lists of possible sins. On the contrary, there are warnings against Sabbath observance on the part of those who are the children of God under grace.

Galatians 4:9-10 condemns the observance of "days, and months, and times, and years." These were usually observed with a view to meriting the favor of God and by those who would be thoughtful of God at one time and careless at another.

Hebrews 4:1-13 contemplates the Sabbath as a type of the rest (from his own works) into which the believer enters when he is saved.

Colossians 2:16-17 plainly instructs the child of God *not* to be judged with respect to a Sabbath day, and infers that such an attitude toward the Sabbath is reasonable in view of all that Christ has become to one who is now of the new creation (Col. 2:9-17). In this passage most evidently reference is made to the weekly Sabbaths, rather than to those special or extra Sabbaths which were a part of the ceremonial law.

Romans 14:5 declares that when the believer is "persuaded in his own mind" he may esteem all days alike. This does not imply a neglect of faithful worship, but rather suggests that, to such a one, *all* days are full of devotion to God.

Because of the fact that in the New Testament the Sabbath is never included as any part of the Christian's life and service, the term "Christian Sabbath" is a misnomer. In this connection it may be noted that in place of the Sabbath of the law there is now provided the Lord's Day of the new creation which far exceeds the Sabbath in its glory, its privileges, and its blessings.

C. The Sabbath in the Coming Age

In full harmony with the New Testament doctrine that the new Lord's Day is related only to the church, it is prophesied that the Sabbath will be reinstated — thus superseding the Lord's Day — immediately upon the completion of the out-calling of the church and her removal from the world. Even in the brief period of the Tribulation which must intervene between the end of this age and the age of the kingdom, the Sabbath is again in view (Matt. 24:20); but prophecy especially anticipates the Sabbath as a vital feature of the coming kingdom age (Isa. 66:23; Ezek. 46:1).

D. The Resurrection of Christ and the First Day of the Week

The first day of the week has been celebrated by the church from the resurrection of Christ to the present time. This fact is proven by the New Testament records, the writings of the early fathers, and the history of the church. There have been those in nearly every century who, not comprehending the present purpose of God in the new creation, have earnestly contended for the observance of the seventh-day Sabbath. At present, those who specialize in urging the observance of the seventh day combine these appeals with other unscriptural doctrines. Since the believer is appointed of God to observe the first day of the week under the new relationship of grace, confusion arises when that day is invested with the character of, and is governed by, the seventh-day Sabbath laws. All such teachings ignore the New Testament doctrine of the new creation.

E. The New Creation

The New Testament reveals that the purpose of God in the present unforeseen dispensation is the out-calling of the church (Acts 15:13-18), and this redeemed company is the new creation, a heavenly people. While it is indicated that marvelous glories and perfections are to be accomplished for this company as a whole (Eph. 5:25-27), it is also revealed that they *individually* are the objects of the greatest divine undertakings and transformations. Likewise, as the corporate body is organically related to Christ (1 Cor. 12:12), so the individual believer is vitally joined to the Lord (1 Cor. 6:17; Rom. 6:5; 1 Cor. 12:13).

Concerning the individual believer, the Bible teaches that (1) as to sin, each one in this company has been cleansed, forgiven, and justified; (2) as to his possessions, each one has been given the indwelling Spirit, the gift of God which is eternal life, has become a legal heir of God, and a joint-heir with Christ; (3) as to his position, each one has been *made* the righteousness of God by which he is accepted in the Beloved forever (2 Cor. 5:21; Eph. 1:6), a member of Christ's mystical body, a part of His glorious bride, and a living partaker in the new creation of which Christ is the Federal Head. We read: "If any man be in Christ, he is a new creature [creation]: old things [as to position, not experience] are passed away; behold, all things are become new. And all [these positional] things are of God" (2 Cor. 5:17-18; cf. Gal. 6:15; Eph. 2:10; 4:24).

Peter, writing of this company of believers, states, "but ye are a chosen generation" (1 Pet. 2:9), which means a distinct heaven-born race, or nationality — a stock, or kind — which has been directly created by the power of God. As the first Adam begat a race which partook of his own human life and imperfections, so Christ, the last Adam, is now begetting by the Spirit a new race which partakes of His eternal life and perfection. "The first man Adam was made a living soul; the last Adam was made a quickening [life-giving] spirit" (1 Cor. 15:45).

Having partaken of the resurrection life of Christ, and being *in Christ*, the believer is said to be already raised (Rom. 6:4; Col. 2:12-13; 3:1-4). However, as to his body, the believer is yet to receive a glorious body like the resurrection body of Christ (Phil. 3:20-21). In confirmation of this we also read that when Christ appeared in heaven immediately following His resurrection, it was as the "firstfruits," implying that the whole company that are to follow will be like Him (1 John 3:2), even to their glorified bodies.

In the Word of God, the new creation — which began with the resurrection of Christ and consists of a born-again, heavenly company who are *in Christ* — is everywhere held in contrast with the old creation, and it is from that old and ruined creation that the believer is said to have been saved and delivered.

As the Sabbath was instituted to celebrate the old creation (Exod. 20:10-11; 31:12-17; Heb. 4:4), so the Lord's Day celebrates the new creation. Likewise, as the Sabbath was limited in its application to Israel as the earthly people of God, so also the Lord's Day is limited in its application to the church as the heavenly people of God.

F. The Lord's Day

In addition to the fact that the Sabbath is nowhere imposed on the children of God under grace, there are abundant reasons for their observing the first day of the week.

1. *A new day is prophesied and appointed under grace.* According to Psalm 118:22-24 and Acts 4:10-11, Christ in His crucifixion was the Stone rejected by Israel the "builders"; but through His resurrection He has been made the Headstone of the corner. This marvelous thing is of God, and the day of its accomplishment is divinely appointed as a day of rejoicing and gladness. Accordingly, Christ's greeting on the resurrection morn was "All hail!" (Matt. 28:9, which is more literally, "O joy!"), and being "the day which the Lord hath made," it is rightfully termed "The Lord's Day."

2. *Observance of the first day is indicated by various events.* (a) On that day Christ arose from the dead (Matt. 28:1). (b) On that day He first met His disciples in the new fellowship (John 20:19). (c) On that day He gave them instruction (Luke 24:13-45). (d) On that day He ascended into heaven as the "firstfruits," or wave sheaf (Lev. 23:10-12; John 20:17; 1 Cor. 15:20, 23). (e) On that day He breathed on them (John 20:22). (f) On that day the Spirit descended from heaven (Acts 2:1-4). (g) On that day the Apostle Paul preached in Troas (Acts 20:6-7). (h) On that day the believers came together to break bread (Acts 20:6-7). (i) On that day they were to "lay by in store" as God had prospered them (1 Cor. 16:2). (j) On that day Christ appeared to John on Patmos (Rev. 1:10).

3. *The eighth day was the day of circumcision.* The rite of circumcision, performed on the eighth day, typified the believer's separation from the flesh and the old order by the death of Christ (Col. 2:11), and the eighth day, being the first day after a completed week, is symbolical of a new beginning.

4. *The new day is of grace.* At the end of a week of toil, a day of rest was granted to the people who were related to God by works of the law; while to the people under grace, whose works are finished in Christ, a day of worship is appointed which, being the first day of the week, precedes all days of work. In the blessing of the first day the believer lives and serves the following six days. A day of rest belongs to a people who are related to God by works which were to be accomplished; a day of ceaseless worship and service belongs to a people who are related to God by the finished work of Christ. The seventh day was characterized by unyielding law; the first day is characterized by the latitude and liberty belonging to grace. The seventh day was observed with the hope that by it one might be acceptable to God; The first day is observed with the assurance that one is already accepted of God. The keeping of the seventh day was wrought by the flesh; the keeping of the first day is wrought by the indwelling Spirit.

5. *The new day has been blessed of God.* Throughout this age the most Spirit-filled, devout believers to whom the will of God has been clearly revealed have kept the Lord's day apart from any sense of responsibility to keep the seventh day. It is reasonable to suppose that if they had been guilty of Sabbath-breaking, they would have been convicted of that sin.

6. *The new day is committed only to the individual believer.* It is not committed to the unsaved. It is certainly most misleading to the unsaved to give them grounds for supposing that they will be more accepted of God if they observe a day; for apart from the salvation which is in Christ, all men are utterly and equally lost. For social or physical reasons a day of rest may be secured to the benefit of all; but the unregenerate should understand that the observance of such a day adds nothing to their merit before God.

It is not committed to the church as a body. The responsibility to the observance of the first day is of necessity committed to the individual believer only, and not to the church as a whole; and the manner of its celebration by the individual is suggested in the two sayings of Christ on the morning of His resurrection: "O joy!" and "Go tell." This calls for ceaseless activity in all forms of worship and service; such activity contrasts with the seventh-day rest.

7. *No command is given to keep the first day.* Since it is all of grace, a written requirement for the keeping of the Lord's Day is not imposed, nor is the manner of its observance prescribed. By this wise provision, none are encouraged to keep the day as a mere duty; it is to be kept from the heart. Israel stood before God as immature children under tutors and governors and needing the commandments which are given to a child (Gal. 4:1-11); the church stands before God as adult sons. The believer's life under grace is clearly defined, but it is presented only as the beseechings of God with the expectation that all shall be done *willingly* (Rom. 12:1-2; Eph. 4:1-3). There is little question as to how a well-instructed, Spirit-filled believer (and the Scripture presupposes a normal Christian to be such) will be occupied on the day which commemorates Christ's resurrection and the new creation. If the child of God is not yielded to God, no unwilling observance of a day will correct his carnal heart, nor would such observance be pleasing to God. The issue between God and the carnal Christian is not one of outward actions, but of a yielded life.

8. *The manner of the observance of the Lord's Day may be extended to all days.* Christ was not more devoted to His Father on one day than on another. Sabbath rest could not be extended to all days alike; but while the believer may have more time and freedom on the first day of the week, his worship, joy, and service which characterizes the keeping of the Lord's Day should, as far as possible, be his experience every day (Rom. 14:5).

Questions

1. Explain the provision in Israel for a Sabbath, a sabbatic year, and the year of jubilee.
2. Of what period was the sabbatic year typical?
3. What does the word "Sabbath" mean?
4. What is the background of the Sabbath prior to the law of Moses?
5. According to Scripture, when was the Sabbath first observed and by whom?
6. Were non-Israelites ever required to observe the Sabbath?
7. What did Christ do about the Sabbath?
8. After Pentecost, is there any record of Christians keeping the Sabbath or being commanded to keep the Sabbath?
9. Why is the term "Christian Sabbath" incorrect?
10. When does prophecy indicate the Sabbath will be observed again?
11. Why do Christians observe the first day of the week as the Lord's Day?
12. What are some of the outstanding features of the new creation?
13. To what company is observance of the Lord's Day limited?
14. Was observance of a new day prophesied?
15. What important events took place on the first day of the week?
16. How is the first day of the week related to circumcision?
17. How do you contrast observance of the seventh day and observance of the first day as to meaning?
18. How do you explain the fact there is no command given concerning observance of the first day and no regulations as to how it should be observed?
19. In what sense may observance of the Lord's Day be extended to every day?

42

The Gentiles in
History and Prophecy

A. The Gentiles in the
Program of God

In both history and prophecy, three major divisions of humanity
may be observed in Scripture, stated simply in 1 Corinthians
10:32 as the purpose of God relating to the Jews, to the Gentiles,
and to the church of God. To this can be added the ministering
of God to and through angels which usually is not considered a
major element of human history or prophecy.

In contrast with God's purpose for Israel as the primary means
of divine revelation and special dealing and the channel through
which Christ could come, and His purpose for the church to
reveal supremely His grace, God's purpose for the Gentiles
seems to be related to demonstrating His sovereignty and His
omnipotence.

B. Early Prophecies Concerning
the Gentiles

In one sense, Gentile prophecy began in the Garden of Eden,

as the Gentile participated to some extent in the purpose of God in salvation. Early in Genesis, prophecy is given concerning the flood of Noah's time which wiped out the human race except for Noah and his family. Likewise, history records the judgment of God upon the Gentiles at the time of the Tower of Babel (Gen. 11:1-9). Beginning in Genesis 12, however, the human race is divided into two classes as God begins to introduce the promised seed which would come from Abraham, Isaac, and Jacob. All others continued in their place as Gentiles. The dealings of God with Gentiles in relation to Israel are basically recorded in Scripture.

The first great Gentile power was Egypt, and in Egypt Israel grew from a small family into a great nation, as recorded in the first five books of the Old Testament. While in due time Israel became a great nation under David and Solomon, the ten tribes were carried off into captivity by the second great Gentile power, Assyria, in 721 B.C. The judgment of God inflicted on Israel by the Assyrians was faithfully prophesied in the years preceding the event and just as faithfully fulfilled.

The major role of the Gentiles in relation to Israel, however, begins with the Babylonian empire, the third in a series of great empires but the first of four empires which became the subject of Daniel's prophecies.

C. The Times of the Gentiles

To Daniel the prophet were given two of the three major programs of God, that is, the program of God for Israel and the program of God for the Gentiles. In a series of divine revelations beginning with the dream of Nebuchadnezzar in Daniel 2, and continuing with subsequent revelations to Daniel, God revealed that four great empires beginning with Babylon would characterize the period of Gentile dominion over Israel. This is seen in the great image of Daniel 2: the head of gold represented Babylon; the upper part of the body of silver, the empire of the Medes and the Persians; the lower part of the body of brass, the empire of Greece; and the iron legs and feet, the empire of Rome. This truth is reinforced in Daniel 7, where the four beasts represent the same four empires.

Daniel lived to see the second empire (the Medes and the Persians) conquer Babylon in 539 B.C., as recorded in Daniel 5. Two hundred years later the Grecian Empire led by Alexander the Great conquered the remnants of the empire of the Medes and Persians. Then in the second century B.C. the Roman Empire began its rise to power and became the greatest and most influential empire of all time.

The period of the four empires beginning with Babylon is referred to by Christ as "the times of the Gentiles" (Luke 21:24) and is characterized by Jerusalem's being under Gentile control. While for brief periods Gentile control of Jerusalem has been relinquished, no final deliverance of Jerusalem from the power of the Gentiles will be fulfilled until the second coming of Christ.

Most of the times of the Gentiles have already been fulfilled as seen in the rise and fall of Babylon, Medo-Persia, Greece, and Rome. The last stage of the Roman empire, however, symbolized by the feet of the image in Daniel 2 and by the ten-horn stage of the beast of Daniel 7, has not had literal fulfillment. The fourth beast, according to Scripture, will be destroyed by the Son of Man coming from heaven, as portrayed in Daniel 7 or in the smiting stone of Daniel 2 which destroys the image of Nebuchadnezzar.

Based on these prophecies, many interpreters believe a future revival of the Roman empire is in prospect which will come about after the church has been raptured and taken to heaven, but before the second coming of Christ to set up His kingdom. This situation will arise in what Scripture refers to as "the time of the end" (Dan. 11:35) and will be a dominant factor in world history and prophecy as they relate to the period leading up to the Second Coming.

Following the completion of the times of the Gentiles at the second coming of Christ to the earth, Gentiles who are saved and on earth in the millennial kingdom will enjoy also special blessing from God, as will be brought out in later study of the millennial kingdom.

Taken as a whole, the biblical outline of prophecy concerning the Gentiles is the outline of world history, which explains many events of the past and casts a shadow on the future. Present world conditions are in line with everything the Bible prophesies and seem to indicate a rapid approach to the consummation in the time of the end which will be preceded by the rapture of the church and will include the events relating to the time of the end and the second coming of Christ to bring His millennial kingdom.

The present age does not seem to advance the fulfillment of

Gentile prophecy and does not seem to be in the foreview of the Old Testament prophesied program for the Gentiles. It is as if the prophetic foreview were suspended on the day of Pentecost, to be resumed on the day of the Rapture. Nevertheless, trends in world development at present seem to foreshadow a setting of the stage for the end of the age, with the implication that the present age is nearing the close and the fulfillment of Gentile prophecy is about to be resumed. The study of Gentile prophecy is, accordingly, an important aspect of the total prophetic program and provides many insights in understanding what God is doing today and what God purposes to do in the future.

Questions

1. Explain how the Gentiles are one of three major divisions of humanity in the present age.
2. Summarize the early history of Gentiles before Abraham.
3. What were the first two great Gentile empires, and how was each related to Israel's history?
4. What two major programs of God were revealed to Daniel?
5. Name the four empires revealed to Daniel as the outline of Gentile world history.
6. What are "the times of the Gentiles" and how are they described by Christ in Luke 21:24?
7. When, according to Daniel, will the times of the Gentiles be ended?
8. What is promised to the Gentiles after the second coming of Christ to the earth?
9. How is the present church age related to the times of the Gentiles?
10. Can we expect future fulfillment of the last stage of the times of the Gentiles?

43

Israel in History and Prophecy

A. *Israel in Relation to the Dispensations*

The history of Israel begins in Genesis 12 with the call of Abraham and is a major theme of the Old Testament. In the New Testament gospels and the Acts, additional insight is given on the state of Israel in the first century, with other allusions to Israel both historic and prophetic in the rest of the New Testament.

Israel is involved in all the dispensations beginning with the dispensation of promise (see Chapter 20, "The Dispensations"). In the dispensation of promise, the covenant with Abraham lays the broad basis for all God's dealings with Israel in subsequent generations. The dispensation of the law beginning in Exodus 19 is the major dispensation of the Old Testament and conditions Israel's life until it is fulfilled on the cross. Most of Israel's recorded history relates to the dispensation of law.

In the dispensation of grace, Israel shares with Gentiles the privileges of grace, both in salvation and as the rule of life. In the future dispensation of the kingdom, Israel again takes a prominent role in possessing her promised land and being subject to Jesus Christ as her King. Although disproportionately small compared with the Gentiles, Israel plays a prominent role in the entire history of the world from Abraham to the end (for further details, see Chapter 20).

B. Israel in Relation to the Covenants

Closely connected to the dispensations are the biblical covenants. Israel has a major role in each of the biblical covenants beginning with the covenant of Abraham in Genesis 12 (see Chapter 21, "The Covenants").

The five covenants are major factors in Israel's history and prophecy. As previously pointed out, the Abrahamic covenant is the basis for Israel's program. The Mosaic covenant conditions the life of Israel in the dispensation of law and relates to all the Old Testament beginning in Exodus 19. The Palestinian covenant relates particularly to Israel's possession and dispossession of the land, anticipating, however, the ultimate permanent possession in the millennial kingdom. The Davidic covenant conditions Israel's relationship to the Davidic kingdom and anticipates prophetically the future kingdom where Christ will reign on earth in the Millennium, with David resurrected and acting as His royal prince. The new covenant prophesied in the Old Testament relates to Israel's blessings in the kingdom and replaces and contrasts with the Mosaic covenant. The detailed relationship of each of these covenants to Israel was presented in Chapter 21.

C. The Old Testament History of Israel

Although properly the history of Israel begins with Jacob, who was given the name Israel, the history of Israel usually includes the life story of Abraham and Isaac, the grandfather and father of Jacob. Abraham, originally a resident of Ur of the Chaldees, went with his father about a thousand miles northwest to Haran and there became a wealthy herdsman. Upon his father's death, in obedience to God, Abraham with his wife Sarah and his nephew Lot came to the promised land, another thousand miles toward the southwest from Haran. In the Promised Land, God began to deal with Abraham.

God had promised Abraham in the important Abrahamic covenant that he would become a great man, that he would be the father of a great nation, and that through his posterity the entire world would be blessed. As previously brought out in the study of the Abrahamic covenant (Chapter 21), these promises have been literally fulfilled. Miraculously, after Abraham and Sarah were too old to have children, Isaac was born. Then in due time Jacob and Esau were born to Isaac and Rebekah, with Jacob the younger twin chosen by God to be the head of the nation Israel.

The account of the lives of Abraham, Isaac, and Jacob takes up Genesis 12-50 and evidently is important to God especially, when taking into consideration that the whole creative narrative took only two chapters (Gen. 1 – 2), and the whole story of the fall into sin took only one chapter (Gen. 3). From the divine standpoint, the history of Israel is the key to history as a whole.

In keeping with the prophecy to Abraham in Genesis 15:13-14, Israel made her way to Egypt in the time of famine. They found their way prepared by Joseph, who had risen to great authority in Egypt. Abraham and his family were welcomed to the land of Egypt and were cared for during the lifetime of Joseph.

The Israelites' several hundred years in Egypt ended disastrously, however, when a change of rulership took away their privileged status, and they became slaves. In their bondage they cried to the Lord, and the Lord raised up Moses and Joshua to lead them out of Egypt into the Promised Land. Although Israel failed God at Kadesh-barnea (Num. 14), and they wandered for forty years in the wilderness as a result, ultimately God enabled them to conquer the land on the east side of Jordan and after Moses' death to cross the Jordan and conquer much of the Promised Land.

Their return to the Promised Land and establishment as a nation prospered through the lifetime of Joshua, but Israel soon departed from God and went on a moral spiral downward as recorded in the Book of Judges.

God then raised up Samuel the prophet, who in large measure reestablished Israel spiritually and laid the basis for the glories of the kingdom under Saul, David, and Solomon. Although Saul failed as the first king of Israel, his successor David as a great warrior was able to conquer much of the territory belonging to the Promised Land.

David's son Solomon extended his sway until he put under tribute most of the area originally mentioned to Abraham, from the river of Egypt to the River Euphrates. His violation of God's command not to multiply wives and depend on horses for military strength (Deut. 17:16-17) prepared the way for the divided kingdom and the rapid decline of Israel's strength after him. Solomon's children were raised largely by heathen wives who were unsympathetic to the law of God. Shortly after Solomon's death, the ten tribes of the North (Israel) withdrew and had a succession of wicked kings. God's judgment descended on them in the Assyrian captivity in 721 B.C. The two remaining tribes of the Southern Kingdom (Judah), although having some godly kings, followed the same downward course and were led into captivity in 605 B.C. by the Babylonians.

At the conclusion of the seventy years of the Babylonian captivity, in keeping with the promise recorded in Jeremiah 29:10, Israel again was able to go back to the land. The Book of Ezra records the people's return and their struggles for twenty years to rebuild the Temple, and Nehemiah completes the story with the rebuilding of the walls of Jerusalem and the city itself about a century later. Israel back in the land, however, did not follow the Lord and was under the dominion of the Medes and Persians for 200 years; then she was caught in the warfare between Syria and Egypt after the death of Alexander the Great in 323 B.C.

Meanwhile, the power of Rome began to expand with the conquest of Sicily in 242 B.C. Jerusalem itself was subdued by the Roman General Pompeius in 63 B.C. Israel was treated cruelly by the Romans, who carried off hundreds of thousands of Jews into slavery. Ultimately, on Roman authority Jesus Christ was crucified, and later (in A.D. 70) the city of Jerusalem was destroyed, with Israel subsequently scattered all over the world and driven from her homeland. It was not until the twentieth century that Israel began to return to her land and became reformed as a national entity and a recognized political state in 1948.

D. *The History of Israel and Fulfilled Prophecy*

The history in the Old Testament is largely in fulfillment of the great prophecies of Scripture. Literally hundreds of prophecies have been fulfilled. In keeping with the prophecies given to Abraham, Israel became a great nation. The Old Testament predicted three dispossessions of the land of Israel, and these were fulfilled (1) in her descent into Egypt and subsequent bondage and release, and the return to the land, (2) the Assyrian and Babylonian captivities which removed Israel once again from the land, and her subsequent return after seventy years in Babylon, and (3) her dispossession once again after the destruction of Jerusalem in A.D. 70. The broad movement of Israel possessing the land and being dispossessed of it formed the important background for her entire history (Gen. 15:13-16; Deut. 28:62-67; Jer. 25:11-12; cf. also Lev. 26:3-46; Deut. 30:1-3; Neh. 1:8; Ps. 106:1-48; Jer. 9:16; 18:15-17; Ezek. 2:14-15; 20:23; 22:15; James 1:1).

Important to the history of Israel are the prophecies given concerning the character and destiny of Jacob's sons (Gen. 49:1-28). Numerous other prophecies are given in the Old Testament concerning God's dealings with the twelve tribes of Israel.

Another important theme of prophecy and its fulfillment relates to the Davidic kingdom. In keeping with the Davidic covenant, the throne is promised to David and his seed forever (2 Sam. 7:16; Ps. 89:35-36; Jer. 33:21; Dan. 7:14). Promises both of blessing and cursing were fulfilled literally as God dealt with Saul, David, and Solomon and succeeding kingdoms of Judah and Israel.

E. The Prophecy of Israel's 490 Years

One of the major prophecies given through Daniel is recorded in Daniel 9:24-27. Here, according to the information given by the angel Gabriel to Daniel, "seventy weeks" or seventy sevens (490 years) were to comprise Israel's future history. Daniel was told (9:24), "Seventy weeks are determined upon thy people and upon thy holy city, to finish the transgression, and to make an end of sins, and to make reconciliation for iniquity, and to bring in everlasting righteousness, and to seal up the vision and prophecy, and to anoint the most Holy."

The prophecy was to begin with the command to restore and to build Jerusalem (Dan. 9:25), and 483 years of the total of 490 years were to be fulfilled before the Messiah the Prince would come. While scholars have differed greatly in their interpretation of this passage, probably the best view is to begin this period of 490 years with the time of Nehemiah's reconstruction of Jerusalem in 445 B.C. It would then culminate about A.D. 32, approximately the time when Christ died on the cross. Recent scholarship has placed the death of Christ as late as 33 A.D., although most interpreters date it A.D. 30 or earlier.

According to Daniel's prophecy, after the Messiah Himself was to be cut off — which would occur after the 483 years but apparently before the last seven years of the prophecy — Jerusalem itself would be destroyed (Dan. 9:26). This historically was fulfilled in the destruction of Jerusalem in A.D. 70.

It is implied in Daniel's prophecy that there is a considerable period between the end of the 483 years, or the 69 "weeks," and the beginning of the last seven years, or seventieth "week," as it includes two events separated by forty years. The last week was to be characterized by a covenant apparently made with a future prince related to the people who destroyed the city. As the people who destroyed the city of Jerusalem were Romans, "the prince that shall come" (Dan. 9:26) will apparently be a ruler of a revived Roman empire. Many interpreters view this as still a future event which will occur after the church has been raptured.

This future ruler will make a seven-year covenant with the people of Israel described in Daniel 9:27. The covenant will be broken in the middle of the week, and the last three and one-half years will be a time of persecution and trial for Israel. This period is the subject of extended prophecy in Revelation 6-18 and ends at the second coming of Christ in Revelation 19. Of special interest is the prediction that this future ruler will cause sacrifice and oblation to cease and will make the Temple desolate. This implies a future temple in Jerusalem and a resumption of the sacrificial system of Moses by Orthodox Jews in the period preceding the second coming of Christ.

It is significant that the first 483 years have been literally fulfilled. Jerusalem was rebuilt in the first 49 years as indicated in Daniel 9:25. The Messiah was cut off after 483 years. The events of the last week are yet future and provide a chronology for the end time leading up to the second coming of Christ.

F. Prophecy Concerning the Advent of the Messiah

From 1 Peter 1:10-11 it is clear that the prophets of the Old Testament were unable to distinguish the two advents of the

Messiah. So perfectly was the present age a secret in the counsels of God that, to the prophets, the events which were fulfilled at His first coming and those which are yet to be fulfilled at His second coming were in no way separated as to the time of their fulfillment.

Isaiah 61:1-2 is an illustration of this. When reading this passage in the synagogue of Capernaum, Christ ceased abruptly when He had concluded the record of those features which were predicted for His first advent (Luke 4:18-21), making no mention of the remaining features which are to be fulfilled when He comes again. In like manner, the angel Gabriel, when anticipating the ministry of Christ, combined as in one the undertakings which belong to both the first and the second advents (Luke 1:31-33).

According to Old Testament prophecy, Christ was to come both as a sacrificial, unresisting Lamb (Isa. 53:1-12) and as the conquering and glorious Lion of the Tribe of Judah (Isa. 11:1-12; Jer. 23:5-6). Considering these two extensive lines of prediction, there is little wonder there was perplexity in the minds of the Old Testament prophets as to the "manner of time" when all this would be fulfilled (1 Pet. 1:10-11).

Prophecy stipulated that the Messiah must be of the tribe of Judah (Gen. 49:10), of the house of David (Isa. 11:1; Jer. 33:21), born of a virgin (Isa. 7:14), in Bethlehem of Judea (Mic. 5:2), that He must die a sacrificial death (Isa. 53:1-12), by crucifixion (Ps. 22:1-21), rise again from the dead (Ps. 16:8-11), and come to earth the second time (Deut. 30:3) on the clouds of heaven (Dan. 7:13). Jesus of Nazareth has fulfilled or will fulfill every requirement of prophecy concerning the Messiah as no other claimant can ever do.

G. Prophecy Concerning the Last Dispersion and Regathering of Israel

Most important in the Old Testament prophecies concerning Israel are those related to Israel's final dispersion and final regathering. By the Assyrian captivity of the Northern Kingdom and the Babylonian captivity of the Southern Kingdom, and as a national punishment for sin, the whole house of Israel was taken from off the land and in due time was scattered among the nations of the earth. This was in fulfillment of multiplied prophecies (Lev. 26:32-39; Deut. 28:63-68; Neh. 1:8; Ps. 44:11; Jer. 9:16; 18:15-17; Ezek. 12: 14-15; 20:23; 22:15; James 1:1). In no case would Israel's national entity be lost even through centuries of dispersion (Jer. 31:36; Matt. 24:34). They refused the divine offer and provision for their regathering and kingdom glory which was made by their Messiah at His first advent (Matt. 23:37-39); at Kadesh-barnea, where their wilderness experience was extended (Num. 14:1-45), their chastisement was continued and will be continued until He comes again. At that time He will regather His people into their own land and cause them to enter into the glory and blessedness of every covenant promise of Jehovah concerning them (Deut. 30:1-10; Isa. 11:11-12; Jer. 23:3-8; Ezek. 37:21-25; Matt. 24:31).

H. Prophecy Concerning the End Time

As intimated in the brief study of Daniel 9:27, Israel will have a dramatic future role in end-time events leading up to the second coming of Christ. According to Scripture, there are four major movements to Israel's future in relation to the end of the age.

1. *Israel was prophesied to be reconstituted as a political state.* In order to make a covenant with the "prince that shall come," it was necessary for Israel to be formed again as a political state. This, of course, was dramatically fulfilled in May 1948 when Israel was recognized as a nation and given a portion of the Promised Land as her possession. In years which followed, her territories have been enlarged and her strength increased, until Israel today, although small in number, is a major factor in world affairs. This is a prelude to other prophecies to be fulfilled.

2. *As indicated in Daniel 9:27, Israel will enter into a covenant with a Gentile Roman ruler of the Mediterranean, a covenant planned for seven years.* This will introduce the covenant period in which Israel will have a measure of peace and security. In this period, undoubtedly many more Jews will go back to the Promised Land, and Israel will prosper financially as well as politically.

3. *The covenant with Israel, however, will be dramatically broken in three and one-half years after it is formed, and Israel will become a persecuted people instead of a favored people.* This is "the time of Jacob's trouble" (Jer. 30:7) and the Great

Tribulation (Dan. 12:1; Matt. 24:21; Rev. 7:14). Further attention to this period will be given in the next two chapters.

4. *Israel's glorious restoration in the millennial kingdom will follow the second advent of Christ and continue throughout the thousand years of Christ's reign on earth.*

The importance of understanding the four stages of Israel's restoration is seen in the fact that the first stage has already taken place and the second stage will most probably not take place until after the church is raptured. The stage is being set for dramatic end-time events in which Israel will have a major role.

I. Prophecy Concerning the Messianic Kingdom and the Day of the Lord

In respect to the amount of Scripture involved, there is no theme of Old Testament prophecy comparable with that of the Messianic kingdom. Lying beyond all the predicted chastisements that are to fall on Israel is the glory which will be hers when her people are regathered into their own land, with unmeasured spiritual blessings under the glorious reign of their Messiah-King. This vision was given to all the prophets. As certainly and literally as Israel, in fulfillment of prophecy, was removed from the land and caused to suffer during these many centuries, so certainly and literally will she be restored to marvelous blessings in a redeemed and glorified earth (Isa. 11 – 12; 24:22 – 27:13; 35:1-10; 52:12; 54 – 55; 59:20 – 66:24; Jer. 23:3-8; 31:1-40; 32:37-41; 33:1-26; Ezek. 34:11-31; 36:32 – 37:28; 40:1 – 48:35; Dan. 2:44-45; 7:14; Hos. 3:4-5; 13:9 – 14:9; Joel 2:28 – 3:21; Amos 9:11-15; Zeph. 3:14-20; Zech. 8:1-22; 14:9-21).

Old Testament predictions concerning the kingdom are often a part of the predictions concerning the return of the King. When these two themes are combined into one, it is termed "the day of the Lord," which refers to that lengthened period extending from the rapture of the church and the judgments following this event on the earth, to the end of His millennial reign (Isa. 2:10-22; Zech. 14).

There are a number of indications that the day of the Lord will begin as soon as the rapture of the church occurs. The major events of the day of the Lord, accordingly, seem to include the Great Tribulation and God's judgments on the world preceding the second coming of Christ, as well as the judgments which attend the second coming of Christ and the entire thousand-year reign of Christ on earth.

Because many of the great prophecies were not fulfilled by the time the Old Testament was completed, the additional revelation of the New Testament is essential to presenting the complete and detailed account of both many fulfillments of the Old Testament and also many prophecies yet to be fulfilled. The story of Israel in history and prophecy has to a large extent been fulfilled, but great future events are yet ahead. Evidence is accumulating that the end time when Israel will again come into its own is very near. Additional details are given in the chapters which follow.

Questions

1. When does the history of Israel properly begin in Scripture?
2. How is Israel related to the dispensations beginning with Abraham?
3. Name the five covenants which are major conditions of Israel's history and prophecy.
4. Summarize the main events of the lives of Abraham, Isaac, and Jacob as outlined in Genesis.
5. Describe the history of Israel from Joshua to Samuel.
6. Summarize the history of Israel during the reigns of Saul, David, and Solomon.
7. Describe the division of the kingdom of Israel after Solomon, and describe the Assyrian and Babylonian captivities.
8. How was Israel restored to the land, and the Temple in Jerusalem rebuilt, after the Babylonian captivity?
9. Summarize the relationship of the Roman Empire to Israel.
10. What are the three dispossessions of her land and dispersion of the nation Israel?
11. What important promises were given in the Davidic covenant?
12. What is included in the 490 years of Israel's history described in Daniel 9:24-27?
13. When did this period probably begin?
14. What two events took place after the sixty-ninth week, or 483 years, of the program?
15. Why do many expositors feel the last seven years are still future?
16. What are the major events of the last seven years, according to Daniel 9:27?
17. Where are the last three and one-half years of Israel's history described in detail in the New Testament?
18. Describe the mingled picture of the first and second comings of Christ in the Old Testament.

19. What are some of the specific prophecies found in the Old Testament relating to the coming of the Messiah?

20. In view of the fact that Israel was regathered from the first two dispossessions of the land, why is it reasonable to assume that the third regathering will be fulfilled also?

21. What is the first of the four movements which relate to Israel's future in the end of the age, and why does the fulfillment of this movement imply the others will follow?

22. What is the second movement in Israel's restoration which is still future?

23. What is the third movement in Israel's restoration, and how does it relate to the Great Tribulation?

24. What is the fourth movement in Israel's restoration, and how does it relate to the millennial kingdom?

25. In view of the fact that God has already begun to restore Israel, what does this imply as to the imminency of the rapture of the church?

26. What are some of the important prophecies relating to Israel's blessing in the millennial kingdom?

27. What is meant by "the day of the Lord," and what periods does it include?

28. In view of the literal fulfillment of Israel's prophetic program in the past, what does this teach concerning the certainty of literal fulfillment of Israel's future program?

44

Events Preceding
the Second Coming of Christ

A. Major Events of the Present Age

As the present age of grace unfolds, many prophecies are being
fulfilled. The general character of the age is presented in seven
parables in Matthew 13. In the parable of the sower, which is
introductory in nature, the varied reception to the truth of God
is described. Truth sometimes falls on the hard, beaten path
where it is destined to be eaten by the fowls. Other falls on
ground that is too shallow and stony, and while beginning to
spring up it is killed for lack of roots. Other falls on good ground
but is infested with thorns, which choke it. Only a portion of
the seed falls on good ground and brings forth fruit a hundred-
fold, sixtyfold, or thirtyfold (Matt. 13:1-9, 18-23).

The parable of the tares sown among the wheat indicates the
danger of false profession which will not be judged until the
time of harvest (vv. 24-30, 36-43). The parable of the mustard
seed indicates the rapid growth of Christendom from a small
beginning to a large movement (vv. 31-32). The parable of the
leaven speaks of evil intermingled with the good meal until the
whole is permeated (vv. 33-35). The hidden treasure of Mat-

thew 13:44 probably refers to Israel hidden as to its national entity in the present age, but nevertheless bought by Christ in His death. The pearl of great price (vv. 45-46) seems to speak of the church as that for which Christ died, a major feature of the present age during a period when Israel's national identity is somewhat hidden. The final parable of the dragnet (vv. 47-51) illustrates the separation of the saved from the unsaved at the end of the age.

In general, Matthew 13 speaks of the entire period between the first and second comings of Christ without reference to the rapture or the particulars of the church as the body of Christ. It describes the sphere of profession of faith and the mingled picture of good and evil. The dual development of both good and evil throughout the age, climaxing in judgment and separation, characterizes the period. There is no justification for postmillennialism, with its concept that the kingdom of God will finally triumph through preaching of the Gospel and human effort. On the other hand, there is no ground for pessimism, because God will fulfill His purpose. Some seed will fall on good ground and bring forth fruit. There will be wheat among the tares and good fish among the bad. The nineteen hundred years since Pentecost have demonstrated the accuracy of this great prophecy of Matthew 13.

A similar picture of the present age with focus on the end of the age is found in Matthew 24. There, in verses 4-14, nine signs of the end are given: (1) false christs (v. 5), (2) wars and rumors of wars (v. 6), (3) famines (v. 7), (4) pestilences (v. 7), (5) earthquakes (v. 7), (6) martyrs (vv. 9-10), (7) false prophets (v. 11), (8) abounding iniquity and cooling ardor for Christ (v. 12), (9) the gospel of the kingdom to be preached in all the world (v. 14).

Another feature of the present age will be the growing apostasy on the part of the unsaved within the professing church. 2 Peter 2 – 3 summarizes the progression in four categories: (1) denial of the person and deity of Christ (2:1), (2) denial of the work of Christ that He bought us when He died on the cross (2:1), (3) moral apostasy over departure from moral standards (2:2-22), (4) departure from the doctrine of the second coming of Christ and the judgments related to it (3:1-13). Other passages contribute to the doctrine of apostasy in the New Testament (1 Tim. 4:1-3; 2 Tim. 3:1-9; Jude 3-19). All these prophecies of encroaching apostasy in the church are being fulfilled beginning with the first century and continuing to the present. The ultimate apostasy will take place after the church is raptured and only the unsaved portion of the professing church is left in the world.

The present age, in terms of the purpose of God in calling out His church, will be brought abruptly to its close at the Rapture. This event — nowhere dated in the prophecies of the Old Testament — describes the dramatic removal of the church from the earth as the dead in Christ are raised and living Christians are caught up to heaven without dying (1 Cor. 15:51-58; 1 Thess. 4:13-18). This event will bring to a close the purpose of God in terms of the church as a separate company of saints, and the departure of the church will set the stage for the major events leading up to the second coming of Christ to the earth to set up His millennial kingdom. Three major periods may be observed between the Rapture and the Second Coming: (1) the period of preparation, (2) the period of peace, (3) the period of persecution.

B. *The Period of Preparation Following the Rapture*

The event of the Rapture, removing every saved person from the earth, will be a dramatic intervention in human history. It will signal the beginning of a series of events which will rapidly move on to a great climax at the second coming of Christ. Obviously, the removal of all Christians from the earth will have an effect upon world history as a whole and will permit the demonstration of evil in the world and the fulfillment of the satanic purpose in a way never before possible.

The first phase immediately after the Rapture will be a period of preparation for the major events which follow. These events will relate to the three major areas of prophecy, which concern the church, Israel, and the Gentiles.

1. *The professing church will remain on earth after the Rapture.* Although the issue of whether the true church will go through the Tribulation has been debated, many expositors believe the church as the body of Christ will be caught up at the Rapture, leaving only the professing church — composed entirely of unsaved individuals on the earth — to fulfill prophecies relating to Christendom.

The professing church after the Rapture is symbolized by the harlot of Revelation 17, pictured astride the scarlet-covered beast bespeaking the political power of that time. Her dominion is over the whole world, symbolized by the many waters (Rev. 17:1, 15). From the description it seems clear that the world church now in its earlier form is seen here in its stage of complete apostasy with every true Christian removed. Religiously, the period after the Rapture accordingly will be a movement toward a world church and a world religion, devoid of redeeming features of true Christian doctrine.

2. *For Israel the period of preparation will be a time of revival.* According to Romans 11:25, Israel's present blindness will be alleviated, and many in Israel will have their eyes opened to the fact that Jesus Christ is indeed their Messiah and Savior. In the days immediately following the Rapture, thousands of Jews will probably turn to Christ, availing themselves of Scripture and books on Christian doctrine which Christians leave behind, as well as works relating Scripture to the hope of a Messiah which many Jews already possess. They undoubtedly will have an insatiable curiosity to answer the question as to what happened to the Christians who disappeared. Their search will be rewarded and many will be converted. As in the first century of the church, the Jews will immediately become the ambassadors for the Gospel, winning both their own people and Gentiles to Christ; the renewed work of evangelism will thereby be undertaken throughout the world. The fact that Jews are already scattered all over the world, knowing many of the world's languages, points them up as natural missionaries to their particular locale so undoubtedly many will be brought to Christ. As in the first century, however, not all Jews will turn to Christ and salvation will be only for those who believe.

3. *Politically in relation to the Gentiles, the time of preparation will involve the revival of the ancient Roman Empire.* As brought out in previous discussion, the feet stage of Daniel 2 and the ten-horn stage of the fourth beast of Daniel 7:7 have never been fulfilled. This prophecy, with the added light given in Revelation 13, indicates that the Roman Empire will be revived in the form of ten nations banding together into a confederacy. The Common Market in Europe may well be the forerunner of it, but the center of political power would seem to be in the Mediterranean rather than in Europe and probably will include the major nations of North Africa, Western Asia, and Southern Europe.

Once again the Mediterranean will become a "Roman lake." When these ten nations are joined together, a ruler will emerge described as the "little horn" of Daniel 7:8, who apparently will be a dictator who gains control, first of three, then of all ten nations. He will be the strong man politically of the Middle East and will work with the world church to gain world power. Once he is firmly established, the stage is set for the second major period, the period of the covenant.

C. The Period of Peace

According to Daniel 9:27, when the dictator of the Middle East emerges as the "Prince that shall come" (Dan. 9:26), he will make a covenant with Israel for a seven-year period. The details of this covenant are not given in Scripture, but it is implied as a covenant of protection. Apparently the dictator desires to settle the controversy between Israel and the nations surrounding Israel; he uses the device of setting up a protectorate for Israel and by this means brings a measure of peace and tranquility to the political situation in the Middle East. While there is no indication that this will be a period of complete peace, Israel is made secure, relatively speaking, and apparently is granted privileges in commerce and a freedom from tension which has not characterized her life since the nation was formed in 1948. Undoubtedly the changed situation will inspire many more Jews to return to their ancient land, and Israel will prosper financially.

During this period also, the world church will continue to grow in power, working with the ruler in the Mediterranean area to accomplish worldwide religious dominion. In like manner, the evangelization of Israel will continue and many will turn to Christ. On the other hand, many will also return to Orthodox Judaism. In this period a temple will apparently be built in Jerusalem and Orthodox Jews will renew the Mosaic system of sacrifices which have not been offered since the Temple was destroyed in A.D. 70. This is implied in Daniel 9:27, where it is predicted that the sacrifices will cease, a fact supported by Daniel 12:11 which speaks of the daily sacrifice being taken away. Obviously, sacrifices could not be stopped unless they had been reactivated, and reactivation of the sacrifices requires a temple in Jerusalem. Exactly when the temple will be rebuilt no one knows, but it will be in operation apparently during this time of peace.

The tranquility of the Middle East will be shattered, however, by a dramatic event described in Ezekiel 38 – 39, an attack upon Israel by Russia and her allies. Interpreters of Scripture have disagreed in their analyses of this event and their placing of it in the chronology. According to Ezekiel 38, it comes at a time when Israel is at peace and at rest, a period which corresponds to the situation following the covenant with the Roman ruler. The attack, moreover, is more than an assault on Israel because it challenges the whole covenant relationship between the Mediterranean ruler and Israel and is, in effect, a Russian bid for control of the Middle East politically and commercially. Because it is a surprise attack, however, there is no record of armies being marshalled against the invaders. Instead God intervenes supernaturally to save His people and wipes out the invading force by a series of catastrophies described in Ezekiel 38:18-23. This war shatters the period of peace and prepares the way for the next and final period.

D. The Period of Persecution

The destruction of the Roman army not only ends the peace of the preceding period, but brings a dramatically changed world situation. Apparently, at that time there is a balance of power between (1) the ruler of the Middle East and the nations aligned with him, and (2) Russia and the nations aligned with her. With the Russian armies temporarily destroyed, the ruler of the Middle East seizes the opportunity to proclaim himself a world dictator. Over night he seizes control politically, economically, and religiously. He proclaims himself ruler over every kindred, tongue, and nation (Rev. 13:7), and Daniel predicts that he "shall devour the whole earth, and shall tread it down, and break it in pieces" (Dan. 7:23). He likewise seizes control of the entire world economically, and no one can buy or sell without his permission (Rev. 13:16-17).

For Israel it is also an abrupt reversal, as the ruler breaks his covenant with her and overnight becomes her persecutor. This introduces what Jeremiah 30:7 describes as the time of Jacob's trouble. Elsewhere, the same period is described as the Great Tribulation (Dan. 12:1; Matt. 24:21; Rev. 7:14). Israel's trials begin with the sudden stopping of their sacrifices (Dan. 9:27; 12:11; Matt. 24:15). Israel, accordingly, is advised by Christ to flee at once to the mountains (Matt. 24:16-20). It will be a time of unprecedented trouble for Israel, and thousands of Jews will be massacred (Zech. 13:8). The Temple itself will be described and an idol of the world ruler set up in it (Rev. 13:15), and at times the ruler himself will sit in the Temple to be worshiped (2 Thess. 2:4). This is the abomination of desolation described in connection with the stopping of the sacrifices. The world ruler will also set himself up as god and demand that everyone worship him under pain of death (Rev. 13:8, 15).

This final period will begin in the middle of the seven years originally planned for the covenant and, accordingly, will last for forty-two months (Rev. 11:2; 13:5; cf. Dan. 7:25; 9:27; 12:11-12).

Because of his complete blasphemy and persecution of both Jew and Christian, the world ruler of the Mediterranean — often referred to as the Antichrist and described in Daniel 9:26 as "the prince that shall come" — will become the object of fearful divine judgment. All this is described in Revelation 6 – 19. Details of these events are recorded in the breaking of the seven seals (Rev. 6:1 – 8:1), the sounding of the seven trumpets (Rev. 8:2-21; 11:15-19), and the outpouring of the seven vials or bowls of the wrath of God (Rev. 16).

Unprecedented judgments will take place on the earth. Christ has described it in Matthew 24:21-22 as a period so terrible that if not stopped or terminated by the second coming of Christ it would have resulted in the extermination of the entire race. Wars, pestilence, famines, stars falling from heaven, earthquakes, demon possession, and great disruption of natural forces in the world apparently destroy a majority of the world's population.

The resulting disorder brought on by these disasters creates opposition to the world ruler of the Middle East. He is unable to fulfill his promises of peace and plenty. As a result, worldwide revolution takes place and major portions of the world rebel against his authority. This climaxes in a gigantic world war described in Daniel 11:40-45 and in Revelation 9:13-21; 16:13-21. The nations of the world are locked in struggle, the battle seesawing back and forth with great armies from the South, great armies from the North, and a huge army from the Orient descending on the Holy Land to fight it out. At the height of this conflict, Jesus Christ returns in power and glory to bring to judgment the wicked men gathered in this struggle and to establish His own millennial kingdom.

Taken as a whole, the events leading up to the second coming of Christ are described in considerable detail in both the Old and New Testaments. The period is a dramatic sequence of tre-

mendous events unequaled in any other portion of history or
prophecy. Many indications that the world is moving on to just
such a climax makes all the more pointed the teaching of Scripture concerning the imminency of the Lord's return for His
own at the Rapture.

Questions

1. What does the parable of the tares teach concerning the general
   character of the period between the first and second comings of
   Christ?
2. Name the other six parables of Matthew 13, and indicate their
   general teachings.
3. Taken as a whole, what does Matthew 13 teach concerning the entire period between the first and second comings of Christ?
4. Does Matthew 13 give any justification for the teaching of postmillennialism?
5. What are the nine signs of the end of the age found in Matthew
   24:3-14?
6. What are the four major aspects of apostasy predicted in 2 Peter
   2 — 3?
7. After the Rapture occurs, what three major periods follow which
   lead up to the second coming of Christ to set up His kingdom?
8. What will be the situation for the church, Israel, and the Gentiles
   in the period of preparation which follows the Rapture?
9. In what sense will the church be on earth after the Rapture?
10. What will be Israel's important role in the period of preparation?
11. What important political events will take place in the period of
    preparation?
12. Describe the situation for Israel and the world church during the
    period of peace following the covenant with Israel.
13. What will shatter the tranquility of the Middle East at the close
    of the period of peace?
14. Describe the sudden change, as the period of persecution begins,
    in relation to Israel, the world, and the world church.
15. What judgments will God pour out on the world during the
    period of persecution?
16. Describe the final, gigantic world war.
17. In the light of world preparation for these events, what is indicated
    about the imminency of the Rapture?

45

The Great Tribulation

A. *The Great Tribulation in Contrast With General Tribulation*

Much confusion has arisen in the doctrine of the Great Tribulation because of failure to distinguish between the general trials and sufferings of the people of God and the specific period of the Great Tribulation described in the Old and New Testaments. The concept of tribulation implies a time of pressure, affliction, anguish of heart, and trouble in general. A situation of tribulation is, accordingly, a common experience of the human race resulting from its sin and rebellion against God and from the conflict between God and Satan in the world.

According to Job 5:7, "Man is born unto trouble, as the sparks fly upward." Christ assured His disciples in John 16:33, "in the world ye shall have tribulation." The trials of Job in the Old Testament and the problems of Paul with his thorn in the flesh in the New Testament are symptomatic of the human race constantly in trouble and bearing many types of affliction. These have characterized the human race since Adam and will continue to some extent until human history has run its course, although greatly alleviated in the time of the millennial kingdom.

In contrast with these general intimations of trial and trouble as they afflict the race, Scripture speaks of a special time of trouble at the end of the age, specifically a time of great tribulation which will continue for forty-two months leading up to the second coming of Christ.

B. The Old Testament Doctrine of the Great Tribulation

As early as Deuteronomy 4:29-30 Israel was warned to turn to the Lord when she was in her time of tribulation in the latter days. This particular time is brought into focus by the prophet Jeremiah. In Jeremiah 30:1-10, he predicts that this time of trouble will be preceded by a partial return of the children of Israel to their land: "For, lo, the days come, saith the Lord, that I will bring again the captivity of my people Israel and Judah, saith the.Lord: and I will cause them to return to the *land that I gave to their fathers, and they shall possess it*" (v. 3).

Immediately following, in verses 4-7, is described the period of trouble which will come upon them after they have returned to the land. Israel will be in travail as a woman giving birth to a child. The time of tribulation is described specifically in Jeremiah 30:7: "Alas! for that day is great, so that none is like it: it is even the time of Jacob's trouble; but he shall be saved out of it."

Israel is given the promise that, though she will endure this great time of trouble, God will eventually break her yoke of bondage and she will no longer serve the Gentiles. Instead, according to verse 9, "they shall serve the Lord their God, and David their king, whom I will raise up unto them." This prophesies the millennial kingdom, when David will be resurrected and with Christ reign over the house of Israel. Accordingly, Israel is given reassurance not to be dismayed; it is God's purpose that eventually "Jacob shall return, and shall be in rest, and be quiet, and none shall make him afraid" (v. 10).

The time of Jacob's trouble, or the Great Tribulation, is in view in Daniel 9:27 after the covenant is broken. Here it is revealed specifically that it will be half of the seven-year period, or three and one-half years. "The prince that shall come" (Dan. 9:26) "shall confirm the covenant with many for one week" (v. 27), that is, will make a covenant for seven years. He will break the covenant in the middle of the week — that is, after three and one-half years — and "he shall cause the sacrifice and the oblation to cease" and will bring about the abomination of the Temple.

Daniel 12:11 adds the information, "And from the time that the daily sacrifice shall be taken away, and the abomination that maketh desolate set up, there shall be a thousand two hundred ninety days." This is approximately three and one-half years with a few days added, and the time period apparently includes the second coming of Christ and the early judgments which follow. The blessing described in Daniel 12:12 which will come after 1,335 days includes not only the time of great tribulation, the second coming of Christ, and the judgments, but also the establishment of Christ's blessed millennial reign upon the earth. Accordingly, the time period for the Great Tribulation is specified as forty-two months, or three and one-half years.

The Great Tribulation clearly will end with the second coming of Jesus Christ. According to Daniel 7:13-14, the period concludes with the Son of Man coming from heaven and all nations coming under His dominion. The wicked king and government which precede the second coming of Christ will be destroyed (Dan. 7:26), and the everlasting kingdom will be brought in which will, of course, be characterized first by the millennial kingdom, then by the ultimate government of God in the new heaven and the new earth. The Old Testament doctrine is relatively complete, but to this, New Testament revelation can be added.

According to Daniel 11:36-39, the end time will be characterized religiously by an atheistic religion headed up by the world ruler. He is described in these verses as an absolute ruler who disregards all previous gods and magnifies himself above God. He honors only the god of forces, that is, the god of war. He is a materialist and an atheist. His kingdom ends in a gigantic war described in verses 40-45. Armies from the South, from the North, and from the East push on him. Although apparently he is able to resist them for a time, the battle is still raging at the time of the second coming of Christ, which ends the Great Tribulation.

C. The Doctrine of the Great Tribulation in the New Testament

When asked by His disciples when His second coming would

occur and the age would end, Christ gives to them first of all a series of signs which have been for us, for the most part, already fulfilled, events and situations which characterize the age between the first and second comings of Christ (Matt. 24:3-14).

Then, in Matthew 24:15-29, Christ, in answer to their question about specific signs, describes the Great Tribulation itself. He warns that it will begin when men see "the abomination of desolation, spoken of by Daniel the prophet, stand in the holy place" (v. 15), referring to the desecration of the Temple and the Mediterranean ruler's putting himself in God's place in the Temple. He warns the children of Israel that when this event occurs, which will apparently be identified as a specific event on a given day, they are to flee for their lives to the mountains.

Christ declares in Matthew 24:21-22, "For then shall be great tribulation, such as was not since the beginning of the world to this time, no, nor ever shall be. And except those days should be shortened, there should no flesh be saved: but for the elect's sake those days shall be shortened." Christ here clearly identifies the period as the Great Tribulation in contrast with all other periods of trouble. It is going to be so great in its extent that it will eclipse anything the world has experienced before.

The Tribulation will be so severe that unless it is shortened (literally, terminated), no human being would be left alive upon the earth. This does not imply, as some have taken from the word "shortened," that it will be less than forty-two months. It simply means that unless it were terminated by the Second Coming, the Great Tribulation would exterminate the entire human race. "For the elect's sake" — whether referring to saved Israel or saved Gentiles or both — Christ's return, while a time of judging for the world, will be a time of deliverance for the saved.

In the verses which follow, our Lord describes some of the characteristics of this period. There will be false prophets and false christs (Matt. 24:23-24). There will be false reports that Christ has come secretly (v. 26). He warns His disciples that no one should be deceived at that time, for the second coming of Christ will be a public event as the lightning shines out of the East even unto the West (v. 27). The Tribulation itself is also described in verse 29 as a time when "the sun shall be darkened, and the moon shall not give her light, and the stars shall fall from heaven, and the powers of the heavens shall be shaken." This will be followed by the return of Christ.

The description of the Great Tribulation given by Christ in answer to the disciples' question is confirmed by additional information in Revelation 6 — 18. A scroll with seven seals, described in Revelation 5:1, is unrolled in chapter 6.

As each seal is broken, great catastrophes begin to overtake the world. This begins with the first seal, describing world government (Rev. 6:1-2). This is followed by war (vv. 3-4), famine (vv. 5-6), and the death of the fourth part of the earth (vv. 7-8). The fifth seal represents the martyrs who die in that period (vv. 9-11), and great disturbances in the heavens — including the stars falling from heaven and a great earthquake on the earth, with the sun becoming black and the moon like blood (vv. 12-14). The impressive display of divine power in the world inspires fear on the part of unbelievers, who call on the mountain to fall on them to save them from "the great day of his wrath" (vv. 15-17).

When the seventh seal is broken (8:1), there comes out of it another series of seven described as trumpets of the angels (Rev. 8:2 — 9:21; 11:15-19). These great judgments for the most part are catastrophes upon the natural world which result in great loss of life, with the third part of the earth consumed with fire, a third part of the sea becoming blood and destroying a third part of the creatures in the sea, and stars from heaven falling upon a third part of the rivers (8:7-11). The fourth trumpet concerns the stars; a third part of the sun, moon, and stars is darkened, and prediction is given of the terrible disasters which will follow with the next three trumpets.

The fifth trumpet (9:1-12) pictures unsaved men tormented by demons for five months in terrible agony, but unable even to take their own lives. The sixth trumpet (9:13-21) relates to the great army which comes from the Orient and crosses the River Euphrates to participate in the great war at the end of the tribulation period. The seventh trumpet (11:15) is near the end of the period and anticipates the coming of Christ and the establishment of His kingdom.

The seventh trumpet, however, issues into another series of seven judgments which fall in rapid succession, described as vials or bowls of the wrath of God in Revelation 16. Each of these is even more destructive than the trumpet judgments, and they constitute the final outpouring of the wrath of God upon the earth, preparatory to the second coming of Christ Himself.

The sixth vial is related to preparation for the great battle of God which centers in a place called Armageddon, giving basis for calling this the battle of Armageddon. Here the kings of the earth and their armies are gathered to battle according to Revelation 16:14. The seeming contradiction of Satan inspiring the kings of the earth to rebel against the ruler which Satan himself has put upon the throne of world government is apparently solved by this fact: Satan gathers his forces under their illusion that they are fighting it out for world power, but actually they are being marshalled by Satan to oppose the armies that will accompany Christ when He returns to the earth (Rev. 19:14).

The final vial, described in Revelation 16:17-21, consists of a great earthquake which levels the great cities of the world and brings Babylon into judgment and causes islands and the mountains to disappear. The climax is a great hailstorm, with hailstones weighing a talent — that is, over a hundred pounds — which destroy what is left. The world is in chaos and in destruction and in war at the time of the second coming of Christ.

What a false dream it has been for some theologians to imagine a world getting better and better, gradually being subdued by the Gospel, and in this way being brought into obedience to Christ! Rather, Scripture describes the world in an awful climax of wickedness and rebellion against God, headed by a world ruler who is an atheist, a blasphemer, and a persecuter of all who are identified with God.

The righteous kingdom of God on earth will be brought in by the second coming of Christ, not by human effort, and will be a dramatic judgment upon wickedness in the world as well as a wonderful deliverance for those who have put their trust in Christ in those tragic days.

The fact that the Great Tribulation is so terrible, designed for the unbeliever and for the blasphemer rather than for the child of God, is another reason why many believe that the rapture of the church will occur before this awful time of trouble. Significantly, the church is never mentioned in any passage relating to the Great Tribulation; though men will come to Christ who are described as saints or holy ones, never are the specific terms used that would relate them to the church. Instead, they are saved Jews and saved Gentiles, many of them subject to martydom, and only a relatively few survive in the period.

Taken as a whole, the Great Tribulation is a prelude to the second coming of Christ, making clear how necessary divine intervention in the world scene is — both for judgment of the wicked and for deliverance of the saints — and providing a sharp contrast between the darkness of the hour of the Tribulation and the glory of the kingdom which will follow.

Questions

1. Distinguish between tribulation in general and the Great Tribulation.
2. What is the first reference in Scripture to the future time of the Great Tribulation?
3. What is the order of events at the end of the age, according to Jeremiah 30:1-10?
4. How does the Great Tribulation relate to the prophecy of Daniel 9:27?
5. What event signals the breaking of the covenant and the beginning of the Great Tribulation?
6. What will characterize the religion of the Great Tribulation?
7. Describe the war at the end of the Great Tribulation according to Daniel.
8. What event will bring the Great Tribulation to a close, according to Daniel?
9. According to Christ, what event begins the Great Tribulation?
10. What is Israel to do in the period of the Great Tribulation, according to Christ?
11. What would happen, according to Christ, if the Great Tribulation were not terminated by His second coming?
12. What are some of the events and situations immediately preceding the second coming, according to Matthew 24?
13. How is the second coming of Christ itself described in Matthew 24?
14. According to Revelation 6:1 — 8:1, what events are related to the breaking of the seven seals?
15. According to Revelation 8:2 — 9:21, what events are related to the sounding of the seven trumpets?
16. What is the situation described by the outpouring of the seven vials in Revelation 16?
17. Describe in detail the results of the seventh vial being poured on the earth.
18. How does the description of the seals, trumpets, and vials demonstrate that the postmillennial view of a world gradually getting better and better is not supported in Scripture?
19. How will the righteous kingdom of God be accomplished in the world?
20. How do the graphic judgments of the Great Tribulation support the doctrine of the Rapture as a preceding event which provides comfort and inspiration to Christians?

46

The Second Coming of Christ

A. *The Importance of the Second Coming*

In previous study of the doctrine of the Second Coming, the major facts concerning the Rapture, the coming of the Son of God for His saints (Chapter 12), and the coming of Christ with His saints (Chapter 13) have already been presented. Here, the second coming of Christ with His saints to establish His kingdom will be considered in its place as a major event in the prophetic program. Coupled with this study are the chapters which follow, dealing with the important themes of the resurrections, the judgments of God on Israel and other nations, and the millennial kingdom. These great themes combine to provide the scriptural goal of history, which in large measure determines the interpretation of the entire Bible.

In both the Old and New Testaments the importance of the coming of Christ to establish His kingdom is set forth in many passages. The doctrine, as revealed, is far more than a simple ending of human history; it is rather a grand climax which brings the program of God to its highest point. For this reason, all systems of theology which tend to ignore or minimize the doctrine of the second coming of Christ and the extensive volume of Scripture dealing with Christ's kingdom on earth are inadequate and can be justified only by denying the plain, literal meaning of the many prophecies and ignoring extensive scriptural revelation.

The second coming of Christ, along with the kingdom which follows it, is in fact, the very heart of the progress of Scripture and is the major theme of Old Testament prophecy. The great covenants of Scripture relate to God's program — especially these covenants with Abraham, Israel, and David, and the new covenant. Much of the revelation of the Psalms and the major and minor prophets revolves around this great theme. Great prophetic books like Daniel, Zechariah, and Revelation focus on the subject of the second coming of Christ and the consummation of history and the kingdom. For this reason, the doctrine of the Second Coming in large measure determines the total theology of the interpreter of the Bible and justifies the attempt to order prophetic events yet to be fulfilled in considerable detail in faithfulness to the extent of scriptural revelation.

B. The Old Testament Prophecies of the Second Coming

While the rapture of the church is a New Testament doctrine and is never mentioned in the Old Testament (because the church as such was a mystery, not revealed in the Old Testament), the second coming is embedded in many Old Testament passages.

Probably the first of the clear prophecies concerning the second coming of Christ is in Deuteronomy 30:1-3. In this prophecy concerning the regathering of Israel to her land, it is predicted that Israel will return to the Lord spiritually and that then the Lord "will turn thy captivity, and have compassion upon thee, and will return and gather thee from all nations, whither the LORD thy God hath scattered thee" (v. 3). The expression "will return" indicates an act of intervention of God in the situation, and in the light of later Scripture it is clearly linked to the return of Christ Himself.

The Psalms, although they constitute the book of worship of the Old Testament, frequently refer to the return of Christ. After the introductory description of the righteous, in contrast with the wicked in Psalm 1, Psalm 2 immediately describes the major contention of God with the nations. Although the rulers of the world desire to reject God and His rule over them, God declares His purpose: "Yet have I set my king upon my holy hill of Zion" (2:6). The psalm goes on to predict that this king in dealing with the wicked "shalt break them with a rod of iron; thou shalt dash them in pieces like a potter's vessel" (v. 9).

The trilogy of Psalms 22, 23, and 24 presents Christ as the Good Shepherd, who would give His life for His sheep (John 10:11); the Great Shepherd, who ever lives to intercede for His own (Heb. 13:20); and the Chief Shepherd, who is coming as the King of Glory to reward faithful shepherds (1 Pet. 5:4). Psalm 24 pictures the millennial situation: "The earth is the Lord's" (v. 1). The gates of Jerusalem are exhorted to be lifted up to admit the King of Glory (24:7-10).

The reign of Christ from Zion is mentioned in Psalm 50:2. As will be seen later, in the study of the Millennium, Psalm 72 describes Christ as having come to the earth to reign over all nations. Psalm 89:36 speaks of Christ's throne as being established in fulfillment of the Davidic covenant following His second coming. Psalm 96, after picturing the honor and glory of God, exhorts the heavens and the earth to rejoice "before the Lord: for he cometh, for he cometh to judge the earth: he shall judge the world with righteousness, and the people with his truth" (v. 13).

The present position of Christ at the right hand of the Father is described in Psalm 110, but it is also predicted that the day will come when He will rule over His enemies and His power will go out of Zion (vv. 2, 6). It is clear from these many prophecies that the truth of Christ's second coming and His reign on earth is a major, not a minor, revelation of the entire Old Testament.

This is confirmed as a principal theme of the major and minor prophets. In the great prophetic utterance of Isaiah 9:6-7, Christ is described as a child born who is at the same time the "mighty God." His government upon the throne of David is described as never terminating. An extensive picture of the results of the second coming of Christ in establishing His kingdom is painted in Isaiah 11 – 12, which will be discussed in the study of the millennial kingdom. The introduction of the kingdom reign, however, depends upon the doctrine of a literal second coming to the earth and the display of divine power judging the wicked. The scene is also mentioned in Isaiah

63:1-6, where the judgment of Christ upon the earth at His second coming is graphically described.

In the prophecies of Daniel concerned with the times of the Gentiles and God's program for the nation of Israel, the consummation of both is related to the coming of the Son of Man from heaven (Dan. 7:13-14). This passage gives a clear description of the Second Coming: "I saw in the night visions, and, behold, one like the Son of man came with the clouds of heaven, and came to the Ancient of days, and they brought him near before him. And there was given him dominion, and glory, and a kingdom, that all people, nations, and languages, should serve him: his dominion is an everlasting dominion, which shall not pass away, and his kingdom that which shall not be destroyed." Daniel had anticipated the same truth in interpreting Nebuchadnezzar's vision and had predicted in Daniel 2:44 "a kingdom, which shall never be destroyed."

Most of the minor prophets likewise take up this theme, and especially the Book of Zechariah. According to Zechariah 2:10-11, the Lord declares, "Sing and rejoice, O daughter of Zion: for, lo, I come, and I will dwell in the midst of thee, saith the LORD. And many nations shall be joined to the LORD in that day, and shall be my people: and I will dwell in the midst of thee, and thou shalt know that the LORD of hosts hath sent me unto thee." This is clearly a reference to the millennial earth and the reign of Christ subsequent to His second coming. Even more specific is Zechariah 8:3-8: "Thus saith the LORD; I am returned unto Zion, and will dwell in the midst of Jerusalem: and Jerusalem shall be called a city of truth; and the mountain of the LORD of hosts the holy mountain" (v. 3). Verses 4-8 picture the streets of Jerusalem full of boys and girls playing and the children of Israel gathered from all over the world dwelling in the midst of Jerusalem.

Zechariah 14:1-4 dramatically pictures the second coming of Christ Himself, coming at the height of the world war which has engulfed the Middle East and the city of Jerusalem. Zechariah states, "And his feet shall stand in that day upon the mount of Olives, which is before Jerusalem on the east, and the mount of Olives shall cleave in the midst thereof toward the east and toward the west, and there shall be a very great valley; and half of the mountain shall remove toward the north, and half of it toward the south" (v. 4).

This graphic description of the division of the Mount of Olives at the time of the second advent of Christ makes clear that no event of the past can compare with His second coming. The ridiculous interpretation that the Second Coming was fulfilled on the day of Pentecost or in the destruction of Jerusalem in A.D. 70 is not only contradicted by later prophecies which look forward to the second coming of Christ as a future event (as in the Book of Revelation), but is here supported by the fact that the Mount of Olives today remains unchanged.

When the feet of Christ touch the same Mount of Olives from which He ascended in Acts 1 it will signal a change in the topography of the whole area about Jerusalem, in preparation for the kingdom which will follow. Accordingly, the second coming of Christ in the Old Testament is not to be explained away as some past event, some contemporary spiritual experience — such as the coming of Christ for saints when they die — or any of the other explanations which are totally inadequate to explain the scriptural revelation. Rather, the second coming of Christ in the Old Testament is the grand consummation of world history, in which the Son of God comes to claim the world for which He died and to exert His power and His authority over the world that would not have Christ reign over it.

C. The Second Coming of Christ in the New Testament

In the New Testament revelation concerning the second coming of Christ, a new factor is introduced with the revelation of the rapture of the church. In the Old Testament the predictions of the first and second comings of Christ were often mingled, and prophets had difficulty distinguishing the two events. With prophecies concerning the first coming now fulfilled, there is no longer any problem in distinguishing the prophecies relating to His suffering as contrasted with those relating to His glory.

In the New Testament, however, because of similar terminology in describing the coming of Christ *for* His saints and the coming of Christ *with* His saints, it is not always clear which event is in view; the decision in each case must be based upon the context. The subject of a future coming of Christ, however, is a major theme of the New Testament, and it is estimated that one out of twenty-five verses refers to it in one way or another. At least twenty major passages may be selected as contributing the major elements of the New Testament revelation (Matt. 19:28; 23:39; 24:3 — 25:46; Mark 13:24-37; Luke 12:35-48; 17:22-

37; 18:8; 21:25-28; Acts 1:10-11; 15:16-18; Rom. 11:25-27; 1 Cor. 11:26; 2 Thess. 1:7-10; 2 Pet. 3:3-4; Jude 14-15; Rev. 1:7-8; 2:25-28; 16:15; 19:11-21; 22:20).

In addition to the facts brought out in the previous study of Matthew 13, major points of emphasis may be noted.

1. *The second coming of Christ is posttribulational and premillennial.* The literal interpretation of the prophecies relating to the second coming of Christ not only makes clear that it is the prelude for the casual event which establishes the reign of Christ on earth for a thousand years, but also serves to distinguish it from the rapture of the church, Christ coming for His saints.

The tendency has been, on the part of those who spiritualize prophecies relating to a future kingdom on earth, to merge the prophecies of the Rapture and the prophecies of Christ's second coming into one event, occurring at the same time, thereby making the Rapture a postribulational event. The same literal interpretation of the Second Coming which leads to the conclusion that it will be followed by the millennial kingdom on earth also serves to distinguish it from the rapture of the church. The events are clearly different in their purpose, character, and context.

In *The Rapture Question,* by John F. Walvoord, fifty reasons are set forth for holding that the Rapture is pretribulational and the second coming of Christ to establish His kingdom is posttribulational. Likewise, in *The Millennial Kingdom* by Walvoord, the arguments for a literal kingdom on earth are set forth, historically and theologically. While theologians will continue to disagree on these subjects, the issue is determined largely on the principles of interpretation employed. Those who interpret prophecy literally, and who consistently take into consideration the details of prophecy, can support adequately the conclusion that the second coming of Christ is posttribulational and premillennial.

The descriptions of the second coming of Christ in all the major passages relating to it make clear that His return is personal. This is, of course, supported by the revelation of the angels in Acts 1:11, who informed the disciples as they were gazing up into heaven, "This same Jesus, which is taken up from you into heaven, shall so come in like manner as ye have seen him go into heaven." This refers to the second coming of Christ to the earth, rather than to the Rapture. Just as He personally went to heaven, so He will personally return. This, of course, is supported by other major passages such as Matthew 24:27-31 and Revelation 19:11-16.

The same passages which indicate that His return will be personal also make clear that it will be a bodily return. While the deity of Christ is omnipresent and can be in heaven and earth at the same time, the body of Christ is always local and is now at the right hand of God the Father. In His second coming, Christ will bodily return, — just as He bodily ascended. This is supported by Zechariah 14:4 — "His feet shall stand in that day upon the mount of Olives" — and by the fact that His return is said in Acts 1 to happen the same way as His ascension.

In contrast with the Rapture, where there is no evidence that the world as a whole will see the glory of Christ, the second coming to the earth will be both visible and glorious. Christ Himself described His return as lightning shining from the East to the West (Matt. 24:27). Just as the Ascension was visible in Acts 1:11, so His second coming will be visible, and Christ "shall so come in like manner as ye have seen him go into heaven."

Christ said in Matthew 24:30, "They shall see the Son of man coming in the clouds of heaven with power and great glory." The main point of the Book of Revelation is that Christ will be revealed to the world in His second coming and subsequent kingdom. According to Revelation 1:7, "Behold, he cometh with clouds; and every eye shall see him, and they also which pierced him: and all kindreds of the earth shall wail because of him." They will see Christ not as the lowly Nazarene in suffering and in death, or even in His resurrection body in which the glory was somewhat veiled while Christ was yet on earth.

The second coming of Christ will fully display the glory of the Son of God as revealed earlier to John in Revelation 1:12-18 and described in detail in Revelation 19:11-16. The Second Coming, accordingly, will be one of the most dramatic events of all time and will be the climax of the whole program of God beginning in the Garden of Eden when Adam sinned and lost the right to rule.

The second coming of Christ is also intimately related to the earth and is not a meeting in space as is the rapture of the church. Many passages speak of Christ as reigning in Zion, coming to Zion, or going from Zion, all references to the literal city of Jerusalem (Pss. 14:7; 20:2; 53:6; 110:2; 128:5; 134:3; 135:21; Isa. 2:3; Joel 3:16; Amos 1:2; Zech. 14:1-4; Rom. 11:26). According to Scripture, not only will His feet touch the Mount of

Olives, but His return is in connection with destroying the armies which will be attempting to conquer Jerusalem (Zech. 14:1-3).

The second coming of Christ will be attended by all the holy angels and all the saints of all ages who are in heaven. It is the coming of Christ *with* His saints rather than *for* His saints. Although an important purpose of the Second Coming is to deliver afflicted saints still living on earth, the description of the event in Matthew 25:31 states that all the angels will be with Him. Revelation 19:11-21 is even more explicit, where the armies from heaven are described as following Him. These undoubtedly include both the holy angels and the saints in heaven. The Second Coming will be a time of the gathering of all the elect — those resurrected, those translated, and even those in their natural bodies on the earth. All participate in one way or another in this dramatic event related to the Second Coming.

The stated purpose of the Second Coming is to judge the earth (Ps. 96:13). This will be brought out in subsequent studies of the judgment of Israel, the judgment of the nations, and the judgment of Satan and the fallen angels. In Matthew 19:28 Christ told the twelve apostles they would join Him in judging the twelve tribes of Israel. Matthew 25:31-46 describes the judgment of the Gentiles on earth at the time of the Second Coming. Ezekiel 20:35-38 predicts the judgment of Israel at the time of the Second Coming. Those who die during the time of persecution preceding the Second Coming will be raised and judged, according to Revelation 20:4.

The same truth is brought out in the various parables dealing with the end time in the Gospels, and frequent mention of this truth is found in Scripture (Luke 12:37, 45-47; 17:29-30; 2 Thess. 1:7-9; 2:8; Jude 15; Rev. 2:27; 19:15-21). The earth — which is now being permitted to manifest its sinfulness and its unbelief and, for the most part, is living as if God did not exist — will be brought under the righteous judgment of God.

The judgment, as extensive as it is, however, will not completely destroy the earth. The judgment by fire, described in 2 Peter 3:10, will not take place until the end of the Millennium when the present earth and heaven are destroyed and a new heaven and a new earth created.

The day of the Lord, which begins at the Rapture and includes in its introduction the judgments preceding and immediately following the Second Coming, concludes with the end of the millennium and with the final destruction of the present heaven and earth. The triumph of sin in our modern world is temporary. The triumph of the righteousness of God is sure.

The major purpose of the return of Christ is to deliver those who have survived martyrdom during the Tribulation, both among Israel and among the Gentiles. If the second coming of Christ were delayed indefinitely, according to Matthew 24:22, the catastrophic judgments poured out on the earth would destroy the entire race. This Tribulation is cut short by the second coming of Christ to deliver the elect from this fate. Israel is described as saved or delivered in Romans 11:26-27. This is supported by Luke 21:28; where the second coming of Christ is referred to as "your redemption." In the Old Testament, passages such as Zechariah 14:4 also describe this deliverance.

The second coming of Christ, however, not only brings judgment on the wicked and deliverance for the righteous, but introduces a new spiritual state which will be considered in the study of the Millennium. The same event which brings judgment to the wicked brings a new spiritual revival to those who have trusted in the Lord. This is supported by Romans 11:26-27 and is embodied in the new covenant of Jeremiah 31:31-34.

Christ's return has also the central purpose of reestablishing the Davidic kingdom. In the discussion of the relationship of the church to the Gentiles in the counsel at Jerusalem in Acts 15, it is brought out that the earlier prophecies of Amos 9:11-15 predicted the order of Gentile blessing first, to be followed by reestablishment of the tabernacle of David. This was to coincide with Israel's regathering and reestablishment in the land, never to be scattered again (Amos 9:14-15; cf. Ezek. 39:25-29). The physical return of Israel, the reestablishment of the Davidic kingdom, and the outpouring of the spirit of God upon the house of Israel (Ezek. 39:29) combine to prepare Israel and the world for the glories of the kingdom to follow. According to Ezekiel 37:24, the Old Testament saints will participate in the kingdom, with David raised up to be a prince over Israel under Christ. It was the purpose of God, as announced to the Virgin Mary in Luke 1:31-33, that Christ should come to reign over the house of Israel forever.

Taken as a whole, the second coming of Christ is a tremendous event occurring at the close of the Great Tribulation and introducing the millennial kingdom. It will be a personal and bodily return which will be visible to the entire world and will be the manifestation of the glory of God. It will be related to the earth rather than to heaven and specifically to Jerusalem in the Mount of Olives.

Christ in His return will be accompanied by the holy angels and the saints. His purpose in His return is to judge the world, to deliver those who have trusted in Him whether Jews or Gentiles, to bring spiritual revival to Israel and the world, to reestablish the kingdom of David and to introduce the final dispensation of His kingdom on earth for a thousand years. In the context of this event, the doctrine of the resurrection and judgments relating to the Second Coming may now be considered.

Questions

1. What are some of the great themes related to the doctrine of the Second Coming?
2. How extensive is the doctrine of the Second Coming in the Old Testament?
3. What does Deuteronomy 30:1-3 contribute to the doctrine of the Second Coming?
4. How does Psalm 2 deal with the Second Coming?
5. What great themes are unfolded in Psalms 22, 23, and 24?
6. Summarize truth about the second coming of Christ and the millennial kingdom in Psalms 50, 72, 89, 96, and 110.
7. What is contributed by Isaiah 9:6-7?
8. How does Daniel 7 describe the Second Coming?
9. What are the contributions of Zechariah 2, 8, and 14 to the doctrine of the Second Coming?
10. How does Zechariah 14 refute the idea that Christ has already fulfilled the promise of His second coming?
11. What difficulty did the Old Testament prophets have in distinguishing the first and second comings of Christ?
12. What corresponding difficulty is found in the New Testament in distinguishing the Rapture and the second coming of Christ to set up His kingdom?
13. Summarize the evidence that the second coming of Christ to the earth to set up His kingdom is posttribulational and premillennial.
14. How does premillennialism depend upon principles of interpretation of Scripture?
15. Demonstrate that the second coming of Christ is a personal coming.
16. What evidence supports the conclusion that Christ will return bodily in His second coming?
17. Contrast the extent to which Christ will be seen by the world at the Rapture with the extent at the second coming to establish His kingdom.

18. How is the second coming of Christ intimately related to the earth in contrast with the Rapture?

19. Who will accompany Christ in His second coming from heaven to earth?

20. Summarize the teaching that Christ will judge the earth in His second coming.

21. Distinguish the judgments which will occur before the Millennium from those which will come at the close of the Millennium.

22. How does the return of Christ relate to delivering the saved in the Great Tribulation?

23. To what extent does the second coming of Christ inaugurate a new spiritual state?

24. How does the return of Christ relate to the reestablishment of the Davidic kingdom?

25. Summarize the main facts that relate to the second coming of Christ as an important event.

47

The Resurrections

Much confusion has been introduced in prophetic interpretation by the unsupported theory that all men will be raised at the same time. This simplistic prophetic program ignores the details given in the prophetic Scripture concerning the various resurrections. Instead of one general resurrection, Scripture presents as many as seven resurrections, some of which are past, others separated by long periods of time such as resurrections which precede or follow the thousand-year reign of Christ. The Scripture clearly teaches that all will be raised in their time and place and that human existence goes on forever. The study of the doctrine of resurrection provides an important outline in the prophetic program related to this central truth of Christian faith and hope.

A. The Resurrection of Jesus Christ

First in order of the resurrections is the resurrection of Jesus Christ, presented in prophecy in the Old Testament (as in Psalms 16:9-10), presented historically in the four gospels, and dealt with theologically in the New Testament beginning with the Book of Acts. Unquestionably the resurrection of Christ is a doctrine of central importance upon which all Christian faith and hope rest, as Paul argues at length in 1 Corinthians 15. In consideration of the facts supporting the conclusion that there is more than one resurrection, it is important to note that all must agree that the resurrection of Christ is a distinct event which has already occurred.

B. The Resurrection of the Saints in Jerusalem

At the time of the resurrection of Christ, a token resurrection also took place, according to Matthew 27:52-53. This passage states that at the time of the death and resurrection of Christ, "the graves were opened; and many bodies of the saints which slept arose, And came out of the graves after his resurrection, and went into the holy city, and appeared unto many."

No explanation is anywhere given concerning this unusual event. While the graves were opened at the time of the death of Christ, it appears that the saints themselves were not raised until Christ Himself was raised, for Scripture makes plain that Christ is the firstfruits, the first to be raised from the dead in the resurrection body which would never be destroyed. By contrast, others restored to life, as in the case of Lazarus, undoubtedly died again and were reburied, but Christ arose never to return to the tomb.

The probable meaning of the resurrection of saints at the time of Christ's resurrection, which apparently included a relatively small number of individuals, may be found in the levitical offering which it fulfilled. The third of the feasts of Jehovah (see Lev. 23:9-14) involves the ceremony in which, at the beginning of the harvest, the Israelites would bring a handful of the unthreshed grain to wave it before the Lord and to offer appropriate sacrifices in recognition of their expectation of the coming harvest. The resurrection of the saints in Jerusalem at the time of the resurrection of Christ constituted the firstfruits and demonstrated that Christ was not alone in His resurrection, but that He was the forerunner of the great harvest to come, of which these saints were the token resurrection.

Although some have interpreted the references in Luke as merely a restoration to life like that of Lazarus, the fact that it occurred at the time of the resurrection of Christ would indicate a permanent resurrection, and undoubtedly these saints were caught up to heaven after they had fulfilled their mission. In any event, it is another historic resurrection which confirms the concept that all resurrections cannot be compressed into one great future event.

C. The Resurrection of the Church

As previously brought out in the studies of the coming of Christ for His saints and the doctrine of the Rapture, the dead in Christ will be raised at the time of the return of Christ for His own, and together with living Christians, who will be translated, will meet the Lord in the air and go to heaven. According to 1 Thessalonians 4:13-18 and 1 Corinthians 15:51-58, both the resurrected saints and the translated saints will receive resurrection bodies which will be patterned after that of Christ's own resurrection body (1 John 3:2). The resurrection of the church is the first massive resurrection and is the forerunner of others to follow.

D. The Resurrection of the Old Testament Saints

Although the Old Testament constantly assumes the doctrine of resurrection, as stated in Job 19:25-26, it is not the subject of extensive prophecy. Such references as are found, however, seem to place the resurrection of the Old Testament saints at the time of the second coming of Christ to the earth, rather than His coming for His saints at the time of the Rapture.

Daniel 12 describes the Great Tribulation in verse 1 and the resurrection in verse 2 as a subsequent and climactic event in relation to it; in this case it would be clear that the Old Testament saints are not raised at the Rapture but rather at the time of the establishment of the kingdom. The same implication is found in the Job passage, where resurrection is connected with the time when the Redeemer will stand on the earth.

In a similar way, the doctrine of resurrection in Isaiah 26:19-21, the awaking of dead bodies from the earth, is related to the time when Christ comes to judge the world. It is also significant that the particular phrase, "the dead in Christ," is used to describe those raised at the Rapture (1 Thess. 4:16). The expression "in Christ" describes the present believer's position in Christ due to baptism of the Spirit, which occurred for the first time in Acts 2 and is not used of Old Testament saints. While interpreters of Scripture will continue to differ, and some will include the Old Testament saints with the Rapture, the burden of evidence seems to relate it to the second coming of Christ to the earth. In any event, all the saints of the Old Testament as well as the church are raised before the Millennium.

E. The Resurrection of Tribulation Saints

Special mention is made of the resurrection of those who died as martyrs in the Tribulation as being raised in connection with the second coming of Christ to establish His kingdom. In Revelation 20:4 John writes that he saw "the souls of them that were beheaded for the witness of Jesus, and for the word of God, and which had not worshipped the beast, neither his image, neither had received his mark upon their foreheads, or in their hands; and they lived and reigned with Christ a thousand years."

This statement is explicit that the martyred dead of the Tribulation will be raised when Christ comes to establish His kingdom. Revelation 20:5 declares, "But the rest of the dead lived not again until the thousand years were finished. This is the first resurrection." A natural question follows as to how this resurrection could be first when there have been other resurrections preceding it, such as the resurrection of Christ, the resurrection of the church, and the resurrection of the Old Testament saints.

The answer is that the term "the first resurrection" refers to all resurrections of the righteous even though they are widely separated in time. They all are "first," that is, before the final resurrection of the wicked. Accordingly, the term "first resurrection" applies to all the resurrections of the saints regardless of when they occur, including the resurrection of Christ Himself.

F. The Resurrection of the Millennial Saints

Scripture in no passage clearly predicts the resurrection of the millennial saints, and some have concluded that saints who enter the Millennium will never die. Scripture, of course, is also silent about a rapture of living saints at the end of the millennial kingdom. Both these items of prophecy are of no immediate concern to saints living today, and truth relating to it can be disclosed after Christ's return to set up His kingdom.

The presumption is, however, that some saints who survive the tribulation time will be already advanced in age, and in any case it is doubtful whether anyone will survive for the entire thousand-year reign. Even Adam and the early Christians did not live to attain the age of one thousand years. Accordingly, it may be assumed that even those who are saved will die in the Millennium even though their life may be greatly prolonged.

According to Isaiah 65:20, "There shall be no more thence an infant of days, nor an old man that hath not filled his days: for the child shall die an hundred years old; but the sinner being an hundred years old shall be accursed." This statement, on the one hand, indicates that life will be greatly lengthened, that is, that at the age of 100 a person is still in his youth. In the Millennium, believers who are old men will fill out their days, meaning that they will live to a ripe old age. On the other hand, this does not state that they will not die. By contrast, a person dying at the age of 100 will do so because of sin, and death will come as a form of judgment.

The evidence remains that there will probably be saints who die in the Millennium and that they will be raised at the end of the millennial kingdom. This doctrine, however, is not built upon explicit Scripture, but is probably the best explanation. At the same time millennial saints are raised, undoubtedly living millennial saints will be raptured or taken from the earth without dying in the same fashion as the church is raptured. This will be in preparation for the destruction of the present earth and heavens.

G. The Resurrection of the Wicked

The final resurrection is a resurrection apparently related only to those who are wicked. According to Revelation 20:11-15, in connection with the judgment at the great white throne, all the dead not previously raised are resurrected and stand before God to be judged. This is the final resurrection before the creation of the new heavens and the new earth. The details of this judgment will be considered in a later chapter.

Taken as a whole, Scripture is plain that all men are destined to be raised. As Daniel summarizes it, "Many of them that sleep in the dust of the earth shall awake, some to everlasting life, and some to shame and everlasting contempt" (12:2). Although men may die, all will be raised, but the resurrections will not be the same. The resurrection of life is a glorious resurrection in which the bodies of believers will be patterned after the resurrection body of Christ.

The resurrection of damnation, however, is an awful spectacle. Men will be given bodies that will last forever, but bodies that are sinful and subject to pain and suffering. Like the devil and his angels, they will exist forever in the lake of fire. This compelling fact has driven men to carry the Gospel to the ends of the earth so as many as possible may be snatched as brands from the burning (Jude 23) and delivered from the wrath of God which is sure to come upon the ungodly. For the righteous, however, the doctrine of resurrection is the basis of our hope and, although the last generation of the church will be raptured without dying, for the great majority of the world resurrection from the grave has been God's method of transforming a body suited for earth to a body that is suited for His glorious presence.

Questions

1. Will all men who die be ultimately raised from the dead?
2. Who is the first person to be raised from the dead?
3. Explain the resurrection mentioned in Matthew 27:52-53.
4. Describe the resurrection of the church.
5. What evidence supports the conclusion that the resurrection of Old Testament saints will occur at the time of the second coming of Christ to the earth?
6. What does the Scripture reveal about the resurrection of tribulation saints?
7. Will saints die in the millennial kingdom?
8. What will happen to the living saints at the end of the millennial kingdom?
9. Describe the resurrection of the wicked dead.
10. Contrast the resurrection body of the saved with the resurrection body of the lost.
11. Why does the doctrine of eternal punishment constitute an impelling motive for preaching the Gospel to every creature?

48

The Judgment of
Israel and the Nations

In connection with the second coming of Jesus Christ, judgments on both Israel and the nations are included in the great events which establish His kingdom on earth. The judgments begin apparently with the judgment of resurrected saints of the Old Testament, both the Israelites and the Gentiles, and resurrected saints of the tribulation period, both Israelites and Gentiles. Attending the event also, however, are a separate judgment of those among Israel still living on the earth and another judgment for Gentiles still living on the earth. These latter judgments have to do with the separation of those counted worthy to enter the kingdom from those who are counted unworthy and are excluded.

A. The Judgment of Resurrected Israel and the Gentiles

The doctrine of resurrection is a familiar truth of the Old Testament, as discussed in the preceding chapter. In addition to the resurrection which takes place at the rapture of the church, there is also a resurrection of righteous dead in connection with the second coming of Christ to establish His kingdom. As previously noted, this is mentioned in Daniel 12:2, Isaiah 26:19, and Job 19:25-26. Resurrection of Israel is also seen in connection with the restoration as a nation at the time of the Second Coming. In Ezekiel 37 in the vision of the valley of dry bones, we learn that while the restoration of the dry bones to a living body is symbolic of the restoration of the nation Israel, it is also the time when Israel will be brought out of their graves (37:12-14). Here the symbolic and the literal seem to be combined. In the same chapter David is pictured as a resurrected person serving as a king over Israel under Christ. In general, the Old Testament gives a firm faith to all who would believe in the resurrection from the dead.

In Revelation 20 the resurrection of the martyred dead of the tribulation time is said to take place in connection with the second coming of Christ. It probably is combined with the resurrection of the Old Testament saints. Those resurrected are said to live and reign with Christ a thousand years (Rev. 20:4) and are apparently rewarded much in the same way as the church is rewarded at the judgment seat of Christ. Their faithfulness to God even unto death and their service rendered are recognized in their sharing in the reign of Christ upon earth.

Some confusion has arisen because of the fact that the church is also said to reign with Christ. Scripture seems to indicate that all the righteous raised before the Millennium will share in some way in the millennial reign, each in his own order and according to the sovereign purpose of God. The church will reign as the bride of Christ; the resurrected saints will reign in their respective capacities as saved Israelites or saved Gentiles. An illustration is afforded in the Book of Esther, where Esther reigned as queen while Mordecai reigned as the king's prime minister. Both Esther and Mordecai reigned, but in different ways and in different capacities. So it will be in the Millennium.

Accordingly, it may be concluded that the righteous dead of both Israel and the Gentiles will be raised at the time of the second coming of Christ, and this resurrection will include all who are not involved in the resurrection and translation at the rapture of the church.

B. The Judgment of Living Israel

When Christ returns in His second coming, He will also deliver

His people Israel from their persecutors. Many will have already been put to death (Zech. 13:8), but those who survive will be delivered by Christ when He comes (Rom. 11:26). All the Israelites who are delivered from their enemies, however, are not worthy to enter the kingdom, as some of them are unsaved. They will be gathered before the Lord and judged (Ezek. 20:33-38). Fulfillment will first be made of the regathering of every Israelite from the entire world (Ezek. 39:28). In Ezekiel 20:35-38 the Lord states, "And I will bring you into the wilderness of the people, and there will I plead with you face to face. Like as I pleaded with your fathers in the wilderness of the land of Egypt, so will I plead with you, saith the Lord God. And I will cause you to pass under the rod, and I will bring you into the bond of the covenant: And I will purge out from among you the rebels, and them that transgress against me: I will bring them forth out of the country where they sojourn, and they shall not enter into the land of Israel: and ye shall know that I am the Lord."

On the basis of this text, regathered Israel is divided into two classes of people — those who have accepted Jesus as their Messiah and Savior and are counted worthy to enter the kingdom, and those who are still rebels, unbelievers, and are excluded and put to death. While Israel as a nation is a favored nation, and while God has showered special blessings upon them, personal salvation still depends upon individual faith and relationship to God.

As it has been through ages past, so at this time there are those who are counted "true Israel" (that is, saved) and those who are Israel only in name, who are unsaved. As Paul expresses it in Romans 9:6, "For they are not all Israel, which are of Israel." In Romans 9:8, he describes the unsaved as "the children of the flesh" who are "not the children of God." The purging of the rebels will leave in Israel only the truly redeemed, and it will be their privilege to enter the land and possess it, in contrast with the unsaved, of whom God states, "They shall not enter into the land of Israel" (Ezek. 20:38).

C. The Judgment of Living Gentiles

The judgment of the nations concerns God's individual judgment on the Gentiles in contrast with His judgment on Israel. This judgment is described by our Lord in Matthew 25:31-46 as a judgment which immediately follows His second coming. In verse 31, it is said to occur in this way: "When the Son of man shall come in his glory, and all the holy angels with him, then shall he sit upon the throne of his glory."

In the description which follows, the Gentiles are described as sheep and goats intermingled gathered before a shepherd. Differing in kind, they are divided one from another, the sheep being placed on the right hand of the King and the goats on the left. Then the King invites the sheep to enter the kingdom. To them he states, "Come, ye blessed of my Father, inherit the kingdom prepared for you from the foundation of the world: For I was an hungred, and ye gave me meat: I was thirsty, and ye gave me drink: I was a stranger, and ye took me in: Naked, and ye clothed me: I was sick, and ye visited me: I was in prison, and ye came unto me. Then shall the righteous answer him, saying, Lord, when saw we thee an hungred, and fed thee? or thirsty, and gave thee drink?" (vv. 34-37).

When the sheep ask the question as to when these deeds of righteousness were done, the King replies in Matthew 25:40, "Verily I say unto you, Inasmuch as ye have done it unto one of the least of these my brethren, ye have done it unto me."

Then the King turns to those on the left hand and declares unto them, "Depart from me, ye cursed, into everlasting fire, prepared for the devil and his angels" (v. 41). The King goes on to say they have not done these same deeds of kindness which He has ascribed to the sheep. The goats respond, "Lord, when saw we thee an hungred, or athirst, or a stranger, or naked, or sick, or in prison, and did not minister unto thee?" (v. 44). The King replies, "Verily I say unto you, Inasmuch as ye did it not to one of the least of these, ye did it not to me" (v. 45). The goats are then declared to be cast into everlasting punishment, but the righteous are ushered into the blessings of eternal life.

This passage has created some misunderstanding because of the emphasis on works. A superficial study would seem to indicate the sheep are saved because of their works, and the goats are lost because of their lack of works. The Bible, however, makes clear that salvation is never by works in any dispensation. Even the Mosaic law which emphasized works never had among its promises salvation as a reward for faithful works. Rather, the norm for all dispensations is stated in Ephesians 2:8-9: "For by grace are ye saved through faith; and that not of yourselves: it is the gift of God: Not of works, lest any man should boast."

Because of man's innate depravity, being born with a sinful

nature, and because of his position in Adam, his first parent who sinned against God, all men are born lost and in themselves are without hope. Only on the basis of the sacrifice of Christ could anyone be saved in the Old or New Testament (Rom. 3:25-26). The law of works is only a road to condemnation, whereas the law of faith is the way of salvation (Rom. 3:27-28). If this is well established in other Scritpure, how can the judgment of the sheep and the goats be explained?

The principle involved in this judgment is of works as an *evidence* of salvation, not of works as a *ground* of salvation. While faith alone can save, it is also true that faith without works is dead, that is, it is not true faith (James 2:26).

The works of the sheep are especially significant in the context of the Great Tribulation through which these people have passed. In this period there will be worldwide anti-Semitism, and many Israelites will be killed. Under those circumstances, for a Gentile to befriend a Jew, even "one of the least of these my brethren" (Matt. 25:40) would be significant.

In fact, for a Gentile to befriend a Jew at a time when Jews are being hounded to death would be to endanger his own life and freedom. The only possible reason for such kindness under these circumstances, in a time of great satanic deception and hatred of the Jews, would be that the Gentile is a believer in Christ and Scripture and recognizes the peculiar position of Israel as the chosen people of God.

Accordingly, while kindness to a Jew might not be especially significant under ordinary circumstances, in this context of worldwide suffering for Israel kindness to a Jew becomes the unmistakable mark of true salvation in Christ. Thus, while the sheep are not saved on the basis of their works, their works demonstrate that they are saved. It is the principle of being known by one's fruit.

In this judgment the righteous Gentiles are allowed to enter the kingdom. They are not given the Promised Land, which belongs only to Israel, but they are allowed to live in the millennial earth, in a time of unprecedented blessing for both Gentiles and Israelites.

The goats, on the other hand, are cast into everlasting fire. Whether this means they are cast into Hades, to be resurrected later and cast in the lake of fire, or whether it refers to immediate entrance to the lake of fire is not entirely clear; in any case they go to everlasting punishment and are denied the privilege of being citizens for the millennial kingdom.

The judgment of God upon the Gentiles is another reminder that God observes our works and that our works should demonstrate our faith. Even small deeds of giving water to the thirsty and food to the hungry are not unnoticed by a loving God who is concerned for His people. This passage is another reminder that proper recognition of human need about us, and kindness and good will to our fellowman, is one of the choice evidences of a transformed heart that comes through faith in Jesus Christ. The God who does not allow a sparrow to fall to the ground apart from His will is also concerned about all the small problems of His creatures. One who has the heart of Christ will have a heart for the people of God.

Taken as a whole, Scripture makes clear that at the second coming of Christ all the righteous will be resurrected and judged before the millennial kingdom is fully inaugurated. Only the wicked remain in the grave, awaiting their judgment at the great white throne at the end of the Millennium.

Questions

1. What judgments will occur in connection with the second coming of Christ?
2. What resurrections will occur in connection with the judgments at the second coming of Christ?
3. What is the nature of the reward given those who are judged?
4. How can you explain that both the church and other saints will reign with Christ?
5. What is the particular judgment on living Israelites at the time of the second coming of Christ?
6. Describe the judgment of the sheep and the goats.
7. Does this judgment teach that salvation is by works?
8. Explain the difference between works as an evidence of salvation and works as a ground of salvation.
9. Why are the works attributed to the sheep especially significant in view of the Great Tribulation?
10. What practical application can be made of the fact that God regards small deeds of kindness as being important?
11. Who of the dead will remain in the grave after the beginning of the Millennium?

49

The Millennial Kingdom

A. *The Concept of the Kingdom of God*

In general, in Scripture the kingdom of God refers to the sphere of God's rule in the universe. Because God has always been sovereign and omnipotent, there is a sense in which the kingdom of God is eternal. Nebuchadnezzar, the king of Babylon who was humbled by God, bore testimony to this when he said, "I blessed the most High, and I praised and honoured him that liveth forever, whose dominion is an everlasting dominion, and his kingdom is from generation to generation: And all the inhabitants of the earth are reputed as nothing: and he doeth according to his will in the army of heaven, and among the inhabitants of the earth: and none can stay his hand, or say unto him, What doest thou?" (Dan. 4:34-35).

The universal rule of God was challenged, however, in eternity past by Satan and the angelic beings who joined him in rebellion against God. Although God demonstrated His sovereignty by judging the rebels, the entrance of sin into the world introduced the divine program to demonstrate God's sovereignty in human history. This involves the concept of a theocratic kingdom, that is, a kingdom in which God is the ultimate Ruler even though He works through His creatures.

Adam, when he was created, was given dominion over the earth (Gen. 1:26, 28). Adam and Eve, however, in disobedience to God partook of the forbidden fruit. In his fall into sin Adam lost the right to rule, and thereafter the sovereignty of God insofar as it was committed to men was delegated to certain chosen people whom God allowed or chose to be rulers. Accordingly, throughout history some men have been permitted to rule. Daniel, for instance, reminded Belshazzar of this when referring to the fact that God chastened Nebuchadnezzar "till he knew that the most high God ruled in the kingdom of men, and that he appointeth over it whomsoever he will" (Dan. 5:21).

In the Old Testament, a major demonstration of the theocratic kingdom was in the kingdom of Israel beginning with Saul, David, and Solomon. Gentile rulers as well, in the sovereign purpose of God, were permitted a sphere of political rule. This general concept of government under God's permission and direction is mentioned in Romans 13:1, where Paul writes, "Let every soul be subject unto the higher powers. For there is no power but of God: the powers that be are ordained of God."

In addition to the sovereignty of God manifested in political governments and their rulers, Scripture also bears testimony to a spiritual government, in which God rules in the hearts of men. This has been true ever since the beginning of the human race, and the spiritual kingdom includes all who are willingly subject to God, whether men or angels. Paul referred to this spiritual concept of the kingdom in Romans 14:17 when he wrote, "For the kingdom of God is not meat and drink; but righteousness, and peace, and joy in the Holy Ghost."

In the gospel of Matthew further distinction is made in the use of the terms "the kingdom of heaven" and "the kingdom of God." Many interpreters regard these expressions as synonymous, as Matthew frequently uses the term "kingdom of heaven" in similar verses where the other gospels use the term "kingdom of God." While the terms themselves are very similar, their usage seems to indicate that the kingdom of heaven is a wider term than the kingdom of God, including the sphere of profession — as in the parable of the wheat and the tares, where the kingdom of heaven apparently includes the tares, and in the parable of the dragnet, where the kingdom of heaven seems to include the good and the bad fish (cf. Matt. 13:24-30, 36-43, 47-50).

The kingdom of God, on the other hand, is not considered a sphere of profession but a sphere of reality as illustrated in John 3:5, where Christ told Nicodemus, "Vereily, verily, I say unto thee, Except a man be born of water and of the Spirit, he cannot enter into the kingdom of God." Most expositors, however, prefer the view that there is no essential difference in the two kingdoms.

A more important distinction, however, lies in the contrast between the kingdom in the present age and the kingdom in the Millennium. The kingdom in the present age has its major features declared to be "mysteries," that is, revelations not given in the Old Testament (cf. Matt. 13); but the kingdom in its millennial form will be fulfilled after the second coming of Christ and is not a mystery.

There is also involved the distinction between the kingdom which is unseen — the rule of God in the hearts of believers in the present age — and the visible and glorious kingdom which all will see in the earth after the Second Coming. This distinction is quite important and essential to contrasting the present age as a sphere of divine rule with what will exist in the millennial kingdom.

Three major interpretations have been advanced in relating the kingdom concept to the millennial kingdom. The premillennial view interprets Scripture as teaching that the second coming of Christ will occur first and be followed by a thousand-year reign of Christ on earth before the eternal state of the new heaven and the new earth is brought in. It is called premillennial because the coming of Christ is before the millennial kingdom.

A second view known as amillennialism denies there will be a literal millennial kingdom on earth. Generally speaking, this view holds that Christ will return in His second coming and immediately usher in the new heaven and the new earth with no intervening thousand-year reign. This view interprets many passages in the Old and New Testaments that refer to the millennial kingdom as being fulfilled in a nonliteral way, either in the present experience of the chruch on earth or the experience of the church in heaven.

A third view is the postmillennial one. This interpretation believes that the Gospel, in the present age, will ultimately triumph in the world and bring in a golden period when to some extent the righteousness and peace prophesied for the millennial kingdom will be fulfilled. It is called postmillennial because it views the second coming of Christ as the climax of this golden age, as the end of the millennium. Postmillennialism of the conservative sort often pictures a literal thousand years in which Christ reigns supreme in the hearts of men. The more liberal type is similar to views of evolution and contemplates gradually advancing progress in the world culminating in a golden age. Because the entire trend of history in the twentieth century has given little ground for believing that the cause of God will be advanced in the world by human means, most interpreters today are either amillennial or premillennial.

While many arguments are advanced for and against the concept of a literal Millennium, the solution is determined by the extent to which the prophecies of Scripture are interpreted literally. In this discussion it will be assumed that prophecy should be interpreted in the same literal sense as any other theme of divine revelation. Accordingly, many predictions of the Old Testament as well as the classic chapter of Revelation 20 in the New Testament are interpreted to mean literally what they state — that a literal thousand-year reign of Christ will take place in the earth after His second coming and before the new heaven and the new earth are created. For detailed arguments presenting the various views on the Millennium, see Walvoord's *The Millennial Kingdom,* which is a detailed discussion of this question.

B. The Millennial Kingdom, a Rule of God on Earth

In contrast with the amillennial view, which regards the kingdom of God as primarily a spiritual rule in the hearts of men, many passages support the conclusion that the kingdom is a literal kingdom on the earth in which Christ will actually be the supreme political ruler as well as the spiritual leader and object of worship. This concept is presented extensively in both the Old and New Testaments.

In Psalm 2, where the rebellion of the nation against God is recorded, the Son of God is instructed, "Ask of me, and I shall give thee the heathen for thine inheritance, and the uttermost parts of the earth for thy possession" (v. 8). That this is not a spiritual rule but an actual political rule is brought out in the next verse, "Thou shalt break them with a rod of iron; thou shalt dash them in pieces like a potter's vessel" (v. 9). This certainly could not refer to the church or to a spiritual rule in heaven, but rather pictures an absolute monarch who will put down wicked men and bring them into subjection.

Another major passage emphasizing the earthly character of the kingdom is Isaiah 11, where Jesus Christ as a descendant of David is described as bringing righteous judgment on the earth and punishing the wicked. Isaiah 11:4 states, "but with righteousness shall he judge the poor, and reprove with equity for the meek of the earth: and he shall smite the earth with the rod of his mouth, and with the breath of his lips shall he slay the wicked." Frequently in the passage, the *earth* is mentioned (as in Isaiah 11:9), and God's dealings with the nations in recovering Israel from all over the earth are described.

Almost innumerable other verses either state or imply that the kingdom will be on earth (cf. Isa. 42:4; Jer. 23:3-6; Dan. 2:35-45; Zech. 14:1-9). The description of the rule of Christ on earth in the millennial kingdom in these passages certainly does not describe the present age nor does it describe heaven. Any reasonable fulfillment would require a literal kingdom on earth following Christ's second advent.

C. Christ as King of Kings in the Millennium

Many Old and New Testament passages combine their testimony that Christ will be the supreme ruler over the earth. Christ, as David's son, will sit upon the throne of David (2 Sam. 7:16; Ps. 89:20-37; Isa. 11; Jer. 33:19-21). When Christ was born He came as a King, as announced by the Angel Gabriel to Mary (Luke 1:32-33). As a King He was rejected (Mark 15:12-13; Luke 19:14). When He was crucified He died as the King of the Jews (Matt. 27:37). In His second advent He is described as "KING OF KINGS, AND LORD OF LORDS" (Rev. 19:16). Literally hundreds of verses in the Old Testament either state or imply that Christ will reign on earth. Some of the more important texts are especially clear (Isa. 2:1-4; 9:6-7; 11:1-10; 16:5; 24:23; 32:1; 40:1-11; 42:1-4; 52:7-15; 55:4; Dan. 2:44; 7:27; Mic. 4:1-8; 5:2-5; Zech. 9:9; 14:16-17).

One of the features of the millennial kingdom is that David will be resurrected and rule as a prince under Christ (Jer. 30:9; 33:15-17; Ezek. 34:23-24; 37:24-25; Hos. 3:5). This situation certainly does not exist in the church today and requires the second coming of Christ and the resurrection of the Old Testament saints before the prophecy can be fulfilled.

D. Major Features of the Government of the Millennium

As scripture bearing on the future kingdom on earth brings out, there are at least three important aspects of Christ's rule in His millennial kingdom.

1. *Many passages testify to the fact that the rule of Christ will be over the entire earth, far beyond the boundaries of any previous earthly kingdom or the kingdom of David himself.* In establishing this worldwide government, God fulfilled His purpose that man should rule the earth. Although Adam was disqualified, Christ as the Last Adam is able to fulfill this goal as mentioned in Psalm 2:6-9. According to Daniel 7:14, the Son of Man "was given . . . dominion, and glory, and a kingdom, that all people, nations, and languages, should serve him: his dominion is an everlasting dominion, which shall not pass away, and his kingdom that which shall not be destroyed." The same thought is mentioned in Daniel 2:44; 4:34; 7:27. The universality of the rule of Christ in the earth is also mentioned in Psalm 72:8; Micah 4:1-2; Zecharaiah 9:10.

2. *The government of Christ will he one of absolute authority and power.* Christ will rule "with a rod of iron" (Ps. 2:9; Rev. 19:15). All who oppose Him will be punished by destruction (Ps. 2:9; 72:9-11; Isa. 11:4). Such an absolute rule does not characterize the rule of Christ over His church or over the world in the present age and could be fulfilled only if Christ had a literal reign on earth following His second advent.

3. *The government of Christ in the Millennium will be one of righteousness and peace.* This is brought out in such classic passages as Isaiah 11 and Psalm 72.

These unusual characteristics of the kingdom are made possible by the introductory judgments of Israel and the Gentiles (discussed in the preceding chapter) and by the fact that Satan is bound and rendered inoperative. The only source of evil in the world will be the sin nature of men still in their human flesh. The separation of the tares from the wheat (Matt. 13:24-30) and the separation of the good from the bad fish (Matt. 13:47-50) are preparatory for the kingdom rule of Christ. The Millennium will begin with all adults converted as true believers in Christ. Children who are born in the Millennium will be subject to the righteous rule of Christ and be punished even to the point of physical death if they rebel against the King (Isa. 65:17-20; Zech. 14:16-19). Open sin will be punished and no one will be allowed to rebel against the King in the millennial kingdom.

E. The Special Place of Israel in the Millennial Kingdom

During the period of the millennial kingdom, Israel will enjoy a place of privilege and special blessing. In contrast with the present church age, where Jew and Gentile are on the same plane and have the same privileges, the people of Israel in the Millennium will inherit the Promised Land and will be the special objects of God's favor. It will be the time of Israel's regathering, reestablishment as a nation, and renewal of the Davidic kingdom. At long last Israel will possess the land permanently and in its entirety.

Many passages bear on this subject. In the millennial kingdom the Israelites will be regathered and restored to their ancient land (Jer. 30:3; 31:8-9; Ezek. 39:25-29; Amos 9:11-15). Having been brought back to the land, Israel will be the subjects of the revived Davidic kingdom (Isa. 9:6-7; 33:17, 22; 44:6; Jer. 23:5; Dan. 4:3; 7:14, 22, 27; Mic. 4:2-3, 7). The divided kingdoms of Israel and Judah will once again be united (Jer. 3:18; 33:14; Ezek. 20:40; 37:15-22; 39:25; Hos. 1:11). Israel as the wife of Jehovah (Isa. 54; 62:2-5; Hos. 2:14-23) will be in the privileged place above Gentile believers (Isa. 14:1-2; 49:22-23; 60:14-17; 61:6-7). Many passages also speak of the fact that Israel will be spiritually revived (Isa. 2:3; 44:22-24; 45:17; Jer. 23:3-6; 50:20; Ezek. 36:25-26; Zech. 13:9; Mal. 3:2-3). Many other passages give additional information concerning the blessed estate of Israel, their spiritual revival, and their enjoyment of fellowship with their God.

Although the Gentiles will not have title to the Promised Land, they too will have abundant blessings, as brought out in many Old Testament passages (Isa. 2:2-4; 19:24-25; 49:6, 22; 60:1-3; 62:2; 66:18-19; Jer. 3:17; 16:19). The glory of the kingdom both for Israel and for the Gentiles will far exceed anything that the world has experienced before.

F. Spiritual Blessings in the Millennium

Although the Millennium is correctly described as the political rule of Christ on earth, the characteristics of the kingdom will provide a context for abundant spiritual life such as no previous dispensation has made possible. This, of course, is due to the fact that Satan is bound, open sin is judged, and universal knowledge of the Lord is realized. According to Isaiah 11:9, "the earth shall be full of the knowledge of the Lord, as the waters cover the sea."

Many promises are given of inward spiritual blessing as provided in the new covenant. Jeremiah 31:33-34 declares, "But this shall be the covenant that I will make with the house of Israel; After those days, saith the Lord, I will put my law in their inward parts, and write it in their hearts; and will be their God, and they shall be my people. And they shall teach no more every man his neighbour, and every man his brother, saying, Know the Lord: for they shall all know me, from the least of them unto the greatest of them, saith the Lord: for I will forgive their iniquity, and I will remember their sin no more." It will be a period of righteousness (Ps. 72:7; Isa. 11:3-5) and universal peace (Ps. 72:7; Isa. 2:4). The spiritual conditions will also make possible unusual joy and blessing for the people of God (Isa. 12:3-4; 61:3, 7).

Although there is no evidence that the Spirit of God will baptize believers into a spiritual unity such as is true in the church today, there nevertheless will be the indwelling power and presence of the Spirit in believers in the Millennium (Isa. 32:15; 44:3; Ezek. 39:29; Joel 2:28-29). Because of the unusual situation, there will undoubtedly be greater spiritual blessing in the world as a whole in the Millennium than in any previous dispensation.

As a center for worship, a millennial temple is described in Ezekiel 40 − 46. In this temple sacrifices are offered which differ somewhat from the Mosaic sacrifices. Interpreters have differed as to whether they should be taken literally or should be explained in some other way. There is no solid reason for not accepting both the temple and the sacrificial system as literal prophecy.

Although the death of Christ has brought to an end the Mosaic law and its system of sacrifices, the sacrifices mentioned by Ezekiel seem to be memorial in character, looking back to the cross even as the Old Testament sacrifices looked forward to the cross. In the Millennium, with its unusual spiritual blessings, the terribleness of sin and the necessity of the sacrifice of Christ may be more difficult to comprehend than in any previous dispensation. Accordingly, the sacrificial system seems to be introduced as a reminder of the necessity of the one sacrifice of Christ which alone can take away sin. If the Old Testament sacrifices were suitable anticipation of the death of Christ, a similar means could be employed in the Millennium in the sense of a memorial.

In any case, there is clear evidence that the Millennium will be a time of unusual spiritual blessing and a period in which righteousness, joy, and peace will characterize the earth.

The abundant spiritual blessings will also issue in important social and economic advances over any previous period. The fact that all will have justice and that the meek will be protected will assure equity in social and economic matters. Probably the majority of men will know the Lord. The earth itself will have the curse upon its productivity lifted (Isa. 35:1-2), and there will be abundant rainfall (Isa. 30:23; 35:7). In general, there will be prosperity, health, and both physical and spiritual blessings such as the world has never known.

The millennial situation will also include important changes in the earth, some of them brought about by the great catastrophies of the Great Tribulaton and others related to the second coming of Christ. A great valley will extend to the east of Jerusalem, where the Mount of Olives now stands (Zech. 14:4). Another unusual feature of the period is that Jerusalem will be exalted above the surrounding territory (Zech. 14:10). As a whole, the Promised Land will once again be the garden spot of the world, the center of God's kingdom in the earth, and the place of unusual blessing. In many respects, the millennial kingdom will be the golden age, the climax of earth's history, and the fulfillment of God's purpose to establish His Son as the supreme ruler over the universe.

Questions

1. What in general is the meaning of the kingdom of God?
2. In what sense is the kingdom of God eternal and universal?
3. How did the entrance of sin introduce the concept of a theocratic kingdom?
4. How did Adam's fall result in God committing to certain men the right to rule?
5. How was the kingdom of Israel a special demonstration of the theocratic principle?
6. In what sense is the rule of God in the heart different from His theocratic kingdom?
7. What distinctions do some make between the terms "kingdom of heaven" and "kingdom of God"?
8. What important distinctions should be made between the present form of the kingdom and the future form of the kingdom in the Millennium?
9. What is meant by the premillennial interpretation of Scripture?
10. What is meant by the amillennial interpretation of Scripture?
11. What is meant by the postmillennial interpretation of Scripture?
12. What is the principle of interpretation involved in these differing views?
13. What does Psalm 2 contribute to the idea of a literal kingdom on earth?
14. What is revealed in Isaiah 11 concerning the earthly kingdom?
15. Why is it unreasonable to make the word "earth" represent heaven in these passages?
16. What does the Old Testament reveal about Christ as the supreme ruler over the earth as David's son?
17. What Scripture supports the concept that David will be resurrected and rule as a prince under Christ in the millennial kingdom, and how does this require a future kingdom on earth?
18. Support from Scripture the fact that Christ will rule over the entire earth, far beyond the boundaries of the Davidic kingdom in the Old Testament.
19. What evidence may be offered that the government of Christ will be one of absolute authority and power?
20. What evidence is found in Scripture that the kingdom on earth will be one of universal righteousness and peace?
21. How do the judgments on Israel, the Gentiles, and Satan at the beginning of the Millennium prepare the way for a righteous kingdom?
22. What special place is given to Israel in the millennial kingdom, and what will be the characteristics of blessings conferred upon her?
23. What special blessing will be given to the Gentiles in the millennial kingdom?

24. What evidence is there of unusual spiritual blessing in the millennial kingdom for all?
25. What ministry of the Spirit will be found in the Millennium?
26. What is taught concerning a millennial temple and a system of sacrifices in the Millennium?
27. In view of the fact that Christ died on the cross, how can such sacrifices be explained?
28. What important social and economic advances will be observed in the Millennium?
29. How will the productivity of the earth be changed in the Millennium?
30. What important changes in the topography of the earth will occur in the Millennium?
31. Summarize the unusual blessings which will characterize the millennial kingdom.

50

The Judgment of
Satan and Fallen Angels

A. *The Judgment of Satan at the Cross*

The conflict between God and Satan began with the fall of
Satan from his original holy state long before Adam and Eve
were created (see Chapter 22). Throughout the history of man,
various judgments fell on Satan, including the judgment in the
Garden of Eden which was inflicted on the serpent and the
pronouncement anticipating Satan's ultimate downfall given in
Genesis 3:15. There Satan was informed that the seed of the
woman "shall bruise thy head, and thou shalt bruise his heel."
This referred to the conflict between Satan and God that resulted in the crucifixion of Christ. Although Christ died on the
cross, He was raised from the dead, and this is referred to as
"thou shalt bruise his heel." By contrast, Satan had a deadly
wound that would prove his complete downfall — expressed in
the sentence, "it shall bruise thy head." Christ in His death
accomplished a lasting victory over Satan.

Reference to this same truth is found in John 16:11, where
Christ indicated that the Holy Spirit, when He came, would
convince the world "of judgment, because the prince of this

world is judged." Satan's judgment was pronounced at the cross, and Satan was held guilty of rebellion against God, which made necessary the sacrifice of Christ in order to save fallen men.

An earlier incident in the life of Christ also anticipated Christ's victory over Satan. When the seventy sent out to preach and perform miracles returned, they declared in Luke 10:17, "Lord, even the devils are subject unto us through thy name." Christ in reply said, "I beheld Satan as lightning fall from heaven" (10:18). This was a prophetic anticipation of Satan's ultimate downfall.

B. Satan Cast Out of Heaven

At the beginning of the Great Tribulation, forty-two months before the second coming of Christ, according to Revelation 12:7-9, a war takes place in heaven between Michael, the leader of the holy angels, and Satan (described as "the dragon") and "his angels" (referring to fallen angels). Satan and the fallen angels are defeated and "the great dragon was cast out, that old serpent, called the Devil, and Satan, which deceiveth the whole world: he was cast out into the earth, and his angels were cast out with him (Rev. 12:9).

As brought out in Revelation 12:10, Satan had been engaged in ceaseless accusation of the brethren and had "accused them before our God day and night." The accusing work of Satan, first introduced in Scripture in the Book of Job, is finally brought to an end then, in anticipation of the ultimate judgment on him. Beginning at this point in the prophetic program, approximately forty-two months before the second coming of Christ (cf. Rev. 12:6), Satan and the wicked angels are at long last excluded from heaven. The defeat of Satan which began when he was unable to tempt Christ, made evident by the casting out of demons by Christ and His followers, and rendered sure by the death of Christ on the cross, is now rapidly coming to its climax. Satan, already judged and declared guilty, now is about to find his judgment executed against him.

C. Satan Bound and Cast into the Abyss

At the second coming of Christ, judgment is inflicted, not only upon a blaspheming world and its rulers, but also upon Satan and fallen angels. In Revelation 20:1-3, John writes, "I saw an angel come down from heaven, having the key of the bottomless pit and a great chain in his hand. And he laid hold on the dragon, that old serpent, which is the Devil, and Satan, and bound him a thousand years, And cast him into the bottomless pit, and shut him up, and set a seal upon him, that he should deceive the nations no more, till the thousand years should be fulfilled: and after that he must be loosed a little season."

In this graphic vision, a further advance in the judgment of Satan is recorded. John not only sees Satan bound and cast into the abyss, or the bottomless pit, and confined there, but also is told the reason for this action. The purpose is that Satan will be unable to deceive the nations until the thousand years of the millennial kingdom are past. While this truth is conveyed to John in a vision, the interpretation of the vision is plain. Satan is unable to deceive the world any longer as he has done ever since Adam and Eve were created.

The vivid fact that Satan is bound during the thousand-year reign of Christ is another important evidence that the millennial kingdom is still future and is not to be identified with any present rule of God. It is very obvious in Scripture that Satan is not bound now, as brought out in the previous study of Satan (see Chapter 23). Any literal fulfillment of Revelation 19 — 20 requires the second coming of Christ to occur first and the binding of Satan to follow immediately afterward. Six times in Revelation 20 the thousand-year period is mentioned, with events preceding and events following. The binding of Satan clearly occurs before the thousand years begin.

While nothing is said in this passage concerning the fallen angels, it may be assumed they are also confined at this point, just as they were cast out of heaven with Satan forty-two months before. There is no record in any millennial passage of Satanic activity until the very end, when Satan is loosed for a short period of time.

D. The Final Judgment of Satan

Revelation 20:7 says: "And when the thousand years are expired, Satan shall be loosed out of his prison." The next verse declares that he "shall go out to deceive the nations which are in the four quarters of the earth, Gog and Magog, to gather them together to battle: the number of whom is as the sand of the sea." Led by Satan, a host of those who had only outwardly professed to follow Christ now show their true colors. These are children born in the Millennium, forced by circumstances to profess faith in Christ, but never actually born again. Now in open rebellion they encircle "the camp of the saints" and "the beloved city," Jerusalem. Their lot is one of immediate judgment and, according to Revelation 20:9, "Fire came down from God out of heaven, and devoured them."

Immediately thereafter, according to verse 10, "The devil that deceived them was cast into the lake of fire and brimstone, where the beast and the false prophet are, and shall be tormented day and night for ever and ever." This is the final doom of Satan, for his destiny is eternal fire which God prepared for the devil and his angels (Matt. 25:41).

The fallen angels are also judged, because they followed Satan's original rebellion against God (Isa. 14:12-17; Ezek. 28:12-19). According to 2 Peter 2:4, "God spared not the angels that sinned, but cast them down to hell, and delivered them into chains of darkness, to be reserved unto judgment." "Hell" here refers to Tartarus, a place of eternal punishment, and not Hades, where the wicked dead go prior to being cast into the lake of fire (Rev. 20:13-14).

The judgment of angels is also mentioned in Jude 6, where it is revealed, "And the angels which kept not their first estate, but left their own habitation, he hath reserved in everlasting chains under darkness unto the judgment of the great day." When this statement is joined with other passages referring to the fall and judgment of Satan and the wicked angels, it becomes clear that — while Satan and some of the angels are allowed a measure of freedom and because of this carry on a ceaseless warfare against the holy angels and the people of God on earth — other angels are bound and not allowed freedom. All, however, are destined for judgment at "the judgment of the great day," referring to the judgment on Satan and all the fallen angels which will take place after the close of the millennial kingdom.

Although in the providence of God Satan and the fallen angels have exerted great power and influence on the world and have ceaselessly opposed God, their ultimate defeat is sure and their eternal judgment follows. Christians afflicted by Satan, however, as Job was in the Old Testament, can rest in the fact that their victory ultimately is assured and the enemies of God will be judged in His time. That their punishment is endless is borne out by the fact that the beast and the false prophet cast into the lake of fire at the beginning of the Millennium are still there at the end of the Millennium. As Scripture makes clear, there are only two ultimate judgments, one the unending bliss of heaven, the other the unending torment of the lake of fire.

Questions

1. What prediction was given in the Garden of Eden of Satan's ultimate downfall?
2. What did Christ indicate in Luke 10:18 and John 16:11 concerning Satan's ultimate downfall?
3. Describe the war which takes place in heaven between Michael and Satan, and its outcome.
4. What has Satan been doing in heaven throughout the history of man?
5. Describe the downfall of Satan at the beginning of the Millennium.
6. How literally should we take the binding of Satan, and how does it affect the millennial kingdom?
7. What is the outcome of the loosing of Satan at the end of the Millennium?
8. Describe those who join Satan against Christ at the end of the Millennium.
9. What is the outcome of their rebellion?
10. Describe Satan's final judgment and that of the fallen angels.
11. How can Christians be reassured amid their spiritual conflict of their ultimate victory?

51

The Judgment of
the Great White Throne

A. The Last Judgment of the Great White Throne

As the final climax to human history at the conclusion of the millennial kingdom, Scripture records the judgment of the great white throne (Rev. 20:11-15). In contrast with previous judgments of the righteous, and various judgments of God upon Israelites and Gentiles living in the world, this is the final judgment; in the context it is seen to refer only to the judgment of the wicked.

B. The Destruction of the Heaven and the Earth

Before the judgment of the great white throne takes place, it is declared in Revelation 20:11, "the earth and the heaven fled away; and there was found no place for them." Human history having now run its course, the old creation is destroyed as expressed in Revelation 21:1: ("... the first earth were passed away; and there was no more sea." 2 Peter 3:10-12 refers to this event and describes the dramatic destruction in these words: "The heavens shall pass away with a great noise, and the elements shall melt with fervent heat, the earth also and the works that are therein shall be burned up" (v. 10). In the next verse, it declares "all these things shall be dissolved" (v. 11), and in verse 12 these concepts are combined when it says "the heavens being on fire shall be dissolved, and the elements shall melt with fervent heat." Because of the destruction of the present earth and heaven, the judgment of the great white throne apparenly takes place in space.

C. The Resurrection of the Wicked Dead

According to Revelation 20:12, John "saw the dead, small and great, stand before God." Revelation 20:13 adds, "The sea gave up the dead which were in it; and death and hell delivered up the dead which were in them." All the wicked dead are here resurrected and stand before God to be judged. That the Judge is the Lord Jesus Christ Himself is clear from John 5:27, where it states that the Father "hath given him authority to execute judgment also, because he is the Son of man."

D. The Books of Human Works Opened

Revelation 20:12 declares, "The books were opened: and another book was opened, which is the book of life: and the dead were judged out of those things which were written in the books, according to their works." The next verse repeats this condemning fact: "They were judged every man according to their works." Here the result of grace spurned is stated in stark terms. There is no forgiveness apart from Christ (Acts 4:12), and those who refuse His grace inevitably must be judged for their sins.

In addition to consulting their works, the Book of Life is examined for their names. Whether, as some believe, that the Book of Life is simply the record of those who have eternal life, or as others have held that it is the record of all living from which has been erased everyone who is unsaved, the result is the same. If their names are not found, they have not received eternal life. Their doom is then pronounced, and in Revelation 20:14-15 it is recorded, "And death and hell were cast into the lake of fire. This is the second death. And whosoever was not found written in the book of life was cast into the lake of fire."

Although some of those judged here may have been relatively good in comparison with others who were relatively bad, the lack of eternal life is the damning fact. All who do not have eternal life are judged on the basis of their works and rejection of Christ and are cast into the lake of fire. The tragedy is that, according to Scripture, Christ died for them as well as for those who are saved.

According to 2 Corinthians 5:19, "God was in Christ, reconciling the world unto himself, not imputing their trespasses unto them." In 1 John 2:2 Christ is declared to be "the propitiation for our sins: and not for ours only, but also for the sins of the whole world." These cast into eternal punishment could have been saved if they had turned to Christ. Their hopeless estate is due, not to a lack of love of God nor to any unavailability of the grace of God, but rather to the fact they would not believe. Those who never had an opportunity to hear the Gospel are condemned upon their rejection of the testimony of God in the natural world (Rom. 1:18-20). They too rejected what light they had and are justly condemned for their unbelief. The judgment of the great white throne is the sad ending for all who will not have Christ as their Savior and Lord.

Questions

1. What major difference may be seen between the judgment of the great white throne and previous judgments?
2. Where does the judgment of the great white throne take place, and how is this contrasted to previous judgments?
3. Describe the destruction of the present earth.
4. What does Scripture reveal concerning the resurrection of the wicked dead?
5. What is the basis of the judgment of the wicked dead?
6. What is the tragedy of the judgment of the wicked dead?
7. How is the revealed end of the lost an incentive to win souls for Christ?

52

The New Heaven and
the New Earth

A. *The New Heaven and*
the New Earth

In Revelation 21:1, following the judgment of the great white throne and the destruction of the first heaven and the first earth, John writes, "I saw a new heaven and a new earth: for the first heaven and the first earth were passed away." The new heaven is not described at all, and all that is stated about the new earth is, "There was no more sea" (Rev. 21:1). The strange silence of Scripture on the appearance of both the new earth and the new heaven is nowhere explained. Instead our attention is directed immediately to the holy city of the new Jerusalem.

B. *The General Description of*
the New Jerusalem

John records what he saw in these words: "I John saw the holy city, new Jerusalem, coming down from God out of heaven, prepared as a bride adorned for her husband (Rev. 21:2). The immediate problem that faces all interpreters is the meaning of what John saw. If one accepts the plain statement, John saw a holy city described as New Jerusalem in contrast with the old earthly Jerusalem which had been destroyed when the earth was destroyed. The city is described as coming "from God out of heaven." It is most significant that the city is not said to be created, and it apparently was in existence during the preceding period of the millennial kingdom, possibly as a satellite city above the earth; as such, it may be the millennial home of the resurrected and translated saints. It is quite clear from descriptions of the millennial earth that no city like the New Jerusalem was on earth itself. Some believe Christ was referring to the New Jerusalem when He declared in John 14:3, "I go and prepare a place for you." Here in Revelation the New Jerusalem is seen coming out of heaven, apparently destined to rest upon the new earth.

John further describes the city "as a bride adorned for her husband." Some have understood this is to be a reference to the church as a bride. However, as later revelation brings out, the New Jerusalem includes all the saints of all ages, and it is, therefore, preferable to consider this merely a descriptive phrase rather than a typical reference. The New Jerusalem is lovely, just as the bride adorned for her husband is lovely. Accordingly, while the city is a literal city, it has the loveliness of a bride.

Although comparatively few passages in the Bible deal with the subject of the new heaven and the new earth, the truth is not introduced for the first time in Revelation. In Isaiah 65:17 God declared, "For, behold, I create new heavens and a new earth: and the former shall not be remembered, nor come into mind." This verse occurs in a context of the millennial earth, and some feel it is referring to renewed Jerusalem in the millennium. However, it may be preferable to consider it as a reference to the New Jerusalem which will be on the new earth as seen in the background, while the renewed Jerusalem in the Millennium is seen in the foreground, as in Isaiah 65:18.

Another reference is in Isaiah 66:22, where it states, "For as the new heavens and the new earth, which I will make, shall remain before me, saith the LORD, so shall your seed and your name remain." While the earthly Jerusalem is destroyed at the end of the Millennium, the New Jerusalem will remain forever just as the seed of Israel will remain forever.

In 2 Peter 3:13, another prediction is made of the new heavens and the new earth, characterized as the place "wherein dwelleth righteousness." Throughout Scripture, accordingly, it may be concluded that the new heaven and the new earth are considered the ultimate goal of history and the final resting place of the saints.

Having introduced the new heaven and the new earth and the New Jerusalem, John proceeds to describe their major characteristics in Revelation 21:3-8. There God will dwell with men and will "be their God." Sorrow and death and pain will be abolished, as John states, "For the former things are passed away" (v. 4). This is confirmed in verse 5 by the statement, "Behold, I make all things new."

In the New Jerusalem Christ, as the Alpha and Omega promises, "I will give unto him that is athirst of the fountain of the water of life freely. He that overcometh shall inherit all things; and I will be his God, and he shall be my son" (vv. 6-7). By contrast, the unsaved described by their works and lack of faith are declared to "have their part in the lake which burneth with fire and brimstone: which is the second death" (v. 8). In contrast with the first death, which is physical and spiritual, the second death is eternal separation from God.

C. Vision of the New Jerusalem

John is invited to behold "the bride, the Lamb's wife" and is carried away "in the spirit to a great and high mountain" (Rev. 21:9-10). Here John sees the New Jerusalem descending out of heaven from God.

In the description which follows, in Revelation 21, the New Jerusalem is declared to have "the glory of God"; the city is brilliant with light "like unto a stone most precious, even like a jasper stone, clear as crystal" (v. 11). Although the jasper is sometimes used of stones of various colors, and most jasper stones today are not clear, the stone in view here is declared to be precious and clear as crystal. The impression must have been one of incredible beauty and brilliance.

The verses which follow describe the city itself as surrounded by a great wall over 200 feet high, with twelve gates in the wall attended by twelve angels. On the gates are the names of the twelve tribes of Israel. The city is square in shape and faces north, south, east and west, indicating that apparently there are directions in the new earth as there are in the present earth. The wall rests upon twelve foundations which, according to verse 14, bear the names of the twelve apostles.

The city is measured and found to be 12,000 furlongs or approximately 1,500 miles square, and it is equally high. This has raised the question as to whether the city is in the form of a cube or a pyramid. It probably is preferable to consider it a pyramid, as this explains how the river can flow down its sides as pictured in Revelation 22:1-2.

In general, all the materials of the city are translucent and permit light to pass through without hindrance. Even the gold is like clear glass (21:18). The foundations of the wall of the city bear the names of the twelve apostles, representing the church, and are garnished with twelve beautiful stones offering every color in the rainbow and, in the brilliant light of the city, providing a breathtakingly beautiful sight (vv. 19-20).

The gates of the city are declared to be large, single pearls, and the street of the city is transparent, pure gold (v. 21). The city has no temple because God dwells in it (v. 22) and has no need of sunlight or the moon or the stars, for the glory of God and the Lamb provides the light (v. 23). The saved among the Gentiles ("the nations") walk in the light of the city and enter freely by the gates, which are not shut because "there shall be no night there" (v. 25).

The inhabitants of the city, according to this description, include the saints of all ages. Not only Israel and the Gentiles are mentioned, but also the twelve apostles who represent the church. This is in keeping with the description of Hebrews 12:22-24, which itemizes those in the New Jerusalem as including "an innumerable company of angels," "the general assembly and church of the firstborn, which are written in heaven," "God the Judge of all," "the spirits of just men made perfect," and "Jesus the mediator of the new covenant." From this it may be concluded that the church will be in the New Jerusalem, as well as "the spirits of just men made perfect" — referring to all the saints not included in the church, both Jews and Gentiles — and the angels, and Jesus as the Mediator of the new covenant.

In his further description of the New Jerusalem, John describes "a pure river of the water of life, clear as crystal, proceeding out of the throne of God and of the Lamb" (Rev. 22:1). The tree of life bearing twelve kinds of fruit is described as being in the middle of the street of the city and on each side of the river and providing for the healing or the health of the nations (Rev. 22:2).

If this is a description of the eternal state, the question has.

been raised why healing is necessary. The difficulty is resolved if the translation is accepted, "for the health of the nations." It may be that the fruit of the tree of life in addition to the water of life is the explanation of the endless existence of the bodies the saints will have in eternity.

In further descriptions of the city, John states, "There shall be no more curse: but the throne of God and of the Lamb shall be in it; and his servants shall serve him" (v. 3). Their blessed estate is that they will be able to see God face to face and will have His name in their foreheads (v. 4). John repeats the fact that the new city will be brilliant and not need artificial light, and he concludes with the word from God, "Behold, I come quickly: blessed is he that keepeth the sayings of the prophecy of this book" (v. 7).

Considering the fact that the new heavens and the new earth will be the eternal abode of the saints, it is remarkable that there is comparatively little description of it in the entire Scripture. It is clear that the Bible is primarily intended to provide light for our present path. At the same time, a sufficient glimpse is given of the glory that is to come, to beckon us on in our life of faith. Undoubtedly there is much more to be revealed than the brief glimpses we have here in these concluding chapters of the Book of Revelation.

Although God has revealed to some extent to His people what "eye hath not seen, nor ear heard, neither [what] have entered into the heart of man" (1 Cor. 2:9), there is undoubtedly much more that God will reveal to man in eternity. The half has not been told, and our great God will delight to the endless reaches of eternity to manifest his love and grace to those who have received Jesus Christ as their Savior and Lord.

The Bible, which alone discloses the wonders of heaven, is equally explicit in its declarations concerning the conditions under which sinners of this fallen race may enter there. Notwithstanding, multitudes are assuring themselves they will be privileged to enter heaven who, at the same time, are giving no heed to those counsels of God in which He explains the only way given among men whereby they must be saved. Not every person will be found in heaven; that glory and bliss is for the redeemed. Redemption is absolutely dependent on a personal acceptance of the Redeemer. Such acceptance is a transaction most simple and yet so vital and conclusive that the trusting soul will be assured above all else that he is depending only on Christ for salvation.

Questions

1. What is revealed concerning the new heaven and the new earth?
2. Why is the New Jerusalem described as a bride adorned for her husband?
3. What is the significance of the fact that the New Jerusalem is not said to be created at that time?
4. How does this cast some light on the possibility that the New Jerusalem may be the home of resurrected and translated saints during the Millennium?
5. What do Isaiah 65:17 and 66:22 reveal concerning the new heavens and the new earth?
6. How does 2 Peter 3:13 characterize the new heavens and the new earth?
7. What are some of the principal characteristics of the new heaven and the new earth spiritually as revealed in Revelation 21:3-8?
8. What is the general picture of the New Jerusalem as John sees it in Revelation 21:11?
9. Describe the shape, wall, and gates of the New Jerusalem as seen by John.
10. What evidence is there that Israel and the angels will be in the New Jerusalem?
11. What are the length, width, and height of the city?
12. What possible explanation can be made of the shape of the city?
13. What characterizes all the materials of the city, and how does this relate to its brilliance?
14. Describe the breathtaking beauty of the precious stones of the foundation of the city.
15. What is the significance of the names of the twelve apostles being on the foundation of the city?
16. Why does the city have no temple and not need the light of the sun or the moon or the stars?
17. Are saved Gentiles also in the city?
18. What evidence can be offered that all the saints of all the ages will be in the New Jerusalem?
19. What does Hebrews 12:22-24 contribute to the identification of the inhabitants of the New Jerusalem?
20. How do the water of life and the tree of life possibly relate to the endless existence of the bodies of the saints in the New Jerusalem?
21. What will the saints do in the New Jerusalem?
22. How do you account for the fact that apart from these closing chapters of the Book of Revelation there is little revelation of the eternal state in the Bible?
23. In the light of this Scripture, why is it so important to be sure one has been saved by faith in Christ?

Index of Subjects

Scripture Index